A GAZETTEER OF BRITISH, SCOTTISH AND IRISH GHOSTS

A GAZETTEER OF BRITISH, SCOTTISH AND IRISH GHOSTS

PETER UNDERWOOD

Two Volumes in One

BELL PUBLISHING COMPANY
NEW YORK

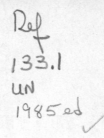

Library of Congress Cataloging-in-Publication Data

Underwood, Peter, 1923-
  Gazetteer of British, Scottish, and Irish ghosts.

  Originally published: A gazetteer of British Ghosts, and A gazetteer of
Scottish and Irish ghosts. London : Souvenir Press, 1971-1973. (Frontiers
of the unknown)
  Bibliography: p.
  Includes index.
  1. Ghosts—Great Britain. 2. Ghosts—Ireland. I. Underwood, Peter,
1923-   Gazetteer of British Ghosts. II. Underwood, Peter, 1923-
Gazetteer of Scottish and Irish ghosts. III. Title.
BF1472.G7U485 1985   133.1'0941   85-18634
ISBN: 0-517-49201-6

hgfedcba

To my wife

JOYCE ELIZABETH

for everything

CONTENTS

ILLUSTRATIONS

PART I: A GAZETTEER OF BRITISH GHOSTS

PART II: A GAZETTEER OF SCOTTISH AND IRISH GHOSTS

ix

INTRODUCTION

There are more ghosts seen, reported and accepted in the British Isles than anywhere else on earth. I am often asked why this is so and can only suggest that a unique ancestry with Mediterranean, Scandinavian, Celtic and other strains, an intrinsic island detachment, an enquiring nature, and perhaps our readiness to accept a supernormal explanation for curious happenings may all have played their part in bringing about this state of affairs.

Another question I am repeatedly asked is whether I believe in ghosts and my answer is that belief does not come into it as far as my work in this field is concerned. I try to investigate and study reports of these phenomena dispassionately but I am impressed by the wealth of evidence for ghosts and hauntings: strikingly similar reports from all over the world since the beginning of recorded history. I am quite certain that I have spoken to many people who are genuinely convinced that they have seen apparitions, phantoms, spectres, spirits, ghosts—call them what you will.

My interest in ghosts and haunted houses probably stems from the fact that my maternal grandparents lived in a reputedly haunted house and as a child I heard all about ghosts and soon found that other people believed that they, too, lived with them. As a boy I was intrigued that adults should take the subject seriously and I began to collect notes of hauntings and then press-cuttings and reports; a collection that has today grown into an enormous collection of data on the subject, and from this material, the result of over thirty years study of the subject, I have selected most of the famous cases of haunting and many hitherto unpublished accounts of ghostly phenomena to offer a representative selection of apparently paranormal activity throughout the British Isles.

The entries marked with an asterisk are those about which I have personal knowledge, either having interviewed the witnesses, carried out an investigation of the case, or visited the place in question myself; and I hope that in reading

xi

between the lines it will be possible to glimpse my opinion on some of these fascinating mysteries. It is interesting to note, for example, that there are often children up to and around the age of adolescence in the affected houses who may be conscious or unconscious participants in the disturbances and I have also often noticed in such houses a dominating mother or a woman who is unhappy or frustrated. I mention these points not as an explanation but as a simple statement of fact.

The entries are arranged in alphabetical order of the place where the ghost has been sighted or where the curious happenings have occurred, something that has never been attempted before on this scale. I hope the work will be of value as a reference book and as a guide to ghost-hunting, although I must emphasize that the inclusion of a haunted house in this volume does *not* necessarily mean that the house is open to the public. At the end of each entry I have indicated a nearby hotel which may be of assistance to those who plan a visit or itinerary to some of these haunted places. I did consider referring readers to various volumes containing fuller details of some of the cases included but decided against this because many well-known hauntings are dealt with, with varying reliability, in many books. The select bibliography at the end of this work includes most of the best books of true ghostly experiences published to date.

I would like to acknowledge the help I have received from many correspondents and people I have talked to, for their co-operation extending over many years; to my wife for inexhaustible patience and understanding; to my daughter for reading the first draft and for many helpful suggestions; and particularly to my son Chris who has provided most of the excellent photographs.

I am always interested to receive first-hand or reliable accounts of ghosts and haunted houses: a subject that has interested me for almost as long as I can remember and will probably continue to interest me until, perhaps, I become a ghost myself!

PETER UNDERWOOD

The Savage Club,
    London S.W.1

Part I
A GAZETTEER OF BRITISH GHOSTS

Abbots Langley, HERTFORDSHIRE.

Here the apparition of a former housekeeper has been seen from two different angles at the same time.

From enquiries on the spot it appears that the house-keeper, Anne Treble, was treated badly by the wife of a former rector soon after the First World War. Anne lies buried in the churchyard but her ghost is said to have been seen in three places: walking between the church and nearby vicarage; appearing at Mass on All Soul's Day inside the church; and in her old bedroom at the vicarage, where the daughter of a former rector used to wake up and see the back of the ghostly Anne, seemingly looking out of the window towards the church. An interesting and unusual aspect of the case is that the face of Anne used to be seen and recognized at the same time in cottages facing the rectory, just over the road!

I traced a former rector who found the ghost very active when he first moved into the vicarage and told me that while deciding on alterations to the rambling Queen Anne house, the local builder pointed to the fireplace which stood out from the wall in what, the rector was to learn, was the haunted room, and said gloomily: 'Not much use repairing that; it will be out again within six months.' Asked to elaborate, he continued: 'Annie it was; died a horrible death in this room and the place will never be free of her.' Nevertheless the fireplace was repaired—and within six months it fell out again! Now the rector began to make searching enquiries. He consulted a surveyor and asked whether subsidence could have caused this to happen, not once but on at least three previous occasions? The surveyor blamed bad workmanship. Again the fireplace was repaired and within a few months it was out again. Since then it has remained unrepaired.

Soon after moving into the vicarage the rector met a

parish priest who had been assistant curate at Abbots Langley and who told him that on All Soul's Day, ten years previously, he had seen the manifestation of an unknown woman at Mass in the church; a woman who disappeared when the priest had turned to give the Invitation and who had not been seen at all by the priest's wife. The curate's description was found to correspond exactly with that of a former vicar's housekeeper—and when the curate and his wife went to the vicarage with the rector after the service, the haunted fireplace was found to be newly cracked!

A year later an Irish vicar saw the same woman in his congregation and reported the facts of the matter to his bishop with the result that Bishop Michael Furse, in full canonicals, exorcized the house in accordance with the mediaeval Service of Exorcism. Thereafter, apart from a mysteriously broken grate, the church and vicarage had peace for some years, although the succeeding incumbent's wife kept the door of what was now the 'guest room' (!) locked because of unaccountable noises.

Another assistant curate heard footsteps approaching him from the west end of the church, when he was there alone late one night, and he felt some clothes brush past his face as he knelt in prayer. He heard the footsteps continue towards the east end of the church, then they ceased. He has reminded me that this occurred on the evening of All Hallow's Day.

On several occasions one rector made a point of spending the night of All Hallow's Day in the 'guest room' at the vicarage and keeping particularly vigilant at the Eucharist in the church on that day, but he saw no materialization; nor has the young daughter of the present rector who told me, very proudly, that she sleeps in the haunted room!
Langley Hotel, Kings Langley, Herts.

Aberdovey, MERIONETHSHIRE, WALES.

Here the ghostly bells of Aberdovey are still said to be heard occasionally, their ringing approaching from the sea on still summer evenings.

Much of the coast-line of Wales has altered beyond recognition since the days of the Romans. Today it is difficult to imagine someone standing on the hills above Aberdovey, looking seawards and seeing 'a rich and fertile plain and prosperous cities with marble wharves and churches whose towers resounded with beautiful peals and chimes of bells stretching for miles towards the west'. The encroaching sea now covers these cities but at low tide the sunken tree trunks of the submerged forests may still be seen sometimes between Aberdovey and Towyn.

The story of the sea's triumph is told in the legend of Seithenin the Drunkard, one-time Lord High Commissioner to Gwyddno Garanhir, lord of Ceredigion, whose rich dominions were protected from the insatiable sea by strong sea walls and dykes. The care and preservation of these walls were entrusted to Seithenin who, however, spent days and nights feasting at his palace by the sea, heedless of the stormy waves and the weakening walls. One night the raging seas rolled in and the wall was washed away. The cities and their inhabitants were lost for ever, only a handful of men escaped, but among them was Talieson the king's bard and his songs tell the story of the fair cities under the sea and of how the bells of Mantua, the greatest city swallowed up by the sea, may now and then be heard; distant-sounding chimes, sweet and low, like a call to prayer or the rejoicing for some forgotten victory.

Penhelig Arms Hotel, Aberdovey, Merionethshire, North Wales.

Abbotsford, ROXBURGHSHIRE, SCOTLAND.

The home of Sir Walter Scott, the novelist, for the last twenty years of his life. Scott died in 1832. He had built the villa, which he called Abbotsford, and between 1817 and 1825 added farm buildings to make a picturesque estate which today contains many Scott relics.

It was in 1818, during some of the alterations, that Sir Walter complained of a 'violent noise, like drawing heavy boards along the new part of the house'. The next night, at the same hour, two a.m., the noises were heard again and on this occasion Scott investigated 'with Beardie's broadsword' under his arm, but could discover no reason or cause for the sounds. At the time of the disturbances, George Bullock, Scott's agent who was responsible for the alterations at Abbotsford, died suddenly.

The George and Abbotsford Hotel, Melrose, Roxburghshire, Scotland.

Airlie, KIRRIEMUIR, SCOTLAND.

Music, like the wail of bagpipes and the beating of a drum, faint but definite, is said to herald the approach of the death of the head of the Airlie family and the ghostly Airlie drummer has been heard, it is claimed, for generations.

A former minister of Airlie published a history of the famous old Scottish family and gave fully documented and corroborated proof of this 'drum of death'.

In 1881 the drum was heard by Lady Dalkeith and Lady Skelmersdale and they remarked at the time that what they heard sounded like the traditional Airlie Drummer. The death of Lord Airlie in America took place the same night and it was discovered that the sound of the Drummer was heard approximately an hour before his death. After the death of the last Lord Airlie in 1968, Lady Airlie (whose second son, Mr Angus Ogilvy, married Princess Alexandra in 1963) informed me that as far as she knew the drum of death had not been heard.

Royal George Hotel, Perth, Scotland.

Alwinton, NORTHUMBERLAND.

A lonely spot here is said to be haunted by a cowled monk-like figure which appears to have no face, hands or feet and seems to hover above the ground. The haunting was investigated by the Newcastle Institute of Psychic Research in 1967.

The White Swan Hotel, Alnwick, Northumberlandshire.

14

Amersham Common, BUCKINGHAMSHIRE.

When actor Dirk Bogarde lived at Bendrose House, an old farmhouse where Cromwell is reputed to have stayed, he told me that the oldest bedroom, a gloomy, timbered chamber, was definitely haunted. While he was there seven people slept in the room at different times and, without previously being aware of the others' experiences, all discovered themselves waking suddenly between three and four in the morning with the feeling that an electric shock was passing through their bodies. The experience seemed to last about four minutes. In addition, unexplained footsteps were heard from one particular corridor.
Crown Hotel, Amersham, Bucks.

Arundel, SUSSEX.

Arundel Castle, the ancestral home of the Dukes of Norfolk, has twelfth-century and perhaps earlier foundations, although the present building is mainly nineteenth century in mediaeval style, and there are four ghosts: a girl, a boy, a dandy and a white bird.

The castle is first mentioned in the will of King Alfred the Great. The third Duke of Norfolk was an uncle of Catherine Howard, fifth wife of King Henry VIII, and the castle has been owned by the Norfolk family since 1580.

A story of unrequited love led to the occasional appearance of a young girl, dressed in pure white, who has been seen on still, moonlit nights in the vicinity of the tower on the brow of the hill, called Hiorne's Tower, from the top of which the love-lorn girl threw herself in desperation.

The great kitchen of the castle is said to be haunted by the ghost of a former kitchen boy who was ill-treated by the head cellarer two hundred years ago. He died young and his ghost has been heard, and more rarely seen, cleaning the pots and pans as if his very life depended upon it, long after the kitchen staff have retired to bed.

The ghost of a dandy dates from the days of King Charles II. This figure, also known as the 'Blue Man', has been seen at night poring over old books in the library. He is dressed in blue silk and there he sits ... nobody knows what he is looking for or why he cannot find it.

The 'White Bird' of ill portent flutters against the windows of the castle when the death of one of the Howard family is imminent and there are those who claim to have seen the bird just before the death of the last Duke of Norfolk.

For good measure the sounds of Cromwell's cannon have been heard from time to time here, battering the ramparts of the castle as they did under the command of Sir William Waller over three hundred years ago.
Norfolk Arms Hotel, Arundel, Sussex.

Ascot, BERKSHIRE.

Where a phantom horseman was long reputed to ride at night near a spot where a new road roundabout was laid in January, 1967.
Berystede Hotel, Ascot, Berks.

*Aspatria, CUMBERLANDSHIRE.

When Gill House was used as a hostel for members of the Women's Land Army during the Second World War there were many reported incidents which were never satisfactorily explained. These included strange noises and 'horrible smells' which were only experienced during the hours of darkness; a phantom shape which was seen walking through closed doors; and one girl awoke with the feeling that she was being strangled. Two W.L.A. chiefs decided to spend a night in the 'haunted dormitory' but left before the morning. The local vicar heard raps travelling around the room and at one time the disturbances became so bad that the affected room was closed. The late Canon W. J. Phythian-Adams, Canon of Carlisle, investigated this case at the time and showed me the papers and reports about the haunting. We discussed some of the unusual phenomena experienced at the house when it was occupied by girls; we decided that it was difficult to decide how many of the reported incidents

16

Aylsham, NORFOLK.

Nearby Blickling Hall, that lovely symmetrical seventeenth-century house of mellowed red brick, probably stands on the site of the birthplace of Anne Boleyn and there seems no doubt that Anne enjoyed many months of happy childhood hereabouts. She died by the executioner's axe on Tower Green on May 19th, 1536, and every anniversary (notwithstanding the alterations in the calendar over the years) a phantom coach drawn by headless horses and driven by a headless coachman is said to convey her ghost, carrying her head on her knees, towards the Hall where coach and horses and Anne vanish into thin air.

When news reached old Blickling Hall of the execution of Anne and her brother George (Lord Rochfort) apparitions of four headless horses were said to have been seen racing over the countryside dragging a headless man behind them. The man's head was safely tucked beneath one arm, his hair was tangled and spattered with blood and the grisly vision was completed by the accompaniment of a pack of 'shrieking demons!' Travelling in a straight line the visitation was said to have to cross twelve bridges before morning brought release. Another version of the story states that Sir Thomas Boleyn (Anne's father) is doomed each year to drive over forty bridges in the county, followed by a pack of yelling demons.
Bell Hotel, Norwich, Norfolk.

Ballechin House, STRATHTAY, NEAR DUNKELD, PERTHSHIRE, SCOTLAND.

A haunted house that was the source of controversy as long ago as 1897 when such public figures as Lord Onslow, Andrew Lang and F. W. H. Myers had letters on the case published in *The Times*. There is still considerable discussion on the curious 'Haunting of B—— House', as it is called, today.

In 1892 Lord Bute was told of the haunting by a Jesuit priest, Father Hayden, S.J., who said that he had heard loud and unexplained noises there while sleeping in one of the rooms. He changed his room but the loud noises seemed to follow him and he heard something which he described resembling 'a large animal throwing itself violently against the bottom of the bedroom door'. He also heard raps and shrieks. The following year Father Hayden met by chance a young woman who had been a governess at Ballechin House some twelve years previously and she told him that she had left because so many people complained of queer noises in the house. She volunteered this before Father Hayden told her he had been to Ballechin but it was subsequently established that the noises had occurred in the two rooms which he had occupied there.

In 1896 the house was let to a family for twelve months. They left after eleven weeks, forfeiting more than nine months rent, having heard rattling, knocking, tremendous thumping on doors, heavy footsteps and other noises they could not explain. Bedclothes were pulled off beds; a silky rustling noise was heard when no lady was present; groans, frequently accompanied by heavy knocking sometimes aroused the whole household; a fanning sensation was reported, as though a bird were flying around; the sound of heavy breathing was heard—and felt; and an icy coldness usually preceded the manifestations.

Lord Bute rented the mansion and arranged for two psychic investigators, Colonel Lemesurier Taylor and Miss A. Goodrich-Freer (Mrs Hans Spoer) to carry out research. They reported on the first morning after their arrival 'a loud clanging sound' which was heard throughout the house and this noise was repeated at frequent intervals for two hours. The sound of voices was heard, and footsteps in locked and empty rooms; the noise of something being dragged along the floor; pattering sounds; explosive bangs; thumps; knockings and other noises were reported by these experienced observers.

Messages were received during experiments with an Ouija board and one communicator, giving her name as 'Ishbel', asked the investigators to go at dusk to a nearby glen. This they did and Miss Freer reported seeing, against the white snow background, a slim black figure, a woman dressed like a nun, moving slowly up the glen. She disappeared under a tree. Miss Freer subsequently reported seeing the same figure many times; sometimes weeping, sometimes talking 'in a high note, with a quality of youth in her voice'.

The case is a puzzling one and a recent assessment of Miss Goodrich-Freer is of little help in elucidating the mystery.
Queen's Hotel, Blairgowrie, Perthshire, Scotland.

Barbreck, ARGYLLSHIRE, SCOTLAND.

A mysterious 'hooded maiden' has been seen repeatedly on this estate on Loch Craignish, in the valley of the River Barbreck between Ardfern and Ford. The figure of a girl with long hair and a pale face has been seen sitting on a rock, wearing a skirt of a dark but unidentified tartan. She seems to be wearing a hood which hides her features. She always disappears when shepherds or fishermen approach her.
Caledonian Hotel, Oban, Argyll, Scotland.

Barnack, NORTHAMPTONSHIRE.

The old fourteenth-century rectory had a 'Haunted Room' troubled by a ghost called 'Button Cap'. Novelist and historian Charles Kingsley spent much of his childhood at Barnack where he wrote sermons and poems *at the age of four*. He knew all about 'Button Cap' and used to say that he had heard the ghost walk across the room in flopping slippers many times; often it would turn over the leaves of the book young Charles was reading.

The ghost was believed to be a former rector of Barnack who wore a flowered dressing-gown and a cap with a button on it. During his life he was said to have defrauded a widow and orphan and his restless ghost was thought to be searching for the incriminating deed.

There seems to be no account of anyone seeing the figure but anyone who spent any time in the 'Haunted Room' always heard him; sometimes making a noise like barrels rolling about. In later years Kingsley put the noise down to rats!
George Hotel, Main Road, Stamford, Lincs.

Basingstoke, HAMPSHIRE.

Both Kingsclere Road, particularly in the vicinity of a plot
of land known for hundreds of years as Catern's Grave and a
nearby hilltop, have long been regarded as haunted. There
are many reports of muttering dark figures being heard and
seen in the shadows of a clump of fir trees; reports that go
back over fifty years.

A visitor on the road beside Catern's Grave approached
what he thought was a man lighting a cigarette in his
cupped hands but when he reached the figure he found it to
be a monk, hands held before him in prayer. 'He had fixed,
staring eyes,' this witness told me, 'his face was grey and
lined and as I looked at him I found myself being drawn
towards him. Although I tried to pull back, I was at first
unable to do so; but at length I turned and started to run.
Then it seemed that his spirit or being pushed mine out of
me and possessed my body. Halfway along a path we had a
terrific struggle; I felt myself shaken until my whole body
ached and quite suddenly, I found that I had shaken off whatever had possessed me. It was a very unpleasant experience
and I will never go that way alone again at night-time.'

A Basingstoke man once overtook a procession of muttering men along the Kingsclere Road; he hurried past them
and then noticed a glow in the darkness. Suddenly he felt
blows raining down on his back as though the muttering
men were trying to drive him away from Catern's Grave. He
ran desperately and succeeded in escaping.
Red Lion Hotel, London Street, Basingstoke, Hants.

Basingstoke, HAMPSHIRE.

Bramshill House, near Basingstoke, was built in 1327 and
has long had the reputation of being haunted. An ancient
chest in the panelled gallery is said to have been the 'death
bed' of a young bride who died on the eve of her wedding.
A former queen of Rumania, while staying at Bramshill
House, was among those who claimed to have seen the young
bride's ghost walk at night through the Long Gallery, wearing a white, ankle-length gown.

There is also an apparition of a 'Green Man' seen near the lake in the grounds where, according to legend, the Black Prince was drowned and the house has always been associated with an early Prince of Wales who died in mysterious circumstances at Bramshill with more than a suspicion of murder by poison.

In recent years the property has been occupied by a police training college.

Red Lion Hotel, London Street, Basingstoke, Hants.

*Battle, SUSSEX.

The great Abbey was founded by King William I (William the Conqueror) to commemorate his victory over King Harold in 1066 and was built on the actual spot where the battle was fought. By founding the Abbey he sought to atone for the awful slaughter and show his gratitude for victory.

On the spot where Harold fell and the gorgeous gem-studded standard was captured, a High Altar was built within the Abbey Church but all that now remains to mark the site is a fine fir tree. It is here that the famous 'bloody fountain' is said to have sprung up after a shower, a sign of the immense efflux of Christian blood that was shed here.

The 'fountain of blood' is still reported to be seen occasionally by visitors and the figure of Harold himself, complete with arrow through his eye and dripping with blood, has been reported on occasions, sorrowfully surveying the dismal scene.

George Hotel, Battle, Sussex.

Bedford, BEDFORDSHIRE.

The Right Honourable Joseph Bradshaw Godber, a former Secretary of State for Foreign Affairs, lives with his wife and sons at nearby Willington Manor, a gracious seven-bedroomed Elizabethan house that has been in the possession of the Godber family for many years. At one time it belonged to Sir John Gostwick, Master of Hounds to King Henry VIII, but having twice been burnt down over the centuries, it is now largely Georgian in aspect.

Mr Godber has not seen or heard the ghost but Mrs Godber has heard it many times. 'Often the dogs have woken me by their barking at three a.m. on the dot and I have heard footsteps and a tinkling bell. My husband used to say that it was the grandfather clock, but when that broke down, the sounds were still heard.'

There is no story or legend to account for the noises although they may possibly be connected with a skeleton found bricked up in a wall during some rebuilding in the early part of the century.

Lion Hotel, Bedford, Beds.

*Berry Pomeroy Castle, NEAR TOTNES, DEVON.

You approach the ruins of Berry Pomeroy Castle along a winding glen banked high with shrubs and trees when suddenly you find the ruins before you, perched on a spur of the hillside; a strange, deserted place—said to harbour at least two ghosts.

Here, from the Norman Conquest until 1548, lived the family of de la Pomerai; in that year the castle was sold to the Lord Protector Somerset and his son, 'Lord' Edward Seymour built most of the Seymour mansion which stands, gaunt and gutted, within the precincts of the old castle.

Elliott O'Donnell told me that he had traced back reports of the haunting of Berry Pomeroy Castle many hundreds of years but that it became widely known when an eminent physician, Sir Walter Farquhar, referred to it in his memoirs. He recounts how he was called one day to attend the wife of the Steward of the Castle, who was seriously ill. While waiting to see the patient he was shown into a lofty, oak-panelled room which had a flight of stairs in one corner leading to a room above. As he was looking round the room the door opened and a beautifully-dressed lady entered, wringing her hands and obviously in great distress. Taking no notice of the occupant, she walked across the room, mounted the stairs and then paused and looked directly at the physician who saw, before she disappeared from sight, that she was very young and of a remarkable beauty. At length the doctor saw his patient who was so ill that he returned

24

to the castle the following morning when he was pleased to find her much better. Afterwards he discussed the marked improvement with his patient's husband and, during the course of conversation, remarked on the beautiful lady he had seen on his previous visit, expressing curiosity as to her identity and cause of her mental anxiety, whereupon he was surprised to find the Steward very upset. He was told that the figure he had seen was a ghost and that her appearance always preceded the death of someone closely associated with the castle. The apparition had been seen shortly before his son was drowned and nothing would convince him that his wife would not die. Sir Walter did his best to reassure the distracted man, pointing out again that his wife's condition had improved vastly; but within a few hours the lady was indeed, dead.

On making enquiries, Sir Walter learned that the ghost was that of the daughter of a former owner of Berry Pomeroy Castle who was as wicked and cruel as she was lovely and who, because of her many crimes and licentious living, was doomed after her death to haunt forever the home of her forebears and the scene of some of her evil deeds. Sir Walter also traced accounts of the haunting during which the beautiful but evil lady lured those who saw her to some unsafe spot in or near the castle, where they were liable to have a serious accident.

Perhaps the best-known story of haunted Berry Pomeroy concerns another lady owner of the castle, one of two sisters, Margaret and Eleanor de Pomeroy, who both loved the same man. Lady Eleanor was mistress of the castle at the time and she was so jealous of her beautiful sister that she caused her to be imprisoned in the castle dungeons where she was starved to death; and now, on certain nights it is said, she rises from her dungeon, leaves St Margaret's Tower in flowing white robes and walks along the ramparts, beckoning those who see her. Another apparition at Berry Pomeroy is an unidentified woman in a long, blue, hooded cape who is thought to have smothered her baby and cannot find rest: according to some sources she is a young daughter of one of the Pomeroys and the murder took place in one of the upper chambers.

Many visitors have remarked on the indefinable sense of

deadness and evil, of loneliness and desolation at Berry Pomeroy, and a number of photographs taken here have included shadowy figures which cannot be explained. In 1968 a visitor took her two children of seven and nine there for a picnic, expecting them to romp and explore and enjoy themselves. Instead they kept sedately by their mother's side for most of the time and when they did venture into the ruins they soon ran back to say that it was horrid and they wanted to go home. When one remembers the young knights who plunged to death with their horses into the valley of the north side, rather than be taken as slaves by their enemies; of the unhappy Lady Margaret starved to death in the dungeons; of that other Pomeroy who killed her offspring and of the tragic and violent happenings here over the years, perhaps it is not surprising that something remains which can be picked up occasionally by some people, especially the young.

Palace Hotel, Paignton, Devon.

Bettiscombe House, SEE *Marshwood Vale.*

Bildeston, SUFFOLK.

The fifteenth-century Crown Inn has long had the reputation of being haunted. Twenty years ago I went there following reports of mysterious footsteps being heard in the rambling old inn; once they were heard by a policeman whose investigations were as completely unsuccessful as those of everyone else who has tried to discover the origin of them over the years. There are many reports too of 'touchings' and loud hammering noises; at one time the landlord thought that the latter could be accounted for by youths hammering at the front door of the inn but when next the knocks came, the landlord, ready for them this time, slipped quickly upstairs and looked out of a window which gave him an uninterrupted view of the front step. There was no one there but the hammering noise continued.

A British Legion secretary told me that once when he was in the bar, he pointed to a man wearing an overcoat and

old-fashioned hat who was standing in the private part of the house and asked the landlord who the stranger was. The landlord turned round but the figure had vanished and it seems that there had in fact been no human being there.
Great White Horse Hotel, Ipswich, Suffolk.

Bisham Abbey, BERKSHIRE, NEAR MARLOW, BUCKINGHAM-SHIRE.

A Tudor house, now belonging to the Central Council of Physical Recreation, it was long reputed to be haunted. A Preceptory of the Knights Templars that became a stately Abbey formerly occupied this site and the mansion that remains is essentially the same building that King Henry VIII gave to his discarded Queen, Anne of Cleves.

Richard Neville, Earl of Warwick, known as the king-maker, knew Bisham and his bones are buried hereabouts. The property passed into the hands of the Hoby family, one of whom, Sir Thomas Hoby, had custody of the Princess Elizabeth during the reign of Queen Mary. He must have been a gentle goaler for after her accession, Elizabeth appointed him Ambassador to France, and it is the ghost of his wife, the Lady Elizabeth Hoby, that has for so long been alleged to haunt this beautiful old house.

Lady Hoby was a scholar; she wrote Greek and Latin verse and composed religious treatises. The haunting of Bisham Abbey, handed down from generation to generation, is in accord with her character, for such a highly accomplished and intellectual person might well have had little patience with a dull child, slow at learning, such as her son William is said to have been. His work was slovenly and untidy and his copy-books were usually full of ink blots. His mother seems to have been in the habit of severely chastising the boy and one day, perhaps when his copy-books were really disgraceful, she thrashed him so unmercifully that he died.

Soon afterwards, Lady Hoby herself died and not long after her death her ghost was reported to be seen gliding from a bedroom, in the act of washing bloodstains from her hands, in a basin of water which floated before her 'without visible means of support'. This is the ghost which has been repeatedly seen over the centuries, recognized by comparing it with old family portraits, still hanging in the hall. Lady Hoby is represented with a very white face and hands and dressed in the coif, weeds and wimple of a knight's widow. Those who have seen her always say that she appears in the negative (speaking in the photographic sense), with black face and hands and white dress.

The same figure has been reported in the grounds and two boys, returning late one evening from fishing, saw an unexplained figure as they walked along the river bank by Bisham: an old woman dressed in black and sitting in a boat. Both she and the boat disappeared as the watchers approached. There have been reports in the past, too, of visitors being woken up in the night by the sound of foot-steps shuffling along corridors no longer there and sometimes there is the sound of hysterical weeping. When Admiral Vansittart lived at Bisham he ridiculed the idea of ghosts until one night when he played a late game of chess with his brother in the panelled room where Lady Hoby's portrait hangs. 'We had finished playing,' he said, 'and my brother had gone up to bed. I stood for some time with my back to the wall, turning the day over in my mind. Minutes passed. I looked round. It was Dame Hoby. The frame on the wall was empty! Terrified, I fled the room.'

During alterations in 1840, workmen are said to have found some antique copy-books pushed into the wall between the joists and the skirting, beneath a sixteenth-century window-shutter and several of these books, on which young William Hoby's name was written, were covered with blots. Unhappily this evidence is the only known reference to the existence of William Hoby. The copy-books were later lost. Lady Hoby had four children by her first husband: Edward, Elizabeth, Anne and Thomas and by her second husband one son, Francis, who is recorded as having died in his infancy. Edward and Thomas grew to manhood and were knighted; the two girls died within a few days of each other in 1570.

George and Dragon Hotel, The Causeway, Marlow, Bucks.

Blackburn, LANCASHIRE.

A few miles north of Blackburn on the way to Preston, stands mediaeval Samlesbury Old Hall with its two 'ghost' lovers. One is a lady in white who is said to have been the daughter of a previous owner of Samlesbury Hall and the other a knight who loved her. The girl's brother slew the knight, so goes the story, and the ghosts of the lovers are said to be seen occasionally in the vicinity of the murder, hovering above the present level of the ground.
Barton Grange Hotel, Preston, Lancs.

Blandford, DORSET.

Long-vanished Eastbury Park was built by George Dodington in the middle of the eighteenth century and allowed to fall into ruin by a later owner, Earl Temple, who found himself unable to afford such a huge place. At one time he even offered £200 a year and free residence to anyone who would take the mansion and keep it in repair.

Earl Temple, it seems, had a fraudulent steward named Doggett and it is his ghost which haunts or haunted the road and long drive from the park gates to the house. He, according to tradition, robbed his employer, oppressed the tenants and eventually shot himself.

On the stroke of midnight, on certain unspecified nights of the year, a coach with headless coachmen and headless horses was said to drive out of the park, pick up Doggett and return to the house where he would alight from the coach, enter the house and proceed to the panelled room where he had shot himself. The sound of a pistol shot would again be heard, ending the ghostly episode.

Doggett was recognized by his knee-breeches which were always tied with a yellow silk ribbon and when workmen exhumed his body, during the demolition of the neighbouring church where he was buried, his legs were found to have been tied together with yellow silk ribbon—and the material was as bright and fresh as the day it had been tied, nor was the body decayed. Little wonder that the local people averred that he was a vampire.
Crown Hotel, West Street, Blandford Forum, Dorset.

Blickling Hall, SEE *Aylsham*, NORFOLK.

***Borley*, ON THE BORDERS OF ESSEX AND SUFFOLK, NEAR LONG
MELFORD.**

Here is the site of 'the most haunted house in England',
Borley Rectory, built in 1863 and destroyed by fire in 1939.
Everyone who lived in the house and literally hundreds of
visitors asserted that they heard, saw or felt things they could
not explain. The famous Borley 'nun' has been seen by dozens of reputable witnesses including three former rectors
of the parish, visiting clergymen, doctors and two of the
present occupants of the cottage near the site. The full story
was published by famous psychical researcher Harry Price
in his books: *'The Most Haunted House in England'*
(1940) and *The End of Borley Rectory* (1946). His findings
and handling of the case was attacked by three members of
the Society for Psychical Research in 1956 (after Price's
death) but an Examination by another member of the same
Society published in the 'Proceedings' of the S.P.R. in 1969
rehabilitated Price and the haunting remains as baffling and
as fascinating as any in the annals of psychical research.
Certainly there exists more evidence for this haunting than
for any other alleged haunted house anywhere in the world.
   In the 1900s Borley Rectory, as a haunted house, had
everything: it was a gaunt, ugly, isolated monstrosity approached by a winding, lonely, overshadowed country lane.
The red-brick house had a window bricked up here, a wing
added there, and the whole impression was grotesque and
ominous—and yet the place held a strange fascination for
its successive inhabitants: the Rev. H. D. E. Bull who built
the house and added to it as his family increased and who
died there in the haunted Blue Room in 1892; his son,
the Rev. Harry Bull from 1892 until he too died there in the
Blue Room in 1927; the Rev. Guy Eric Smith, an Anglo-
Indian, from 1928 to 1930; the Rev. Lionel Foyster from
1930 to 1935 and, although he never really lived in the
house, the Rev. Alfred C. Henning from 1936 to his death
in 1955. Subsequently many curious happenings have been
reported from the site of the vanished rectory, the vicinity

of the cottage and the church just across the road.

The rambling rectory acquired a 'haunted house' reputation almost as soon as it was occupied and the Rev. and Mrs H. D. E. Bull knew all about the legend that a monastery formerly occupied the site and that a monk, attempting to elope with a nun from a nearby nunnery, had been hanged and the nun bricked up alive. The ghostly nun was supposed to walk each July 28th. I talked with several of the children of the Rev. H. D. E. Bull and in particular with Ethel Bull, the last to survive, and she told me of the remarkable experience she had with three of her sisters on the afternoon of July 28th, 1900. She and Freda and Mabel were returning from a garden party in the late afternoon and as they reached the rectory gate they all saw a nun-like figure gliding slowly along a path that had long been known as the 'Nun's Walk'. The face of the figure was not visible and they heard no sound but the 'nun' appeared to be solid and Ethel thought she might be telling her beads. Ethel and Mabel stood by the gate watching the figure while Freda ran into the house and fetched a fourth sister, Elsie, who also saw the figure and thinking there was nothing strange about it, went forward to ask what she wanted; whereupon the figure vanished. Mr P. Shaw Jeffrey, M.A., a former headmaster of Colchester Grammar School told me that he visited the rectory in either 1885 or 1886 and saw the 'nun' several times.

Mr Shaw added that Harry Bull told him: he, too, had seen the ghost nun, both before and after he took over the living of Borley. I talked too with a resident of nearby Cavendish who used to go to the rectory for instruction in Latin when Harry Bull was rector. Once when he was spending the night there the Rev. Harry Bull came to his bedroom door after everyone in the rectory had been awakened by a loud peal of bells. Mr Bull was much perturbed by the ringing for which there seemed to be no normal explanation; he was concerned lest it foretold misfortune for himself or his family. On another occasion Harry Bull, 'a puckish, lovable man', said that if he was dissatisfied with his successor, he would try to make his presence felt from beyond the grave in some singular and unusual way—'such as throwing moth-balls about: that's it, moth-balls; then you'll know it's me'.

After Harry Bull's death moth-balls did in fact fly about the deserted rectory. A doctor who knew Harry Bull described him to me as 'one of the most normal men you could meet'. Harry Bull told many people that he had seen the ghost nun; that he had seen and heard phantom coach-and-horses and had witnessed a wealth of varied psychic phenomena which left him in no doubt but that the rectory was haunted.

Eric Smith and his English wife were the third occupants of the haunted rectory and it was not long before the Smiths were puzzled and alarmed to find curious and quite inexplicable things happening in and around the house. Mrs Smith saw what she took to be a horse-drawn coach with lights on in the drive; rooms in the rectory lit up mysteriously; bells rang, footsteps were heard and she would frequently complain of the curious occurrences to neighbours and friends. Mr Smith, too, heard and saw things for which he could find no explanation; once he heard words like *'Don't, Carlos, don't!'* when he was near the archway on the first floor leading to the chapel. Soon he appealed to a daily paper for assistance and they sent down Harry Price who lost no time in obtaining evidence pertaining to the haunting from all the principal witnesses, little thinking that twenty years later he would still be occupied with this enigmatic case. The Smiths welcomed Price and his investigators; they supplied him with details of their experiences; entertained him and gave him facilities for his researches and repeatedly asked him to produce a printed report on the case. His initial book on the haunting was received by them enthusiastically and with no criticism whatever; but within nine months they left the rectory (giving as their reason 'lack of amenities') residing at Long Melford for another nine months when they moved to Norfolk, and later to Kent. Mr Smith died in 1940; Mrs Smith now lives in East Anglia her memories of Borley Rectory, of Harry Price and of her husband, confused and muddled.

In October, 1930, the Rev. L. A. Foyster (a relative of the Bulls) and his much younger wife Marianne moved into the rectory and from then until they left almost exactly five years later, the unusual happenings at Borley reached their zenith. Messages were discovered on walls and pieces of paper—appealing for *'Light'*, *'Mass'* and *'Prayers'*—bottles

Bramber, Sussex, a village where ghostly children run after passers-by and vanish when they are spoken to. *Photo: Chris Underwood*

Haunted Berry Pomeroy Castle, near Totnes, Devon, persistently haunted by the beautiful Margaret de Pomeroy who walks the ramparts in flowing white robes on certain nights. *Photo: West of England Newspapers Ltd.*

The Black House, Higher Brixham, Devon, used by the monks when they were building nearby St. Mary's Church, harbours the ghost of a monk. Unexplained footsteps and curious happenings have been reported here for many years. *Photo: Chris Underwood*

Borley Rectory, Essex. Probably the earliest photograph in existence of 'the most haunted house in England' that was mysteriously destroyed by fire. The Rev. H. D. E. Bull and his wife are on the veranda.

materialized and flew about and de-materialized; articles appeared and disappeared; noises of practically every description were reported; phantom figures were seen. Things were so bad and so regular that the Rev. L. A. Foyster kept a diary of events and circulated among his family details of the curious happenings. Among the contemporary evidence in my possession for this period is the testimony of Dom Richard Whitehouse, a nephew of Lady Whitehouse of Arthur Hall, Sudbury. Dom Richard approached me in 1956 with a view to our meeting and discussing Borley in detail; the result was a lengthy discussion in London followed, at my request, by a written and signed account of his evidence and views. This letter or statement of facts puts fairly and squarely on record an independent account of the psychic phenomena occurring at Borley at this period, for Dom Richard witnessed movement of objects without human contact; pencilled wall-writing; an unexplained outbreak of fire; door-locking and un-locking; bell-ringing and other inexplicable noises and the materialization and de-materialization of bottles. His evidence alone, it has been suggested to me, establishes the haunting of Borley Rectory for all time. (I reproduced this evidence in the *Examination of the Borley Report*' published by the Society for Psychical Research in their Proceedings in March, 1969.) Other contemporary evidence for paranormal activity at the rectory at this period includes that of Captain V. M. Deane. He told me at a meeting of The Ghost Club in 1948 that there is not the slightest shadow of doubt: in good light showers of bottles and stones fell amongst observers who saw the phenomena with their own eyes, heard them with their own ears and handled the objects, thus using three of the five senses. Mr Guy L'Estrange, J.P. has told me about the bottles he saw thrown and broken; how one missed his ear by about an inch and of the tremendous din caused by the violent ringing, 'by no human hands', of the thirty bells in the hall. The Rev. L. A. Foyster died in 1945; Marianne who has lived a strange and unhappy life now resides in Canada where, under pressure, she has told conflicting stories of her life at Borley Rectory, the people she met there and her subsequent life.

After the departure of the Foysters the haunted rectory

was empty. Harry Price had the foresight and ingenuity to rent the property for a year for the purpose of scientific investigation. He arranged a rota of investigators of high integrity who spent varying periods at Borley and their detailed reports provide further evidence of unexplained happenings. The principal investigator was Sidney H. Glanville, a retired consulting engineer, with whom I spent many hours both in London and at his home at Fittleworth. Glanville became deeply interested in the Borley haunt as a scientific problem and he compiled a typed manuscript with pasted-in photographs, cuttings, booklets, posters, tracings and plans that became known as *'The Locked Book of Private Information'* after Price acquired it, had it bound in morocco and fitted it with a Bramah lock. Glanville became convinced of the genuineness of the Borley haunting based on his own experiences and the evidence he had obtained firsthand from witnesses; all of which he collated and presented in his scrap book of Borley. With his permission I took a verbatim copy of the 'Locked Book' to add to my Borley Dossier.

Other people, apart from the occupants and investigators experienced curious happenings at Borley and the inhabitants of the rectory cottage had their own stories to tell over the years: the Coopers, who lived there from 1916 to 1920 told me of the 'padding' noise they heard night after night, of the 'black shape' in their bedroom with its distinctive smell; of the ghostly coach-and-horses and the hooded figure Mr Cooper saw in the courtyard; the Arbons who were at the cottage in the 1930s have curious experiences to relate; the Turners, there from 1947 to 1950 reported many strange things at the time; and the Bacons and the Williams who are there now have also testified to many unexplained occurrences. In 1926 a journeyman-carpenter saw the sad-faced figure of a nun, waiting at the gate of the rectory on four successive mornings as he walked up the lane on his way to work; on the last occasion it occurred to him that she might want help so immediately he had passed her, he turned, but she had vanished and he never saw her again. Years later a local doctor had an almost identical experience. Clive Luget, Rector of Middleton, told me many interesting details about the haunting for he was actively associated with several suc-

34

cessive rectors of Borley and he entertained no doubts as to the authenticity of the numerous manifestations he and others had witnessed there.

The property was sold to Captain Gregson in December, 1938 and in February, 1939 (seemingly fulfilling a planchette prediction made eleven months earlier) the place was gutted by fire. Later that year Dr A. J. B. Robertson organized and controlled a Cambridge Commission which conducted investigations and experiments at what was left of the rectory. These inquiries continued until 1944 and the detailed report issued later shows that peculiar temperature variations were scientifically recorded; a luminous patch was seen; footsteps were heard; knocks and other noises were heard—on one occasion eighteen knocks in a row—stones were thrown; strange smells were noticed; unexplained lights were seen. All this evidence was presented soberly and factually by Mr Robertson, M.A., a Fellow of St John's College, Cambridge, holder of an honours degree in chemistry, a Doctor of Philosophy and a member of the Society for Psychical Research.

Over the Christmas holiday of 1939, the Rev. Canon W. J. Phythian-Adams, D.D., Canon of Carlisle, read *'The Most Haunted House in England'* and produced a brilliant theory involving a young French Roman Catholic brought to this country in the seventeenth or eighteenth century, betrayed and murdered and her remains buried on the site. The Canon suggested digging and Price dug in the cellars and found human remains which medical experts believed to be those of a young woman; in particular a jaw bone showed evidence of a deep-seated abscess which must have caused considerable pain to the owner. It is interesting that many witnesses of the ghost nun have described her as 'miserable', or with 'face drawn' or with a 'pale face' or 'sad' and never as looking happy or laughing. The remains were buried in Liston churchyard and thereafter the Canon and Price kept up a lively correspondence until that day in 1948 when Price had a sudden heart attack and died. When he left Carlisle, Canon Phythian-Adams, with whom I discussed Borley and its mysteries both in London and at my home, presented me with all his correspondence pertaining to the Borley haunting and this too is in my Borley Dossier.

Since the death of Harry Price I have collected a wealth of first-hand contemporary evidence for unexplained happenings at Borley, both in the vicinity of the rectory site and in the nearby church and churchyard. There are many reports of unexplained footsteps in and around the church: they come from such diverse witnesses as an archaeologist, a nursing sister, a Sunday school teacher, a visiting rector and his wife, a student, a headmistress, a poet and literary consultant. They include a member of The Ghost Club who, one September evening of the full moon, heard heavy footsteps hurriedly approach the church, yet when he stood up in the church porch ready to greet whoever was coming along the path, the sounds ceased instantly.

There are reliable reports of unexplained organ music being heard from the locked and empty church. Among witnesses for this phenomenon are Mrs Norah Walrond (Norah Burke, the novelist), the Rev. A. C. Henning, a visitor to Borley, Mrs A. G. Wilson and her thirteen-year-old sister-in-law, Vivienne Wilson, who both heard the sounds at the same moment. Early in 1970 the sounds were heard yet again during the course of investigations by a party of scientists.

The nun-like figure has been seen many times since the destruction of the rectory, both on the rectory site and in the churchyard. The present occupants of the cottage are Mr and Mrs R. Bacon, their children, Terrence and José and Mrs Bacon's father, Mr Williams. All have experienced curious happenings which they cannot explain in rational terms. Terrence claims to have seen the 'nun' three times and Mr Williams to have seen her once. In 1952 I interviewed a Mr Cole of Great Cornard who once saw in Borley churchyard, in 1951, a nun who looked rather sad and seemed to be sheltering under a tree. She looked quite normal and wore a black hood, a white collar, a golden-coloured bodice and a black skirt which stood open about eight inches down the front disclosing a blue under-dress. When Mr Cole approached the figure, she suddenly disappeared. In 1949 the Rev. Stanley C. Kipling of Barnoldswick, Lancashire, visited Borley to read the lesson at the funeral of a friend. As he stood at the west door he saw the figure of a veiled girl in the churchyard and as he watched, she passed behind

36

a shrub to another close by and then vanished. He told me that she appeared to be a 'frail' girl, aged about eighteen to twenty-three and he distinctly saw the shape of a nun's hood on her head from which the thick veiling hung. A couple of months later two 'ghost-hunters' reported seeing a figure in black walk silently towards the priest's door at Borley church. No sound broke the silence of the night although the figure appeared to be walking on the pathway. No door opened and the figure simply disappeared. In 1956 Mr Peter Rowe, a retired Bank of England official, member of The Ghost Club and of The Society for Psychical Research, went to Borley with a friend to whom he was telling the story of the Borley nun. Mr Rowe stopped his car by the gate to the rectory garden and his friend turned towards Mr Rowe as he listened to the story and so had his back to the rectory site. He failed to see a nun-like figure with head-gear flowing behind her, run past the gate with short, quick steps, towards the south-east end of the old rectory garden. Mr Rowe was quickly out of the car and examining the site of the rectory but there was no sign of a nun; indeed there was no sign of anyone on or near the rectory site apart from Mr Rowe and his friend. From the fact that the black habit which the figure wore was not voluminous, Mr Rowe gained the impression that she was a novice. In 1970 the ghost nun was reported to have been seen again.

Curious odours were experienced when the rectory still stood and this phenomenon too has survived the fire. Unexplained smells of incense, of violets completely out of season, of corpse-like smells and distinctive, heavy smells, often lo─ 'ized and stationary even if a wind was blowing; all have been reported at Borley.

Among the unusual noises reported since the rectory fire are numerous raps (once experienced by B.B.C. producers); the noise of a panting dog which seemed to follow the late Mrs Williams along the Nun's Walk; noises of heavy furniture being moved and of crashing crockery, when nothing has been moved or broken; and voices, happy and laughing, that Mr Turner heard night after night for a fortnight when he was clearing the old Bull orchard. In 1970 distinct thuds were heard on the rectory site which seemed to have no normal explanation.

Careful examination of the evidence for the haunting of Borley Rectory suggests that this was a unique case, perhaps caused by successive occupants of a similar psychic awareness or sensitivity living in a house built on the site of an earlier building with a tragic history. But whatever the reason, this is a truly remarkable case of haunting which will be dealt with in detail in the *Borley Omnibus*, now in active preparation.
Bull Hotel, Long Melford, Suffolk.

Boscombe, HAMPSHIRE.

Twenty-eight-year-old secretary Margaret Best was repeatedly tucked into bed by a 'ghost' for over nine months in 1964.

She told me that she would wake up in the middle of the night conscious that 'something' was in the room although she never saw anything; then she would feel the bedclothes being tucked in all round her divan bed. She would lay still, not daring to let the presence know that she was awake and soon the 'influence' in the room would go away. Occasionally objects in the room were moved, too. A curious feature of the case was the fact that the 'ghost' seemed to visit the flatlet at more or less regular intervals.

Sometimes Margaret Best had the impression of being strangled and she discovered marks on her throat consistent with this actually happening. The disturbance ceased as mysteriously as it began.
Fircroft Hotel, Owls Road, Boscombe, Bournemouth, Hants.

Bramber, NEAR STEYNING, SUSSEX.

A village that is reputed to have ghostly children that run after passers-by, begging for food.

Eight hundred years ago when Bramber Castle was owned, together with forty manors, by William de Breose, King John suspected the loyalty of the powerful lord and demanded his children as hostages. Although the family fled to Ireland, they were captured and taken to Windsor Castle, where they were starved to death. The story of the ghosts of these starved children used to be well-known in the vicinity of Bramber.

Usually about Christmas time the emaciated figures of a little boy and a little girl would be seen gazing wistfully at the ruins of their former home, and sometimes they would be seen in the village, at night time, begging for food. Starved and in rags, the pathetic ghosts would pursue anyone who saw them, holding out their hands in mute appeal. Should anyone attempt to speak to them, they simply vanished.

Three Tuns Inn, High Street, Steyning, Sussex.

Brede Place, NEAR RYE, SUSSEX.

Once described by the architect Sir Edwin Lutyens, who designed the Cenotaph in Whitehall and the British Embassy at Washington, as the most interesting haunted house in Sussex.

In 1350 one of King Edward III's knights, helped by monks, erected this mediaeval manor house. In 1570 the Oxenbridge family added two wings and the following owners, the Frewens (one of whom was related to Sir Winston Churchill, who planted a golden yew tree here on one of his visits) restored the house and improved the garden, adding much period furniture, tapestries and pictures. The present owner is Mr Roger Moreton Frewen who told me of the history and hauntings associated with his beautiful home.

In the eighteenth century the house was a favourite haunt of smugglers and it is thought that a horror story about a former owner, Sir Goddard Oxenbridge, was invented to keep prying eyes away from it. He was presented as a giant ogre who devoured babies. Eventually, the story goes, the children of East and West Sussex succeeded in capturing the giant and sawed him in half with a wooden saw at a spot marked on the map as Groaning Bridge. The story was spread around that various portions of the luckless giant would appear in different parts of the house for ever!

The chapel and its adjoining rooms are particularly haunted and perhaps this fact has some connection with the bones of a priest that were found buried underneath the original altar during restoration in 1830, wearing a gilt cross round his neck. One owner used to say that she could draw a line through the house to divide the part that was evil and that which was not. 'The rooms adjoining the chapel,' she stated, '—which used to have a room over it but which was so haunted that it had to be taken down—and the dungeons beneath the house are certainly haunted.'

In 1936 sculptress Clair Sheridan, née Frewen and her son Dick, made the house their home. After Dick's death, his mother became much drawn to the occult and saw several ghosts at Brede: Marthe, a Tudor maidservant who is said to have been hanged from an oak tree in the grounds and haunted the dell where she died, Father John, a priest who lived at Brede hundreds of years before and other ghostly visitants.

During the 1939-45 War members of the British Army were at Brede Place and there were several reports of ghostly monks being seen by various officers. Some Canadian officers also had a number of ghostly encounters. Chairs and tables moved without anyone being near them; boots and other articles of clothing were shifted and found hidden in odd parts of the house. On one occasion the ghost of Father John is said to have walked through a file of men in one of the corridors.

George Hotel, Rye, Sussex.

Bristol.

In the early 1900s a fine house in the best residential part of Bristol was reputed to be haunted by a 'horrible, pale-faced' servant girl. She was said to have been the natural daughter of a wealthy man who owned the house some fifty years earlier. A half-witted, hunch-backed creature, she always wore a cheap pink dress and lived a miserable life, half-starved and often beaten, until in the end she drowned herself in a pool in the garden.

A widowed colonel's wife and her three daughters took a long lease of the house in the early part of this century and settled comfortably into the house but were unable to obtain a housemaid for several weeks; yet, soon after they moved in, one of the daughters passed on the stairs a young girl, in a pink dress, busily sweeping with brush and pan as if her very life depended upon it. Thinking that her mother must have obtained a temporary maid, the daughter gave the girl no more than a glance but the impression that she obtained was distinctly unfavourable; the girl appeared to be untidy and sluttish, her cap was soiled and askew, she was practically hump-backed and she had such a white, unhealthy face. The ghost girl was next seen by another daughter of the colonel's widow. This time she seemed to be aware of the daughter's presence and slithered down the stairs, grinning hideously over her shoulder as she closed a door behind her.

Montague Summers, that remarkable student of ghosts, witchcraft and vampires, told me that when he visited the house, he also saw a most repulsive-looking and dishevelled little maid in a dirty pink frock, near the front door. The creature grinned and then slipped away through a red baize door at the back of the hall.

A week later one of the colonel's daughters, alone in the house at the time, went down to the basement to fetch some hot water and was astonished, when she pushed the kitchen door open, to see the girl in the pink dress, apparently busy at the kitchen range, with her back towards the door. 'What on earth are you doing here?' the daughter of the house asked. The figure swung round, an impudent leer on her white face and without a word of explanation, scuttled off into an adjoining room, from which there was no other exit. At last, the widow's daughter thought, I'll catch you face to face; but the scullery was empty and of the mysterious girl in the pink dress there was no sign. Suddenly frightened, she turned and ran upstairs, pausing to recover breath on the landing when, to her horror, she saw, grinning at her through the landing window, thirty feet from the ground, the white face of the ghostly housemaid she had left a moment before in the kitchen! 'How I got out of the house I don't know,' she told Montague Summers; but she was found in the porch in a dead faint and was so ill afterwards that she went to Brighton to recover which took several months. By then her mother and sisters had left the house and found another, without a ghost.

Montague Summers told me that the family who moved in after the colonel's widow stayed less than a month; and the next tenants left abruptly within an even shorter time. As stories of the ghost spread the house stood empty and as Summers was fond of saying, he was sure it would always be empty—except for the ghost-maid.

Dunraven Hotel, Upper Belgrave Road, Bristol.

Burford, OXFORDSHIRE.

The ancient Priory, hard by the River Windrush that ran red with blood twelve hundred years ago after a battle between the kingdoms of Mercia and Wessex, is said to be haunted by a little brown monk and by the sound of a bell that rings at two o'clock in the morning. Little is known of the origin of either haunting.

Richard, Earl of Warwick (1428-71) was one of the Lords of Burford. King Charles II came here with Nell for there is still a room called 'Nell Gwynne's Room'. King William II stayed here. A Lord Abercorn was tried for murder of a man whose body was found in the grounds, while in the nineteenth century the place became neglected and was avoided by the local people because it was said to be haunted. Sir Archibald Southby bought it some sixty years ago, restored and repaired the property but never had any luck there. Lady Southby always said it was 'very haunted' and would never be peaceful until it went back to the church, for Augustinian monks were here before recorded history.

In 1947 the Priory passed into the hands of the Anglo-Catholic Church and some twenty sisters of the Benedictine order now reside in the Priory itself while the old Rectory houses the convent's chaplain and the gardener and his wife. Both houses are haunted.

At the old Rectory there are stories of articles being thrown about, of screams being heard from an empty room, of things disappearing in front of one's eyes and of an overwhelming atmosphere of sadness.

The figure of a man dressed like an old-fashioned gamekeeper has been seen by the sisters, carrying an out-of-date gun under his arm and walking right through anything that is in his path. The sound of singing has been heard in the garden, not far from the old monks' burial ground. The little brown monk has been seen by many people in the entrance hall of The Priory. Lady Southby used to say that visitors frequently saw the strange figure in the hall and a relative of one of the sisters saw the same figure on two occasions. Another visitor saw a monk in brown habit on the path leading to the chapel and the same form has been glimpsed, it seems, in the chapel itself and in one of the corridors outside the nuns' cells.

In this strange, silent place footsteps have been repeatedly heard that have no normal explanation, doors have opened and closed, distinct knocks have been heard on doors and walls and the mysterious bell has been heard to ring on many, many occasions. It always rings at two o'clock in the morning, the time that the mediaeval monks of Burford were called to worship.

The Cotswold Gateway Hotel, Burford, Oxon.

Bury St Edmunds, SUFFOLK.

The remains of the mighty abbey which once housed the shrine of St Edmund, King of the East Angles, who was martyred by the Danes, include the Gateway where occasionally ghostly, monk-like figures have been reported. When I was there in 1942 I met several local people who told me of their personal experiences in and around the Abbey Gateway, a place which has been described as 'one of the most spiritually-powerful spots in England'. Some years ago a former Rector of Risby, the Rev. A. F. Webling, told me that he had received messages from his two dead sons and that several of the former Abbey monks 'influenced' him when he was writing a book on the last years of St Edmund's life. One dead Abbot had told him that St Edmund's body had been taken out of the sarcophagus and placed in another part of the church where it was buried deep as a protection against defilement. There was some talk years ago of excavation on the site of the transept facing the high altar, in the hope of discovering the saint's remains,

but as far as I know this was never undertaken.
Suffolk Hotel, Bury St Edmunds, Suffolk.

*Caister, LINCOLNSHIRE.

The local church has long been reputed to be haunted by a monk who plays the organ. In January 1967 the vicar, Canon Ernest Pitman, decided to end the story once and for all by placing a tape-recorder in the old church one night and locking the door. Next morning when he ran the tape, there were footsteps echoing through the empty church and loud and clear notes from the church organ—with banging noises that were not part of the traditional ghost story!
Yarborough Hotel, Old Market Place, Grimsby, Lincs.

Caldmore Green, WALSALL, STAFFORDSHIRE.

The old White Hart Inn has a haunted attic where a mummi-fied baby's arm was once found. There is a story, too, of an elderly maid who committed suicide here in the early 1900s. A few years ago the licensee heard curious noises and cries which appeared to come from the attic and when he inves-tigated he found the imprint of a tiny hand on a dust-covered table in the attic. He had heard the noises before and thought there must be a logical explanation but after his visit to the attic and the evidence of a former licensee's wife who woke up one night to find a white form standing by her bed, he had second thoughts about the place not being haunted.
George Hotel, The Bridge, Walsall, Staffs.

Cambridge, CHRIST'S COLLEGE.

A haunting known as 'the college mystery' concerns a mul-berry tree in the Fellows' Garden, planted by Milton where, on certain nights of the full moon, a tall, elderly, stooping figure is seen at midnight. It is thought to be the ghost of Christopher Round who murdered another Fellow and

lived in repentance for forty years. The figure walks in the solitude of the garden with his hands behind his back; occasionally a heavy and ponderous step, for which no explanation has ever been discovered, is heard mounting the staircase of the college to the first floor.
Blue Boar Hotel, Cambridge, Cambs.

*Canterbury, CITY WALL, SUDBURY TOWER.

Eighty-year-old Charles Denne told me that he had dwelled here with a ghost for twenty years. It all began when he retired one evening to his bedroom at the top of the tower, where he lived all alone. After a busy day repairing shoes, he was having a rest before getting his evening meal when he heard someone knocking at his bedroom door; there were three distinct knocks and then the door opened. Although he knew that he was alone on the premises, Mr Denne told me that he did not feel afraid as he saw that his late visitor, apparently as solid and substantial as himself, although wearing very out-of-date clothes and what looked like a grey robe, walk slowly towards his bed. Mr Denne said that he felt a strong feeling of friendliness emanating from the stranger and as he rose from his bed to offer the visitor his hand in welcome, the strange figure with its grey square-cut beard, bowed three times—and disappeared. Mr Denne never saw the figure again but he often felt the presence in his bedroom and on occasions he was aware of a pair of hands 'tucking him in' at night-time. He often heard strange tapping noises which sometimes came before he had the feeling that his 'visitor' was in the room with him.
Chaucer Hotel, Canterbury, Kent.

*Chatham, KENT.

Two neighbouring houses in Magpie Hall Road are reported to have been haunted at night for over twenty years by unexplained noises, rappings and footsteps—noises which always stopped when a light was switched on. Time after time, the occupants told me, footsteps followed by rapping

45

as though someone wanted to come in, were heard from the vicinity of the stairs and bedrooms; sometimes the rapping sounded louder and more violent than at others but always it stopped when a light was switched on. It usually began about midnight and sometimes went on till about five o'clock. Years ago a man committed suicide in one of the houses by cutting his throat and in the same house a previous occupant complained that she had seen a 'form' she could not account for.

King's Head Hotel, Rochester, Kent.

Cheam, SURREY.

The Century Cinema was the scene of curious and unexplained happenings a few years ago, when sounds of shuffling feet were heard by some of the cinema staff, including the manager, apparently coming from the empty stage. When some of them, with three local reporters, held a midnight watch in the silent cinema they all heard the mysterious shuffling noise on three occasions from the right-hand side of the stage. The noises, which could not be traced to mice or any other rodent, may have had some connection with the disappearance of a workman who helped to build the cinema some forty years ago. His lunch-bag and hat were found hanging on a nail near the part of the building which is now the stage and his wages were never collected. He seems to have disappeared without trace and some people have wondered whether something happened to him and whether the ghostly shuffling footsteps that are heard from time to time are his.

Drift Bridge Hotel, Reigate Road, Epsom, Surrey.

*Cheltenham, GLOUCESTERSHIRE.

There is a large house here, formerly a school and now divided into flats, where the ghost of a nun used to appear each New Year's Eve at six-fifteen p.m.

Miss Margot Vincent Smith, formerly of Randolph Crescent, Edinburgh, was a nurse at the house when the building was used as a girl's school and she first saw the apparition in 1939. She was shown the figure, some fifty yards from the house at the far end of the open play-ground, by the headmaster, from an upstairs window. As they watched, the figure moved backwards into a sitting posture, although no seat was visible. It appeared to be wearing a white habit, complete with hood. The headmaster asked Miss Smith to remain watching while he descended to see whether the figure was also visible from a lower floor window, but a moment later it vanished.

Miss Smith, who was interviewed at Wandsworth Training College in 1951, stated that she also saw the apparition the following New Year's Eve, but on that occasion the figure appeared at seven-fifteen p.m. one hour later—because British Summer Time was in force. The 'nun' was seen at the precise spot as the previous year. On this occasion Miss Smith and the headmaster went to the edge of the play-ground. The figure seemed to be solid and looked as clear-cut and distinct as when viewed from a distance. There was bright moonlight. When the headmaster directed a torch on to the figure, the light immediately went out and the torch could not be made to work. They intended to attempt to speak to the figure on this occasion but the headmaster, after his experience with the torch, made no attempt to do so. Miss Smith, with no obstruction between her and the ghostly form, began to feel somewhat uneasy and the watchers retired to the school-house. Soon after 1940 Miss Smith left the school.

I had been in touch with Professor H. H. Price, a past-President of the Society for Psychical Research and at that time Wykeham Professor of Logic at Oxford, concerning the case and we decided to visit Cheltenham together and try to find out whether the 'nun' had put in any appearances in recent years. We found the house and located the owner who told us that she had no knowledge of the haunting. She would not permit an investigation under any circumstances and so we had to give up what had promised to be an interesting exploration of a recurring manifestation.
Queen's Hotel, Cheltenham, Glos.

Chenies Manor House was visited by King Henry VIII with Anne Boleyn and, seven years later, with Catherine Howard. King Charles I came here as a prisoner of the Parliamentarians in 1648. It is now owned and occupied by Lt.-Col. Alastair MacLeod Matthews and his charming wife, Elizabeth.

They moved into the house in 1956 and realized immediately that they had a ghost for they were disturbed in the small hours of the morning by heavy and distinct footsteps and the creaking of floorboards. They investigated and traced the sounds to an anteroom of the apartment which Queen Elizabeth I had occupied nearly four hundred years before.

Once Lt.-Col. Matthews heard limping footsteps outside his bedroom and noticed that the time was about two o'clock as he got out of bed and followed the sounds. He traced them to the vicinity of the ancient gallery where two hundred of Cromwell's men were reputed to have slept.

More recently, the Matthews had house-guests and it was arranged that they should occupy the Pink Room—until Mrs Matthews pointed out that there was no wardrobe in that room nor a convenient place where one could be installed. Her husband then consulted the plans of the house and discovered that there used to be a small prayer room in the corner of the room above although there was no corresponding space in the Pink Room. He took measurements which showed that there certainly should be a room of some kind in the corner of the Pink Room. It was decided to have the wall broken down and use the space that must be there for a wardrobe. After they had broken down two-and-a-half thicknesses of brickwork they found themselves in a space which was in fact a priest's hiding hole. The wall of the little room bore a year in the 1660s and, quite distinctly, the date of September 9th. A door was duly hung to the room. Some time later, after the visitors had been and gone, the Matthews' children were being rather troublesome at night and Lt.-Col. Matthews decided to sleep in the Pink Room. It was a very windy night, he told me, and he read himself to sleep with a candle, for electric light had not then been installed in that part of the house. The door to the little room had a 'Suffolk latch' and since the night was so boisterous, Matthews made sure that he gave the door a really good pull to before settling down for the night. He was quite certain that the door was absolutely secure and all the windows tightly closed. Suddenly a puff of wind blew out his candle so he decided to settle down for the night. He awoke early in the morning to find the windows and the door to the little room wide open, and when he eventually arose he discovered that the date was September 9th!

The Bedford Arms Hotel, Chenies, Bucks.

Chilton Cantelo, SOMERSET.

For over two hundred years the skull of Theophilus Brome has been kept at Higher Chilton Farm.

Tradition asserts that he requested that his head should be preserved at the farmhouse near the church when he died in August 1670. Repeated attempts to inter the head have resulted in 'horrid noises', heard throughout the farmhouse. In the 1860s a sexton began to dig a hole to bury the head but when his spade broke into two pieces, he declared that he would never again attempt 'an act so evidently repugnant to the quiet of Brome's head'. Brome was probably actively engaged in the Civil War and may have given the directions about the preservation of his head on account of the practice at the time of the Restoration for the bodies of those who had been against the monarchy to be taken from their burial-places and for the heads to be cut off and exhibited. During restoration of the church Brome's tomb was opened and the skeleton found inside—minus the head. It seems likely, therefore, that the head, or rather the skull, preserved in a special cabinet over a door in the hall at the farmhouse is indeed that of Theophilus Brome.

Portman Arms Hotel, East Chinnock, Yeovil, Somerset.

Claydon House, SEE *Middle Claydon*, NEAR AYLESBURY, BUCKINGHAMSHIRE.

Coggeshall, ESSEX.

There are many reports of local ghostly visitations; vague accounts of inexplicable happenings at the Abbey and at the Gatehouse, at Cradle House, Guild House and at some of the cottages. At number 47 Church Street in 1966, the occupants, Mr and Mrs Michael Grant and their two daughters, Isabel and Rebecca and son, Simon, were convinced that paranormal occurrences took place ever since they had moved into the house four years previously.

The rambling old house used to be an inn and later the residence of a baker. Still later (about 1959) it was reconstructed by a local builder but it still has a distinctly weird atmosphere. No reports of curious happenings seem to have been recorded before the reconstruction, but during the rebuilding a hidden room was discovered on the ground floor and it is in the vicinity of this room that most of the unexplained phenomena have occurred.

There is now a modern door leading from the previously hidden room into the present morning room. This door will suddenly open and shut by itself for no apparent reason, when there is no breath of wind. The door of the kitchen, too, has opened by itself—just like the doors in the hall. Curious smells, the unexplained appearance of objects, a sudden sensation of coldness, footsteps and the feeling that a 'presence' is in the house have all been reported by the Grants. Mr Grant said that sometimes 'there seems to be a eerie mist flitting past the bottom of the stairs', at other times the same thing has been seen at the top of the stairway. Pictures have fallen off walls in various rooms, quite inexplicably, but the Grants were not worried by the happenings, merely curious.

Cradle House, near Markshall Old Rectory, is said to be visited from time to time by ghostly white monks who dance in the garden, coming in through the gate near the little brook. The property now forms two cottages but it used to be known for its hidden stairway and recesses where the monks from Coggeshall Abbey held secret meetings.

The Guild House, Market End, has a small room under the eaves of the roof and here a mysterious light has been seen. After experiencing an overwhelming impression that

someone was in the room, occupants have sensed, or seen, an unidentified 'little man' who stood at the foot of the bed.
Red Lion Hotel, Colchester, Essex.

Connemara, IRELAND.

At Renvyle House many séances took place with such literary luminaries as W. B. Yeats, James Joyce and Oliver St John Gogarty taking part. Yeats always maintained that he personally raised the ghost of a remote member of the Blake family, who used to own the property; a man who had strangled himself with his own hands. It is said that the ghost still haunts the house.
Renvyle House Hotel, Killary Harbour, Connemara, W. Ireland.

Cookstown, COUNTY TYRONE, NORTHERN IRELAND.

A model council house was reported by the occupants Mr and Mrs Mullan and by visitors to be haunted by an indistinct figure resembling a man. He was claimed to have been seen by a number of people in the vicinity of the house. Inside the property unexplained footsteps were heard many times, pacing the floor of one of the bedrooms.
Conway Hotel, Belfast, N. Ireland.

*Cranford Park, MIDDLESEX.

Hardly anything remains now of the dark and ominous mansion, for so long the seat of the Fitzhardinge Berkeleys. It was a member of that illustrious family, the Hon. Grantley Berkeley, who first told of the ghost in the kitchen of the old house. He, together with his brother, returned home late one night, went down into the kitchen in search of food and there both distinctly saw the tall figure of an elderly woman. As they entered she walked from one side of the room to the other. Thinking she must be one of the maids, they called out to her, but by then the figure had reached the other side where she vanished. Puzzled, they searched diligently but could find no trace of the woman or of how she could have vanished. Grantley Berkeley's father used to describe a man he once saw in the stable-yard and who, on being challenged, vanished as completely and inexplicably as the woman in the kitchen.

Grenada Hotel, Lampton Road, Hounslow, Middlesex.

Creslow, NEAR AYLESBURY, BUCKINGHAMSHIRE.

Creslow, the smallest parish in the county has, or had, the largest field: the 'great pasture' containing three-hundred-and-twenty-seven acres and a romantically-situated old house, now vastly altered, that once had a famous 'haunted room'. The surrounding 'Creslow pastures', long celebrated for their exceptional fertility, were once Crown property. Cattle and produce from these fields supplied the tables of the monarchs from Queen Elizabeth I to King Charles II. Creslow Manor House was originally built by the Knights Templars who acquired the land in 1120 and added to by the Knights Hospitallers of St John of Jerusalem. In succeeding years much has been destroyed and much added, notably the gabled Elizabethan octagonal turret and groined crypt or dungeon. The confiscation of monastic property during the reign of Henry VIII made Creslow pass to the Crown, with more alterations. Some seventy years ago the chapel, once attached to the manor house, was a stable and the farmyard formerly part of a graveyard. There is still Tudor panelling and plaster decorations in parts of the house which must have been even more picturesque, romantic and isolated among high trees a hundred years ago when its haunted room gained and held its reputation.

It was about 1850, it seems, that a former High Sheriff of Buckinghamshire visited Creslow to attend a dinner-party. His house was some miles distant and as the weather turned stormy, he was pressed to stay the night—provided that he had no objection to sleeping in the haunted room. He said he was interested in the possibility of meeting a ghost, for he did not believe in the supernormal; being a strong and fit man, he was convinced that any practical joker would more than meet his match—should anyone think to 'play the ghost' that night.

Accordingly the room was prepared. He desired no fire or night-light but took with him a box of matches so that he might light a candle if he wished to do so. He armed himself with a cutlass and a pair of pistols—amid much joking between himself and his hosts.

Morning came, clear and bright after the stormy night and the other guests gathered round their host and hostess in the breakfast room. Someone remarked that the visitor who had slept in the haunted room was not present. A servant was dispatched to summon him but soon returned, saying that his repeated knocking had brought no answer and that a jug of hot water left outside the room an hour before, was still there. Two or three of the gentlemen went up to the chamber and after also knocking loudly several times, entered—to find the room empty! No servant had seen anything of the guest, but, since he was a county magistrate, it was thought he had left early to attend a meeting. Then it was found that his horse was still in the stable; and so, at last, perplexed and a little worried, the guests sat down with their hosts to eat and were in the middle of their breakfast when in walked the missing guest!

He had, he said, locked and bolted his room on entering it the night before, then proceeded to examine carefully the whole place. Only when quite satisfied that no living creature but himself was in the room and that every entry was sealed did he go to bed, expecting to have a good night's rest. But shortly after dropping off to sleep he was awakened by the sound of light footsteps, accompanied by a rustling noise, like that of a silk gown. He got up quietly, lit a candle, and searched the room but could find nothing to account for the noise which had ceased as soon as his feet had touched the floor. He looked under the bed, in the fireplace, up the chimney and at both doors which were fastened and locked as he had left them. Glancing at his watch he found the time was a few minutes after midnight. Since all seemed quiet again, he returned to bed and was soon asleep. Then he was awakened again, by the same noises—but this time they were much louder: he heard the violent rustling of a stiff silk dress and distinct footsteps which told him, he thought, exactly where the figure was in the room. This time he sprang out of bed, darted to the spot where he felt the figure must be and tried to grasp the intruder in his arms. But his arms met and there was nothing there. The noise moved to another part of the room and he followed it, groping near the floor to prevent anything passing under his arms but still he found nothing. Eventually the sounds died away at the doorway to the crypt and the visitor returned to bed, leaving a lighted candle burning, but more than a little perplexed at being totally unable to detect the origin of the noise or account for its cessation when he lighted the candle.

Mr D. G. Hares told me in 1967 that the inside of the house had been extensively altered and no room remained as it once did; he had no personal knowledge of any ghost at Creslow.
Bell Hotel, Aylesbury, Bucks.

Crowborough, SUSSEX.

Windlesham Manor was the home of Sir Arthur Conan Doyle for the last twenty years of his life and he and his wife were buried in the garden until their bodies were exhumed and placed in the family vault in 1955. The house was first reputed to be haunted in 1968 when the manageress of the property (now a home for retired gentlefolk) said that she had seen no ghost but had sensed an extraordinary atmosphere. Certainly, the local people regarded the house as haunted. Sir Arthur died at the Manor in 1930, at the age of seventy-one, a dedicated spiritualist.
Country House Hotel, Croft Road, Crowborough, Sussex.

Cumnor, NEAR ABINGDON, BERKSHIRE.

Here, before it was destroyed, stood Cumnor Hall, the scene of Amy Robsart's mysterious death after her 'fall' down a staircase; a death probably engineered by Queen Elizabeth

I and Amy's husband, Robert Dudley, Earl of Leicester, one of the Queen's favourites.

When the hall was demolished in 1810 the ghost of Amy Robsart was said to have haunted the place of her death for two-hundred-and-fifty years. Her figure was most often seen in the vicinity of the fatal staircase but her ghost is also said to have made such a nuisance of itself by frequenting Cumnor Park that nine parsons were called from Oxford to 'lay the ghost'. They duly 'laid' her in a pond, known afterwards as 'Lady Dudley's Pond', and it was said that thereafter the water would never freeze in it. However, her apparition seems to have survived the exorcism and her ghost was still said to revisit at intervals the scenes of her past life. Amy Robsart's ghost is also reported to have appeared to her husband to warn him of his approaching death.
Crown & Thistle Hotel, Abingdon, Berks.

Cwm, NEAR RHYL, WALES.

The 'Blue Lion Inn' is reputed to be haunted by a farm labourer, John Henry, who was murdered here in 1646. The present landlord, Mr S. Hughes, who owns a private menagerie, will tell you that he has found different cages opened mysteriously during the night and his pets missing. Once Mr Hughes caught a glimpse of the ghost and he and many other people have heard footsteps at the old inn which cannot be explained.
Hotel Marina, Rhyl, Flint, Wales.

*Dartmoor, DEVON.

Two miles north of Widecombe-in-the-Moor there is a lonely stretch of countryside with a roadside grave where fresh flowers have appeared mysteriously for years.

Jay's Grave is said to be the final resting place of a young girl, Mary Jay, who hanged herself in a barn which used to stand on the site of the grave. According to the custom of over a hundred years ago, she was buried in unconsecrated ground on the spot where she committed suicide. Ever since, it is said, fresh flowers have appeared on Mary's grave and no one has ever discovered where they come from.

From time to time there are stories too of unexplained figures being seen in the vicinity of the grave. In August 1967 a seventeen-year-old girl and her fiancé saw someone, or something, crouching over the grave as they passed the spot in a car. Rosemary Long described how the crouched figure straightened itself and stood up as they passed, looking like a huddled man at the head of a grave. He appeared to have a dark blanket over his head and body and around the bottom of the blanket there was a white line. The blanket stopped about a foot above the ground; yet there were no legs to the figure and no face was visible. Other local people and visitors have had similar experiences there.
Wooder Manor Hotel, Widecombe-in-the-Moor, Devon.

Dartmoor, DEVON.

According to legend the ghost of Sir Francis Drake (1545-96) has been seen on the moor, riding with a pack of spectral hounds whose cries are so terrible that any dog hearing them dies on the spot! (My wife and I once spent a night on Dartmoor and our dog whined and was restless the whole night.) It is also said that Drake's ghost sets out for Plymouth from Tavistock in a black coach or hearse, drawn by four headless horses—and, some say, preceded by a dozen goblins whose eyes flash fire and whose nostrils emit smoke!
White Hart Hotel, Moretonhampstead, Devon.

Deddington, OXFORDSHIRE.

In 1962, after the death of the vicar, the Rev. Maurice Frost, who had lived there for nearly forty years, the vicarage was thought to be haunted by his ghost. Servants fled when Mr H. Campbell Jarrett, who came from Italy to settle his cousin's estate, claimed that a mysterious hand stopped him leaving the drawing room. Between eight-thirty and nine o'clock in the morning the beds were pressed down with nobody touching them; there were noises in the study and

coughs in the drawing room, when no human being was in the rooms. Mr Jarrett believed his cousin's ghost had returned to the vicarage to wind his antique clocks and look after his favourite books. Mrs Betty Spencer, one of the maids at the vicarage, said she thought she heard Mr Jarrett cough in the drawing room and decided to clean his bedroom—but found him upstairs, sitting on the bed, tying his shoe laces—so, presumably, she heard a ghost cough.
Hotel Russell, Deddington, Oxon.

Disley, CHESHIRE.

Lyme Park, enlarged in 1726 and 1817, is said to have been given to Sir Thomas Danvers as a reward for his bravery at Caen and Crécy, by the Black Prince. The house and park both have ghosts: at the house unearthly peals of bells have been repeatedly heard and the long gallery is known as 'The Ghost Room' because a 'lady in white' has been reported to walk here on many occasions. She is thought to be Blanche, who died of grief when her betrothed, Sir Piers Legh, was brought back dead from Agincourt. His phantom funeral procession has been seen winding its way through the park, followed by the same faithful and inconsolable spirit figure seen in the house.

Years ago a skeleton was found here in a tiny secret chamber under 'The Ghost Room' but whether they were the bones of a forgotten priest, a hidden offspring, a runaway or a secret enemy of the family, no one knows.
Alma Lodge Hotel, Buxton Road, Stockport, Cheshire.

*Dorchester, DORSET.

Nine miles east of Dorchester, one and a half miles east of Waddock crossroads, stands the cottage where T. E. Lawrence lived after he left the Royal Air Force in 1935. Here the ghostly form of Lawrence of Arabia has been seen and the roar of a powerful motorcycle has been heard at dead of night.

Soon after his death stories began to circulate that a figure in Arab costume had been seen entering Clouds Hill at night and since then there have been persistent reports that his ghost has been there. I know one person who is quite convinced that she had seen Lawrence, long after he was killed, on the Brough Superior motorcycle which he so loved to ride at night in the lanes and roads in this quiet area.

Farm workers have heard the noise of a motorcycle roaring towards them in the early hours but always the noise stops abruptly just when the hearers expect to see it. Perhaps that last tragic journey that Lawrence took has somehow become impressed for ever upon the atmosphere.

I have talked with men who served with Lawrence and I like to think that the moving spirit of the Arab revolt does in fact visit again the little cottage he called Clouds Hill, where he found some peace at the end of a troubled life.
Antelope Hotel, South Street, Dorchester, Dorset.

Driffield, YORKSHIRE.

Burton Agnes Hall, a fine Tudor mansion and one of the stately homes of England, designed by Inigo Jones and decorated by Rubens, still contains the skull of Anne Griffith in the Great Hall, in accordance with her dying wish three hundred years ago.

In the reign of the first Queen Elizabeth the property was owned by the three daughters of Sir Henry Griffith who spared no expense in improving their property. None was keener on this work than Anne, the youngest of the three sisters. She became obsessed with and seemed to live only for the beautiful house. One day, while visiting friends, she was attacked and robbed by footpads and left for dead. She was found barely alive and lingered only a few days at her beloved Burton Agnes Hall but before she died she beseeched her sisters to preserve her head within the walls of the house for ever. She added that if this wish was not granted she would endeavour to return from the grave and make the house uninhabitable for any human beings. Her sisters duly promised but after she had died they decided that her gruesome wish had been the wandering of a dying mind and her body was duly interred in the family vault.

Not many days had passed however before the sisters were

58

reminded of their promise when loud crashing noises were heard for which no cause could be discovered and a few nights later the reverberating slamming of doors awakened the entire household. Again, no cause could be found for the noises. Inexplicable groans echoed through the corridors night after night and at length the sisters consulted their vicar who advised them to keep the promise they had made to their dead sister. When the corpse of Anne was disinterred her body was found in perfect condition but headless; where the head should have been, they found a grinning skull. After the skull had been installed in the Hall, no further mysterious noises were heard until, many years later, a mischievous servant-girl threw the skull on to a passing farm cart, whereupon the horse stopped dead in its tracks and would not move. The driver whipped the animal unmercifully but sweating with terror, the horse stood its ground. At length the servant admitted what she had done; the grisly relic was taken indoors again and the cart went on its way.

Later owners of the mansion refused to regard the story seriously and they buried the skull in the garden. However, they had so much bad luck that they decided to bring the skull back into the house and only then did things improve for them.

In the 1860s a visitor to the Hall scoffed at the story of the skull and did not believe in the haunting until he heard noises like hob-nailed boots in his bedroom and doors banging all over the house. By morning he had changed his mind and never spent another night at Burton Agnes.

Today the skull is built in behind a great carved screen where it cannot easily be removed and on the staircase of the Hall there hangs a large oil-painting of Anne, strikingly depicted in black, together with her two sisters, looking down into the house she loved.

The Bell Hotel, Driffield, E. Yorks.

Ealing, MIDDLESEX.

A haunted photographer's studio, built about 1900, attracted the attention of Dr George Owen in 1967 and resulted in an unusual film which told the story of the disturbances, including interviews with witnesses, depicted the scenes of the haunting and re-created some of the haunting.

When he rented the derelict hall the photographer did not know that in the house next door a woman and a child had been murdered and that an airman had been hanged for the crime in 1943; but he and his staff soon experienced incidents which convinced them that supernormal agencies were at work. Lamps hanging from the ceiling swung in unison, footsteps sounded on the unfrequented floor, people were touched, voices were heard. Convinced that the place was indeed haunted, the photographer and his staff held séances at which a dead airman purported to communicate, spoke of an aircraft which at the relevant date was on the secret list and insisted that he had not been guilty of the crime for which he had been hanged. Various marks, consistent with the story he was relating, appeared mysteriously on his neck and arm. It seemed certain that as the photographer was a young boy at the time, he could have had no direct knowledge of either the murder, which was described in some detail, or the secret aircraft.
Carnarvon Hotel, London W.5.

East Bergholt, ESSEX.

The local Friary used to have the reputation of being haunted. At night there is a distinctly eerie atmosphere in this area which includes the church just across the road, where the bells are hung in a bell-cage behind the church—after, it is said, numerous unsuccessful attempts to hang the bells in the church belfry during which at least one man was killed.

During the Second World War soldiers were stationed at the Friary and at that time one particular door which led into the sergeants' mess would unlatch itself every night at ten minutes to eleven and open to a distance of about eighteen inches; a distinct drop in air temperature would precede this apparent phenomenon and soldiers playing cards in the room would purposely stop at this time to wait for the door to open; each night it would regularly 'oblige'. On five different (but not consecutive) nights, arrangements were made for men to be situated on either side of the door, armed with clubs, to see whether anyone was playing tricks, but invariably the temperature would drop and the door open and no explanation was ever found for the curious happening.

One night a young soldier of about eighteen was lying on his bed alone in another room when he saw the door, which connected with the next room, open by itself. He claimed he saw a vague, indistinguishable shape enter the room; next he felt a pair of icy cold hands being placed on his face. Terrified, he screamed for help whereupon whatever it was in the room with him, immediately disappeared. Next morning his hair had turned from jet black to white. Thereafter all the soldiers refused to sleep in that particular room and it was eventually sealed off.

On account of the reputation that it had acquired with officers and men no one used a certain door at the Friary at this period, a door which led into a passage and was the quickest and most direct way into the building. Without exception, they would all go a long way round to the front entrance and then walk back through the building along narrow winding passages with recesses in the walls, marked with the names of those buried in them. The Friary was formerly St Mary's Abbey, a Benedictine nunnery.
Red Lion Hotel, Colchester, Essex.

Edgehill, WARWICKSHIRE.

Within a year of the first battle of the Civil War, fought on this hilly ridge in 1642, a pamphlet was published, describing the ghostly re-appearance of the troops who fought and perished here. Witnesses quoted included clergymen, a Justice of the Peace and several Army officers who had recognized some of the combatants.

The story goes that on the Christmas Eve following the battle local people heard the sound of far-off drums, accompanied by groans and shouts and all the noise of battle. Then suddenly, there appeared in the air battalions of soldiers, with flags flying, drums beating and with the infantry discharging small arms and cannon. The phantom battle is said to have continued for two or three hours until the Royalists took flight and soon afterwards the aerial apparitions vanished.

Witnesses hurried to Keinton and signed declarations of what they had seen with the result that many people from the surrounding countryside went to Edgehill the following evening—and there witnessed themselves the same dreadful vision.

A week later the spectral struggle seems to have been repeated yet again, lasting an hour longer this time; and it was seen once more on the ensuing night.

Stories of the strange spectacle reached the ears of King Charles I at Oxford and he immediately dispatched Colonel Lewis Krike, Captain Dudley, Captain Wainman and other officers to inquire into the matter. This the worthy gentlemen did and in fact themselves witnessed the phantom battle and recognized some of the combatants; all this they testified on oath before the King.

Periodically there are reports of the noise of battle still being heard at Edgehill on the anniversary of the struggle (October 23rd). The Rev. John C. Dening (with whom I have spent many hours discussing ghosts) visited the vicinity a few years ago and succeeded in locating a number of people who had heard what they thought were sounds of the battle fought over three hundred years earlier.

White Lion Hotel, High Street, Banbury, Oxon.

Elm, NEAR WISBECH, CAMBRIDGESHIRE.

Rambling, two-hundred-year-old Elm Vicarage is said to be haunted by a monk who died over seven-hundred-and-fifty years ago and by a bell that tolls a death-knell.

Some years ago I was in touch with the rector and his wife and learned that Mrs Bradshaw was the only one who heard the tolling bell, but her husband, the Rev. A. R. Bradshaw, would invariably hear of a death in the parish next day. This happened, I was told, thirty-one times in two-and-a-half years!

In common with so many cases this haunting began with

accounts of unexplained footsteps. These were heard, night after night, soon after the Bradshaws went to live at Elm Vicarage. At first the rector would get up and go in search of an intruder but after some extremely cold nights, wandering about the house, unable to find any normal cause for the nocturnal footsteps, or even locating exactly where they came from, Mr Bradshaw gave up trying to discover their origin. The mysterious footsteps continued until a ghostly monk, Ignatius, appeared.

Mrs Bradshaw told me that when she brushed against the ghostly monk one evening in an upstairs corridor, 'he' said: 'Do be careful.' Mrs Bradshaw, with commendable pluck, asked the visitor who he was and received the reply: 'Ignatius, the bell-ringer.' The form appeared to be wearing a brown monk's habit and sandals. After that first occasion Mrs Bradshaw met the monk many times and gradually learned his history. It seems that he died over seven hundred years ago in a monastery that used to occupy the site of the present rectory.

Ignatius said that one of his responsibilities had been to watch the flood waters rising in the nearby Fens and to warn his brothers if there was any danger. One night he was asleep and did not ring the warning bell when the waters rose to a dangerous level. The water rushed in, some monks were drowned and Ignatius was in disgrace.

I asked Mrs Bradshaw to describe exactly how Ignatius usually became visible and whether he always appeared at the same spot. She told me that she had seen him in various parts of the house, sometimes in the upstairs corridor where he had first appeared, sometimes in the parlour, occasionally elsewhere. He appeared first as a fine outline, then gradually emerged into the figure of a man aged about thirty-three with 'dark curly hair and thin ascetic features'. It was usually dusk when she saw him and he was always dressed in a brown monk's habit that looked old and worn.

One September night Mrs Bradshaw was going to sleep, as she occasionally did, in a bedroom usually reserved for visitors. Afterwards this room was used as a box room and the door kept securely locked. The family dog invariably slept on Mrs Bradshaw's bed but this night he whimpered and cried and repeatedly ran out of the room. He had to be brought back three times and at length he was persuaded to stay.

Mrs Bradshaw put out the light and went to sleep. She awakened with the feeling that something was being tied around her neck. She reached for her torch and discovered that a tendril of wisteria from the wall outside the bedroom window had made its way through the open window and lay across her throat. She tore it away and then felt the bed-clothes being pulled from her. Terrified, she felt herself being violently picked up and thrown sideways across the bed. Speechless with fright, she became aware of a vague black shape looming over her and through what appeared to be a haze, a pair of gnarled hands materialized and clutched at her throat. She tried hard to scream but no sound would come. The hands tightened their hold now and she had to use every ounce of her willpower to fight the increasing pressure for she found that she was powerless to defend herself physically. Suddenly she saw Ignatius. He came towards her, reached for the twisted hands clutching at her throat and pulled them away. As the pressure on her throat relaxed, Mrs Bradshaw dropped back exhausted on to the bed. She hardly had time to catch her breath before she became aware of the horrible vague creature bending over her again. It had a huge head and a red face. The dog was on the bed, snarling and fighting something invisible. Summoning all her remaining strength, Mrs Bradshaw tore herself free and rushed into her husband's room. The marks on her throat remained for almost a week. The first her husband knew of the episode was when he was awakened by his wife, but he confirmed to me that her throat was badly bruised and that the marks remained visible for days.

When she next saw Ignatius, Mrs Bradshaw asked him who had attacked her and she was told that he was a man who had been murdered in that room. Later Ignatius told Mrs Bradshaw that he would not be seeing her so often in the future; his having saved her life had gone some way towards completing his penance and he was hopeful of complete forgiveness and rest.

At all events Mrs Bradshaw is quite convinced that a ghost saved her life that night.
Duke's Head Hotel, King's Lynn, Norfolk.

Bosworth Hall at Husbands Bosworth, Leicestershire, where Mrs. Constable Maxwell's family have always lived. Lady Lisgar, an occupant during the nineteenth century, still haunts the delightful Georgian-cum-Victorian mansion. *Photo: Chris Underwood*

The ruins of Bramber Castle, Sussex, where the ghosts of the children of William de Breose have been seen around Christmas time.
Photo: Chris Underwood

The fifteenth-century 'Crown' inn at Bildeston, Suffolk, where ghostly happenings have been reported in most of the rooms. *Photo: Len Faiers*

Farnham Parish Church, Surrey, where ghostly chanting has been heard; a ghostly procession seen; and a female figure has entered the church on many occasions – and then disappeared.
Photo: Chris Underwood

Emneth, NORFOLK.

A lonely hundred-year-old cottage was occupied for several years by a fitter and his former beauty-queen wife. As long as they lived here, mysterious things happened: windows opened inexplicably, the radio, television set, cooker and alarm clock were all switched on, on different occasions, when no living person was in the room, door latches rattled, locks were undone, ornaments were smashed and furniture broken. Mr Thorpe said, in 1967: 'There is a strange atmosphere here, as though someone were in the spare room.' *Duke's Head Hotel, King's Lynn, Norfolk.*

Epworth, ISLE OF AXHOLME, LINCOLNSHIRE.

One of the best documented cases of poltergeist infestation concerned the parsonage of the Rev. Samuel Wesley (1662-1735), which, with alterations, is still standing. The disturbances took place during December, 1716 and January, 1717 and the evidence is contained in letters received by the rector's eldest son Samuel (1690-1739) from his mother and other members of the family. In addition the Rev. Samuel Wesley himself wrote an account of the haunting. It was at the same parsonage that John Wesley (1703-91) was born, one of the nineteen children of the Rev. Samuel Wesley. At the time of the curious happenings he was thirteen-and-a-half years old.

The first recorded incidents were 'several dismal groans' followed by a 'strange knocking', usually three or four at a time. This continued for a fortnight and was heard in various parts of the house but most frequently in the nursery. Every one in the house heard the knockings, which grew in intensity and number: often nine loud knocks would be heard very near the Rev. Samuel Wesley's bedstead. He never found anything to account for the noise or saw anything to explain them. One night noises came from the bedroom above that which was occupied by the Rev. Samuel Wesley and his wife, sounding as though people were walking about. This was followed by the noise of running footsteps up and down the stairs. When they reached the bottom

65

of the stairs the noise of rattling money was heard at their feet and then the noise of dozens of bottles being smashed.

The following night Samuel Wesley asked a friend, the rector of a nearby parish, to spend a night at the house. As the three sat up waiting, the knockings were heard in the very early morning. Sometimes a rasping noise would be heard, as if a clock were being wound up; and the sound of a piece of wood being planed—but more frequently the knocks, three at a time, silence, and then three again, continuing for many hours. Once the rector, looking in at the nursery to ensure that the children were asleep (the younger children usually slept through the disturbances) heard several loud and deep groans and then more knocking.

Soon the noises increased in volume and the Wesleys were disturbed day and night. They became utterly convinced that 'it was beyond the power of any human creature to make such strange and various noises'.

A maid was so frightened by hearing a 'most terrible and astonishing noise as of someone expiring' at the door of the dining room that she dared not move from one room to another by herself. One of the daughters, Hetty, while sitting on the stairs waiting for her father saw 'something like a man' come down the stairs behind her, with a loose nightshirt trailing behind him—which caused her to flee to her room!

Another apparition was seen by Mrs Wesley under one of the girl's beds, something 'like a badger' but apparently without any head; it seemed to run directly under Emily's petticoats. The same form was seen one evening in the dining room when a servant entered: it ran past him and through the hall under the stairs. He followed with a candle but could find no trace of it. Later he saw it again in the kitchen and this time he likened it to a white rabbit. The stairway seemed to particularly attract this ghost and the sounds of footsteps were heard going up and down them, at all hours of the day and night, dozens of times; vast rumblings were heard and a gobbling noise, like a turkey cock.

Sometimes the latch of the Wesley's bedroom door would be lifted when everyone was in bed and one night, when there was a great noise in the kitchen and the latch of the yard door was also lifted, another of the daughters, Emilia,

66

went and held it tight on the inside. Still it lifted up and the door itself was pushed hard against her although nothing was visible outside. The Rev. Samuel Wesley was frequently interrupted while at prayer by loud noises and he was pushed by an unseen force three times. He followed the noises into practically every room in the house and would sometimes sit alone and ask to be told what it wanted—but he never heard any articulate voice, only once or twice two or three feeble squeaks. The ghost, or poltergeist, came to be called 'Old Jeffrey' after a former occupant who had died in the house.

It was noticed that soon after the noises began, the wind usually rose and whistled loud around the house; often the sounds seemed to be in the air in the middle of the room; and a mastiff which had barked violently the first time 'it' came, never did so afterwards but seemed to be conscious of it before the family and would run, whining or silent, to shelter.

Independent accounts of the disturbances were recorded by members of the family and visitors and the Rev. John Wesley, in 1720, enquired into the whole matter, speaking to each of the people concerned. He compiled an account which was published in three issues of *The Arminian Magazine* and reprinted sixty-four years later in the same periodical. This certainly suggests that he was as convinced of the authenticity of the disturbances when he was over eighty as he had been when he was twenty.

Harry Price has pointed out that the poltergeist seemed to centre on Hetty Wesley, then aged about nineteen. There are reports of her 'trembling strongly in her sleep' and of her confused breathing and flushed face prior to and during 'visits' from 'Old Jeffrey' who seemed to follow her about the house and to have a particular predilection for the bed on which she was lying.

After about two months the disturbances ceased as mysteriously as they began.

Mount Pleasant Hotel, Rossington, near Doncaster, Yorks.

Faringdon, BERKSHIRE.

The lonely hundred-year-old Oriel Cottage, Wicklesham Road, was the scene of 'ghostly rumblings, bangings, cold draughts and strange shadows' in 1963 and 1964. Police stayed a night and reported: 'There is no doubt there are strange noises ... there is nothing the police can do about it.' A mysterious shape was seen by twenty-one people who stayed a night at the cottage and they all felt a cold draught around their feet for which they could find no rational explanation.

'We are sick with fear,' the family said in December, 1963; 'it's all so uncanny.' The family then consisted of Mr and Mrs Norman Wheeler and their children Colin (nineteen), Betty (fifteen), Joy (ten) and Rosalie (five). At the height of the disturbances the girls were afraid to go upstairs for a fortnight and slept huddled round the living-room fireplace. Yet the Wheelers had lived at the cottage, undisturbed, for eighteen years.

The mysterious knockings and bangings brought Mrs Wheeler to the edge of a nervous breakdown. Mr Wheeler ripped up floorboards to try to find the source of the noises and architects checked the walls for flaws but could find no material cause for the noises.

A medium identified the entity as a troublesome lodger who had lived at the cottage prior to the Wheelers moving in and who had committed suicide. After a thirty-minute exorcism service by Canon Christopher Harman, a member of the Churches' Fellowship for Psychical and Spiritual Studies, the Wheelers reported that the disturbances had ceased.
Crown and Thistle Hotel, Abingdon, Berks.

*Farnham, SURREY.

The 'Hop Bag Inn', Downing Street, was once on the main coach route, when coaches were drawn by horses. In those days the inn was called the 'Adam and Eve'. In recent times the sounds of horses and heavy wheels have been heard in the courtyard.

A visitor staying at the inn was awakened by the sounds

one night and when she looked out of her window into the yard, where the sounds seemed to originate, it was quite deserted. It was a bright moonlit night but nothing could be seen that might have accounted for the loud and distinct noises. There is a story associated with the inn that goes back to the old coaching days when a coach came over Long Bridge and pulled into the yard here for the driver to break the news to a waiting girl that the lover she was waiting for would not come for her. He had been shot dead by highwaymen. If the mysterious sounds heard here have their origin in this coach of bygone days, it is only one of several phantom coaches that are said to haunt the vicinity of Farnham.

Bush Hotel, The Borough, Farnham, Surrey.

Farnham Parish Church, SURREY.

There are a number of apparently well-authenticated ghost stories associated with this pleasant church. During the last war a firewatcher reported hearing men's voices, chanting what sounded like Latin from within the dark and empty church. He investigated and noticed a number of tiny pinpoints of light at the far end of the nave; he saw them moving and realized that the moving lights were candles being carried in procession round the interior. Far from being frightened, he only felt a deep sense of peace. Only afterwards when he thought about what he had seen, did he begin to have a feeling of apprehension. Of all the nights he spent in the vicinity of the church, this was the only time he saw or heard anything of a ghostly nature; but he could never be shaken on this particular experience.

A visitor, kneeling at the back of the church, raised her eyes and saw a pre-Reformation High Mass being celebrated at the altar. She watched, spellbound, the gold-clad celebrant and his brightly-dressed assistants wreathed in the rising incense smoke. She said afterwards that the church seemed half-full of people, some motionless, others moving up and down the north aisle; but unlike the celebrants, they were colourless and shadowy. She strained her ears for the sound of ghostly music but the arrival of the rector and a church-

69

warden shattered the strange atmosphere and she found the church suddenly empty—as it had been when she arrived.

A former curate used to say that he saw on occasions a semi-transparent veil descend during the preaching of the sermon, cutting off the chancel and altar and figures and lights moving dimly behind the veil. Other visitors to the church have experienced the same 'vision'. This curate, in the company of another parson, saw a little old lady enter the church while the church bell was ringing for evensong, but when they followed her they found she had disappeared and that the church was deserted. This happened not once but several times and it seems certain that the little old lady was no physical being.

Bush Hotel, The Borough, Farnham, Surrey.

Felbrigge, NEAR NORWICH, NORFOLK.

Noble Felbrigge Hall, built on the site of an older Felbrigge residence, was long the home of the Windhams, a family that included the patriotic statesman, William Windham and the notorious 'mad Windham' who died in 1866. Later the house passed to the Kitton family and one of the Miss Kittons told the traveller and author, Augustus Hare (1834-1903): 'Mr Windham comes every night to look after his favourite books in the library. He goes straight to the shelves where they are: we hear him moving the tables and chairs about. We never disturb him though, for we intend to be ghosts ourselves some day and to come about the place just as he does.'

Bell Hotel, Norwich, Norfolk.

Fernhurst, NEAR HASLEMERE, SUSSEX.

On the eastern side of Fernhurst, near Blackdown Hill, there are a few remains of Verdley Castle. According to legend this was the place where the last bear was killed in Sussex—and perhaps in England. It was slain on Christmas Day in the Great Hall of old Verdley, where it had sought refuge from the locals who had discovered the poor beast in

70

the snow nosing for food. It is said that at this time of the year the growls of the cornered beast and the shouts of the yokels have been heard in the vicinity.
Georgian Hotel, Haslemere, Surrey.

Flansham Manor, FLANSHAM, NEAR FELPHAM, SUSSEX.

In the 1930s the manor was a guest house. Many visitors seemed to have 'bumped' into a phantom called Cuthbert. The deep lounge hall has a small gallery running overhead which goes through a doorway at one end and connects with bedrooms. One night all the residents and guests were out except for the owner and a friend. Suddenly they both heard footsteps coming from the passage upstairs at the other end of the gallery. They knew there was no one else in the house but decided to investigate and when they walked across the hall and looked up at the gallery they saw the door slowly closing. No living person was in fact in the house, except themselves. Years before a child sleeping in a bedroom that had a connecting door to what is now a bathroom was awakened night after night by strange sounds, thuds and bumps, seemingly coming from actually within the room, almost as though someone or something was being dragged out of the cupboard, along the floor and through the haunted doorway.
Clarehaven Hotel, Wessex Avenue, Bognor Regis, Sussex.

Forrabury, CORNWALL.

Forrabury has long had a tradition of ghostly bells sounding from beneath the waves. They are supposed to have originated with the conveyance by sea of new bells for the local church. All went well until the captain of the boat used profane language, whereupon a violent storm broke and the ship sank with all hands. There are local people, too, who claim to have seen phantom boats with phantom crews rowing silently to the spot where the ship sank.
Tolcarne Private Hotel, Doctor's Corner, Boscastle, Cornwall.

*Fulmer, BUCKINGHAMSHIRE.

Near this delightful village there is a ford which runs across
the road. Many people have reported hearing curious and
apparently ghostly noises hereabouts. One man, a technician
at nearby Pinewood Film Studios, heard the sound of a
horse and trap which sounded quite distinct; yet there was
no sign of any such vehicle. The noise did not seem to be
advancing, but sounded as though the trap was in one spot,
yet moving. Another witness said she heard the sounds of
hooves at one side of a field near the same spot, not once but
many times. The same noise had been heard by a friend of
hers.
Royal Hotel, Slough, Bucks.

Fyvie, ABERDEENSHIRE, SCOTLAND.

Fyvie Castle is famous for its ghost room, a murder room and
a secret chamber. In 1920 the famous 'green lady ghost' is
said to have been seen wandering forlornly and silently
along the corridors and disappearing through the panels of a
dark, wainscotted apartment. A few years before a monster
fungus had grown up in the gun-room and when masons and
carpenters had removed the plant and were repairing the
room, they discovered a complete skeleton. This discovery
seemed to signal the commencement of psychic disturbances
and Lord Leith gave instructions for the skeleton to be rebuilt into the wall, whereupon 'normality' returned.
Kintore Arms Hotel, Inverurie, Aberdeenshire, Scotland.

Galashiels, SELKIRKSHIRE, SCOTLAND.

Nearby Buckholm Tower (ruins) is reputed to be haunted
by a former Laird of Buckholm; weird stories are told of
strange noises heard in the dungeon and there is talk of an
everlasting bloodstain on an old beam.

Two hundred years ago a laird of Buckholm, a man called
Pringle whose family still owns the property, ill-treated his
young wife and ten-year-old son so badly that she ran off

with the boy. Left on his own, the laird's behaviour became wild and violent and his great delight, in those days of the Covenanters, was to hound these upholders of the forms of worship no longer countenanced by law. He kept two ferocious dogs, the terror of the local inhabitants, expressly for this cruel purpose.

Known as a local supporter of the Government, the laird was called upon one day by a captain of the Dragoons, to assist in breaking up an unlawful assembly of Covenanters on nearby Ladhope Moor. Delighted to assist, Pringle shrewdly guessed where the gathering would take place. But when he arrived on the spot, he found that the assembly had somehow received warning and had disbanded—all except one old man, Geordie Elliot, whose wife had once been in the Pringle service. His son, too, had stayed by his father's side when the old man had been thrown from his horse and was badly hurt. Both were known as Covenanters.

The wicked laird of Buckholm was for disposing· of both men on the spot but the captain decided that they might be able to give information about their fellow Covenanters. It was arranged that Pringle should hold them prisoner for the night and that the captain would send an escort for them the following day.

Back at the Tower the prisoners were thrown into the dungeon which exists to this day with its grisly row of iron hooks suspended from the ceiling.

When the captain and his troops had left, the laird dined and soaked himself with brandy, well-pleased with the day's work. The hours passed and brandy followed brandy.

Hours later the servants were awakened by loud cries from the direction of the dungeon where the prisoners had been left for hours. They heard the laird stagger and curse as he made his way downstairs. Fearful sounds reached their ears and several servants hovered at the dungeon door when at length the laird stumbled out muttering something like 'swine should be treated as swine...' He staggered towards the main door and there, when he had opened it, stood an old woman. Pringle stopped dead in his tracks. It was Isobel Elliot looking for her menfolk. The laird muttered some drunken oath and dragged her to the dungeon. A piercing scream broke from the old woman's lips when she saw, suspended from the hooks like carcases of swine, the bodies of her husband and her son.

Screaming and wild-eyed the distraught woman ran out of the dungeon, fell headlong and sobbed uncontrollably. The drunken laird stood looking down at her, perhaps for the first time realizing the enormity of his crime. Slowly old Isobel rose to her feet and in a quiet tone she cursed Pringle for what he had done. She called down the vengeance of God upon him, so that the memory of his evil deeds, like hounds of hell, should haunt and pursue him, waking and sleeping, and he should find no place of refuge in this life or in eternity.

After that Pringle firmly believed that he was haunted; he would imagine frequently that ghostly hounds were at his throat night and day. Before long he died a painful death, full of horror at the last moments which were accompanied by convulsions as if his body was being worried and torn to death.

As the first anniversary of the laird's death approached, a ghostly figure was seen in the vicinity of the Tower, running for his life from baying hounds. On the eve of the anniversary the baying of dogs and the sound of someone calling desperately for help were heard; there was also the noise of hammering on the great door. A terrified old retainer called out to ask who was knocking and a voice answered, asking to be admitted 'for mercy's sake'; it sounded like the voice of the dead Laird of Buckholm! The faithful man-servant at length plucked up enough courage to throw open the door but as he did so there was only silence and nothing to see in the dark night.

Next night, on the actual anniversary of the death of the laird, the baying of hounds was heard for the third time, coming now from the dungeon and again a voice the old servant recognized cried out for help. Everyone in the place was terrified and stood listening to the dreadful commotion in the dungeon: baying hounds, frenzied breathing, blood-curdling screams—and finally silence.

Every June, it is said, these same sounds are heard by those who are able to hear them, from the depths of the dark and mysterious dungeon of Buckholm Tower.
Douglas Hotel, Galashiels, Selkirkshire, Scotland.

Gateshead, CO. DURHAM.

A council house in Bronte Street, occupied by the Coulthard family, was the scene of 'poltergeist' activity in 1963 and 1964. Exorcism was carried out by a local clergyman but had no lasting effect. Ornaments were thrown, bottles smashed, slippers shot up from the floor, plates and crockery crashed down and chairs and other objects were moved. The householder fled and appealed for alternative accomodation.
Springfield Hotel, Gateshead, Co. Durham.

Gill House, ASPATRIA, CUMBERLAND; SEE *Aspatria.*

*Glamis Castle, GLAMIS, ANGUS, SCOTLAND.

The oldest inhabited and most impressive castle in Scotland is famous for the story of the Monster of Glamis and the secret room. It was in this splendid castle that Duncan was murdered by Macbeth and a bloodstain remained for ever where King Malcolm II is said to have been killed—so that the whole floor was boarded over. The place is, as might be expected, haunted by several ghosts. Among them, the little Grey Lady—so I was told when I was there in 1968— had been seen quite recently by the present Lord Strathmore.

The Dowager Countess Granville saw her one sunny afternoon, kneeling in one of the pews; the sun, coming through the windows, shone through the outline of the little figure. Lord Strathmore walked into the chapel one afternoon and saw the same figure in the identical place; once he saw her walk into the chapel. Others have seen the same form but who she is, nobody knows.

High up in the uninhabited tower of Glamis there is a room where, in the days of King James II of Scotland, one Alexander, fourth Earl of Crawford, known as 'Earl Beardie', quarrelled while gambling with a Lord Glamis and two chieftains. They were cursing God when the Devil suddenly appeared and they were doomed to play dice for ever in that room. The cook at the castle will tell you that she has heard the rattle of dice and stamping and swearing coming from that empty room at dead of night.

The legend of the Monster of Glamis relates that somewhere around 1800 a monster was born to be heir of Glamis; misshapen to an awful degree, he had no neck, only minute arms and legs and looked like a flabby egg; but he was immensely strong and a special room was built in the castle where he was kept from the eyes of everyone. His existence was known only to four men at a time: the Earl of Strathmore, his eldest son, the family lawyer and the factor of the estate. Each eldest son was told the secret and shown the rightful Earl when he reached the age of twenty-one. There are still records at Glamis, showing that a secret chamber was built there in 1684 and since the monster is said to have lived to an incredibly old age (some think, he only died in 1921) the secret may account for so many Lord Strathmores being unhappy men. A Lady Strathmore is said to have asked one of the factors outright about the story—for no Countess of Strathmore was ever told of the monster—and the factor refused to satisfy her, saying, 'It is fortunate you do not know the truth, for if you did, you would never be happy.' The present Lord Strathmore knows nothing about the monster, presumably because the creature was dead when he reached his majority, but he has always felt that there was a corpse or a coffin bricked up somewhere in the walls.

A former Lord Halifax was convinced, after spending a night there, that the Blue Room at Glamis was haunted. He thought he saw the ghost of 'Earl Beardie' and recounted how two visiting children often saw shadowy figures flitting about the castle in the vicinity of the Blue Room, where they would not sleep. Sir Shane Leslie told me that the ghost of 'Beardie' had been seen by one of his aunts when she stayed at Glamis.

The small dressing room off the Queen Mother's main bedroom used to be haunted. People who slept there often felt the bedclothes being pulled off but there have been no disturbances since the room has been turned into a bathroom.

Among the other haunted places at Glamis there is the room where the door opens by itself every night—even when it is bolted or wedged by some heavy object. There is a tongueless woman who runs across the park, pointing in anguish to her wounded mouth. 'Jack the Runner', a strange thin figure races up the long drive to the castle. A madman walks a certain portion of the roof on stormy nights, a spot known as 'The Mad Earl's Walk'. A ghostly little black boy has been seen sitting by the door of the Queen Mother's sitting room and is thought to have been a page boy who was badly treated. Noises of hammering and loud knocking are heard in a room in the oldest part of the castle. A female figure has been seen hovering above the clock tower, surrounded by a reddish glow, she is thought to be a Lady Glamis who was burned to death on Castle Hill, Edinburgh, charged with witchcraft and with being concerned in an attempt to poison King James V. A tall figure once walked into a room occupied by a Provost of Perth, clad in a long, dark cloak, fastened at the throat with an unusual clasp. A woman with mournful eyes and a pale face peers out of an upper lattice window, hands clutching at the panes. There are indeed ghosts aplenty at Glamis and whether one visits this historic and ancient pile in brilliant sunshine or on a stormy night, it is not difficult to believe that strange happenings have taken place here.

Once a party of youngsters decided to try to discover the locality of the secret room. They visited every room in the castle—the total is over a hundred—and hung towels and sheets out of the windows to mark them. They were sure that they had visited every room but when they gathered outside they counted seven windows in the massive castle with nothing hanging from them. The mystery of Glamis was still unexplained.

County Hotel, Forfar, Angus, Scotland.

Gloucester, GLOUCESTERSHIRE.

Some ten years ago there was an old house, where a vicar used to live, at a little village on the outskirts of Gloucester, almost hidden from the road by high trees.

Beneath the house there was a rambling kitchen unused in living memory but at times sounds that seemed to originate from this room suggested that people were walking about. One day the vicar went to see whether he could discover the causes of the noises and, standing in the centre of the old kitchen, he saw the figure of a monk. The vicar asked whether he could help the monk who, by way of reply, looked sadly at him, walked across the kitchen and, when he had almost reached the opposite wall, vanished.

After this the vicar saw the monk on several occasion, in the old kitchen and the figure always vanished a few seconds after being seen. It never spoke and always had a sad look on its face. The vicar began to make enquiries and discovered that there had once been a monastery nearby but now only a few ruins marked the site.

One day the vicar noticed that the floor of the old kitchen seemed to be sagging in the middle and thought that he had better see about getting it repaired. When workmen took up the floor, it was found that the flooring rested on two huge wooden beams which were almost rotted through with damp and age. Beneath them was a large and deep tank of water—possibly the water supply of years gone by. After the flooring had been repaired and replaced, the ghostly monk was never seen again.

New County Hotel, Southgate Street, Gloucester.

*Grantchester, CAMBRIDGESHIRE.

Rupert Brooke (1887-1915), the famous First World War poet, lived here at the Old Vicarage, a lovely house with a garden which must still be largely unchanged since those days, when it was the subject of one of his most famous poems.

Ever since they went to live there in 1911 (the occupants told me a few years ago) they heard a noise like someone walking about the top floor and moving books; they thought nothing of the sounds and were not in the least frightened.

My friend Christina Hole suggested that the unexplained footsteps, heard coming through the garden towards the sitting room, are those of the poet, re-visiting the house he loved.

In his well-known poem Brooke refers to 'the falling house that never falls'; this is an odd little semi-ruined house at

the bottom of the garden and, I am told, it can be a very eerie place after dark. Curious poltergeist manifestations used to occur there at night-time, small objects being spilled out of boxes and arranged in strange little patterns. The most stringent precautions were taken to detect whether any living person had been able to get into the building during the night and once the disturbances occurred after snow had fallen yet there was no sign of any footsteps.
Blue Boar Hotel, Cambridge.

Great Bealings, NEAR WOODBRIDGE, SUFFOLK.

Bealings House was the scene of a classic story of paranormal bell-ringing in 1834. The occupant of the Georgian mansion at the time, Major Edward Moor (1771-1848) a Fellow of the Royal Society, retired from the East India Company and author of a book on Hindu mythology, described the occurrences in a letter to his local paper and subsequently published a short volume on the case which includes accounts of unexplained bell-ringing at other places throughout the country.

On Sunday, February 2nd, 1834, Major Moor, on returning home from church, was told that the dining-room bell had rung three times between two and five o'clock. The following day the same bell again rang three times during the afternoon and the last time, just before five o'clock, it was heard by Major Moor. Next day he was out and returning shortly before five o'clock he learned that all the bells in the kitchen had been ringing violently—and as he was being told this a peal of bells sounded from the kitchen. There were (and still are) nine bells in a row in the kitchen, about a foot apart, ten feet from the floor, and on enquiry Major Moor learned from the cook that the five bells on the right were the ones affected: these were the ones situated in the dining room, the drawing room over the dining room, an adjacent bedroom, and two attics over the drawing room. While he was looking at these bells, which he was told had rung frequently since about three o'clock, the same five rang violently and with such force that he thought they would be shaken from the fastenings. Major Moor's son was with him

79

at the time and also witnessed the ringing; he had previously seen the bells ringing and had also heard them once before. In addition the cook and another servant were present in the kitchen. About ten minutes later there was another peal and a quarter of an hour later yet another.

At six o'clock, when Major Moor and his son were sitting down to dinner in the breakfast room, the bell of that room rang once, as if it had been pulled, although no one was near it at the time. During the meal the five bells previously affected rang every ten minutes or so and continued to do so at longer intervals when the six servants were at dinner in the kitchen until a quarter-to-eight when the ringing stopped.

Next day, Wednesday, February 5th, a peal of bells was heard at eleven o'clock in the morning when Major Moor, his son and grandson were in the breakfast room and while several of the servants were in the kitchen. Major Moor went to the kitchen and five minutes later the same five bells rang again, very violently, and four minutes later, yet again; one so violently that it struck the ceiling.

From then on the bells rang scores of times and in conditions that convinced Major Moor and his family that no human being was responsible. They rang when no one was in the passage or room concerned or outside the house unobserved. Major Moor saw the bells ring in the kitchen when all the servants were present and he became utterly convinced that the ringing noted by him and his family and others could not possibly have been produced by a living person.

The bell-ringing lasted from February 2nd to March 27th, 1834 when it ceased as abruptly as it began. The cause was never discovered. The original bells, now disconnected, still hang at Bealings House.
Crown Hotel, Woodbridge, Suffolk.

Great Leighs, ESSEX.

St Anne's Castle Inn, which claims to be the oldest inn in England, has long been famous for its haunted room and there are stories of over a hundred people who attempted to spend a night there, at different times, and who had curious experiences to relate.

Noises of various kinds have been reported: thuds, shuffles, bangs and raps from the direction of the stout oak door, the noise of furniture being moved around, a cold draught has been felt, curtains have been torn down, bed-clothes have been ripped off beds and clothing scattered.

One visitor to this former retreat of royalist, monk and highwayman, heard loud cries as he attempted to sleep in the haunted room. As soon as he rose from the bed the noises ceased but they began again when he lay down. This continued time after time and he had no rest until daybreak. Not long afterwards a girl occupied the room for one night and spent most of the time huddled by the window, waiting for the dawn. Several people reported seeing a black shape in the room, especially on one side of the bed.

There are various stories and legends that attempt to justify the manifestations. Perhaps the most persistent concerns the alleged murder of a child in the four-poster that used to stand there, in the presence of the child's mother, a very long time ago. Investigator Harry Price found the contents of the room in a condition comparable to having been 'shaken out of a pepper-pot' when he was there in 1944.
County Hotel, Rainsford Road, Chelmsford, Essex.

Greenwich: NATIONAL MARITIME MUSEUM.

Two visitors from Canada, a retired clergyman and his wife, visited the National Maritime Museum in 1966 and took a photograph in normal opening hours of the Tulip Staircase in The Queen's House, a beautiful building erected by Inigo Jones for Anne of Denmark, consort of King James I, and subsequently completed for Henrietta Maria, wife of King Charles I.

The staircase appeared to be deserted at the time but when the photograph was developed after the Hardys had returned to Canada, there seemed to be a cowled figure climbing the staircase with 'his' left and ringed hand on the stair-rail, preceded by a less clear figure also with a hand on the rail.

The original transparency was sent to The Ghost Club who obtained expert opinion and assurance that there had been no technical interference. The only logical explanation was that there had been a person, or persons, on the stairs. On a further visit to England in 1967 Mr and Mrs Hardy, who are not interested in psychic activity, were interviewed at length at Canada House by Richard M. Howard, then Honorary Secretary of The Ghost Club. He is of the opinion that they are incapable of conscious fraud.

There are no official records of any alleged haunting at the Museum although an official told me that there have been stories of an unidentified figure being encountered in the tunnel beneath the paved way immediately outside the Queen's House; a former employee of the Museum stated that on several occasions he had noticed unexplained 'figures' in the vicinity of the Tulip Staircase; and one of the Warders on duty at the Queen's House used to say that he heard footsteps there which he could not account for.

The Ghost Club organized an all-night vigil at the Queen's House and 'sealed off' certain rooms, placed 'controls' in strategic positions, noted atmospheric conditions, took thermometer readings every ten minutes, used sound recording apparatus, infra-red and standard film in movie and still camera and attempted 'to tempt' the ghosts by resorting to periods of total darkness and silence, using also planchette, table-turning and automatic writing for communication. Among the unexplained noises heard during the course of the investigation were the single peal of a bell, the sounds of muttering, crying and footsteps; while the remarkably clear photograph remains an enigma and, if genuine, probably the best spontaneous ghost photograph in existence.

Eltham Private Hotel, Westmount Road, Eltham, S.E.9.

Grimsby, LINCOLNSHIRE.

A council house was so badly haunted that Mr Ted Barningham, his wife and family left the place in September, 1967 after a 'ghost' appeared on closed circuit television at the house! It was thought to be the entity which had been terri-tying the family for weeks beforehand. This time it appeared on the monitor screen as the head of 'an old man of hideous appearance'. It was seen by a group of six people, including an electrical engineer, who had rigged up the apparatus. A television camera had been placed in the bedroom where most of the disturbances had taken place and after a watch of several hours the face appeared on the monitor screen downstairs. When one of the party rushed upstairs, the face disappeared. The engineer stated that he had tried every possible test with the apparatus but could find no possible explanation for the occurrence.

Ship Hotel, Flottergate, Grimsby, Lincs.

Haltwhistle, NORTHUMBERLANDSHIRE.

Near the remains of the old Roman wall an entire phantom hunt used to be seen galloping past, terrifying the dogs and cats of the neighbourhood who would run for miles to get away from the spectral hounds.

Hadrian Hotel, Wall Village, Hexham, Northumb.

*Ham House, NEAR PETERSHAM, SURREY.

Almost hidden by trees amid the Thames-side meadows between Twickenham and Richmond, one is surprised to come upon stately Ham House, a silent reminder of a more leisurely past, its ancient iron gates unopened since the flight of King James II.

Ham House was built by Sir Thomas Vavasour in 1610 and intended, according to tradition, as a residence for the eldest son of King James I. But the young prince's sudden death in 1612 brought whispers of murder—although it is not Prince Henry who haunts Ham House, but the old Duchess of Lauderdale who is said to revisit the scene of her triumphs and infamies during the days of Cromwell and of King Charles II.

The scheming and powerful Duchess, formerly Countess of Dysart, reputed to have been Cromwell's mistress, was daughter of William Murray, First Earl of Dysart, who built the magnificent great staircase at Ham. Elizabeth, his only child, while still married to Sir Lionel Tollemache, chose for her lover John Maitland and in 1672, with Sir Lionel dead, she married this member of Charles II's Cabal Ministry. He lived to become the unpopular Duke of Lauderdale, favourite of King Charles II. Ham House was enlarged, sumptuously decorated and furnished anew with lavish splendour: these were the compensating deeds of the villainous Lauderdale and his wicked wife who were known to send innocent people to the rack.

For years after her death the Duchess's boudoir remained as she had known it: her silver-headed ebony walking-stick where she had left it. It is this stick which is thought to be the original source of the mysterious tapping noises heard about the history-laden rooms of Ham House. At dead of night that noise would be heard—tap, tap, tap—just as the old Duchess used to hobble about.

The story that is supposed to account for the haunting concerns a butler at Ham whose little girl of six stayed at the house on a visit at the invitation of the Ladies Tollemache. Very early in the morning the child awoke suddenly to see an old woman scratching and clawing at the wall close to the fireplace. At first more curious than frightened, the little girl sat up in bed to see better what was happening but the sound of her movements made the old woman turn round. She came to the foot of the child's bed, grasping the bed-rail with her bony hands and stared long and fixedly at the now terrified child who screamed and buried herself beneath the bedclothes. Hearing the screams, servants and occupants of the house rushed to the child's room and although they saw no old woman, they comforted the child, listened to her story and then turned their attention to the wall by the fireplace. There they found papers which proved that in that very room Elizabeth, Countess of Dysart, had murdered her husband to marry the Duke of Lauderdale.

When I was there in August 1970 I learned of a phantom King Charles Spaniel which is reputed to run yapping along the terrace at the original front of the house (now the back), where colourful herbaceous borders face the long unopened gates of this splendid house.

Richmond Hill Hotel, Richmond Hill, Richmond, Surrey.

*Hampton, MIDDLESEX.

Penn Place, the former home of Mrs Sybell Penn, nurse to the infant Prince Edward, later King Edward VI, is now occupied by Eric Fraser, the artist, who will tell you that his daughter used to see a 'lady in grey' in her bedroom when she was a little girl.

As he showed me the room, Eric Fraser explained that his daughter was only two or three years old at the time and could not have known that the house probably incorporates part of the original house occupied by Mrs Penn, whose ghost, the 'lady in grey', is said to walk at nearby Hampton Court. One morning the little girl said casually, 'I've seen a nice lady in a grey dress. She came to my room last night and I didn't mind.' After that first time, she told her parents on several occasions: 'I saw the grey lady again last night.' After a while the child no longer mentioned the apparition but it may be that the ghost still walks at Penn Place and can be seen by those who have the extra-sensory perception of some children.

Mitre Hotel, Hampton Court, Middlesex.

*Hampton Court, MIDDLESEX.

The Old Court House, where the great architect Sir Christopher Wren lived during the years he was supervising work at Hampton Court Palace and where he died, has been the scene of a remarkable psychic occurrence.

Norman Lamplugh lived here for many years, until the outbreak of the Second World War. On one of the occasions when he held a garden party at the beautiful old house, two of the guests (one of them Norman's brother, Ernest) noticed a little boy of about eight years old threading his way through the groups of guests dotted about the lawn. The two friends were standing on the landing of the main staircase and they were puzzled for two reasons: they knew that no children had been invited to the social event and they were struck by the appearance of the child, for his fair hair was abnormally long and he was dressed in a black-and-white costume of a page-boy of the time of King Charles II! His breeches and doublet appeared to be of black velvet; he wore shiny black shoes with big silver buckles and white hose.

While the two men were discussing the boy, they watched as he easily and quickly wended his way between the guests and approached the stairway. Unhurriedly but with the confidence of someone who knew where he was going and without wasting any time he mounted the stairs and passed the two friends, who were in fact obliged to step back to make room for him. The child took no notice of them but walked on up the stairs to the top of the house and there entered a room which had no exit other than the doorway on to the stairs disappeared. No explanation was ever found for the mystery and as far as I know the phantom child was never seen again, although mysterious and unexplained footsteps are reported in the vicinity of the stairs on the night of February 26th, the anniversary of the death of Sir Christopher Wren.

The spirit of King Henry VIII seems to brood heavily over the mellow Tudor palace itself. He was at Hampton with five of his six wives and it was here on October 12th, 1537, that his third queen, Jane Seymour, bore him a son and died a week later. Her ghost walks here, or rather glides, clad in white, perambulating Clock Court. Carrying a lighted taper she has been seen to emerge from a doorway in the Queens' Old Apartments, wander noiselessly about the stairway and through the Silver Stick Gallery. Quite recently some servants handed in their notice because they had seen 'a tall lady, with a long train and a shining face' walk through closed doors holding a taper and gliding down the stairs.

Another courtyard, Fountain Court, used to be haunted by two male figures which were seen by Lady Hildyard who had grace and favour apartments overlooking the Court. She wrote to the Lord Chamberlain about the figures and also complained about unaccountable rappings and other strange noises at night-time. Her letter was passed to the Board of Works who did nothing; but not long afterwards workmen laying new drains in Fountain Court came across the perfectly preserved remains of two young cavaliers of the Civil War period, buried two feet below the pavement.

It is possible that they were the remains of Lord Francis Villiers and a brother Royalist Officer killed in a skirmish between the king's forces and those of Parliament but at all events after the bones had received decent burial, Lady Hildyard saw no more figures and heard no more unexplained noises.

The famous White Lady of Hampton Court is reputed to haunt the area of the landing-stage and a number of anglers reported seeing her one midsummer night a few years ago. There is also the ghost of Archbishop Laud (whose spirit is also said to appear in the library of St John's College, Oxford, rolling his head across the floor!) which has been allegedly seen by residents at the palace, strolling slowly without a sound (but complete with head!) in the vicinity of the rooms he once knew so well.

An example of the 'residential ghost' is also provided by the spectre of Mrs Sybil Penn, foster-mother of Edward VI. Records show that she was seen by a sentry here in 1881 and there are infrequent reports of her recurring appearances in succeeding years. As the nurse of Henry VIII's only legitimate son, Edward, she anxiously and conscientiously watched over the sickly child and the sound of her voice and the whirr of her spinning-wheel must have been some of the first sounds heard by the young prince. Edward never forgot his old nurse, nor did Mary Tudor or Elizabeth who granted her a pension and apartments at Hampton Court where both Elizabeth and Mrs Penn suffered an attack of smallpox in 1568. Queen Elizabeth survived but remained marked for the rest of her life. Mrs Penn was less fortunate and died on November 6th. She was buried at nearby St Mary's Church, Hampton, which was struck by lightning in 1829 and although Mrs Penn's tomb and monument were removed to the new church, her grave was rifled and her remains scattered. It was not long after this that a family named Ponsonby occupied the rooms in the palace where once Mrs Penn had lived and worked. They soon began to complain of continually hearing the sound of a spinning-wheel and a woman's voice which they could not account for. The sounds seemed to originate through one of the walls in the south-west wing and the noises became so persistent that the Board of Works was called in. They discovered a sealed chamber which, when opened, was found to contain, amid other feminine relics, a much-used spinning-wheel which may have been the one Mrs Penn used so often during her lifetime. It was about this time that a sentry on duty one day outside these apartments, saw a female figure clad in a long grey robe and hood emerging from the former rooms of Mrs Penn and vanishing in front of his eyes. Another sentry deserted his post when he saw the phantom of an old woman in grey pass through a wall. Both asserted that the figures they saw resembled the stone effigy of Mrs Sybil Penn.

Oddly enough the discovery of the spinning-wheel seems to have accentuated the curious happenings and for years afterwards there were continuous complaints about weird happenings in the vicinity of these apartments. Servants declared that they were awakened at night by cold hands on their faces, that they repeatedly heard stealthy footsteps perambulating the floor close to them; mutterings in a sepulchral voice were reported and, on occasions, loud crashing noises were heard at night. They awoke to find the whole apartment bathed in what they described as 'a ghastly lurid light'. Princess Frederica of Hanover, who knew nothing of Mrs Penn, came face to face with a 'tall, gaunt figure, dressed in a long grey robe, with a hood on her head, and her lanky hands outstretched before her'. She, too, declared that the figure resembled the faithful nurse's effigy. The well-authenticated ghost of Mrs Sybil Penn is known as the 'Lady in Grey'.

Perhaps the most famous ghost at Hampton Court is that of Lady Catherine Howard who came here in 1540, a lovely girl of eighteen, as bride of the fat, lame and ageing monarch. After little more than a year ugly rumours began to circulate and it was said that she behaved little better than a common harlot, both before and after her marriage. The night before she was arrested, her first step to the block, she broke free from her captors and sped along the gallery in a vain effort to plead for her life with her husband. But Henry, piously hearing vespers in the chapel, ignored her entreaties and she was dragged away, still shrieking and sobbing for mercy. As you go down the Queen's Great Staircase you can see on the right-hand side the low-roofed and mysterious cor-

The Ferry Boat Inn, Holywell, St. Ives, Huntingdonshire, where the ghost of the unhappy Juliet is reputed to walk each March 17, where she hanged herself many years ago. *Photo: Chris Underwood*

Flansham Manor, Sussex, long reputed to be haunted by unexplained footsteps, thuds, bangs and strange dragging noises. *Photo: Chris Underwood*

The Friary, East Bergholt, Essex, where a door used to open by itself every night at ten minutes to eleven; where the temperature would inexplicably drop and where a young soldier had a terrifying experience.
Photo: Chris Underwood

Ham House near Petersham, Surrey, haunted by the old and powerful Duchess of Lauderdale who murdered her first husband; and by a yapping King Charles Spaniel. *Photo: Chris Underwood*

Hampton Court Palace. Fountain Court used to be haunted by two cavaliers whose bones were unearthed here. *Photo: Chris Underwood*

The present Hinton Ampner Manor House, near Alresford, Hampshire, photographed from the site of the earlier house that was haunted for twenty years; a haunting that is exceptionally well documented in the form of contemporary letters. *Photo: Chris Underwood*

The courtyard of the Hop Bag Inn, Farnham, Surrey, where the sounds of a coach that used to come here years ago have been heard in recent times.
Photo: Chris Underwood

St. John's Priory, Poling, Sussex, where the sounds of Latin chanting, ghostly music and mysterious voices have been heard on many occasions.
Photo: Chris Underwood

ridor containing the room from which Queen Catherine escaped and to which she was dragged back, her screams mingling weirdly with the singing in the chapel. Her ghost re-enacts the grisly event on the night of the anniversary, running shrieking through what has come to be known as the 'Haunted Gallery'. Those who have heard and seen her ghost include Mrs Cavendish Boyle and Lady Eastlake, together with many servants at the palace. All the witnesses say the figure has long, flowing hair but it usually disappears so quickly that no one has time to observe it closely.

A hundred years ago the 'Haunted Gallery' was locked and used as a storage room for pictures but adjoining chambers were occupied as a grace and favour apartment by a titled lady who has recorded that once, in the dead of night, she was awakened by an appalling and ear-piercing shriek which died away into a pulsating silence. Not long afterwards she had a friend staying with her who was awakened by a similar dreadful cry which seemed to come from the 'Haunted Gallery'. After the Gallery was opened to the public an artist sketching some tapestry was startled to see a ringed hand repeatedly appear in front of it but he hurriedly sketched the hand and ring. The jewel was later identified as one known to have been worn by Catherine Howard.

Towards the end of the last century the ghost of Anne Boleyn was reported to have been seen here. Her ghost, dressed in blue, surprised a servant who recognised the figure she had seen, from a portrait in the palace. Anne is a perambulating ghost and is reputed to haunt Blickling Hall, Hever Castle, Salle Church, Rochford Hall, Bollin Hall, Marwell Hall, the Tower of London and the Undercroft of Lambeth Palace!

A police constable with over twenty years experience in the force, once saw a group of ghosts in the palace grounds. Standing by the main gates he noticed a party of people coming towards him along Ditton Walk. They consisted of some eight or nine ladies and two men in evening dress. The constable noticed that the only sound he heard was a rustling as of dresses. When the group drew near he turned and opened the gate for them, whereupon they altered direction and headed north towards the Flower Post Gates. At the same time the party formed itself into a procession two deep with the men at the head; then, to the policeman's amazement and while he was actually watching them, the whole group vanished!

Among other accounts of ghosts at Hampton Court there is the story of two devoted friends of whom one, after the death of her first husband, married a German count and went to live in Germany with her little girl Maud; the other was granted a residence at Hampton Court. One night when going to bed the latter lady saw, climbing without a sound the wide staircase opposite the door of her chamber, the figure of a lady dressed entirely in black except for white kid gloves. Speechless with horror as she recognized her friend, she fainted with a shriek as the apparition drew near to her. A few days later she received a letter from Maud informing her of the death of the Baroness. She hurried to Germany where she learned that her friend had requested, on her death-bed, that she should be buried in black—with white kid gloves. The Baroness had died in Germany on November 9th, the date on which her ghost had been seen by her friend at Hampton Court.

After a costume performance of 'Twelfth Night' at Hampton Court Palace, producer-actor Leslie Finch told me that he was walking towards one of the gateways with Lady Grant, who has apartments at the palace, when he saw a grey, misty figure in Tudor costume approaching them and he felt a sudden coldness. He thought the figure must be one of the actresses and moved to one side to let her pass. His companion looked oddly at him and he discovered that Lady Grant had seen no figure at all but, as the phantom passed, she also had noticed a sudden cold draught of air.

During the 1966 season of *Son et Lumière* at Hampton Court Palace a member of the audience 'saw' the figure of Cardinal Wolsey (who built the palace) under one of the archways and thought that an actor was taking part in the performance of sound and light; a fact that Christopher Ede, the producer, mentioned in his contribution to the 1970 programme.

Mitre Hotel, Hampton Court, Middlesex.

Hastings, SUSSEX.

The castle is said to have been the scene of the first tournament in England, held for Adela, daughter of William the Conqueror. After the castle had ceased to be a stronghold it was used as a religious house and there were frequent reports of ghostly organ music being heard here.

A figure, believed to be Thomas à Becket, has been seen within the precincts of the castle on autumn evenings—never at any other time of the year. There are stories, too, of the sounds of rattling chains and the groans of starving prisoners: perhaps some strange echo from the past. It is said that on certain sunny, misty mornings, a huge mirage of Hastings Castle can be seen far out at sea on the horizon. This might be explained as a result of reflection and refraction of light were it not that the castle appears again in all its former glory, with flags flying from the turrets.

Queen's Hotel, Hastings, Sussex.

*Heathfield, SUSSEX.

Warbleton Priory, an ancient farmhouse near Rushlake Green incorporated parts of an old Augustinian ecclesiastical building and used to house two skulls, thought to be those of a former owner of the house and of the man who murdered him. In common with most houses that harbour skulls, there were vague stories of evil consequences for those who moved them from the house; of cattle drying up and of the person responsible being plagued with continual bad luck and strange noises until the skulls were returned. There was also a bloodstain here that could not be removed.

Years ago when one of the thick walls of the house was being knocked down, workmen are said to have found the two skulls. When the first was discovered it was buried but the following morning the skull is reputed to have worked its way out of the earth and was found on the doorstep of the farmhouse. The skull was then placed in a box and stored on the cross-beams of the house. Later it was placed on a Bible in the front-room where it remained for many years with tenant farmers coming and going; but when one attempted to take the skull with him, screams sounded throughout the house, thuds and knocks were heard, doors and windows slammed and rattled, horses showed signs of fright and there was no peace until the skull was returned to Warbleton.

The second skull was also preserved here for many years and then turned up at a farmhouse some six miles away where the farmer is said to have been plagued with a whirl-wind when he tried to bury it.

It is a good many years now since either of the skulls were at Warbleton and I have been unable to trace any recent ghostly happenings hereabouts.

There was also a curious story associated with the rambling house. On certain moonlit nights a pair of ghostly white hands were said to be seen fluttering at a small window high up near the roof.

The alleged bloodstain was still shown to visitors some years ago and the floor-boards seemed to be distinctly worn in that part of the floor where there was certainly a persist-ent stain of some kind.

George Hotel, Battle, Sussex.

*Hemel Hempstead, HERTFORDSHIRE.

'The King's Arms' has a room where guests have 'restless nights', the wife of the landlord told me a few years ago; and once 'some manifestations' were experienced in the same room. There have been many unexplained noises, too, but the occupants were not distressed—'far from it, we live very happily here' I was told.

Breakspear Motor Hotel, Hemel Hempstead, Herts.

*Henley-on-Thames, OXFORDSHIRE.

The 'Bull' inn, old, dark and unusual, has been the scene, from time to time, of a curious and unexplained smell of burnt candles in one particular part of the bar. It may well be that there was a separate room or passage here at one

92

time for there have been many alterations over the years. One occupant reported seeing a cowled figure bending over him while he was in bed. He was obviously sincere about this and troubled by the experience when I spoke to him; at the same time he was honest enough to admit that others using the same room had not been disturbed.

The Red Lion Hotel, Riverside, Henley-on-Thames, Oxon.

Henley-on-Thames, OXFORDSHIRE: KENTON THEATRE.

In 1969 playwright Joan Morgan's play, 'The Hanging Wood', based on the story of a local girl, Mary Blandy, who was hanged at Oxford in 1752 for poisoning her father, was produced here. As soon as rehearsals began 'unusual incidents' took place. A large mirror 'jumped' off a wall, lights were switched on and off, doors were mysteriously opened and closed. A figure of a girl was reported at the back of the theatre watching the performances, although she was never seen to enter or leave the building. Whenever someone decided to discover who the girl was, the figure disappeared. Once, when some members of the cast were discussing Mary Blandy, a cup jumped about six inches off a table and smashed on to the floor. Miss Morgan said that some years previously, when the trial of Mary Blandy was being re-enacted at Henley Town Hall, a similar unexplained figure was seen by a number of people, including herself.

The Red Lion Hotel, Riverside, Henley-on-Thames, Oxon.

Hereford, HEREFORDSHIRE.

A seventeenth-century haunted house in the centre of Hereford was towed a hundred yards along the street at the end of 1966 to become the showpiece of a new store on the High Street. The old house is once said to have belonged to an apothecary who accidentally killed an apprentice by mixing the wrong medicine for him; whereupon he committed suicide in remorse.

Green Dragon Hotel, Hereford, Herefordshire.

There are many accounts of ghostly experiences at imposing and exceptionally well-preserved Hurstmonceaux Castle, which now houses the Royal Observatory. (This fifteenth-century castle is no longer open to the public.)

Perhaps the best-known story concerns the 'White Lady' who has been seen swimming the moat. Several hundred years ago, when the castle was still the property of the Fiennes family (Sir Roger de Fiennes built the place in 1440), one of the young sons enticed a village maiden into the castle and succeeded in getting her into bed. However, she resisted his advances and sought to escape by swimming the moat—but he dragged her back to the castle and eventually murdered her in what became known as 'the haunted bed'. The bed was still preserved a few years ago. The ghost of the terrified girl has been seen by local people, soundlessly and unsuccessfully swimming for life.

One night in 1910, Colonel Claude Lowther, the owner at that time, met a girl he did not recognize in the courtyard. She was distressed and stood there wringing her hands which he noticed were white and shrivelled. He thought she must be a gipsy girl begging but when he spoke to her, she instantly vanished. Another time he saw a man in riding breeches and velvet jacket near the old bridge over the moat. The figure walked straight at Colonel Lowther who was mounted on horseback, passed right through the horse's head and disappeared.

The Drummer's Hall has long been reputed to be haunted by the ghost of a giant drummer from the days of Sir Roger Fiennes, and the figure is said to have been seen striding along the battlements above the Great Hall, beating a drum and sending showers of sparks cascading from his incandescent drum-sticks. During the last century a story was circulated suggesting that a member of the Dacre family who was supposed to be dead, lived on in the castle in secret with a beautiful young wife. To frighten away the men who came to pay their attentions to the young 'widow', he dressed himself in a drummer's uniform, smeared his clothes and drum with phosphorous and drummed his way along the battlements.

Another ghost at Hurstmonceaux is that of Grace Naylor whose father George bought, in 1708, the property which originally contained exactly as many windows as there are days in a year and as many chimneys as there are weeks. For some reason, that has never been revealed, her governess starved the girl to death in the room with the oriel window on the east side. She was buried in the family vault at All Saints Church, Hurstmonceaux but the sounds of her sobbing used to be heard in the castle and occasionally a female figure would be encountered, floating about the corridors and disappearing through walls.

Beautiful Georgiana Naylor lived at Hurstmonceaux Castle at the end of the nineteenth century, an independent, forceful and eccentric student of the occult. She daily rode a white ass to drink from an enchanted spring in the park, dressed in a white cloak embroidered with mystic symbols, while a tame white doe trotted at her side. One day some hounds fell on the doe and tore it to pieces near the church. Georgiana left Hurstmonceaux and never returned. She died at Lausanne in 1806 and for years afterwards there were reports of her spectre riding a white ass in and out of the deserted rooms at the castle.

Finally stories of the ghosts of Lord Dacre and a poacher have been current locally for centuries and probably date from a fight between the young Lord and his friends when they encountered three of Lord Pelham's keepers, while on a poaching lark. The keeper haunts the field where he died from a blow from Lord Dacre's sword and Dacre himself has been seen in the grounds of the castle wearing a rusty riding cloak and large brass spurs and riding a fine chestnut horse. There are reports of his having been seen in recent years but whenever he is addressed, he turns and plunges into the moat and sinks in a cloud of mist.

White Friars Hotel, Hurstmonceaux, Sussex.

Higher Brixham, DEVONSHIRE.

The old and ominously-named Black House, used by the monks when they were building nearby St Mary's Church, has long had the reputation of being haunted and for years local residents were reluctant to pass it at night.

Not long ago there were stories of various unexplained noises, a mysterious lighting-up of an upper room (once noticed by a police constable) and the apparition of a man, possibly a monk, that used to be seen at one of the upstairs windows of the forty-two roomed house.

The owner, Miss Evelyn Joyce, will tell you that she thinks the ghost, if there is one, must be bored with being earth-bound and plays practical tricks on her—for she has been locked out of the house on more than one occasion. Once the bathroom door was found to have locked itself from the inside and a carpenter had to saw through locks and bolts to break in and release her. Unexplained noises and particularly footsteps, have been reported both inside the fine house with its wonderful carved staircase and also in the garden where, nine feet under the present lawn, traces have been found of the cobbled stable yard of a much earlier building. There is a tradition that the clatter of a horse's hooves used to be heard here, sounding as though they were on cobble-stones.

Churston Court Hotel, Brixham, Devon.

Higher Chilton Farm, SEE *Chilton Cantelo*, SOMERSET.

*Hinton Ampner, NEAR ALRESFORD, HAMPSHIRE.

The Tudor Manor House, demolished in 1793, was the scene of remarkable and unexplained happenings for some twenty years. The house is thought to have been built early in the sixteenth century, replacing a mediaeval building destroyed by fire. Sir Thomas Stewkeley lived here at the end of that century and as a country seat, the sprawling 'E' shaped manor was later occupied by his descendants. One of them, Mary Stewkeley, married Edward Stawell (later Lord Stawell) in 1719. Her younger sister, Honoria, lived with them and when Mary died in 1740 an affair developed between Lord Stawell and his sister-in-law who had continued to live at the Manor after the death of her sister. There were stories of 'wild happenings' and a baby is supposed to have been born and to have been murdered. Honoria died in 1754 and there is a plaque to her memory in nearby Hinton Ampner Church.

Lord Stawell died in 1755 and very soon afterwards a groom at the Manor declared that one bright moonlit night he had seen the 'drably dressed' ghost of the fourth Baron, his former master. Apart from servants, the furnished house was unoccupied for some years except during the shooting seasons. In January, 1765, the property was let to the Ricketts family.

Mrs Mary Ricketts is the chief witness in this case and it is worthwhile noting that she came from a distinguished family, her brother having been created Baron Jervis of Meaford and Earl St Vincent for his naval exploits. Like George Washington, Mary Ricketts was regarded as being unable to tell a lie. In 1757 she had married William Henry Ricketts of Jamaica and when his business took him to the West Indies, which was quite frequently, she stayed at home with their three children.

When the Rickettses moved into the Manor they took with them an entirely new set of servants from London, complete strangers to Hinton Ampner and its tales; but almost immediately the family and servants were disturbed by the continual noise of slamming doors for which no normal explanation was ever discovered. New locks were fitted to all the doors in the house but the unexplained slamming noises continued and six months after the Ricketts moved in, Elizabeth Brelsford, nurse to eight-month-old Henry Ricketts, plainly saw 'a gentleman in a drab-coloured suit of clothes' go into the yellow bedchamber, which was the apartment usually occupied by the lady of the house. The groom, George Turner, maintained that he saw the same 'gentleman in drab clothes' one night. This would seem to be the identical figure seen in the house ten years earlier.

Later the form of a tall woman dressed in dark clothes which rustled like silk was seen and heard one evening by four servants who were in the kitchen. Noises described as 'dismal groans' and 'rustling' were reported soon afterwards, most frequently in the vicinity of bedsteads. A couple of years later, during one of William Ricketts' trips to Jamaica, his wife and all three of the children frequently heard the noise of footsteps and the rustling of silk clothes against the bedroom door; sometimes the footsteps were loud enough to awaken Mrs Ricketts. In spite of persistent searches, no physical explanation was ever found for these noises. A couple of months later Mrs Ricketts again heard footsteps, heavy and distinct; and about the same period she reported hearing the sound of music and heavy knocks which had no physical reality. About a year later a curious murmuring sound was often heard throughout the house, like a wind beginning to rise; and a maid stated that she heard a great deal of groaning and fluttering in her bedroom.

Early in 1770 an old man living at West Meon called at the Manor and asked to see Mrs Ricketts. He explained that his wife had often told him: in her young days a carpenter whom she had known well, had related, how he had once been sent for by Sir Hugh Stewkeley and on his direction had taken up some boards in the dining room to enable Sir Hugh to conceal something beneath them. Afterwards the boards were replaced.

In the summer of 1770 Mrs Ricketts, lying in bed in the yellow bedchamber, 'thoroughly awake' as she put it, for she had retired only a short while before, plainly heard the plodding footsteps of a man approaching the foot of her bed. She felt the danger to be too near for her to ring the bell for assistance so she sprang out of bed and fled to the adjoining nursery, returning with a light and the children's nurse. A thorough search revealed no trace of an intruder or any cause for the noise she had heard. There was only one door to the bedroom, the one leading into the nursery. For some months after this experience Mrs Ricketts was undisturbed in the yellow bedchamber until, having moved to a warmer room over the hall, she sometimes heard in the November, 'the sounds of harmony' and, one night, three distinct knocks. A little later she often noticed a kind of hollow murmuring 'that seemed to possess the whole house', a noise that was heard on the calmest nights.

On April 2nd, 1771, the sixteenth anniversary of Lord Stawell's death, a number of unexplained noises were heard at the house by Mrs Ricketts and some of the servants, including three heavy and distinct knocks. A month later the disturbances increased and by midsummer they had reached a hitherto unparalleled level. The sounds of a woman and two men talking were a frequent phenomenon at this time. These sounds were heard night after night. Usually a shrill female voice first, followed by two deeper men's voices. Although the conversation sounded close at hand, no words were distinguishable. Loud crashing noises and piercing shrieks followed which died away as though sinking into the earth and a nurse, Hannah Streeter, who expressed a wish to hear more, was thereafter troubled every night.

Mrs Ricketts' brother, the future Lord St Vincent, arranged to sit up with Captain Luttrell, a friend, and a servant. Night after night they heard loud noises, as of a gun being let off nearby, followed by groans; there were rustlings, door-slammings, footsteps and other sounds which convinced Captain Jervis and Captain Luttrell that the house was unfit as a residence for any human being.

Early in August, 1771 Captain Jervis left the house and his sister and her children followed soon afterwards. The Bishop of Winchester allowed Mrs Ricketts to live at the Old Palace —the Manor of Hinton Ampner originally belonged to the Priory of St Swithum at Winchester (nine miles to the west) and was the particular perquisite of the Almoner, whose title became attached to the place and gradually became corrupted to Ampner. Later the Bishop of St Asaph offered Mrs Ricketts his house in London where she lived before renting a house in Curzon Street.

There can be no doubt that the experiences at Hinton Ampner Manor House so terrified Mrs Ricketts that she had to leave the place—in particular one curious experience of which she gives no details, merely saying: 'I was assailed by a noise I never heard before, very near me, and the terror I felt cannot be described.'

Towards the end of the Ricketts tenancy of the house a reward of £50, then £60 and finally £100 was offered for the solution of the disturbances; the money was never claimed.

A year after Mrs Ricketts and her family left Hinton Ampner, the Manor was let to a family named Lawrence who endeavoured, by threats to the servants, to stifle reports of disturbances. Little information of the curious happenings undoubtedly experienced at this time leaked out although it does seem that the apparition of a woman was seen. The Lawrences, who were the last inhabitants of the property, left suddenly in 1773 and the house stood empty, apart from its ghosts, for over twenty years, when it was demolished.

The Hinton Ampner case is exceptionally well documented in the form of contemporary letters from Mrs Ricketts to her husband in Jamacia and to the Rev. J. M. Newbolt, Rector of Hinton Ampner. There are also letters from Mrs Ricketts' brother to William Ricketts, and various letters from servants to Mrs Ricketts; but perhaps the most moving evidence is contained in an account, written in 1772, which Mrs Ricketts left for her children and for posterity. This is published in its entirety in Harry Price's *Poltergeist Over England.*

The fourth Baron Stawell's only daughter, who was created Baroness Stawell, married the Rt. Hon. Henry Bilson-Legge and their grand-daughter, an only surviving child, married in 1803 John Dutton, second Baron Sherborne. The present owner, Ralph Stawell Dutton, F.S.A., is their great-grandson.

A new Hinton Ampner House was built about 1793 some fifty yards from the site of the old building and this Georgian house forms the central part of the present building. During the demolition of the old Manor a small skull was discovered under the floorboards in one of the rooms.

The present owner will tell you, as he told me when I was there in June, 1970, that there were some reports of unexplained noises being heard in the new house, usually just before dawn, but between 1936 and 1939 the house was much altered and in 1960 the main part was gutted by fire. Mr Dutton says there have been no apparently paranormal happenings in the present house.
Swan Hotel, Alresford, Hants.

Hinxworth Place, NEAR BALDOCK, HERTFORDSHIRE.

For years on stormy evenings in the autumn strange noises have been heard here. Screams, followed by a thudding noise from the direction of the stairs, the sound of a baby crying, the sound of water gushing from the pump in the yard. A Major R. G. Clutterbuck, who has had connections with

Hinxworth, suggested that the origin of the curious noises dates back many years to the time when some occupants left their small baby in the care of a young nursemaid while they went out one evening. The young boy of the house decided to frighten the girl by draping himself in a sheet and making weird noises. The frightened girl attacked the 'ghost' with a poker and the boy fell down the stairs, screaming. He was found by the cook who tried to restore the dying boy by putting his head under the pump, but to no avail.

Ye Olde George and Dragon Hotel, Baldock, Herts.

Hitchin, HERTFORDSHIRE.

Hitchin Priory was in the possession of the same family for four hundred years. The property incorporates part of a house of White Friars and is reputed to be haunted each June by a cavalier named Goring who was wounded in a skirmish during the Civil War.

Goring sheltered in a mansion known as Highdown House at nearby Pirton, where the small roof chamber he occupied over the porch is also reputed to have ghostly associations. When the Roundheads began to search the house Goring changed his hiding place to a hollow elm (which is still standing) but he was discovered and killed on the spot, while his betrothed watched from an upstairs window. Legend has it that each June 15th he rides, headless, on a white horse to the site of the cell in the grounds of Hitchin Priory.

The Priory is also said to have a ghost of its own: an unidentified 'Grey Lady' who has been seen in recent years outside the building, wearing a long grey dress but no coat, even on cold nights. What she is doing outside the former home of monks, is not known.

The Sun Hotel, Hitchin, Herts.

Holywell, HUNTINGDONSHIRE.

On the edge of the River Ouse, just beyond Holywell, stands

the 'Ferry Boat Inn' haunted, for perhaps nine hundred years, by the ghost of Juliet, a young girl who loved a rough local woodcutter named Tom Zoul so deeply that it became a kind of sickness.

Tom preferred the company of his fellow-workmates to that of the tender-hearted Juliet and, neglected by him, she pined and languished and slowly her heart broke. One wild spring day the grief became too much for her; wearing a pink dress that Tom liked, she hanged herself on a tree beside the river. The date was March 17th.

As a suicide she could not be buried in consecrated ground and she was laid to rest near the river that seemed to share her sadness; the grave simply marked with a plain slab of grey stone.

Many years passed until the builder of the 'Ferry Boat Inn' came along and decided to incorporate Juliet's gravestone in the flooring of the inn, for there are few quarries hereabouts and he was short of stone. There it can be seen to this day, forming part of the inn's stone floor and for many years, people have gathered here on each March 17th to watch for Juliet's ghost which is said to rise from the flagstone and drift out of the inn and towards the river.

A few years ago no less than four hundred people turned up on the anniversary and in 1955 the Cambridge Psychical Research Society sent a team of investigators equipped with electronic detection apparatus but their instruments showed no abnormality.

This is a ghost which everyone knows about but few have seen. 'There are certainly some very odd happenings here,' the landlord told me in 1965, 'quite inexplicable; there is for instance the dog that will not go near the gravestone and of course the local women don't come near the inn on March 17th.'

Golden Lion Hotel, St Ives, Hunts.

Horden, DURHAM.

In 1967 a miner and his wife, living at number 4 Eden Street, were so terrified by many 'ghostly incidents' they were totally unable to explain that they called in their vicar, the Rev. T. Matthews. When his prayers did not end their problems, they decided to move and did so. The family were reluctant to talk about their experiences but insisted that 'ghostly presences' had made themselves indisputably felt in the little house.

The Three Tuns Hotel, New Elvet, Durham City, Co. Durham.

Houghton, NEAR WALSINGHAM, NORFOLK.

Sir Robert Walpole, (1676-1745) first Earl of Orford, statesman and perhaps the first effective Prime Minister of England, built the magnificent Houghton Hall on the site of his old ancestral home. But it is his sister, Dorothy Walpole, whose ghost, dressed in a brown brocade dress, is reputed to haunt the house. She probably spent the happiest days of her life here and her ghost is said to have appeared to the Prince Regent when he was occupying the State Bedroom, causing him to request a different room for the rest of his stay.

The Red Lion Hotel, Fakenham, Norfolk.

*Hoylake, CHESHIRE.

The thirty-two bedroom Royal Hotel, facing the Irish Sea and built in 1797, has an unidentified ghost in tweeds.

Some years ago the proprietor informed me that there had been frequent reports of an unknown ghost in one particular wing of the hotel. Psychic investigator Harry Price spent several days and nights there in 1923 and decided that the manifestations were genuine but that identity could not be established.

Twenty years later a female employee reported seeing, on several occasions, a male figure in knickerbocker tweeds and a cloth cap walk down the corridor from the hall to the ballroom. She said that the rather slight form had an energetic and lively figure and twice when she followed the solid-looking figure, it disappeared quite inexplicably. She realized afterwards that she had not noticed any sound accompanying the experience.

Some years later after the hotel had changed ownership, a barman reported seeing a similar figure pass from the billiards room across the room where the barman stood and disappear along the same corridor. His description stated: 'brown knickerbocker tweeds and cap.'

Years later a maintenance joiner on the staff repeatedly saw an unexplained figure in the same room although his description did not entirely agree with that of the barman.

A few months later unaccountable openings and closings of various doors in the hotel provided further food for speculation. At the time of their respective experiences neither the barman nor the joiner were aware of reports of an unidentified figure seen many years before in the same part of the hotel.

Royal Hotel, Hoylake, Cheshire.

Hurley, BERKSHIRE.

Ladye Place used to be an historic building standing in twenty acres of land in this old world village when I knew Colonel Rivers-Moore who bought the place in 1924. At that time he hardly could have known that in the years to come he would build up an impressive dossier of signed statements from responsible people who witnessed inexplicable happenings at this house which used to be a Benedictine priory.

Colonel Rivers-Moore was interested in archaeology and he began to dig, looking for early foundations, hoping to find confirmation of a charter from the reign of King Richard II which gave Ladye Place as the burial place of Editha, sister of Edward the Confessor. He particularly wanted to find Editha's grave for it was her ghost, the Grey Lady, that according to tradition, haunted his historic home.

Soon after excavation began Mrs Rivers-Moore's brother, a doctor, was staying at Ladye Place. He surprised his hosts one morning by telling them that he had encountered a ghostly monk in the house. Soon after another visitor said she had had some strange experiences which suggested a psychic presence. Following séance messages, the Rivers-Moores unearthed part of the foundation of the Tudor house and some human remains, but they were not those of Editha. Still the digging continued under the guidance obtained at séances and at length a hard base was uncovered, surrounded by tiles, which could have formed the base of an early shrine.

Meanwhile ghostly monks were seen more and more often at Ladye Place. One declared that he had practised black magic. Others were seen by visitors and friends and it became a common occurrence for a monk to be seen, with arms crossed, in the cloisters. But Colonel Rivers-Moore was primarily interested in archaeology and after twenty years at Ladye Place he had exhausted the ground of secrets, except for the resting place of Editha which he may or may not have found. With the cessation of the digging the ghosts went back to rest.

In 1947 Colonel Rivers-Moore put the place up for auction; he moved to Wargrave and later to Scotland where I saw him shortly before he died in 1965, still firmly convinced that he was responsible for disturbing the ghostly monks of Ladye Place and still sure that one day the grave of Editha would be found. I didn't tell him that his beautiful house had been converted into three homes and that his land was sold in lots, some of it for a market garden. Perhaps the ghosts had won their peace at last.
Ye Olde Bell Hotel, Hurley, Berks.

Husbands Bosworth, LEICESTERSHIRE.

Bosworth Hall has a ghost that creaks and groans and a bloodstain that has been damp for three hundred years.

Mrs Constable Maxwell's family have been at Bosworth since time immemorial and although the house so full of rambling corridors and twisting staircases has been altered a good deal, the Roman Catholic atmosphere is still as strong as ever. In Cromwell's days masses had to be held in secret. One day, in those troubled times, Roundhead troops were heard approaching as the Jesuits were celebrating such a Mass, but they were prepared and the priest leapt for the hide hole which was entered from an attic. My friend Granville Squiers, who made a study of secret hiding places, told me of this fascinating one which was large enough to accomodate two or three men comfortably and yet quite invisible, constructed as it was near the fireplace but cunningly camouflaged by a cupboard with a rounded back and a false wall.

In his flight the priest is thought to have knocked over the chalice of consecrated wine or in his haste he cut himself; at all events the dark, waxy stain has remained damp ever since: for the sceptic, an oddity, for the religious, a miracle.

Lady Lisgar, a Protestant widow who married Sir Francis Fortescue-Turvile in 1881, is doomed to haunt Bosworth Hall forever because she refused to allow a priest into the house to administer the last rites to a Roman Catholic servant. Mrs Maxwell recalls a doctor seeing her ghost, when he stayed in the house because she was ill. On his way upstairs from dinner one evening he passed a strangely dressed woman on the stairs and murmured a polite 'Goodnight' but received no reply. When he enquired next morning who the other guest in the house might be he was told that there was nobody. When he described the woman he had seen, Mrs Maxwell's mother recognized her ancestor. 'That was the ghost of Lady Lisgar,' she told the doctor, 'I beg you not to mention the matter to the children.'

The silent ghost of Lady Lisgar has been seen in the Bow Room where she slept and where she died, along corridors she knew and loved, on stairways and in passageways she helped to create for she carried out many changes when she was at Bosworth. But wherever she is seen Mrs Maxwell notes the date and the circumstances in the Black Book of Boswell Hall; and every Easter the rooms are blessed by a priest.

Guests complain that they are awakened by fearful groans and unearthly creaks, quite convinced that the house is full of ghosts. Once a guest was thrown out of a canopy bed with considerable force and landed on the floor. No need to ask that visitor whether Bosworth Hall is haunted!

L'Auberge, Berridge Lane, Husbands Bosworth, Leics.

Igtham Mote, NEAR SEVENOAKS, KENT.

A fourteenth-century manor house, eerie and isolated but perfectly-preserved and occupied from the days of Queen Elizabeth I to the middle of the reign of Queen Victoria by the devout Roman Catholic Selby family. Built at the period when castles were becoming obsolete, it became a mansion, fortified against vicious wandering bands of brigands. There is an escape route behind a chimney and various hiding places. Secret religious services used to be held in the crypt; the chapel door has no less than five locks. In 1872 workmen discovered a fourteenth-century window and a blocked-up doorway in the tower where many visitors have experienced an uncanny coldness. When the doorway was broken down, they found the skeleton of a woman in a cupboard. She is thought to have been Dame Dorothy Selby. An anonymous letter in the Monteagle Collection of the British Museum warns Lord Monteagle not to attend the Houses of Parliament on November 5th, 1605. It was through this letter that the Gunpowder Plot was uncovered. There is evidence to suggest that the letter came from Lord Monteagle's cousin, Dame Dorothy and legend has it that she was walled up in the cupboard as a punishment by the partisans of the Plot. Some years ago a bishop sought to exorcise the ghost in the tower but the peculiar chill remains.
Royal Oak Hotel, High Street, Sevenoaks, Kent.

Ilford, ESSEX.

The old fire station on Broadway is said to have a ghostly fireman, complete with brass helmet. Firewoman Penny White reported seeing this figure, thought to be Godfrey Netherwood, a fireman in the 1890s who was interested in ghosts and hauntings. The same form was observed many times in the old building, but Penny White saw the figure under a stairway at the new fire station in Romford Road! A careful search revealed no explanation.
Cranford Private Hotel, Ilford, Essex.

Ilfracombe, DEVONSHIRE.

The fifteenth-century Chambercombe Manor House has a haunted room which was discovered in 1865 when the owner noticed an extra window where there was no room. After a wall was broken down, a low, dark chamber was revealed with remains of tapestry still hanging on the walls and Elizabethan black carved furniture almost falling to pieces.

Behind the curtains the skeleton of a woman was found lying on the bed and since then weird sounds have been heard at night from the vicinity of this room, hidden for so long. Today the haunted room, situated between the Coat of Arms Bedroom (once used by Lady Jane Gray) and the low-beamed Victorian Bedroom, can be viewed through a hole in the wooden partition of the staircase; a strange mystery that will probably never now be solved. Perhaps it has some connection with the tunnel that ran from here to Hele beach and was reputedly used by smugglers.
Westwell Hall Private Hotel, Ilfracombe, Devon.

Inverness, SCOTLAND.

There is a vague local story of ghostly soldiers led by an officer wearing a gold-laced hat and blue Hussar cloak, riding a grey dragoon horse. The phantom army suddenly vanishes and has never been identified.
Royal Hotel, Inverness, Scotland.

Jay's Grave, SEE *Dartmoor, Devon.*

Kilkenny City, IRELAND.

The vicinity of St John's Parochial Hall is said to be haunted by the ghost of a tall, thin woman using crutches who wears a long coat, no stockings and has flowing white hair. A young nurse and a friend saw the figure twice one evening in May, 1969, when they were returning home from a dance.

'The Marble City' is one of the most interesting old towns in Ireland with its dignified eighteenth-century houses, its castle, the River Nore dividing it in two and its cathedral dedicated to St Canice, the sixth-century saint from whom Kilkenny derives its name.
Castle Motor Hotel, Ferrycarrig Bridge, Wexford, Co. Wexford, Ireland.

Kingham, NEAR CHIPPING NORTON, OXFORDSHIRE.

The century-and-a-quarter-old Langstone Arms Hotel made news in 1964 when noises and a 'white shape' pestered the owner, the manager and customers for several months. The 'form' seemed to re-appear regularly every ten days or so, heralded by mysterious coughing noises and shuffling footsteps. The figure was that of an elderly woman wearing a head-dress which made those who saw 'her' think she must be a nun. She glided along certain corridors in the hotel, but never anywhere else. Once she seemed to pass clean through a glass partition. The Rev. W. Attwood-Evans was sceptical at first but after hearing first-hand evidence from local people, changed his views and investigated the history of the inn but could find no record of a murder or suicide that might have accounted for the ghost.
Langstone Arms Hotel, Kingham, Oxon.

*Knebworth House, KNEBWORTH, HERTFORDSHIRE.

The ancestral home of the Lytton family used to have a haunted room in the east wing where, according to tradition, 'Jenny Spinner' was imprisoned and where she worked hard and long until her mind became deranged and she died. Soon after her death the sound of her spinning-wheel was heard and this sound continued intermittently until the wing was demolished in 1811. The story has some foundation in fact and 'Spinning Jenny' is mentioned in some of the old documents at Knebworth.
Roebuck Motor Hotel, Stevenage, Herts.

Lamberhurst, KENT.

In May, 1906, Mr J. C. Playfair of Furnace Mill discovered that all the horses in his stables had been turned round: their tails were in their mangers and their heads were where their tails should have been!—while one horse was missing altogether!

Eventually it was discovered in a hay-loft although the doorway was barely wide enough for a man to enter and a partition had to be knocked down to get the animal out. Other apparently inexplicable incidents included the movement of several heavy barrels and locked and bolted doors opening by themselves. It is interesting to note that a young son was a member of the household and that two watch-dogs guarded the premises which could not be approached without the occupants being aware of the fact, yet no adequate explanation was ever offered for these strange happenings.

Three miles to the west stand the beautiful ruins of Bayham Abbey with its spectral monks, phantom voices and ghost bells.

The Abbey was founded in 1200. An excellent idea of how splendid the building was can be obtained from the well-preserved ruins of the North Transept, the two Chapels and the Cloisters. There is part of a holy-water stoup here and in a niche, the remains of an ancient tomb. The very air seems permeated with the past and if Bayham is not haunted, it ought to be.

In fact there are many stories of ghostly monks being seen here, sometimes a whole procession slowly wending its silent way amongst the ruins at midnight. Sounds of sweet music have been heard and the noise of revelry; of voices chanting Latin, and bells faintly chiming. The smell of burning incense has also been remarked upon by visitors to this pleasant spot.

Nearby Scotney Castle with its picturesque circular tower rising from the edge of the lake or moat, has the ghost of a murdered man, dripping with water.

In 1259 the castle was held by Walter de Scotney, steward to the Earl of Gloucester. He was induced by William de Valence to administer poison to the Earl and other nobles who were feasting as guests of the Bishop of Winchester.

The Earl's brother and some other guests died but the Earl escaped, with the reputed loss of his nails, teeth and skin. Walter de Scotney was hanged at Tyburn and his estates forfeited. The castle passed into the hands of the Darrells and in 1598 the Jesuit priest Father Blunt was concealed here by the Roman Catholic family. When his hiding place was discovered, he escaped by swimming the moat. A member of the Darrell family, Arthur Darrell, had a fake funeral after he was outlawed, which he attended himself. In the eighteenth century the Darrell family took to smuggling and once entrenched themselves for three days to resist the attack of revenue officers.

It was another skirmish with the revenue authorities that gave rise to the haunting for on that occasion a Darrel killed one of the officers and threw his body into the moat. The murdered man has been seen many times since, dripping with water, hammering at the great door of Scotney, seeking retribution.

Wellington Hotel, Tunbridge Wells, Kent.

Langenhoe, NEAR COLCHESTER, ESSEX.

Until a few years ago a haunted church stood like a sentinel near the Manor House, looking out over the desolate marshes; certainly the most haunted church that I have come across.

As soon as I heard about the curious happenings, I spent several hours with the rector, the Rev. E. A. Merryweather who regaled me with the story of the strange experiences he vouched for. I examined the diary in which he had recorded the events at the time they had taken place. Later he presented me with this diary.

I found Mr Merryweather to be a large, astute and kindly man, then in his sixties, level-headed and sensible, with an infectious sense of humour and a gift for looking on the bright side of things. Before coming to Langenhoe in 1937 he had spent most of his life in the North of England and had previously experienced no psychic manifestations of any kind, nor was he interested in the subject. Doubtless because he was at the church more frequently than anyone else, he had experienced himself much of the allegedly paranormal phenomena.

The first happenings for which he could find no explanation were typical poltergeist activity: door-slamming and paranormal locking. 'Yes, it wasn't long before things happened that suggested to me that there was something odd about the place,' the rector said as I remarked on the date of the first entry in the diary: 'I visited the church on September 20th, 1937. It was a quiet autumn day. I was standing alone in the church, and the big west door was open. Suddenly it crashed to with such force that the whole building seemed to shake. Doors don't usually slam to as if an express-train had hit them, when there is no palpable reason. This aroused my curiosity as to the cause.' Twice during November 1937 the rector's valise, in which he carried his books and vestments, was found to be unaccountably locked while he was in the vestry; all efforts to unlock it proving entirely unsuccessful while in the vicinity of the church, although on each occasion when he was outside in the lane the valise unlocked without any difficulty. On the first occasion a friend of the rector also witnessed this 'locking'.

There was little further to report until 1945 when, on Easter Sunday, there occurred the first of a number of incidents concerning flowers. Mrs Gertrude Barnes and her daughter Irene were helping Mr Merryweather decorate the church before the congregation arrived and had placed some flowers in a vase on a pew while attending to some other matter. A moment later Mrs Barnes found the flowers removed from the vase and laid on the pew. Later there were other incidents when flowers were moved and unaccountably appeared or disappeared.

During the autumn of 1947 Mr Merryweather called at the Manor House and walked into (quite literally!) a tactual phenomenon that is almost unique in the annals of psychical research. He was shown over the house by the late Mrs Cutting and entered a charming front bedroom which Mrs Cutting said she did not use as there was something queer about it; she preferred to sleep in the bedroom facing north even though the view over the marshes was much less attractive. She stayed in the room with Mr Merryweather only a few seconds and then left him, saying as she went: 'I don't like this room.' Left alone, the rector, after admiring the grand sweeping view for a moment, turned from the window—and, as he told me, he 'moved into the unmistakable embrace of a naked young woman'. This singular tactual phenomenon lasted only a few seconds: 'one wild, frantic embrace and she was gone' as Mr Merryweather put it; but the rector was quite emphatic that he had this most unusual experience and had no doubt whatever that it was just as he described it; there existed absolutely no doubt about it in his mind. Nothing auditory, visual or olfactory accompanied the experience.

Several times in 1948 while celebrating Holy Communion, the rector and members of the congregation heard thuds from the direction of the vestry door. Upon investigation nothing was ever visible and no explanation or cause for the noise was ever found. The thuds continued with some regularity for about a month and were afterwards heard intermittently. Reference to the rector's diary shows that they were heard ten times between July and December, 1948; and on November 11th that year, while busy raking coal at the side of the church with an iron rod, the rector suddenly sensed that someone or something was near him in the deserted churchyard. He stuck the rod into the coal and, taking off his biretta, hung it on the end of the rod as a test. To his amazement the hat began to revolve slowly in front of his eyes!

Five minutes later he heard a voice in the empty church. For some time past there had been a certain amount of hooliganism on the part of some boys staying at a nearby village. People had been attacked while out walking in the lonely lanes, so the rector, visiting his isolated church, decided to go armed and selected a wicked-looking dirk or dagger which his son had sent to him from Cyprus. He placed the dagger firmly in his belt beneath his cassock. After the biretta incident Mr Merryweather went into the church and as he was standing before the altar, he felt the dagger suddenly pulled from his belt and as it was flung on the floor at his feet, he heard a female voice say, 'You are a cruel man.' In answer to my question as to the direction from which the voice came, the rector said he thought that it came from the tower end of the church, that is behind him as he faced the altar.

On December 2nd, 1948 the rector and a number of parishioners heard a series of unexplained noises which seemed to originate from the direction of a blocked-up door that used to be a private entrance to the church for the occupants of the Manor House. The noises were described to me as resembling 'an old man's cough'; a moment later a little brass credence bell rang of its own volition; still later a loud 'crack', as of a rifle, came from the same spot and a pile of stained glass was found in the chancel. During the months that followed the credence bell rang several more times without anyone being near it; lamps inexplicably swung (this happened for three days in succession); a lamp mysteriously burst into flames (and it had *not* been recently re-filled). Then, on August 21st, 1949, the rector saw the apparition of a young woman in the church.

He was celebrating Holy Communion at the time. He turned round to read the gospel at the altar and saw, on looking down the church, the figure of a young woman, aged he thought about thirty, wearing a white or grey dress and 'flowing headgear' that reached over her shoulders. She walked from the north side of the church, near the window beside the tower, across the chancel and disappeared into a corner in the south-west. The wall seemed to open, she passed in and then the wall closed again. He noticed, too, that she walked with a slight stoop; from the expression on her face and her attitude, he gained the impression that she was unhappy. She appeared to be about five feet six inches in height and looked like a normal person; nor was she transparent, although she made no sound.

During the severe earthquake of 1884, Langenhoe Church was badly damaged; the tremors lasted almost twenty seconds. Photographs of the west end of the church the morning after the earthquake show the devastation but also clearly indicate a former doorway in the internal tower-wall, several feet to the right of the later doorway. In view of this fact it is interesting to note that Mr Merryweather insisted: the 'phantom girl' vanished into the tower-wall and not through the later doorway. It was not until I began my research into the history of the area and located the photographs taken at the time of the earthquake that Mr

Merryweather saw them for the first time.

During the rest of 1949 incidents included the smashing and disappearance of part of the vestry door-handle, the unexplained locking of the same door, mysterious knocks and footsteps inside the church. I spent the night of September 24th, 1949 in Langenhoe Church with a friend who had become interested in psychical research, John C. Dening, then at the Foreign Office (later to become the Rev. John C. Dening). I had a number of instruments which I set up and I also scattered some 'controls' throughout the church and churchyard. I sealed the doors and windows, ringed a number of objects and even left paper and pencils here and there in case an entity should feel inclined to leave a message! Objects that had moved or had been disturbed were under particular surveillance throughout the night; powdered chalk was spread where the apparition had walked and where footsteps had been heard; threads were strung across the church at strategic points. In fact the psychical researcher's whole armoury was used in an effort to prove scientifically the 'existence' of a paranormal being in the church during the hours of darkness—if one put in an appearance. Unfortunately a thunderstorm raged during most of the night and we may well have missed any auditory phenomena amid the claps of thunder and the sound of rain pattering on the roof. But I don't think we were in luck, for in the morning I found all my apparatus exactly as I had left them and the instruments showed no abnormality. Perhaps the most lasting memory of that visit was the magnificent view from the church tower across the marshes to Mersea Island at the moment when the autumn dawn was breaking.

Early in 1950 Mr Merryweather heard a female voice when he was near the south door. It made a sound resembling 'Ow!' A few months later a bricklayer, who had once been a local bell-ringer, was high up on the empty church replacing tiles, when he heard the church bell chime twice, loud and clear. Previously sceptical of the haunting, this experience caused him to modify his opinion considerably. Mr Merryweather, tongue in cheek, wondered whether the bell-ringing was a sly dig at the local bricklayer who was no longer a church bell-ringer!

In the autumn of 1950 an apparently paranormal odour joined the wealth of unexplained 'phenomena' at Langenhoe, when the rector visited the church on September 14th, and found that a strong smell of violets permeated the whole building—completely out of season.

Later the same month, while in the vestry, Mr Merryweather suddenly heard the voice of a young woman singing in the church; the sounds seeming to originate from the west end of the building. He described the singing to me as resembling Gregorian (plain-song) chanting. As the singing stopped, it was followed by the sounds of a man's heavy footsteps walking 'with slow and sinister tread' up the nave. This was too much for the rector and he moved quickly into the church from the vestry. As he did so, the footsteps stopped abruptly and he could find nothing to account for either the singing or the footsteps.

Exactly a week later the rector paid another mid-week visit and as he entered the churchyard he was surprised to see two workmen crouching in front of the west door, apparently looking through the keyhole! As they became aware of his approach, they beckoned to him to join them and listen. Even as they stood up Mr Merryweather guessed the reason for their interest and, sure enough, the sound of singing came from the locked and empty church. All three listened for a moment and then the singing, seemingly in French, ceased. The rector unlocked the door and took the workmen inside where they searched everywhere, even climbing the tower to satisfy themselves that there was no human being anywhere inside the church.

During the following months a cupboard door was found open although it was always locked before the rector left the church as it contained his vestments; the following Sunday the same thing happened and then a further four times! Never again, either before or after, during the twenty-two years that he was Rector of Langenhoe was this cupboard ever found other than securely locked. On December 24th, 1950 the rector saw another apparition in the church, a figure that walked up the nave towards the chancel, a curious vague form that suddenly appeared from nowhere and proceeded to glide along the nave in front of him. The rector stopped in his tracks and watched the form which seemed to resemble a man in a tweed suit. It disappeared into the pulpit.

On January 28th, 1951 the white impression of a woman's hand was found on the vestry door. The rector had arrived at the church some fifteen minutes before when the imprint had certainly not been there; he had gone into the churchyard to throw some dead flowers away and when he returned there was the full and clear imprint. This was also seen by Mr Merryweather's housekeeper and her daughter. It lasted for ten days and then gradually faded away.

On July 8th, 1951 the rector, during a service, again saw the girl with the flowing head-dress. She was dressed exactly as before but this time she stood facing the credence bell and the old entrance used years before by the inhabitants of the Manor House. As he watched, she seemed to float towards the bricked-up door and disappeared through it. A few weeks later as he arrived at the church one morning he was surprised to hear voices from within. He told me that he had the impression two or perhaps three people were holding a conversation in an undertone in the chancel. One man's voice sounded more distinct than the others although no actual words were distinguishable. A heavy sigh followed and then silence reigned.

On October 12th, 1952 the rector saw yet another apparition in the church. He was singing Psalm CXIX verses 129–136 and had just reached the passage: 'My eyes gush out with water because men keep not my law' when he felt someone was watching him and saw the figure of a young woman, wearing a cream dress. She had an oval face and blue eyes and gave the rector a 'strange, sad look' before she vanished—but the cream dress she was wearing seemed to linger for some time after the wearer had gone.

Other incidents included a 'popping' noise, the rattling of the church door handle, a loud 'bang', more footsteps, the organ lid moved and the curiously quick burning of a candle.

Among several stories locally current to account for the haunting which is very ancient—witnesses of a veiled girl figure were traced back to the turn of the century—perhaps the most consistent one concerns a former rector who is said to have murdered his illicit sweetheart. If there is anything in this story it might account for the figure appearing most frequently to another rector. Certainly, a number of the reported incidents can be made to fit such a theory, especially the whispering (between the sweethearts?) and the final sigh (the fatal move made or the last breath of the victim?). A dagger may have been the weapon used and it could be suggested that the presence in the church of a similar instrument on the occasion when Mr Merryweather took the Cyprus dirk with him, may have revived memories and provoked the remark 'You are a cruel man.' Alternatively, these may have been the last despairing words of the victim, recorded perhaps for ever, on the atmosphere. The thuds on the vestry door may have had their origin in the victim's urgent summons to her lover (?) to admit her; little knowing that she was going to her death. Mr Merryweather's experience at the Manor House may have been a repetition of the exhibition of a girl's conscious or unconscious need for love and the temptation to which a former rector had been subjected. The appearance of a girl assumes significance when the passage of the Psalm heralding her coming is considered, while the smashing of the vestry door handle, the incidents concerning flowers and candles, the singing and the bell-ringing, may all have a symbolic meaning. The connection suggested by the door-slamming and the footsteps are all too obvious.

It is interesting to note that the whole area once formed part of an estate belonging to the powerful Waldergrave family. This included the church (the third to be erected on the site), a shooting-range, the Manor House, a former rectory and several other houses and cottages—all of which have been the scene of alleged psychic disturbances.

I spent many hours with Mr Merryweather during a period extending over twelve years, both at his home on Mersea Island and in the vicinity of Langenhoe Church. I found him to be ready and willing to discuss the curious happenings that he had witnessed, open to questioning and always eager to obtain corroboration or an explanation for the strange occurrences. I believe he was genuinely puzzled by the things that happened to him and if some of them were hallucinations or unconscious mind phenomena, it was only in this single sphere that he experienced these manifestations. Away

from Langenhoe, his life was undisturbed in any psychic sense and he led the quiet and satisfying existence of a country clergyman. Mr Merryweather retired from the ministry in 1959 and the living of Langenhoe was combined with that of a neighbouring parish. Haunted Langenhoe Church, a desolate and silent sentinel, stood for some years alone with its ghosts until it fell into decay and was finally pulled down. On one of my last visits to Mr Merryweather, he presented me with his private notes on the case and a relic from Langenhoe Church: the beautiful little Credence Bell. I hope that it will ring for me one day without a human agency!
Red Lion Hotel, Colchester, Essex.

Leicester, LEICESTERSHIRE.

Mrs Jennie Morrison of Newbold, Verdun, used for the first time in January, 1967 a cotton nightgown with lace trimmings which had belonged to her great aunt who had, in fact, asked to be buried in it. The aunt had died three years before but Mrs Morrison's mother thought the nightdress too good to be used as a shroud and she gave it to her daughter who had cut it down and made it fit. She wore it once and in bed that night felt 'a tremendous force' dragging at her sleeve. 'The nightdress was being pulled so strongly that it nearly hauled me out of bed,' she said. She took the nightdress off and threw it on to the landing outside the bedroom: then she heard a long drawn-out sigh, just like the sound that would be made by an old woman and she is convinced that the sound came from her dead aunt. 'The nightdress is very pretty now,' she said wistfully, 'but I'll never wear it again.'
Bell Hotel, Leicester, Leicestershire.

*Letchworth, HERTFORDSHIRE.

Ghostly footsteps at night are reported to have frightened a dog which rushed, panic-stricken, from an empty room at 'Scudamore', Letchworth Corner in 1946, as Mrs E. M. Walker, managing director of Lloyds', the mowing machine manufacturers, will tell you. She was alone in the house at

about ten-thirty at night and while downstairs, she heard a thud from the room above, followed by footsteps which appeared to cross the room towards the door. She hurried upstairs, thinking that someone had broken into the house but there was no one there and she discovered nothing to account for the noises she had heard. Night after night she heard the same sounds and she began to think that her married son was right when he said it was probably old beams drying out until the curious behaviour of her border collie, 'Bruce'. 'Bruce' used to go everywhere with Mrs Walker's cousin, Mr Edward Halford but nothing would persuade it to enter Mr Halford's bedroom—the room where the noises came from each night at ten-thirty p.m. Once Mrs Walker tried hard to get the dog into the room; she held the dog's collar and tried to force him inside but the dog held back, struggling and growling and once he was free, raced down the stairs and into the garden 'as if the devil were after him'. Mrs Walker feels that the ghost paid its last visit to the house in 1947. She and her family decided that it was the spirit of the man who had three four-hundred-year-old cottages converted into the present house.
Letchworth Hall Hotel, Letchworth, Herts.

Little Burton, SOMERSET.

An early case of poltergeist activity was reported from 'old Gast's House' in 1677. The sound of washing was heard from upstairs by the occupants and visitors who had a damp cloth thrown at them when they began to mount the stairs. When they continued, another cloth was thrown at them. Arriving at the room, where the sounds seemed to come from, they found a bowl of whitish water, some of it spilled over. The witnesses stated that immediately before they had come upstairs the bowl had been downstairs in the kitchen and could not have been carried to where it was now found except through the room in which those present had been gathered.

The same night a tremendous, thunder-like noise was heard, followed by a loud scratching sound in the vicinity of a bedstead; then a violent hammering noise on the bedhead so that the two maids occupying the bedstead cried out for help. When the investigators went into the room a hammer lay on the bed and there were many marks on the bedhead where the blows had landed. The maids asserted that they were scratched and pinched by a hand that was inside the bedclothes and which had exceedingly long nails. They were adamant that the hammer was locked fast in a cupboard when they went to bed. Later, objects were moved, more things were thrown at people, candles were put out, a hideous cry was heard, feathers were plucked out of a bolster and some were thrust into the mouths of those lying in bed.

Two witnesses, James Sherring and Thomas Hillary asserted that when they took up a position at the foot of the bedstead with a candle, they both saw a hand and wrist holding the hammer which kept knocking on the bedhead. One of the articles moved was a pole some fourteen or fifteen feet long which stood in the yard; this was found upstairs in the house, on a bedstead. It was only with the greatest difficulty and the removal of a window that eventually it was taken from the house.

One night at old Gast's House two grand-daughters were in bed together, one aged twelve or thirteen and the other sixteen or seventeen. Suddenly they felt a hand in bed with them which they tied up in a sheet and beat until it was as soft as wool, then placed under a heavy stone—whereupon all was quiet for the rest of the night. In the morning the sheet was still there, held by the heavy stone but when one of the girls declared that she would burn 'the Devil', she found the stone moved and the sheet wet. Stones were also thrown in a bedroom after a candle had been put out and in the morning there was a pile of them on the bed.

Francis Hotel, Bath, Somerset.

Little Gaddesden, BERKHAMSTED, HERTFORDSHIRE.

The Manor House of the Lucies was at one time known as 'The Priory' which suggests that the present house occupies the site of some religious building. There are many ghostly legends associated with the place. Perhaps the most convincing concerned William Jarman, a churchwarden who lived in the old house during the eighteenth century and who committed suicide: some say he hanged himself inside the building, others claim he drowned himself in the village pond which at one time used to be just across the Green from the Manor House.

A century or more ago, fire destroyed much of the old house which Jarman knew but nearby Ashridge House is still extant. Jarman killed himself because he was rejected by an unidentified heiress of Ashridge, which in the eighteenth century was the home of the Earls of Bridgewater. His ghost is reported to have been seen near the village pond.

There are also accounts of curious happenings involving lights at the Manor House. Years ago candles would dip or be extinguished and later the same thing would happen to electric lights. My friend Vicars Bell, author of a history of the parish, told me how he traced a witness who stated that many years ago a former occupant and a visitor were chatting in the drawing room when one after the other the lights were extinguished. The present occupant tells me that Jarman, who is said to have been so troublesome at one time that he was exorcized by 'bell, book and candle', is still reputed to make the lights burn low on a certain day each year but for generations nobody has known which day! In any case the present occupant, Miss Dorothy Erhart, will tell you that there is nothing sinister about the ghostly presence and most people regard him as a benevolent and friendly ghost, just as she does.

Gallows Hill, in the vicinity, has long been reputed to be haunted by the sounds of creaking and clanking that must have been a familiar noise when the long-vanished gallows stood hereabouts. There are reports of the apparition of an unidentified grey man seen to pass silently on dark nights. *Rose and Crown Hotel, Tring, Herts.*

Littlecote, WILTSHIRE, TWO-AND-A-HALF MILES FROM HUNGERFORD, BERKSHIRE.

This magnificent Tudor Manor House has a huge Great Hall

with panelled walls and a grey and white stone floor. Its drawing room boasts of hand-painted Chinese wallpaper and an Aubusson carpet from the Palace of Versailles; the unusual, egg-shaped library is full of interesting and rare volumes, the Dutch Parlour has wall paintings by Dutch prisoners. There is a unique Cromwellian chapel. The historic and beautiful place is set in matchless scenery and possesses several ghosts.

The best-known story dates from Elizabethan times when the rambling and isolated seat of the ancient Darrell family was owned by 'Wild' or 'Wicked' Will Darrell who is said to have murdered a new-born child in particularly horrible circumstances in 1575. The charge is based on a statement made by a midwife, a Mrs Barnes of Great Shefford, who on her death-bed told a magistrate that she had been summoned one dark night to attend in secret a lady about to have a child; she was promised a large sum of money if she would do so. She allowed herself to be blindfolded and was taken by horseback to a house she did not recognize where she delivered a young woman of a child. As soon as it was born, the child was snatched from her by a man and thrown into the fire where he held the infant down with his boot-heel until it was quite dead.

The midwife was too terrified to say much at the time although she had the presence of mind to cut a small piece of material from the bed-curtains and to count the number of stairs as she was led out, blindfolded again. After her 'confession' suspicion centered on 'Wild' Will Darrell as the villain and Littlecote as the house. Darrell was arrested. The connection with Littlecote was established by means of the correct number of stairs given by Mrs Barnes and the corresponding hole in the bed-hangings, but the account of the trial at Salisbury is confused. Littlecote was made over to Sir John Popham, the judge at the trial who took possession of the property on Darrell's death in 1589. Darrell was acquitted.

It was known that Darrell had several mistresses (including his own sister) and any one may have been the unfortunate young mother; or the mysterious birth may have been the result of his liaison with a Miss Bonham whose brother was staying at Longleat at the time. In 1879 a letter was discovered addressed to Sir John Thynme at Longleat from Sir Harry Knyvett, written about the time of Mrs Barnes's death and substantiating the midwife's story. It used to be said that bloodstains appeared from time to time in a mysterious way on the floor of the haunted chamber and according to local tradition the terrible crime is re-enacted by the ghost of the distracted midwife with the child in her arms. However, the original bed went to America and the bed-hangings are comparatively recent.

The ghost of the murdered babe is also said to have appeared suddenly in front of Darrell when he was hunting in Littlecote park and so startled his horse that he was thrown and his neck broken. This place is known to this day as 'Darrell's Stile' and horses have been known to shy frantically at the spot. Also in the park, in front of the entrance gates where once the old Gate House stood, there is an ancient elm tree, known as 'Darrell's Tree'. Legend has it that the tree will flourish with the fortunes of the owners of the house.

Littlecote has belonged to the Wills tobacco family for fifty years now and although the present owner, Major George Wills (who does not live there) will tell you that he has never seen a ghost he is no sceptic. This may be due to the fact that his brother, Sir Edward Wills saw a ghost in the passage beyond the Long Gallery. In 1927, while sleeping in their room which was the first up the few stairs from the Long Gallery, both Sir Edward and his wife were disturbed by the sounds of somebody or something coming up the creaking stairs from the Long Gallery. The third time Sir Edward heard the sounds, he quietly stepped out and saw a lady with a light in her hand which cast a shadow on the ceiling of the passage. Her hair was fair, she was not very tall and wore a pink dress or nightdress. Sir Edward followed the figure that disappeared into the room occupied by his younger brother, the present owner of Littlecote; he however, slept through it all and knew nothing of the affair until told of it by his older brother. One curious thing about this ghost is that it appeared to open the door of the room into which it disappeared.

From time to time terrifying screams have been heard in the small hours from the direction of the bedroom and landing that were the scene of the tragedy while some say they have seen the apparition of the grief-stricken mother with a baby in her arms. Others maintain that the spot is haunted by the frenzied midwife; another version speaks of Darrell himself. Where he appears, the floor can never be kept in repair but constantly moulders away, no matter how often the wood is replaced. When I was there in 1969 I was told of the apparition of a female figure dressed in brown, seen recently by one of the guides at Littlecote. The ghost, if ghost it was, walked along a closed-in-cloister-like passage and out through a doorway on to the lawns on the north side of the house.

Another guide heard footsteps in the Long Gallery; these were also heard by a student guide, when the two were alone in that part of the house. It was on the floor above this gallery that the Little Garrison, under Colonel Alexander Popham, was quartered during the Civil War.

Another of the guides at Littlecote maintains that she saw a woman standing by the herbaceous border in the garden; she disappeared completely a few seconds later. Clairvoyant Tom Corbett told me that he, too, saw a ghost in the garden, a beautiful woman whom he later recognized from a portrait in the house as Mrs Leybourne Popham—although why her ghost should appear no one knows! But at Littlecote, with its history and its atmosphere of the past, one might expect almost anything to happen.

The Bear Hotel, Hungerford, Berks.   .

London, AMEN COURT, NEAR ST PAUL'S CATHEDRAL.

It is worth going out of your way to find this delightful little court with the handsome wrought-iron entrance gates for it is one of the few places where it is still possible to see a piece of the old City wall on Roman foundations that divides the garden of the court from former Old Bailey property. R. H. Barham, author of *The Ingoldsby Legends* lived here when he was a minor canon of St Paul's.

The tall, dark wall that has clearly been extended over the years, bordered part of old Newgate prison graveyard and the path immediately on the other side of the wall was known as Dead Man's Walk for here the hanged criminals were buried in quicklime, after they had used the path to pass to and from their trials.

Over the years there have been persistent reports of a dark shape crawling along the top of this wall at night; the scrape of his boots and the occasional rattle of his chains breaks the uncanny silence that seems to hang around this fateful spot. A clergyman saw the figure several times in 1948.

Three Nuns Hotel, London, E.C.3.

London, BANK OF ENGLAND.

It is not generally known that the Bank of England in Threadneedle Street has a ghost, an apparition that many people have seen wandering about the Bank garden. It is known as the Black Nun.

The story of the haunting goes back to 1811 when Philip Whitehead, a former employee of the Bank was arrested for forging cheques and was condemned to death at the Old Bailey. This tragedy caused Whitehead's sister, Sarah, to lose her reason and for some twenty-five years, the rest of her life, she daily journeyed to the Bank, loitering there and looking for her brother. Some people think she gave the name of The Old Lady of Threadneedle Street to the Bank. She died suddenly and was buried within the Bank premises, in the old churchyard which afterwards became the Bank garden. Here her figure has been glimpsed on many occasions over the years.

Great Eastern Hotel, London, E.C.2.

London, BERKELEY SQUARE.

Colonel A. Kearsey, visiting a relative in the square, was shown into a room where, by the light of the bright fire burning in the fireplace, he saw a woman in a long dress and broad-brimmed hat sitting in an armchair. She was sobbing bitterly and when he went forward and asked whether he could help, she rose from the chair and, without looking at him passed through the heavy curtains and disappeared through the shuttered windows. Later he learned that his hostess's children had reported hearing sobs in that room, while a previous owner had told him that at one time a woman had lived there who had left her husband for another man. She had cried a great deal. After she left, she never returned to the house, but it seemed that her ghost did.

Grosvenor House Hotel, Park Lane, W.1.

*London, 50, BERKELEY SQUARE.

The most famous of all London's hauntings. The house, now occupied by Messrs Maggs Brothers, the well-known antiquarian booksellers, was said to have possessed, years ago, a haunted room in which the ghost caused at least two deaths, in convulsions, for people foolhardy enough to attempt to sleep there. Victorians would not have dreamt of visiting London without a look at 'the haunted house in Berkeley Square'. Lord Lyttleton spent a night in the haunted room, comforted by the company of two blunderbusses loaded with buckshot and silver sixpences, the latter being protection against the powers of evil. He later reported that during the night he fired at an entity that leapt at him from the darkness, that something fell to the floor 'like a rocket' and then disappeared. He had also traced a woman who went out of her mind after spending one night in the house.

Among the many unsubstantiated but persistent stories associated with the building is the account of a little Scottish child that was either tortured or frightened to death in the nursery and whose pathetic little wraith wearing a plaid frock, sobbing and wringing its hands, was said to appear periodically in the upper part of the house.

There is the story, too, of a young lady who lived in the house at one time with her lecherous uncle. To escape his attentions she threw herself out of a top room window and her ghost is said to have been seen, apparently clinging to the window ledge and screaming.

Perhaps the most famous story concerns a curious white-faced man with a gaping mouth whose appearance is said to have terrified two fog-bound sailors who stumbled one night into the house, which stood empty at the time. During the night they were first disturbed by the sound of muffled footsteps mounting the stairs. Something entered the room they were occupying and when one of the sailors, in an effort to escape the horror creeping towards them, fell through the window, his partner succeeded in escaping and was found in a state of collapse outside by a passing policeman. His companion's dead body was found in the garden but the policeman found no trace of the horrible creature that had so terrified the two tough sailors.

During the 1870s the occupants of neighbouring houses told of loud cries and noises emanating from the locked and empty building at night, the sounds of heavy furniture being dragged across bare boards, bells ringing, windows being thrown up and of stones, books and other articles being hurled into the street below.

At one time the haunted room was said to be kept locked and there were stories of a lunatic who died there; others spoke of a housemaid found lying in the haunted room in convulsions. She died next day in St George's Hospital, refusing to give any account of what she had seen because it was 'just too horrible'. A visitor volunteered to spend a night in the room on condition that help would be forthcoming if he should ring. He did and they rushed to his aid. He was found exactly where the housemaid had lain, his eyes fixed upon the same spot. Neither did he ever reveal what he had seen—for he was dead.

Today the house stands much as it was in the days of hansom cabs, and when I called there in June, 1970 I learned that Messrs Maggs had a lease on the whole property since 1939. Nothing really untoward, I was told, has happened there in recent years, though throughout the Second World War fire-watchers used the building night after night. The haunted room was pointed out to me on the top floor. The middle window is the one from which the sailor is said to have fallen, or been pushed. It seems that he was impaled on the spiked railings still bordering the pavement. All the rooms in the property are used by Messrs Maggs who regard the various ghost stories as vague and ancient, as indeed they are; but a hundred years ago anything might have hap-

Ladye Place, Hurley, Berkshire. Following excavations in an attempt to locate the burial place of Editha, sister of Edward the Confessor, ghostly monks were frequently seen here, particularly one who stood with arms crossed, in the cloisters. *Photo: Chris Underwood*

Langenhoe Church, Essex, scene of a wealth of unexplained happenings: a ghostly singing girl, mysterious voices, knockings, odours and movement of objects.

Ludlow Castle, Shropshire, has a ghostly White Lady and a mysterious breathing noise; doors that open and close by themselves and raps and taps that cannot be explained. *Photo: A. A. MacGregor*

Markyate Cell, Hertfordshire, the former home of the wicked Lady Ferrers who used to dress as a highwayman and plague the countryside. After she was shot during one of her escapades her ghost is reputed to have been seen on the winding drive to the house. *Photo: Chris Underwood*

pened in the murky, gas-lit square.
Grosvenor House Hotel, Park Lane, W.1.

London, BIRDCAGE WALK, ST JAMES'S PARK.

Several sentries of the Coldstream Guards, when they were stationed at Wellington Barracks, reported seeing the ghost of a headless woman walking between the Cockpit Steps in Birdcage Walk towards the lake in St James's Park. One guardsman, in his signed statement, reported that it was about one-thirty a.m. when he noticed the figure of a woman, 'rise from the earth at a distance of about two feet before me'. He was so alarmed that he momentarily lost the power of speech as, wide-eyed, he watched the figure, dressed in a red-striped gown with red spots between each stripe, for about two minutes, before it vanished. Another guardsman reported hearing shrieks and shouts at night from an empty building behind the Armoury House; in his subsequent sworn statement he said the voice shouted: 'Bring me a light! Bring me a light!', the voice dying away on the last word. Thinking that someone must be ill, the soldier tried to locate the origin of the cries and shouted back; each time the voice returned, always using the same phrase. Then he heard noises which sounded like sashes of windows being hastily lifted up and dropped, from different parts of the dark and empty building. Twenty years before a sergeant in the Coldstream Guards murdered his wife in a house near the barracks; he cut off her head and threw her body into the lake in St James's Park.
Hotel Meurice, Bury Street, St James's, S.W.1.

London, CHISWICK.

Walpole House in Chiswick Mall, a fine seventeenth-century property, was the home of Barbara Villiers, Duchess of Cleveland and mistress of King Charles II.

She lived here during the latter part of her life with her grandson Charles Hamilton, the son of one of her daughters by the Duke of Hamilton; the young man's father was killed in a duel by the wicked Lord Mohun.

She died in her sixty-ninth year, from dropsy, which had 'swelled her gradually to a monstrous bulk'. At one time famed for her beauty, her accommodating manner and lack of morals caused many a scandal and Charles II acknowledged five of her many children. She must have led a sad life here after the years of pleasure and probably often walked up and down the shallow stairs in the high heels she always wore, gazing wistfully out of the tall windows of the drawing room. It is said that she would raise her hands to the moon-lit sky on occasions, begging for the return of her lost beauty.

It is over two-hundred-and-fifty years since Barbara Villiers died but at certain times the tap-tap of her heels is said to be heard on the stairway and on stormy, moonlit nights, her form has been seen at the window of the drawing room, wringing her hands.

The 'Old Burlington', Church Street, a four-hundred-year-old former Elizabethan ale house, purchased by Mr Richard Strickley in 1963, has a household ghost: Percy, who wears a wide-brimmed black hat and cloak. He had also been seen by previous occupants who described him as 'good-humoured and harmless'. In the courtyard highwayman Dick Turpin is said to have once leapt from an upstairs window to evade the Bow Street Runners, the predecessors of the Metropolitan Police.

Anna Hotel, London, W.6.

London, COCK LANE, SMITHFIELD.

In 1762 a little terraced house (long since disappeared) was the scene of a reported haunting which set the whole country talking and intrigued such personalities of the day as Dr Samuel Johnson, Oliver Goldsmith, Horace Walpole, various ecclesiastical luminaries and even the Duke of York.

In 1759 the house was occupied by Richard Parsons, the hard-up parish clerk of St Sepulchres, Mrs Elizabeth Parsons and their eleven-year-old daughter, Elizabeth. The troubles began when Parsons let rooms to a Willian Kent whose young wife had died in childbirth five years before. Kent's sister-in-law, Fanny, joined him and they lived together at Cock Lane and made wills in each other's favour—a fact which may be significant in the light of later events. Parsons borrowed money from Kent which he was unable to repay and after Kent sued his landlord, he and Fanny moved to fresh lodgings in Clerkenwell, where Fanny died in 1760. But before they left Cock Lane, the little house is said to have been the scene of mysterious happenings which made it one of London's most famous haunted houses.

The affair started when Kent went to the country one Saturday to attend a wedding, leaving Fanny who, not wishing to sleep alone, asked little Elizabeth to share her bed. Violent bumps, rappings, knockings and scratchings began almost immediately and kept Fanny awake. The noises were centred on and around the bed. Next morning Fanny complained to Mrs Parsons who told her the noises must have come from the cobbler next door who sometimes worked all night. However when Fanny found the noises continued the following night, a Sunday, this theory was discarded. She was terrified by the noises and thought they foretold her death.

She did in fact die eighteen months after leaving Cock Lane and during this period no manifestations were reported. But soon after her death fresh disturbances broke out around the bedstead of little Elizabeth Parsons, who is reported to have trembled and shivered uncontrollably at the activities of the 'ghost'. The scratchings and bumps even followed Elizabeth when she visited neighbours and as word spread of the curious happenings, crowds of sightseers thronged the narrow street to gaze at the 'house of wonder' and to pester the Parsons with interminable questions.

By the time-honoured code of one rap for yes, two for no and three for uncertain or don't know, Mary Frazer, the Parsons' servant girl, established contact with an entity who answered questions. The Parsons were told that it was indeed Fanny who was responsible for the noises. Fanny said she had been poisoned by William Kent who had given her arsenic, and she hoped he would hang!

At one stage the 'ghost' promised to accompany little Elizabeth to the vault of St John's Church, Clerkenwell where Fanny was buried (after dying of smallpox) and strike the coffin to convince witnesses of the authenticity of 'Scratching Fanny'. However, when the little girl's hands were held it was noticed that all the noises stopped and no manifestations were produced in the vault of St John's.

After attending one of the séances Oliver Goldsmith published a pamphlet on the affair which was in effect a defence of Kent who was being increasingly annoyed at the charges being levelled at him. The authorities now stepped in to make enquiries and to hold tests. Nothing happened until, at the third 'test' séance with little Elizabeth slung in a hammock, feet and hands extended wide, she was told that unless something *did* happen, her father would be committed to Newgate Prison whereupon the frightened child was detected secreting a small board and a piece of wood inside her dress. This was really the end of the matter except that William Kent indicted Parsons and his wife, the servant Mary Frazer and several others, of conspiring against his life and character. They were duly found guilty and had to pay several hundred pounds to Kent. In addition Parsons was condemned to the pillory and to a year in prison (although the populace, convinced of his innocence, collected money for him). His wife also went to prison for a year and Mary Frazer for six months. Later Elizabeth Parsons is said to have 'confessed' that she had caused all the noises deliberately.

Denis Bardens adds an interesting note to this curious case. Years later, in 1845, a coffin, believed to be that of 'Scratching Fanny', was opened and it was found that there was no discoloration, mouldering or any of the usual disintegration of the body; a state of affairs well in keeping with the administration of arsenic.

Great Eastern Hotel, London, E.C.2.

London, DRURY LANE.

The Theatre Royal possesses the most famous of all theatre ghosts, the 'man in grey', a daytime spectre which has been seen dozens of times at matinées during the last two hundred years, in the vicinity of the upper circle, sometimes occupying a seat but more often walking along the gangway from one side of the theatre to the other where it disappears into a wall.

The figure was seen by the late W. J. McQueen Pope, the theatre historian, who showed me the exact spot where he had observed the tall, upright figure with tricorn hat and long grey cloak, not once but several times. Here, about a hundred years ago, a small room was discovered containing a skeleton of a man with a dagger between his ribs. He is thought to have been the victim of a vicious manager of the theatre in the eighteenth century. At all events, the ghost is regarded as foretelling a successful production at the theatre since it has often been reported either before or during the early days of many successful runs at Drury Lane. It has never been associated with a failure.

The Green Room at the Theatre Royal was the scene of a murder some two hundred years ago when actor Charles Macklin, in a fit of anger, killed another actor in front of the fireplace which can be seen to this day. Macklin was never punished for his crime and a ghost with a thin, ugly and heavily-lined face, answering to his description, has occasionally been seen near the theatre-pit.

This theatre is also haunted by the ghost of much-loved Dan Leno and Stanley Lupino is among those who have claimed to see the unforgettable face of the comedian in a dressing room which the player had used during his lifetime.

Strand Palace Hotel, Strand, W.C.2.

London, EAST ACTON.

St Dunstan's Church was (and perhaps still is) haunted by ghostly monks, sometimes singly and sometimes walking in procession up the central aisle.

When the red-brick church was built a hundred years ago, a stately mansion called Friar's Place stood close by. During the Middle Ages, a chapter of St Bartholomew's the Great of Smithfield existed here. In those days monks, singly and in procession, probably walked where now the big church of St Dunstan's stands.

It is now twenty years since I first visited St Dunstan's at the invitation of the incumbent, the Rev. Hugh Anton-Stevens, and heard from him and his secretary the full story of the remarkable experiences of many people at the church. Mr Anton-Stevens considered his secretary to be one of the best psychics in the country; he believed that she was the medium through whom some of the manifestations occurred.

I learned that a former curate, the Rev. Philip Boustead, always maintained that he had seen ghostly monks in the church in the 1930s. Mr Anton-Stevens had been vicar only a short time (he went there in December, 1944) before he realized that there was something very strange about the church and that ghostly monks did indeed walk there.

'There is no doubt,' he told me, 'that on many evenings up to a dozen monks can be seen walking in procession up the central aisle and into the chancel of St Dunstan's. They wear golden brown habits and are hooded. Apart from myself, three other people, unknown to each other, have seen these figures from time to time. Most interesting, I feel, is a violet-hooded monk who keeps apart from the others and with whom I have had a number of conversations.'

The vicar put me in touch with a member of his congregation who saw the procession of ghostly monks three times from the vestry during evening discussion groups. When glancing at them from the corner of the eye, they were quite clear, I was told; but they seemed to disappear when looked at directly. There has long been a theory that the human eye is a deterrent to psychic phenomena and it is interesting that the vast majority of poltergeist-propelled objects have been seen in flight and when ending their flight or movement—but very rarely is there good evidence for objects seen to commence movement.

One November evening a reporter spent some hours in the church in an attempt to establish whether or not the ghostly monks walked. He dropped off to sleep in the quiet of the church but soon found himself awake again—and was absolutely certain that he was not dreaming. There, walking slowly towards him, were six monks in grey hooded gowns. The reporter, Mr Kenneth Mason of the *Daily Graphic* stood up to bar their way—whereupon they passed right through him!

A churchwarden, previously sceptical of the ghosts, saw a monk himself in the church one evening; the church organist heard music he could not account for and 'felt a presence' in the empty church. Mr Anton-Stevens, after publishing an article on confirmation in the parish magazine which he claimed was dictated by the violet-hooded monk, became distressed by the resulting publicity. Although for the rest of his life (he died in 1962) he always maintained that the ghosts of St Dunstan's had objective reality, he did not encourage active investigation and he talked less and less about the remarkable experiences he had. The late psychic investigator Harry Price decided, after extensive research, that the reports were based on fact and that the procession of ghostly monks appeared in four-year cycles.

Carnarvon Hotel, Ealing Common, London, W.5.

London, EATON PLACE.

One of the best authenticated of London's many ghosts is that of Admiral Sir George Tryon. On June 22nd, 1893, Lady Tryon was giving one of her 'At Home' parties at her house in Eaton Place. The London season was in full swing and the cream of Edwardian high society chatted and moved among the elegant furniture: dandies in tight-waisted frock-coats, military gentlemen in colourful uniforms and ladies resplendent in their frills, laces and jewels. Suddenly there was a hush in the conversation as a commanding figure in full naval uniform walked into the room, without being announced, strode straight across the place—the guests draw-aside to let him pass—and vanished! He was recognized as Sir George Tryon by everyone present.

At that precise moment the body of Admiral Sir George Tryon, just dead, was lying in the wreckage of his flagship, H.M.S. *Victoria,* at the bottom of the Mediterranean. The cause of the collision which resulted in the loss of Admiral Tryon and most of the crew of the *Victoria,* is one of the great naval mysteries.

The Mediterranean Fleet was steaming along in two columns at the time when Lady Tryon was welcoming her guests; Admiral Tryon led one column, Admiral Markham in the *Camperdown* the other. For no reason that has ever been discovered Sir George Tryon suddenly signalled to the two columns of battleships to turn inwards on each other at a given point. His officers and those of the *Camperdown* were amazed. It seemed that a serious accident could not be averted unless the order was retracted but Sir George was adamant and in due course the two lines of ships turned towards each other, the *Camperdown* heading straight for the *Victoria*. Sir George seemed to realize too late the folly of his previous order and he now commanded the crew, 'full steam astern'. But before the manoeuvre could be executed, the *Camperdown* sheared into the *Victoria* and the flagship sank quickly. One of the surviving officers reported that as the ship went down, he heard Sir George cry out that it was all his fault and, with a young midshipman standing beside him—a lad who refused Sir George's order to jump to possible safety overboard—the Admiral went to his watery grave. At the same moment he also appeared in full uniform, with a set and haggard face, in his wife's drawing room, hundreds of miles away in London.

Hotel: 99, Eaton Place, London, S.W.1.

London, GARLICK HILL, OFF QUEEN VICTORIA STREET.

The church of St James, built in 1326, destroyed by the Great Fire and rebuilt by Sir Christopher Wren (1632-1723), was the burial place of no less than six Lord Mayors. It now has an unidentified, mummified body and a ghost.

The mummified corpse of a young man was found under the chancel and is now preserved in a glass-faced receptacle in the vestibule. The body was discovered before the Great Fire of London and buried in a glass coffin near the altar. Nobody knows who the man was: he may have been the first Lord Mayor of London or an embalmed Roman general, Richard Rothing who built the church in King Edward II's reign or even Belin, a legendary King of the Britons. Today he is known as 'Old Jummy Garlick' and, according to reports, he sometimes takes a stroll round the church. An American lady visited the place with her two sons and when the elder boy looked up a staircase to the balcony, he saw the figure of a man, wrapped in a winding-sheet, standing erect, with his hands crossed on his chest. The figure resembled a dried-up corpse and the terrified boy ran back to his mother and dragged her out of the church and into the street.

During the Second World War 'Jimmy' had a narrow escape when a bomb shaved his case in 1942 and penetrated into the vaults below the church but fortunately it did not explode. After that 'Jimmy' was reported to be seen in the body of the church more frequently and other manifestations, including noises and movements of objects, were said to take place but there are no recent reports of similar happenings. 'Jimmy's' mortal remains have been a relic of the church for five hundred years and although he is getting thin on top, he retains his skin, his finger nails and his teeth, and seems good for another five hundred years!

Howard Hotel, Norfolk Street, Strand, London, W.C.2.

*London, THE GARGOYLE CLUB, SOHO.

One of the oldest clubs in Europe, the site of the Gargoyle Club once housed a musketry school belonging to Charles II and at one time Nell Gwynne lived in the same building. Many people, including the owners, staff, members and visitors have reported unusual experiences. Dylan Thomas the poet told me he found the atmosphere fascinating but would never spend a night there on his own for anything in the world. Several witnesses have seen a woman dressed in period costume, a grey shadowy figure in a high-waisted dress with a large flowered hat accompanied by an overpowering odour of gardenias, drifting rather than walking across the floor and disappearing at the lift shaft. A rather incongruous visitor among the strippers who work here! Others say, they have seen a tall figure, cowled and shrouded, on the pavement near the Meard Street entrance to the club.

Regent Palace Hotel, Piccadilly Circus, London, W.1.

One of the sights of University College, built in 1828, is the embalmed body of Jeremy Bentham, the law reformer and natural scientist whose ghost haunts the main corridor.

It was part of Jeremy Bentham's will that his body should be used for the purpose of improving the science of anatomy and this was done when Bentham, the prophet of utilitarianism and reformer, died in 1832. Afterwards the skeleton was re-erected, padding was used to stuff out Bentham's own clothes and a wax likeness, made by a distinguished French artist, was fitted to the trunk. Seated on the chair which he usually occupied, with one hand on his constant 'companion', his walking-stick, called Dapple, and wearing his famous white gloves; with a five-pound note and a pack of playing cards in his pocket, he was enclosed in a moth-proof mahogany case with folding glass doors and deposited at University College where he can be seen to this day.

Legend has it that the great eccentric was mummified against his wishes and the unexplained noises heard from time to time at the College are said to be Bentham rapping on the doors and windows of his cage with his walking-stick to frighten the officials of the College into having him sent away and buried!

He is housed in the cloister near the main entrance and one evening Mr Neil King, Mathematical Master at the University College School, then accommodated in the College buildings, heard the tap-tap-tap of Jeremy's walking-stick in the nearby corridor. He walked towards the open door to take a peep, not really expecting to see anything, but there was Jeremy, complete with white gloves and walking-stick! He walked right up to Mr King and when he reached him, made a sudden dart forward and seemed to throw himself bodily at the teacher—but there was no sensation of impact.

Another time a sound of flying wings and the displacement of books in one particular classroom were attributed to the ghost of Jeremy Bentham and the sound of his footsteps and tap-tap-tap of his walking-stick have, according to reports, been heard many times.

Hotel Russell, Russell Square, London, W.C.1.

London, HAMPSTEAD.

An early Georgian terraced house, formerly occupied by television personality Peter Cook, his wife Wendy and small daughters Lucy and Daisy, is reputed to be haunted by the ghost of H. G. Wells. The ghost of the great visionary novelist and sociologist who used to live at the house has been seen and heard walking around in what became known as the nursery wing.
Clive Hotel, Primrose Hill Road, London, N.W.3.

London, HAMPSTEAD LANE.

In 1947 the manager of 'The Gatehouse' public house collapsed after seeing an apparition here and was taken to hospital suffering from shock. He later left the premises on the advice of his doctor; a spokesman for the owners gave the reason as 'overwork'. The ghost of a white-haired smuggler who was murdered here after an argument over money was clearly seen by medium Trixie Allingham who visited the pub and found the gallery a 'cold, evil place'.
Sandringham Hotel, Holford Road, London, N.W.3.

*London, HAYMARKET.

At the Haymarket Theatre there is a certain dressing room which was always used by John Baldwin Buckstone about a hundred and twenty years ago. Here the ghost of the gentle, kindly actor-manager has been seen from time to time; he is said to rattle doors and open and close them; his footsteps are repeatedly reported to have been heard.

More than one employee has seen the figure of a man in the theatre which has disappeared as they watched. One man identified John Buckstone from a photograph. In 1880, soon after Buckstone's death, his ghost is said to have been seen in Queen Victoria's box, where he was often present during his lifetime and quite recently Dame Flora Robson thought she saw the ghost on stage.

The ghost of Buckstone is not a frightening one. Mrs Stuart Wilson, Chairman and Managing Director of the theatre will tell you that no one could be frightened of him; he returns because he loved the old theatre so much and because he was so intensely happy here. When she hears a rattling at the door or when it unaccountably opens, Mrs Wilson says 'Come in, love' or 'Hallo, you are so welcome' for she, like everyone at the Haymarket, would hate to offend this inoffensive ghost.

Cavendish Hotel, Jermyn Street, S.W.1.

London, HORNSEY, FERRESTONE ROAD.

The Hornsey 'rachety' ghost received considerable publicity in January, 1921, when for several weeks unexplained happenings puzzled the occupants and visitors to the house.

The events began with the sound of loud explosions, almost like small bombs, which greatly startled the Frost family, then occupying the premises. The noises seemed to originate from lumps of coal which exploded both in coal buckets and in the grates of the house. The days passed and still the 'explosions' occurred. A new delivery of coal made no difference. Coal was found upstairs and then proceeded to be projected in all directions although it was never seen in motion; glass globes, vases and china were smashed.

One day the family, which included three children: Gordon, Bertie and Muriel, were at tea when two of the tea-plates rose seemingly unaided into the air and then dropped back again, without breaking. A step-ladder also was lifted into the air and lowered again; two glass dishes flew off the sideboard and broke when they fell to the floor; a book lifted itself from a shelf, dropped to the floor and there twirled round and round before laying still and flat. Once Mr Frost saw one of his sons lifted into the air, chair and all—he caught hold of the chair and replaced it on the floor but five minutes later the same thing happened again. A police inspector stated that a piece of coal which he picked up to examine, broke into three pieces in his hand, and then vanished!

A vicar, the Rev. A. L. Gardiner, visited the house and saw a lump move from its place on a shelf and fall but instead of falling straight down to the floor, it moved outwards into the room for a couple of feet and then dropped lightly. Mr Gardiner stated after his visit: 'There can be no doubt of the phenomena: I have seen them myself.' Another visitor was Dr Herbert Lemerle who stated that he was present when a clock vanished mysteriously.

The strange events (which Harry Price regarded as 'well-attested') began on January 1st, 1921. Little Muriel was so terrified by the disturbances that she died on April 1st; the boy Gordon was frightened into a nervous breakdown and was taken to Lewisham Hospital. It was said at a public meeting held on May 8th, 1921, that the phenomena always occurred in the presence of one of the young boys and that the ghost of their father's sister, who had died a year previously, had been seen by one of the brothers.
The Orchard Private Hotel, London, N.12.

*_London_, KENSINGTON PALACE.

This royal palace, purchased by King William III in 1689, is haunted by the anxious face of King George II looking out of the window over the main entrance.

Queen Victoria was born here and so was Queen Mary, consort of King George V. King William III, Queen Anne and King George II, the last sovereign to use the palace, all died here.

The home of two exiled kings, William III and George II, there still seems to be an air of expectancy and sadness here where two hundred years ago the ailing King George II would frequently gaze from the window of his room and think of the Germany he had left. In October, 1760 the irritable and choleric king was dying. He would often raise himself to look out of the window, up at the curious weather-vane, with its conjoined cyphers of William and Mary, hoping for winds from the right quarter to speed the ships carrying long-overdue despatches from his beloved Hanover. He died on October 25th, 1760, before the winds changed and they say that when there are high winds from the west, a ghostly face peers from the old windows up at the weather-vane just as it did all those long years ago.
De Vere Hotel, Kensington, London, W.8.

Evidence has been collected of an unidentified robed figure having been seen here in daylight through the years. Many visitors, especially those from Eastern countries, sense an un-usual atmosphere as soon as they enter. The church was built by Sir Christopher Wren in 1676 on the site of a previous church destroyed in the Great Fire of London—one that had been founded before the Norman Conquest in 1066. Among those buried in the old church was Henry de Yevele, master-mason to Kings Edward III, Richard II and Henry IV; one of the architects of Westminster Abbey and sculptor of the tomb of the queen of King Richard II; he died in the year 1400.

A former rector, the Rev. H. J. Fynes-Clinton, M.A., told me he had no doubt whatever that the church was haunted by a robed figure which he thought was probably a former priest of St Magnus. His verger at one time, an ex-soldier who was very reliable and unimaginative, found himself within four or five feet of a priest or monk one Sunday evening after service. Everyone had left and he had locked the door. The lights were all on and he was just putting things away in a cupboard behind a side altar when he saw the figure immediately in front of him. He was on the point of asking how he had got in when it bent down and seemed to be looking for something on the floor, so the verger en-quired: 'Have you lost something—can I help you?' The figure straightened up, turned and smiled at the verger and then just faded away in front of his eyes.

A former verger's wife told the rector that she had twice seen a short, black-haired priest wearing a cassock, kneeling before the Blessed Sacrament in the Lady Chapel. Each time when she spoke to it the figure disappeared.

Later a church worker was in the vestry one afternoon doing needlework when a priest in a cassock walked into the room (a modern addition built on the site of a much older building); it circled the table in the middle of the room and then disappeared through a wall. Four years later she saw the same figure in similar circumstances. This time she was sitting at the table in the vestry-room one Saturday afternoon working on embroidery for the church, when she suddenly became aware that someone in a serge cassock was standing by her side. She saw the ribbing of the serge material quite clearly but when she looked upwards she could see no body or face. She suddenly felt very frightened and walked out of the room without looking back. On the third occasion that she saw the figure she was at early Mass one Sunday morning and as she turned her head to make her contribution to the collection, her eye caught a movement behind her. She turned round and saw a priest wearing a cassock walk up the nave and turn into a seat behind her. She took him to be a real person and expected him to go and get a surplice and help as they had no server at the time; when he did not do so she glanced round and found that he was not behind her. When she asked the verger about the priest who had come in during the collection, she was told that no one had entered nor had anyone been moving at that time and no one had occupied the seats behind her.

An electrician working in the church asked who the priest was who watched him so intently and who seemed to be there one minute and gone the next. A choirman ran up from the crypt one Easter, looking very frightened, and said he had passed a robed figure on the stairs who had disappeared into one of the old walls.

An interesting point concerning the stooping figure seen by the verger is that the spot where this took place is exactly over the grave of Miles Coverdale, the sixteenth-century English translator of the Bible; he was a friar and Bishop of Exeter and all the witnesses of this apparition have agreed that the figure they saw wore a cowl or monastic hood.

Howard Hotel, Norfolk Street, Strand, London, W.C.2.

London, ST JAMES'S PALACE.

One part of the palace, which looks like a country house, is reputed to harbour a 'horrible ghost': a small man, his throat slit from ear to ear and with his mouth hanging open, sits up in bed, the head propped precariously against the wall and the body and bedstead drenched with blood.

The awful spectre is said to have its origin in a murder that took place in the haunted room on May 31st, 1810. The debauched Duke of Cumberland, son of King George III, after a night at the opera, retired to his bedroom. Soon afterwards shouts and the sounds of a scuffle were heard but those sounds were not unknown in the Duke's quarters and the servants took no action.

The Duke had two valets, Yew and Sallis, and at length, after things had quietened down, the Duke called for Yew who found the Duke standing in his room, 'cool and composed' but with his shirt-front covered with blood and his sword lying on the floor, bloodstained. The Duke explained that he had been set upon and severely wounded and asked the valet to fetch his physician, Sir Henry Halford. Sir Henry arrived within minutes and found that none of the Duke's wounds were serious and that in fact the only real wound was a deep cut on the Duke's sword hand.

Almost two hours had passed since the Duke had returned to the palace and now, with the wounds dressed and the room re-arranged, the Duke said to Yew: 'Call Sellis.' Yew's sworn statement states that he went to Sellis's room and there found the valet lying perfectly straight in the bed, the head raised against the head-board—and nearly severed from the body. A razor, covered with blood, was found in the room but too far from the body to have been used by Sellis himself or to have been thrown away by him in such a condition.

The Duke, already hated in London, was now openly booed in the streets and he no longer dared to show his face at the opera. At the inquest he stated that Sellis had tried to murder him and had then committed suicide; a suggestion which seemed unlikely in view of the fact that Sellis was a small, weak fellow, while the Duke was a gross, beefy man. The truth seems to have been that the Duke had an affair with Sellis's daughter, who either had a child by him or committed suicide because of his conduct. In order to silence Sellis, His Royal Highness, seizing the poor man as he was in bed and holding him by the hair had cut Sellis's throat with his sword. Then he had probably gashed himself with a razor which he had thrown down on the floor before returning to his own room.

Originally it was King Henry VIII who had acquired the palace for the Crown, pulling down the old leper hospital and building a manor for himself and Anne Boleyn. Another well-known ghost story associated with the palace concerns two notorious women of the Court who were rivals for the affections of King James II: the Duchess of Mazarin and Madame de Beauclair.

The two women, living in retirement, had become friends. They often talked about the possibility of a future life and agreed that whoever died first would, if possible, communicate with the other from beyond the grave.

At length the Duchess of Mazarin died and Madame de Beauclair waited in vain for a message from her friend. As the months passed, she grew sceptical and declared that there was no life after death. She had a heated argument on this subject with a friend who was surprised, some time later, to receive a message from Madame de Beauclair entreating her to come at once if she wished to see her alive. The friend was unwell and hesitated, whereupon she received a still more urgent message, accompanied by a gift of jewelry, imploring her to come immediately.

She hurried to St James's Palace where she found Madame de Beauclair seemingly in the best of health but was told that within a short time Madame would be dead. She had been visited by her dead friend, the Duchess of Mazarin, she affirmed. The ghost of the Duchess had walked round her room, 'swimming rather than walking', had stopped beside a chest and, looking at Madame de Beauclair, had said: 'Between the hours of twelve and one tonight you will be with me.' The midnight hour was close at hand; as the clock began to strike, Madame de Beauclair exclaimed, 'Oh! I am sick at heart!'—and she was dead within half an hour.

There ought to be other ghosts at St James's Palace: perhaps the ghost of King Henry VIII's daughter, 'Bloody' Mary, who died here; or handsome Prince Henry, King Charles I's adored elder brother who also died here in spite of the medicines sent to him by Sir Walter Raleigh from the Tower; or King Charles himself who spent the last few days of his life here, leaving the palace early on that January

145

morning in 1649 to walk across the park for his execution in Whitehall.

There are fourteen crosses on the cobbled stones of an inner courtyard, worn but still visible. They mark the graves of fourteen leprous maidens who were buried here when the palace was a hospital for 'maidens that were lepers, living chastely and honestly in divine service'. They, too, appear to sleep undisturbed.

Hotel Meurice, Bury Street, St James's, London, S.W.1.

London, TOTTENHAM.

Tottenham Museum is housed in Bruce Castle where, each November 3rd, the ghost of Costania, Lady Coleraine, runs screaming through a certain room at dead of night.

Bruce Castle is a late Elizabethan manor house once owned by Sir Rowland Hill (1795-1879) the originator of the penny post, so it is a happy choice for a museum of postal history. Three hundred years ago the jealous Lord Coleraine is said to have kept his beautiful wife locked here, in the room that is now haunted by her screaming ghost. In desperation, she threw herself to her death from the balcony but still her screams and other uncanny sounds are occasionally reported from this impressive building near the parish church.

Some years ago Mr C. H. Rock, B.Sc., A.L.A., the Curator of the Museum, informed me that he had traced a lady who used to live opposite Bruce Castle as a child and she claimed to have heard the screams on November 3rd several years running.

In 1949 thirteen watchers held an all-night vigil on the anniversary of the Lady Coleraine's death and when several of the watchers heard footsteps, the spiral stairs and echoing corridors were immediately searched, but the lady did not put in an appearance on that occasion.

At one-thirty a.m. however all the ghost-watchers noticed a strange chill; but the thing that particularly interested Mr Rock, who joined the watchers, was the peculiar behaviour of a reliable clock, situated immediately above the haunted chamber, which totally failed to strike the hour of one a.m., although it struck midnight and the hours after one a.m.

quite normally.
Pembury Hotel, Stamford Hill, London, N.4.

*London, THE TOWER OF LONDON.

Built by William the Conqueror this venerable collection
of buildings is closely connected with the tragic side of
English history, having been a fortress, a palace, a prison,
an arsenal, even a mint and a menagerie—although it is
best remembered because of the long list of state prisoners
lodged here, so many of whom were executed within its
walls. If tragic deaths and violent happenings can cause
hauntings, then surely the Tower should be ghost-ridden
and, indeed, there are convincing reports, extending over
many years, of curious and inexplicable happenings.

A remarkable story is told by Edward Lenthal Swifte, a
Keeper of the Crown Jewels, a post to which he was appointed in 1814, who resided at the Tower with his family until
his retirement in 1852. One Saturday night in October, 1817
he was having supper with his wife, her sister, and their
young son in the sitting room of the Jewel House (then in
the Martin Tower) and thought by Swifte to have been the
'doleful prison' of Anne Boleyn. The doors and windows of
the room were closed and shuttered that dismal winter's
night and his wife was about to take a drink with her food
when she stopped with the glass half-way to her mouth, and
exclaimed: 'Good God! What's that?' Keeper Swifte looked
in the direction of his wife's gaze and saw a 'cylindrical
figure, like a glass tube', about as thick as one's arm, hovering between the ceiling and the table. Its contents appeared
to be a dense fluid, white and blue, incessantly mixing and
mingling within the cylinder. The shape remained in one
spot for about two minutes and then slowly moved towards
Swifte's sister-in-law, apparently following the shape of the
table. It passed in front of Swifte and his son, then behind
his wife, pausing for a moment over her right shoulder.
(There was a mirror opposite in which she could watch its
progress.) Suddenly Mrs Swifte's nerve broke and she collapsed on to the table, her hands covering her head and
shoulders as she shrieked out, 'Oh, Christ! It has seized me!'

Swifte immediately picked up a chair and struck at the mysterious object which promptly disappeared. Subsequent questioning revealed that while Swifte and his wife had seen the object clearly, neither his son nor his sister-in-law saw anything.

A few days later one of the sentries at the Jewel House maintained that he saw a figure which reminded him of a large bear 'issuing' from under the door of the Jewel Room! He thrust at the form with his bayonet which struck the door and the sentry promptly fainted. He was carried senseless to the main guard-room where he revived to some extent but his nerves were completely shattered and a couple of days later he died.

Sir George Younghusband, a later Keeper of the Crown Jewels, stated that a sentry on duty at the Jewel House (in his time still in the Martin Tower), declared that he often saw the ghost of one of the Earls of Northumberland pass up and down the narrow walk along the edge of the ramparts running on each side of the Martin Tower; a walk known to this day as 'Northumberland's Walk'. Other sentries also saw the ghost and the sentries on duty were doubled.

The Bloody Tower, where the little princes and Sir Thomas Overbury were murdered, where Sir Walter Raleigh was imprisoned and Judge Jeffreys died, was built by King Henry III and has several ghosts. Guido ('Guy') Fawkes, of the Gunpowder Plot fame, was 'examined' here and there are records of agonized groans emanating from the place long afterwards, when no human being was in the former council-chamber. As might be expected, there have been stories also of the pathetic little ghosts of the two murdered princes, King Edward V, acclaimed before he was thirteen although he never lived to be crowned, and his younger brother, Richard, Duke of York, smothered on the orders of Richard, Duke of Gloucester, afterwards King Richard III. Their ghosts have long been reputed to walk, hand in hand, about the palace that became their tomb. Their bodies were hastily buried, first in the basement of the Wakefield Tower and then at the foot of a staircase leading from the White Tower to the Chapel of St John.

The ghost of Anne Boleyn has been seen at the Tower of London, as well as at several other places. Here her ghost has been seen in the vicinity of the White Tower and Tower Green. Sometimes she is seen and her footsteps are heard, sometimes she remains invisible. In 1933 a sentry, hearing approaching footsteps, called out a challenge and saw, floating towards him, the headless body of Anne Boleyn which he recognized by the dress she wore—before he deserted his post in terror. Because that spot was well known to be haunted he was only reprimanded. When Field-Marshal Lord Grenfell (a Member of The Ghost Club) was a lieutenant at the Tower, a similar appearance frightened a guard outside the King's House, where Anne Boleyn spent her last night on earth—in human form. He declared that a headless woman had suddenly appeared in front of him, wearing a dress similar to that he had seen in portraits of Anne Boleyn and when he had received no answer to his challenge he fixed his bayonet and approached to find the weapon made no difference to the advance of the headless woman. He fainted with shock and was charged with being drunk on duty. But at the court martial he told his story and when other sentries testified to similar experiences, he was acquitted.

Anne's ghost has also been seen inside the church within the Tower precincts, the Chapel of St Peter-ad-Vincula (Saint Peter in the Fetters), where her bones lie before the high altar. Years ago a captain noticed a light in the church and asked the sentry on duty outside what the cause was. The sentry said he did not know but he often saw this eerie light and heard strange noises. The officer procured a ladder and when he looked into the church, saw a procession of men and women in Elizabethan dress walking slowly down the central aisle with noiseless tread, headed by a figure that was unmistakable: it was Anne Boleyn. After having paced the chapel several times, the procession and light, for which no origin could be seen, vanished.

Perhaps the most striking ghostly manifestation is that of the execution of the wicked Countess of Salisbury, daughter of the Duke of Clarence, beheaded by order of King Henry VIII. The harrowing scene of her execution is said to be re-enacted on the anniversary of her death; the ghostly Countess being seen and heard, screaming with terror, as she is chased by the phantom executioner who, axe in hand, finally overtakes her and hacks off her head with repeated blows.

In the small chapel in the Wakefield Tower there were reports in the past of the ghost of King Henry VI having been seen there. The persistent stories of his having been stabbed to death as he knelt at prayer, may have some foundation, but I have no record of this particular ghost being seen for many years now.

The ghost of Sir Walter Raleigh is supposed to have been seen from time to time at a spot near The Bloody Tower known as 'Raleigh's Walk' although he was executed at Westminster Old Palace Yard.

The most recent happenings at the Tower for which there appears to be no logical explanation are unexplained footsteps, a shadowy form which disappeared near the Wakefield Tower and a remarkable account from a high-ranking officer at the Tower who saw what he described as a puff of smoke emerge from one of the ancient and long disused cannon. It floated over the ground and appeared to sit on top of a wall. If such an account had not come from an authoritative source, it could be dismissed as a trick of the light—instead, it remains one more curious incident at the haunted Tower of London.

Three Nuns Hotel, London, E.C.3.

London Museum, LANCASTER HOUSE, ST JAMES'S, LONDON S.W.

Some years ago jewels consisting of about one hundred and fifty gold and enamelled necklaces, pendants, rings, stones and ornaments, enclosed in a decayed wooden box, were discovered by workmen near St Paul's Cathedral, during excavations for building a warehouse. They were taken to the house of an official of the London Museum who kept them in his study for a fortnight, informing the Treasury of the find. The jewels arrived about six in the evening on a warm June night; by ten p.m. although the night was still warm, the official and his wife and daughter experienced a sensation of coldness and found themselves shivering in the room where the jewels had been placed. The next day a friend who was interested in the occult called and they discussed the matter with him. While he was in the room containing the jewels he startled the family by stating that he could see, standing by the precious stones, a tall, thin man dressed in Elizabethan costume. The man seemed angry and the student of the occult heard or sensed the apparition say words to the effect that the jewels were his and by what right had they been brought there?

Several years later, after the jewels had been placed officially in the London Museum, then housed at Lancaster House, a professional medium, who knew nothing of what had happened two or three years before, was visiting the museum official at his home when he declared that he could see a tall man standing by the side of the official's daughter who did not like the girl and who might try to do her harm. His description exactly tallied with that of the occult student. The daughter had assisted her father in cleaning the jewels while they were in the house. Another incident concerned a spiritualist who fainted when she was shown the jewels at the London Museum and on recovering stated that she had seen blood on a gold necklet among the jewels and that she had sensed that the woman who wore it had been murdered.
Hotel Meurice, Bury Street, St James's, London, S.W.1.

London, VINE STREET POLICE STATION.

A grim, one-hundred-year-old building haunted by the ghost of a police sergeant who committed suicide in the cells at the turn of the century and who is still reputed to pound with heavy footsteps the station corridors. Locked cell doors have been found unaccountably open. Papers and documents in one of the offices have been discovered scattered and disarranged. One senior detective said in December, 1969, that he had been thoroughly scared on two occasions; each time he had felt the presence of someone else when he was alone in a room. He had made no official report for fear of being laughed at.
Three Nuns Hotel, London, E.C.3.

London, WESTMINSTER CATHEDRAL.

A sacristan on night duty in the locked cathedral in July, 1966 reported seeing a 'black-clad figure' which disappeared as he watched. A spokesman at Cardinal Heenan's London residence stated that 'an extensive search of the cathedral inside and outside, failed to yield any clue and police dogs did not find any scent. Officially, we do not support the theory that it was a ghost, but I have heard it mentioned.' The figure disappeared in the direction of the high altar as the sacristan approached.
Eccleston Hotel, Victoria, London, S.W.1.

London, WILTON ROW, NEAR MARBLE ARCH.

A fashionable public house has long been said to be haunted by a ghostly grenadier.

The 'Grenadier' was once an inn that served as a mess for officers of regiments stationed nearby. The name of the alley that runs beside the pub, Old Barrack Yard, recalls the time when soldiers drilled here. In those days one of the bars was situated where the cellars are now and the present bar served as a dining room for the officers. The story goes that during a game of cards an officer was caught cheating and rough justice was handed out by his companions—a little too rough, it seems, for he was flogged on the spot and staggered down the stairs to the cellar where he died. His ghost is said to haunt the pub to this day.

The fatal game of cards is supposed to have taken place during the month of September and it is during this month that the disturbances at the 'Grenadier' reach their climax. I remember Roy Grigg, a previous licensee, telling me that while he had reservations about the grenadier story, he had no doubt whatever that the place *was* haunted, especially during each September. His Alsatian dog always showed every sign of being terrified during this period, growling and snarling at no visible presence and often trying to scratch and dig its way into the cellar. This curious behaviour of the dog was confirmed by all the occupants of the 'Grenadier' at that time.

One September Roy Grigg's nine-year-old son, lying in bed with the door open, saw what he described as a 'shadow' of someone on the landing. As the boy watched, the shadow grew larger and larger, then became smaller, almost as though someone were approaching the bedroom, then retreating, undecided whether or not to enter. Not long afterwards Mrs Grigg, was changing in her bedroom at midday; believing herself to be alone in that part of the house, she had not troubled to shut the door. Suddenly, when she was half-undressed, she became aware that a man was climbing up the stairs towards her bedroom. She quickly covered herself but when she turned to confront the figure, there was nobody there. As far as can be established no human being was in fact on the stairs at that time; certainly Mrs Grigg, who obviously knew all the men in the pub at the time, did not recognize the person she glimpsed through her bedroom door.

A year later the proprietress of a Hammersmith public house, having a drink in the bar of the 'Grenadier', distinctly saw a man going up the same stairway; a 'man' who seemingly vanished as easily as the one seen by Mrs Grigg.

Mr Grigg told me too about a Roman Catholic friend of his he had known since childhood, who stayed a night at the 'Grenadier' and slept in a bedroom about which he had heard disturbing stories. He therefore hung a rosary over the bed to safeguard his undisturbed sleep. Instead he found himself suddenly awake in the middle of the night and sensed, rather than saw, someone or something, standing at the foot of his bed. The figure seemed to be trying to touch him but almost as soon as he was aware of the presence, it disappeared.

The present landlord Geoffrey Bernerd is equally sure that peculiar happenings occur at the pub; things he is totally unable to explain: knocks, raps, lights switched on during the night, taps turned on, objects moved—these and other phenomena he related during the course of a film made there when I took the B.B.C. to the 'Grenadier' for a programme broadcast one All Hallow's Eve. Bernard's teenage daughter with whom I had a long talk told me she sometimes was very frightened at night for no apparent reason. Occasionally she saw shadows she could not explain.

There were other factors that suggested to me that this young lady may be the focus of the phenomena then occurring at the 'Grenadier'. When I asked her what she did when she had these feelings or saw something she could not explain, usually soon after she had gone to bed, she replied very sensibly that she put her head under the bed-clothes and went to sleep!

The Berkeley Hotel, Wilton Place, London, S.W.1.

Long Melford, SUFFOLK.

At one time the ancient and picturesque Bull Hotel was reputed to be haunted by a poltergeist that threw things about.

This mellow sixteenth-century hostelry was originally a mansion built by a rich 'woolman' in the days when the little town was the centre of the cloth-making industry. The old courtyard at the back is particularly interesting with part of the gallery that at one time surrounded the yard, still preserved.

After receiving reports of various unexplained happenings at the Bull, I approached the manager at that time, a Colonel Dawson, late of the Indian Army. He invited me to spend a night or two there.

On arrival, Colonel Dawson told me that the mysterious happenings began at a time when he had a young nurse-maid looking after his children. When she left nothing untoward happened for a time, but after a new girl took her place, strange things began to occur again. There is a theory that a poltergeist obtains its energy from an adolescent and certainly there is usually a young person present in such cases. The Bull manifestations were interesting because it appeared that the 'geist' was able to attach itself to more than one adolescent. Perhaps the fact that neither girl was at the Bull during my visit accounted for the absence of paranormal phenomena at that time.

Mr Whayman, the head-waiter, told me that he had several times seen objects in flight. Once a heavy copper jug was hurled across the dining room in his direction; at another time a copper urn, which normally stood on a Dutch dresser and was safe-guarded by a ledge, flew through the air as he entered the room, landing on the carpet just behind him. Still another time the same jug was found lying in the middle of the room, having presumably moved there when nobody was present in the room.

One of the first apparently unaccountable incidents concerned the movement of some dining-room chairs. One morning they were found grouped round the enormous fireplace as though people had been sitting there all night. Next, a flower vase was found on the floor in the same room. At the time both these incidents were regarded as being due to lack of attention on the part of members of the staff.

About six months later Colonel Dawson and his wife were having lunch in the dining room when they heard a loud 'click' and the door leading from the hall into the dining room opened of its own accord. The Dawsons noticed that the room felt suddenly cold.

It was in the entrance hall of the Bull in July, 1648 that a yeoman, Richard Everard, was murdered by Roger Greene. The heavy oak door leading from the hall to the dining room was reported to open unaccountably on many subsequent occasions.

One night when he was alone at the inn, Colonel Dawson heard distinct footsteps pass his bedroom door. He quietly brought his dogs upstairs and as soon as they reached the passage outside his bedroom they bristled with fright, absolutely refusing to go along the passage. It was some time before they could be quietened down. Some months later a visitor heard footsteps outside her bedroom door early one morning, followed by a knock on her bedroom door. Thinking it must be her early-morning tea, she called out, 'Come in.' By way of reply, she heard a terrific crash, as though a tray with tea-pot, jug, cup and saucer and other crockery had been dropped and she hurriedly got out of bed to help. When she opened the door nobody was there, nor was there any sign to account for the noise she had heard. Later she established that no one else in the hotel had heard the crash.

I was shown a pewter coffee pot kept in the dining room on a little shelf guarded by a ledge. Once, I was told, this pot had jumped off the six-inch deep shelf, some six feet from the ground, in the presence of nine people having breakfast. It is not unusual for a building three centuries old to have a little dust here and there and this particular shelf was no exception. Colonel Dawson told me that he examined the shelf immediately after the pot had 'jumped' and discovered the slight layer of dust on the shelf had only been disturbed in a clean circle where the pot had stood; there was no displacement of the dust consistent with the pot sliding to the edge of the shelf and then falling over the ledge. So it had to be deduced that the pot had literally jumped.

Two small fires, typical poltergeist activity, were experienced at the Bull, the first occurring in the lounge situated just across the hall from the dining room. A smell of burning from the empty room heralded the discovery of a small hole burning in the carpet, five feet seven inches from the fireplace—where no fire was burning at the time. The other incident also took place in the lounge. This time there was a fire burning there in the heavy fire-basket. After a loud bang had been heard this fire-basket was found in the centre of the room. It was only with some difficulty that it was replaced in its proper position.

I experienced no unusual happenings during my visit to the Bull and Colonel Dawson invited me to pay a return visit at a future date in the hope of witnessing some paranormal activity. But soon afterwards the disturbances ceased as unaccountably as they began and as far as I know nothing untoward happened there for a long time now.
The Bull Hotel, Long Melford, Suffolk.

Ludlow, SHROPSHIRE.

The eleventh-century castle at Ludlow has a ghostly 'White Lady' and a mysterious breathing noise.

Historic Ludlow Castle, in its strong strategic position on the Welsh border, was the last Shropshire fortress to surrender to the Parliamentary Army in 1646. It had been the seat of the Lords President of Wales and began to fall into decay in 1689.

The 'White Lady' haunting is said to date from the days of

King Henry II when Ludlow was the scene of many Border clashes. A maiden by the name of Marion de la Bruyère was among the few retainers left at the castle on one occasion in the absence of its custodian, Joce de Dinan. Marion had an admirer who was attached to the enemies of Ludlow and she was in the habit of lowering a rope, when the opportunity occurred, to enable the knight to visit her at night. This time he did not come alone and while Marion was greeting him, he purposely left the rope dangling. Within a short time a hundred men had swarmed into the castle and Ludlow was in the hands of the enemy. Realizing that she had been betrayed, Marion snatched her lover's sword, slew him and then threw herself over the battlements of the Hanging Tower to her death on the rocks below.

For many years the ghost of 'Marion of the Heath' was said to be seen in the vicinity of the Hanging Tower, wandering among the ruins on dark nights. Now all that seems to remain is a curious gasping or breathing sound that seems to originate half-way up the Garderobe or Hanging Tower. This is thought to be either the expiring gasps of the knight who betrayed the innocent Marion or Marion's deep breathing as she struggled to kill her deceiver. At all events there appears to be no denying this aural phenomenon for which no entirely satisfactory explanation has yet been discovered.

A few years ago I was in touch with Mr J. Didlick, a Ludlow man, who heard the noise several times. He told me that the sounds might be likened to those made by someone in very deep sleep, but he particularly remarked on the loud and distinct quality of the noise which he felt originated high up on the ancient battlements. On the first occasion he heard the noise he was so puzzled that he returned home and asked his wife to accompany him back to the castle, taking care not to tell her what he had heard. But as soon as they reached the spot where he had heard the very heavy breathing, Mrs Didlick stopped and remarked on the curious noise which seemed to come from the castle walls. She was very reluctant to stay anywhere near the spot and subsequent questioning established that she had heard precisely the same noise as her husband.

Mr Didlick told me that he had since heard it on several occasions and each time, although he had searched carefully, he had been unable to discover any material cause. A nest of young owls was a popular suggestion but Mr Didlick assured me that this theory could be discounted as owls do not nest in January and no traces were found to suggest that owls habitually visited the spot. A suggestion that the wind might be responsible was not accepted by Mr Didlick who maintained that on two occasions when he has heard the noise there had been no wind whatever.

Another witness explored the possibility of night birds, either animal or human, being responsible. He maintained that the breathing was too restrained to originate from a human being and too human to come from an animal or bird. A young man and his girl-friend also heard the noise which they described as 'wheezing'; they became frightened and ran from the spot beneath the Hanging Tower.

During the Second World War a family were evacuated to Ludlow from Liverpool and spent four months in part of Ludlow Castle. Soon after they arrived odd things happened: raps and bangs which they could not account for and the mysterious opening and closing of doors. When I was there not long ago I talked to one of the officials and he told me that he was always getting reports of odd happenings in and around the castle.

Ludlow's parish churchyard and rectory are also reputed to be haunted. At the rectory a tall, elderly woman with grey hair dressed in a long, dull-coloured robe has been seen from outside the house when the place has no occupants. Sometimes shuffling footsteps have been heard by those living there. A similar figure, an old woman in a drab dress, has been seen wandering among the tombs and disappearing among the ancient headstones. No one knows who she is or what she wants.

Feathers Hotel, Ludlow, Salop.

Lyme Regis, DORSET.

Nearby Trent Manor House contains a hiding-place used by King Charles II. A legend tells of ghostly horses' hooves thundering past, on the old highway, on certain nights of the year. They are said to have originated in the mysteri-

ous disappearance of a coach and horses, driver and passengers, who all vanished from the face of the earth one dark and stormy night.
Three Cups Hotel, Lyme Regis, Dorset.

*Lympne, NEAR HYTHE, KENT.

Lympne Castle here has been a Roman fortress, an Anglo-Saxon outpost, a Danish stockaded camp, a Norman castle, a home of the Archdeacons of Canterbury (including Thomas à Becket), a Tudor fortified residence, a farm, the haunt of smugglers and a look-out in the Second World War. It also has several ghosts, including one seen by a previous tenant, Mrs Henry Beecham, sister-in-law of Sir Thomas Beecham.

Ancient documents and local folklore tell of six Saxons fleeing from the Normans—a flight perpetuated perhaps for ever because their ghosts (the Normans discovered their hiding place and they met an 'untimely' end) have been seen inside the castle.

Another ghost is that of a Roman soldier who, on watch in the east tower, accidentally fell to his death. Appropriately enough his footsteps are heard mounting the tower steps ... but they never come down.

The present occupants are Mr and Mrs H. Margery who will tell you that they have heard mysterious footsteps and other noises which they are unable to account for.
Clifton Hotel, Folkestone, Kent.

Lytchett-Maltravers, NEAR POOLE, DORSET.

There are several haunted houses in this village of Norman origin where Sir John Maltravers, involved in the murder of King Edward II, lies buried in the churchyard of St Mary the Virgin. The ancient Church Path, once used by survivors of the plague when they abandoned the doomed village in the valley is still the shortest way from the present village to the church. It climbs a hillside, skirts a wood, and then, at the angle where it bears sharply left, we find Whispering Corner. In daylight and at night-time, anxious and urgent

whispering voices have been heard here—as though several people were urgently discussing some pressing subject. But the words are always indistinguishable.
Sandacres Hotel, Poole, Dorset.

Macclesfield, CHESHIRE.

Capesthorne Hall, near Macclesfield, is the ninety-eight roomed home of Sir Walter Bromley-Davenport. Perhaps significantly, all the unexplained happenings here have been reported from the original portion of this ancient towered and domed mansion and none from the middle section of the house which was rebuilt after being destroyed by fire in 1861.

Sir Walter himself saw 'a line of shadowy, spectre-like figures descending the steps into the family vault' in his private chapel and briefly glimpsed a grey form gliding along a corridor in the house.

His son, William, one still, windless night in 1958 when he was twenty-three, was startled by the sound of the bedroom window rattling near his head and awoke to see a detached arm reaching towards the window. Since then the place has been known as 'The Room with the Severed Arm'. William Bromley-Davenport promptly got out of bed to discover the source of the disturbance but the arm disappeared as he approached. He opened the securely fastened window, and looked down at the deserted courtyard, a sheer drop of thirty feet below.

Other witnesses of strange happenings here include Sir Charles Taylor, M.P., who saw a 'lady in grey' hurrying past the foot of a staircase in the west wing as he was going upstairs. His attention was attracted by the 'swish' of her long skirts and he noticed that she floated rather than walked. Another Member of Parliament spent a sleepless night in a bedroom where the door kept opening and then banging shut for no apparent reason.
Bulls Head Hotel, Macclesfield, Cheshire.

The 'Old Burlington',
Church Street, Chis-
wick, a former Eliza-
bethan ale house,
haunted by a ghost in
wide-brimmed black
hat and cloak.
Photo: Chris Underwood

The parish church
of West Drayton,
Middlesex, said to
have been haunted
for a hundred years
by a ghostly black
bird sometimes seen
in the chancel and
sometimes in the
vault beneath the
church. *Photo: Chris
Underwood*

Penkaet Castle, Pencaitland, Scotland, haunted by the ghost of King Charles I, who spent a night in the four-poster bedstead here; John Cockburn a former owner and murderer; and a hanged beggar.

The Tulip Staircase at The Queen's House, National Maritime Museum, Greenwich, with an unexplained and shrouded figure (or figures) climbing the staircase, which is viewed from below. The photograph was taken by the Rev. R. W. Hardy and is perhaps the most remarkable spontaneous ghost photograph ever obtained. *Photograph: The Rev. R. W. Hardy and The Ghost Club*

Manchester, LANCASHIRE.

A house in Cheetham was the scene of curious happenings in 1964, including a child's cries and 'mournful whistling'. A dressing table moved across a bedroom, a pram shook noiselessly while the baby inside slept peacefully and apparitions of an old woman and 'a black figure' were reported. The family tried planchette and seemed to contact a dead man who referred to a baby that had been murdered. In response to the messages obtained, a search of the house revealed a narrow strip of calico sheeting in a chimney; copies of newspapers dated 1922 and a pencilled music score which read similar to the mysterious whistling. Later small bones were discovered beneath the kitchen floorboards but when these were handed to the police, the family were informed that they appeared to be those of a cat or a rabbit!

'The Rover's Return', a fourteenth-century curio shop in Shudehill, says owner Mr Francis Shaw, is haunted by a kilted Jacobite ghost who often appears at the foot of Mr Shaw's bed. The apparition is described as having auburn hair, wearing buckles on his shoes and carrying a dirk. The ghost seemed to be gazing at a portrait of Bonnie Prince Charlie and Flora Macdonald and Mr Shaw gained the impression that it was one James Stewart who came to Manchester with Prince Charlie and was stabbed to death in this old house. Mr Shaw's partner, Mr Robert Stark, an ex-R.E.M.E. man, said that once when he slept alone in the house there was a loud crash from the direction of the cellar as though a stack of bottles had fallen down but when he went to investigate, there was no sign of any disturbance.

Mitre Hotel, Manchester, Lancs.

Markyate, NEAR ST ALBANS, HERTFORDSHIRE.

The curious name of Markyate Cell for the wonderful old house here is derived from the hermitage built by Roger, a monk of St Albans in the early twelfth century. After Roger had been on a pilgrimage to Jerusalem he settled as a hermit at Markyate, under the care of the Abbot of St Albans. He died about 1122 and was buried in St Albans Abbey where his shrine was visited by King Henry III in 1257.

In 1118, Christina, a member of a wealthy Anglo-Saxon family in Huntingdonshire, fled to Markyate to become one of Roger's hermits, when her parents attempted to force her into a marriage against her will. Her presence was kept a close secret for fear of the Bishop of Lincoln's intervention and she was enclosed in a cell measuring only a span and a half, where for four years she sat on hard stone, there being insufficient room to stand, suffering extremes of heat and cold, hunger and thirst. Under these rigorous conditions she acquired, apart from physical ailments, a great reputation for sanctity and in due course she succeeded Roger as head of the hermitage. Christina was renowned for her embroidery and in 1155 samples of her work were sent to Pope Adrian IV. The priory survived until the dissolution of the monastries in the sixteenth century, when much of the building was pulled down but some of the material was incorporated in the new house built by Humphrey Bourchier, Master of the King's Past-times. Bourchier's widow, Elizabeth, married George Ferrers in 1541 and much of the Tudor house is still evident, despite extensive alterations in the nineteenth century. One can discern the general Tudor style of the house from its courtyard; many of the windows are Tudor, too, and so is much of the actual stonework, while the garden, at once peaceful and expectant, is laid out in perfect Tudor style.

During the seventeenth century the lady of the house was Catherine Ferrers: 'the wicked Lady Ferrers' who was married at the age of thirteen to a sixteen-year-old member of the aristocracy named Fanshawe. The marriage was not a success. Perhaps it was the disillusionment of a broken union or maybe just loneliness and frustration that first caused Catherine Ferrers to take to crime but there can be little doubt that it was the excitement of the chase and not the financial and other rewards that came her way when she changed into a highwayman's costume and practised the art of her choice upon the late travellers in the surrounding countryside. She had a secret room built into the kitchen chimney, reached by a concealed stairway and there she kept her three-cornered hat, her buckskin breeches and riding cloak. It was down this secret stairway (which can still be seen today) that she would steal to mount her coal-black horse, to hold up and kill without hesitation, travellers and coachmen on their journeys north and south.

One night during the course of a robbery, she was wounded on nearby No Man's Land and although she managed to struggle home, she expired outside the door which led to the secret stairway. Now the secret was out but the doorway was bricked up and remained so for over a century and a half.

Shortly after her funeral stories began to circulate in the surrounding countryside that her ghost had been seen abroad, riding hell-for-leather on horseback over the tree-tops; while others declared that they had seen her spectral figure swinging in the branches of an old oak tree under which she is thought to have buried the proceeds of her robberies.

In 1840 there was a bad fire at Markyate Cell and some of the men working to put out the blaze asserted that they distinctly saw the ghostly Lady Ferrers beneath a branch of a large sycamore tree near the house. After the fire, Mr Adey, the owner at the time, decided to open the bricked-up doorway but found great difficulty in enlisting workmen locally for it appeared to be common knowledge that the place was haunted and that unaccountable sighs and groans were frequently heard there. At length workmen had to be obtained from London and when they opened the doorway they found that the narrow stone staircase led up to a heavy oak door which they broke down, only to find afterwards that the door opened by means of a concealed spring. The room, however held no secrets, only spiders and bats.

There seems to be good evidence that the ghost of Catherine Ferrers has been seen in the vicinity of Markyate Cell; either riding her black horse, appearing near the branch of a tree, or sitting or standing in the garden. Once she was seen by a number of people at a parish tea; at other times near the kitchen and in other parts of the house. Mr E. A. Sursham and his wife, the occupants when I was there in 1966, told me that their own daughter had seen the figure of an unexplained woman in the garden. The figure disappeared under curious circumstances.

The Noke Hotel, St Albans, Herts.

Marshwood Vale, BETWEEN BROADWINDSOR AND LYME REGIS, DORSETSHIRE.

The lonely Queen Anne mansion in the shadow of the hills, is called 'The House of the Screaming Skull', because of the yellowed skull preserved here and because of the manifestations that are said to have occurred when it was removed from Bettiscombe House.

The story was first related in print by J. S. Udal, a High Court judge and collector of folklore, who, in 1872, told of the human skull that had been at Bettiscombe for many years. He added that according to tradition if it were removed, the property itself would rock to its foundations and the person responsible would be dead within a year.

One legend says that the skull is that of a Negro brought to England by Azariah Pinney (from whom the present owner, Michael Pinney is descended) and who declared, just before he died, that he would never rest until his body was buried in his native land. According to another the skull is that of a black servant who was murdered; still another says that the skull was brought to England by Azariah Pinney and belonged to a faithful old black servant who died in his master's service abroad. The fourth suggests that the skull is that of a young woman who died at Bettiscombe— some say after a long illness, some say, she was murdered. Near its traditional resting place there is a priest's hiding-place, immediately under the roof, which might be connected with the mysterious skull.

Azariah Pinney was the son of the Rev. John Pinney who died in 1705 and lies buried at Bettiscombe. Both Azariah and his brother John joined the ineffectual Monmouth rebellion and were found guilty of high treason by Judge Jeffreys in 1685. John was hanged and Azariah shipped to the West Indies as a slave. It may be that years later he brought back this memento of a trusty servant whom he had named 'Bettiscombe'. At all events it is said that soon after the black servant was buried in the local churchyard, screams were heard, animals on the farm died, crops failed and the house seemed to rock, but that after the body was exhumed and the skull taken into the house, all was quiet.

Among the stories associated with the skull one states that

years ago a tenant threw the skull into the duckpond opposite the house and a few days later spent hours raking the pond until he found the skull; for he had been much disturbed by noises of all kinds during its absence and was only too glad to have it back inside. Another tale tells of the skull being buried nine feet deep and working its way back to the surface. It is said to have been heard screaming at the turn of the century, screams that reverberated throughout the house and were heard by villagers and farm workers. In 1914 the skull is said to have sweated blood.

In 1963 the skull was examined by a professor of Human and Comparative Anatomy at the Royal College of Surgeons who decided that the skull was probably a female aged between twenty-five and thirty, rather small but a normal European one and certainly not negroid.

Stile House Hotel, Pound Street, Lyme Regis, Dorset.

Meopham, KENT.

Where a headless monk is reputed to walk between the Georgian public house and the village church a few hundred yards away across the road. The ghost's path leads between two pillars but whether these have any significance for the headless apparition or, indeed, why the monk is headless and why he walks, no one seems to know. There are, however, reports of the figure having been seen within the last few years.

The old Manor House was haunted during the 1930s and Mr G. Varley, during the six months he was there, saw the ghost on several occasions; once, terrified, he threw a poker at the figure which still didn't move! The cellar door used to be opened several times a day and once Mr Varley was in the lounge when the ghost opened the door. He and his family were always hearing footsteps and mutterings, nearly every night. Psychic investigator Harry Price conducted a broadcast from this haunted house and obtained evidence of a sharp fall in the temperature; one member of the broadcast team who slept in the house, heard unaccountable footsteps.

King's Head Hotel, Rochester, Kent.

Mersea Island, ESSEX.

The ghost of a Roman centurion has long been said to haunt
The Strood. Some accounts say the lonely figure is joined by
other legionaries and a clash of swords is heard across the
quiet saltings.

I remember an elderly inhabitant telling me of how she
thought she had once walked with a ghostly centurion from
Mersea Barrow, on the East Mersea Road, to the Causeway.
She described the steady tramp of a soldier's feet beside
her. She met a friend who also heard the regular and heavy
stamping sounds, but Mrs Jane Pullen of 'The Peldon Rose'
was not in the least frightened: 'Those old Romans do you
no harm,' she would say.

In February, 1970 two naval men were driving over the
Strood when something loomed up suddenly in front of their
dipped headlights; something dark, upright, with vertical
white lines and horizontal white lines across it—perhaps the
metal skirt of a Roman tunic. It was a very clear night yet
they were on to whatever it was almost before they realized
and then they were through it; there was no bump. The
thing seemed to have no definite shape but resembled a
human figure surrounded by a white mist. Both men are
seasoned members of the Royal Navy and used to observation at all times of the day and night.

The unidentified figure of a woman, dressed in a smock
and wearing a tall hat, with a stick tucked underneath her
arm, has been seen sitting on a wall at the corner of the
Colchester Road and High Street: there were reliable reports
that she was seen in November, 1966.
Red Lion Hotel, Colchester, Essex.

Middle Claydon, NEAR AYLESBURY, BUCKINGHAMSHIRE.

Delightful Claydon House, built in 1768 and standing in its
own open parkland, has several ghosts including Sir Edmund
Verney, the King's Standard Bearer at the battle of Edgehill
in 1642, who walks here looking for his hand which was
buried in the family vault.

When Cromwell's men captured Sir Edmund they demanded that he give up the colours but he refused, saying: 'My life is my own, but my Standard is the King's'; so he was killed. But when the Roundheads came to take the Standard from his hand, they could not unlock his death-grip and they cut off his hand with its signet ring. Later in the battle the Standard was recaptured by the King, Sir Edmund's hand still grasping it. Sir Edmund's body had been buried in an unknown grave but his hand was sent home and was interred in the family vault at Claydon. The ring was removed and is now in the possession of the present baronet, Sir Harry Verney, who showed it to me when I was there in 1962 and allowed me to examine the exquisitely beautiful jewel. Sir Harry and Lady Rachel recounted the history of Claydon as we wandered through this magnificent house with the quite exceptionally fine staircase. Its iron balustrade depicts a continuous garland of ears of corn, so delicately wrought that they rustle when anyone walks up the stairs. Sir Harry presented me very kindly with a letter from his sister, Miss Ruth Verney, about the ghost she saw on the Red Stairs here.

As with so many haunted houses, there are convincing reports of unexplained footsteps at Claydon. A forester's wife, who still lives on the estate, has told of hearing very heavy footsteps in the corridor above her when she was at Claydon House in 1923 looking after the children, while everyone else was away. She knew that there was no one in the house at that time, apart from herself and the children who were within sight. The footsteps stopped at what she judged to be the trapdoor entrance to the priest's hole but when she went up there, no one was in sight. Years later exactly the same experience befell her sister who returned home shaking with fright after hearing heavy and distinct footsteps in the empty house.

Sir Harry told me of John Webb, the level-headed and practical estate carpenter who assisted with the demolition of the enormous ballroom that was pulled down some years before. He had been working among the rubble when he chanced to look up and saw a strangely-dressed man standing nearby, looking sadly at the devastation. When the carpenter called out to the man, for he knew the stranger did not belong to the big house, the figure disappeared. There was no cover whatever at the spot where the stranger had stood.

In giving me his sister's account of the apparition she had seen at Claydon, Sir Harry mentioned that this was probably the same figure that other people had seen while staying at Claydon. I cannot do better than quote Miss Verney's letter verbatim:

'I was born in 1879 and it must have been about 1892, when I was thirteen, that I ran up the Red Stairs at Claydon House, and turned left and left again on the first landing and then took a few steps towards the Cedar Room. I noticed without surprise that a man was half-way down from the upper floor. After I got nearly to the door of the Rose Room, I quite suddenly thought, "But who was he?" and I ran back to look. He was gone and there hadn't been time for him to reach the top or the bottom of the flight. I saw him on the third step of the second flight and he was coming down. He was tall, and slender, and wore a long black cloak, beneath the hem of which peeped the tip of his sword: he carried a black hat with a white feather gracefully curled round the crown. That was all I saw. Mother said he was just where the secret stair had been.

'There was a curious little sequel which may or may not have been merely a coincidence. Some time later a little school-friend was coming to spend the week-end. She was, of course, all agog to see the ghost, but in the interval we both forget him completely. We were going up to the top of the Red Stairs and as she put her foot on the third step, she said: "By the bye, *where* did you see the ghost?" Alas! He has never come back. Other people have seen ghosts and heard unaccountable noises. Andrew Lang, sleeping in the Rose Room, was much honoured to be awakened one night and to see a lovely lady in grey, but she quickly vanished into the wall of what had been a secret room.'

Sir Harry Verney keeps an open mind on the question of ghosts and although he hasn't encountered the wraith of Sir Edmund, wandering about the little chapel at Claydon and within the house, looking for his lost hand, I am sure he would treat his ancestor courteously and sympathetically should he ever do so.

White Hart Hotel, Buckingham, Bucks.

Minehead, SOMERSET.

In 1636 there lived at Minehead a family named Leaky:
a respected shipowner, his wife and small daughter and his
widowed mother. Mrs Leaky senior was a much-loved old
lady with a large circle of acquaintances, some of whom, at
times, would lament the fact that one day death must separate them from their beloved but ageing friend. To this the
old lady would reply that while she might be missing from
the convivial gatherings which she also enjoyed—should
her friends meet her after her death—they would, in all
probability, rather they had not seen her.

In due course the old lady died and was accompanied to
her grave by many of her loyal friends. Not long afterwards
there were stories that old Mrs Leaky had been seen about
the town and near the house of her son; stories that were
treated with respect after the experience of a Minehead doctor who recounted that on his way back to town after a
country visit he had met an old gentlewoman whom he had
helped over a style. He found her hand uncommonly cold
which made him eye the woman more closely, whereupon
he observed that in speaking she never moved her lips, nor
her eyes. Somewhat perturbed, the doctor deliberately re-
frained from helping the old lady over the next style. She
went ahead of him and sat upon it, effectively barring his
passage. He turned aside to a gate only to find her sitting
upon that and this strange game went on for some time
until at last the doctor managed to get by and reached the
outskirts of the town where the 'spectre' gave him a kick in
the breeches and told him to be more civil to old ladies
in future! From then on she became more vicious; all the
good nature for which she had been so beloved, disappeared
and she seemed to haunt her son's ships, distracting and
scaring the crews as the ships neared port so that many of
the vessels went aground. Often, it is said, she would appear
at the masthead and whistle in an eerie and blood-chilling
manner, whereupon a storm would arise and wreck the ship.
Owing to this peculiarity, she became known as 'the
whistling ghost'. Before long her son's fortunes diminished
and now she appeared night and day in and about the house
where she had lived. At night her daughter-in-law would

often wake to see the apparition in the bedroom and although she always woke her husband immediately, the figure invariably disappeared before he saw her. The climax came one terrible night when the ghost strangled the five-year-old Leaky child. Her parents heard a terrible scream from the child's bedroom: 'Help! Help! Father, father, grandmother is choking me...' Before the anguished parents could reach the child, she had been murdered.

On the morning of the funeral of the little girl, the distraught mother was tidying her hair when she saw in the looking-glass her mother-in-law looking over her shoulder. Almost paralysed with fright, the poor woman murmured a prayer and then turned to face the horror and implored the apparition in the name of God to say why she plagued the family so. In reply the ghost told her to go to Ireland and visit her uncle, the Lord Bishop of Waterford; who was to be told that unless he repented of the sin (which she said he knew all about), he would be hanged. The horrified and distraught mother asked what sin and was told: murder. Apparently when he lodged at Barnstable and was married to the sister of the ghostly Mrs Leaky, he had a child by her daughter, which, after baptizing it, he had strangled; smoked it over a pan of charcoal 'that it might not stink' and buried it in a chamber of the house ... All this was found to be true and after the bishop did his best to atone for his sins, the ghostly Mrs Leaky was seen no more.
Carlton Plume of Feathers Hotel, Minehead, Somerset.

Minsden, NEAR HITCHIN, HERTFORDSHIRE.

Almost hidden and practically forgotten, the ruins of Minsden Chapel, a fourteenth-century chapel-of-ease, have long been reputed to be haunted by a ghostly monk.

As long ago as 1690 Minsden was reported to be 'totally ruinated, stripped, uncovered, decayed and demolished' but Reginald Hine, the Hertfordshire historian, leased the ruins for his lifetime and cautioned 'trespassers and sacrilegious persons take warning, for I will proceed against them with the utmost rigour of the law and after my death and burial, I will endeavour, in all ghostly ways, to protect and haunt its hallowed walls'. After Hine's tragic death his wife made of the ruins a memorial to her husband and the picturesque walls and arches seem to have been rescued from oblivion at the eleventh hour.

Minsden is traditionally associated with Alice Perrers, mistress of King Edward III, who is charged with stealing her royal lover's rings while he was on his deathbed. She infatuated the old King by 'occult spells' manufactured by her physician who was regarded as a 'mighty sorcerer' but eventually he was arrested on a charge of confecting love philtres and talismans.

All Hallows Eve, the night when ghosts are reputed to hold sway and be able to return and be visible, is the night of the year when Minsden's ghosts manifest and there are many stories of horses and dogs behaving as though they see or sense something invisible to their human companions as they climb towards Minsden Chapel on that night. Elliott O'Donnell told me that one All Hallows Eve he heard sweet music here and thought he caught a glimpse of a white-robed figure standing in one of the archways.

It seems that the ghostly manifestations usually begin with the tolling of the lost bells of Minsden and as the sounds die away the figure of a monk is seen under the ivy-covered arch on the south side. Walking with bowed head he silently mounts steps no longer visible and disappears. After a moment the strains of sweet and plaintive music fill the air but almost as soon as the hearer is aware of the sounds, they cease and all is quiet again.

Reginald Hine gave me permission to spend the night of All Hallows Eve at Minsden some years ago. During the course of a preliminary visit with my brother and a friend, both my friend and I, although ten yards apart, heard, just for a moment, a snatch of music we could not account for, while my brother only a step behind me, heard nothing. We met no ghost during our vigil on All Hallows Eve. Hine never saw the ghost of Minsden although he did see one at Stanegarth (as he reports in his *Confessions of an Un-Common Attorney*) and he recalled that experience vividly when I talked to him about ghosts. He believed in ghosts for the best of reasons: because he had seen one.

The Sun Hotel, Hitchin, Herts.

Cleve Court, a handsome, red-brick early Georgian house bought by lawyer and politician Sir Edward Carson in 1920, stands off a quiet road. A great advocate, he is particularly remembered for his merciless cross-examination of Oscar Wilde in 1895. On becoming a lord of appeal in 1921, he was given a life peerage. He died here in 1935 and his body was taken to Belfast for a State funeral. Lady Carson, who often told me how she loved the house from the first time she had seen it, lived at Cleve Court until she died a couple of years ago.

Lady Carson was as clear-sighted and practical a person as anyone I have met and she was utterly convinced that Cleve Court was haunted. There were noises at night-time, though never during the day: footsteps that sounded like a woman wearing high heels, taps on doors, as though someone were seeking admission, dragging sounds that disturbed visitors, noises of drawers being opened and closed although nothing physical was ever interfered with. Lord Carson tended to dismiss the curious noises but there were occasions when even he was quite mystified. The time, for example, when Lord and Lady Carson were in their bedroom and a light knock sounded on the door. He called out 'Come in', but no one did and there was nobody outside; the Carsons were alone in the house at the time.

Soon after they moved in an old man in the village told them that a previous owner, many years ago, had been a tyrant who kept his wife locked up. She finally died, childless, although her greatest wish had been to have a son or daughter. It was soon after they had heard this story—to which they did not give much attention—that the Carsons began to notice whenever children were in the house, a mysterious 'grey lady' was often seen. Patricia Miller, a great niece of Lord Carson, asked her mother who the lady was who stood by her bed—a lady she had seen before to whom nobody ever talked. Joanna Wilson paid a return visit to Cleve Court when she was about eight years old; she remembered seeing a lady there 'who walks in and out of rooms and whom nobody speaks to' and she wanted to know whether the lady was still at the house. A grandson, Rory

Carson, visited the house when he was fifteen in 1965 but refused to sleep in the old part of the house. A large dog couldn't be made to stay in the room, either.

It was soon after Lady Carson herself saw the 'grey lady' in 1949 that I first met her and she told me of her own experiences. She had been awakened about one-thirty a.m. by her spaniel, Susan, who needed to be let out. Lady Carson put on a dressing-gown and, leaving a light on the landing by her bedroom, took the dog downstairs. As she passed a switch on the stairs she accidentally turned the light off but continued down the stairs and stood waiting for Susan to return indoors. When she did so the dog immediately began to run back up the stairs, then suddenly stopped dead in its tracks. Lady Carson switched on the lights and found the dog whimpering and shivering and looking up the stairs. There, on the landing, a grey-coloured lady was floating noiselessly down towards them. When the figure reached a half-landing, it turned and disappeared through an open door into the old part of the house. Lady Carson described the figure minutely. Although she could not see the face clearly, she was certain that it was a young woman who wore a very full grey dress that reached to her feet, a pale grey lace cape on her neck and shoulders and a white ribbon in her hair. The form appeared to be quite solid but Lady Carson knew by the silence and by the behaviour of her dog that she was seeing a ghost and she was terrified. She told me she had never been so frightened of anything in her life; she felt ice-cold and began to shiver until the figure disappeared from sight.

After reports of Lady Carson's experience appeared in print a former housemaid at Cleve Court wrote to her. The letter related that when she was fifteen years old, she had been busy early one morning in the old part of the house when she had heard footsteps coming along the passage. She had looked up, expecting to see one of the other maids but saw instead a lady in an 'old-fashioned dress'. As the girl got up and prepared to leave the room, the grey lady waved a hand and went away.

Cleve Court is now the home of the Hon. Edward Carson, a former Member of Parliament and Lord and Lady Carson's only son. He was hardly a year old when the family moved to Cleve Court and when he was six he told his mother that he did not like the lady who walked in the passage outside his room. Lady Carson, who knew this could be no 'normal' lady, asked her son what she looked like. 'I don't know,' little Edward replied, 'I've only seen her walking away.' Some years ago Mrs Edward Carson heard footsteps approaching down a passage as she came out of a bathroom. The footsteps seemed to pass her, although she saw nothing. This was the same year that Lady Carson saw the 'grey lady'. She used to say that the apparition was never seen again and footsteps were never heard after that night, but an ex-hospital sister, who knew nothing of the ghost of Cleve Court, will tell you that she, too, heard footsteps pass her bedroom door very late one night. And perhaps if there were children now at Cleve Court the 'grey lady' might appear again.

San Clu Hotel, Ramsgate, Kent.

Morwenstow, CORNWALL.

The thirteenth-century Stanbury Manor has, or had, a haunted chest that is thought to have come to England with the Spanish Armada.

A few years ago the owner, Mr T. A. Ley, told me that when he bought the chest from an antique shop, the proprietor said he was glad to get rid of it for there was something queer about it. He had found that he could never keep anything hanging on the walls near the old cedar chest, which was heavily carved on the lid and sides with such grisly subjects as dismembered limbs and headless bodies.

At Stanbury Manor Mr Ley first had the chest placed in the armoury until a permanent place could be found for it and there the first unexplained incident took place. The morning after the chest had been delivered, Mr Ley had occasion to pass through the place and as he did so, six guns fell off the wall together. He told me that the guns were hung on stout wire which was not broken and none of the hangings had come out of the wall.

The chest was next moved to the Leys' bedroom. The same evening when Mr Ley was assisting his wife in the next room, hanging curtains on a four-poster bedstead, a picture fell off the wall and hit him on the head although he was at least eighteen inches away from the wall at the time. An odd thing about this incident is that although the picture was a heavy one, Mr Ley hardly felt it strike him; it was perhaps a gentle warning of what *might* happen.

Next day Mr and Mrs Ley were working in the same room when three more pictures fell off the walls. Two days later four more pictures came down in the drawing room which is immediately beneath the Leys' bedroom where the chest still stood. Both Mr and Mrs Ley were present at the time. One of the pictures went backwards through some stout pine panelling into a secret passage, which shows the force that was exerted on that occasion. Next day one more picture came down in the drawing-room. None of the wires were broken but most of the pictures that fell were damaged.

Two days later Mr Ley had news of the death of a near relative and he wondered whether there was any connection between the falling pictures and the death, for there were no further disturbances associated with the chest.

A former curate of Newlyn West recognized the photograph of the Morwenstow 'poltergeist chest' (as the press dubbed the case) and related the following story concerning it. Many years ago there lived in the village two ladies who owned the chest. They were elderly and both stone deaf. They used to communicate with each other by writing notes. They lived like recluses and were rarely seen by the local people. During their long lives they had gathered a great deal of junk which they believed to be a valuable collection of antiques. When they decided to put these objects up for sale, the curate went along to examine the articles but found it very difficult to do business with the old ladies as they wrote their usual notes and expected him to do the same. On making enquiries afterwards, the curate learned that when the sisters were young, they had gone to visit some friends and as they arrived late at night, they retired, without unpacking their trunks which they had placed on a chest by the window in their bedroom. In the morning when they awoke their attention was immediately drawn to the chest: although weighed down by the heavy trunks the lid was slowly opening. The two sisters got out of bed and went over, looked inside the chest and 'what they saw was so horrible that they were both struck deaf on the spot'. They would never reveal what they saw. The two old ladies are long dead but the story still persists locally.

When I heard this story I immediately recalled the account of a haunted chest told by a hard-headed surgeon in the Midlands. The bedroom allocated to him when he went to visit a friend was spacious but dreary and a large carved chest stood in one corner. Soon after his arrival, moved by some unexplained impulse, after examining the outside of the chest, he raised the lid. Inside he saw a man lying with his throat cut. With an exclamation of horror and surprise the surgeon let the lid fall but almost immediately re-opened the chest. To his great astonishment, it was completely empty. When he mentioned this curious experience to his host the following morning the latter stared at him in amazement and told him that a former occupant of that room had, in fact committed suicide and his body was found in the chest in the condition described.

If it was the same chest, was a sight such as the surgeon saw horrible enough to strike two young ladies deaf? One wonders whether on re-opening the chest the ladies, too, found it empty—a fact that might well account for their never revealing what they had seen.

Grenville Hotel, Bude, Cornwall.

Newmarket, SUFFOLK, HAMILTON STUD LANE.

In 1927 a native of this East Anglian town, famous for its racecourse, declared that she had seen the ghost of the great jockey Fred Archer mounted on his favourite grey horse, emerge from a copse, gallop noiselessly towards the woman and her daughter (who both saw the apparition) and then vanish mysteriously. The woman was familiar with the winner of more than 2,000 races and was adamant that the figure was Archer—who had then been dead for some forty years. The affair caused something of a sensation and other local people came forward to say that they, too, had seen the phantom horse and rider in the vicinity of Hamilton Stud Lane and also on the heath.

Archer was an outstanding jockey, who won the Derby

five times, but he was known to have a violent temper and be intolerant of rivals. He had been greatly depressed by the death of his wife within a year of their marriage; within two years he was dead himself and lies in the same grave with her. His ghost is thought to be responsible for a number of unexplained mishaps on the Newmarket Course where there have been many instances of horses swerving or slowing or stumbling for no apparent cause.

In 1950 jockey Charlie Smirke said he could not explain why his mount, the Aga Khan's horse Kermanshah, fell in a race at a spot where another horse had fallen the previous year. But jockeys and spectators have, on occasions, seen a white formless shape hovering in the air at this spot at about the height of a horse's head.

White Hart Hotel, Newmarket, Suffolk.

Newton-le-Willows, NEAR WARRINGTON, LANCASHIRE.

Here the ghostly tramping footsteps of the 'chok'd Battalion' are said to be heard sometimes during the month of August. The sounds are reputed to have originated with the Highlanders caught by Cromwell's men here in August 1648, and summarily hanged on nearby trees.

Patten Arms Hotel, Warrington, Lancs.

*Oxford, MERTON COLLEGE.

There have long been stories of a room which cannot be slept in. In 1966 the Warden told me that when he was an undergraduate at Merton in the 1920s he had been told about a haunted room. It was rumoured that a service of exorcism had taken here but this particular room has now become part of the Library and no longer appears to have any ghostly associations.

St John's College. The ghost of Archbishop Laud is said to roll his head across the floor of the Library of the College where he was educated and elected Chancellor of the University of Oxford. Three years later he was made Archbishop of Canterbury but in another seven years he was

impeached for high treason by the Long Parliament, and was executed at the Tower of London in 1645.
Randolph Hotel, Oxford, Oxon.

Pencaitland, EAST LOTHIAN, SCOTLAND.

Fountainhall House or Penkaet Castle, one of the most interesting mansions in Southern Scotland, is haunted by the ghost of King Charles I, by the ghost of John Cockburn, an owner of the property centuries ago and an alleged murderer; and by the ghost of Alexander Hamilton, a beggar, who was hanged.

The sixteenth-century house is full of interest. Its treasures include a crusader's helmet, a Spanish treasure chest and part of the chair used by Mary, Queen of Scotland, when she abdicated her throne. The late Professor Holbourn acquired the property in 1923 and I am indebted to his widow, Mrs M. C. S. Holbourn for details of the local apparently paranormal activity.

The picturesque rubble-built structure with its forestair leading from the courtyard and an interesting circular tower, was at one time owned by Sir Andrew Dick Lauder. He is reported to have been terrified there as a child when he saw an apparition near one of the fireplaces in an upper room.

The manifestations associated with King Charles I seem to have begun when a four-poster bedstead that was once occupied by the king (and bears a reproduction of his death-mask) was moved into the house after being presented to Professor Holbourn by his students.

In 1924 a relative took a visitor to see the room and found the bedclothes disarranged as if the bed had been slept in although Mrs Anderson who was responsible for keeping the room tidy insisted that she had personally left the room, including the bed, perfectly tidy. Shortly afterwards another visitor, looking into the room for the purpose of taking a photograph of the historic bedstead, also found that the bed seemed to have been slept in. He found that the photograph he eventually took was under-exposed and returned to take another. Once again the bedclothes on this haunted bed were found in a disarranged condition. On this occasion Mrs Anderson, after making the bed, had taken the precaution of locking the two doors giving access to the room and making sure that the windows were secured; in addition, two bricks were placed against the main door. Next day the bricks were found to have been moved and although the doors were still locked and the windows closed, the bedclothes were disturbed yet again.

When a party of students spent a week-end at Penkaet rehearsing a play, all except one were awakened during the early hours of the morning by strange sounds. Two of them sleeping in the room containing the four-poster, noticed what they described as 'a ghastly stain' on the wall while the weird noises were going on. But in the morning, when all was quiet, they could discover no trace of the mysterious stain.

Miss Avis Dolphin, a survivor of the *Lusitania* disaster, lived at Penkaet Castle for some years with the Holbourns. One night in 1925, while occupying the King Charles Room, she came to Professor and Mrs Holbourn's bedroom, which was situated directly below, to say that someone was moving about downstairs. Professor Holbourn got up, but by the time they got downstairs all was quiet. However, as they were returning upstairs, they both heard, as they reached the first floor, unmistakable creaking noises, as of a person tossing and turning in the King Charles bed so recently vacated by Miss Dolphin. On another occasion Miss Dolphin felt a light touch on her neck as she climbed upstairs in the dark. She described it as if someone drew the tip of one finger across her throat. About the same period (and certainly in the same year) Mrs Holbourn saw a faint shining light in several of the passages which she was never able to account for.

In 1935 an elderly lady was recovering from an illness at Penkaet and occupying the King Charles bed. Mrs Holbourn's brother was using the bedroom directly below at that time and one morning he awakened Mrs Holbourn to say that, judging by the sounds he had heard, the old lady must have fallen out of bed and was knocking for help. On reaching the room Mrs Holbourn found her friend sleeping soundly.

Sounds of heavy footsteps were frequently heard echoing

179

through the house, together with the noise of heavy furniture being moved about, right from the day the Holbourns moved in. The following year when friends occupied the house while Professor and Mrs Holbourn were visiting the Island of Foula, they complained of loud shrieks and groans heard at night. The doors which were always securely closed at night, were often found open in the morning; some had been locked quite securely. One girl refused to sleep in the house after one night.

After a time the noises and disturbances became less violent and whenever a continuous rattling or tapping was heard, one of the Holbourns would call out: 'Now John, that's childish. Stop it.' The noise usually ceased! Such a well-behaved ghost as John Cockburn soon became known as 'the perfect gentleman'; but some of the other disturbances were not so easily stopped.

One Christmas Eve the family and guests, after singing carols, were gathered around the fire in the music room. Everyone present watched amazed as a piece of oak, carved with the family crest, emerged from its place on the wall, paused for a moment and then returned to its normal position.

Since then a number of objects have moved apparently of their own volition, including large and heavy furniture. Once an antique cabinet, too heavy to be moved by one person, was found shifted right away from its usual place. A brass ewer and basin, brought by Mrs Holbourn's grandfather from Turkey, were placed on top of a cabinet, the ewer on its side. A bath was filled when nobody turned the tap on or off; a strange piece of soap unaccountably appeared in the bathroom; a glass case containing a model of the castle cracked and broke in several places when nobody was near it; clocks and watches stopped when placed near a certain wall—and there was the still unexplained apparition of a small man dressed in a cloak. He was seen by Mrs Holbourn's daughter-in-law to emerge from a cupboard and walk the whole length of one room before disappearing into a solid wall.

Many years ago a local beggar who dealt in wizardry called at Penkaet but received a brusque welcome from the lady of the house who chanced to open the door, which was soon shut in his face. In revenge the spiteful Hamilton resorted to witchcraft and, returning to Penkaet at dead of night, bound the bars of the gate 'with murderous intent'. Two days later the lady of the house, Lady Ormiston and her eldest daughter were dead, struck down by a mysterious illness. But Hamilton did not escape; he was brought to trial and after confessing to being responsible for the two deaths and other felonies, he was hanged on Edinburgh Castle Hill. On certain nights of the year his ghost is said to return to Penkaet to repeat his wicked deed but happily it no longer has any effect.

George Hotel, High Street, Haddington, East Lothian, Scotland.

*Penrith, CUMBERLANDSHIRE.

Just outside Penrith stands Eden Hall, the home of the Musgrave family since the reign of King Henry VI. It is the scene not of a ghost but of a legend, perhaps the most famous of all family legends: the 'Luck of Eden Hall'. The grand house owes its name to the river flowing through the park and is renowned for its lovely gardens as much as for the present, rebuilt structure.

The 'Luck' is said to have come into the possession of the family before history was written, in those magical days when 'fairies were common and were seen by everyone'. The story goes that in those far off times a butler at Eden Hall went to draw water from St Cuthbert's Well, near the house and came upon a company of fairies holding a revel around a curiously designed and painted glass. The butler snatched it up whereupon the fairies tried to wrestle it away from him but realizing that the mortal was more than a match for them, eventually withdrew, leaving him with the glass and vanishing, after warning him: 'If that glass either break or fall, Farewell the Luck of Eden Hall.'

The glass, six inches tall, is a beautiful example of enamelled and engraved glassware, of a yellowish-green colour, patterned in an almost Moorish style in blue and white enamel, heightened with red and gold. It is perhaps rather large for fairies and the more sceptical experts who

have examined it consider that it may have once been used as a chalice and probably came from Spain. When I last heard the 'Luck' was securely locked away in a strong room at the Hall, with the key deposited at the Bank of England.
Edenhall Hotel, Penrith, Cumb.

Penzance, CORNWALL.

'The Dolphin Inn' stands on the waterfront and was the headquarters of Sir John Hawkins in 1588 when he was enlisting Cornishmen to fight the Spanish Armada. Judge Jeffreys is reputed to have held court here in what is now the dining room. The prisoners were kept in the cellars, where the old kitchen range and lavatory remain to this day. More concrete proof was found a few years ago during repairs, that the inn had been used by smugglers. In the old days Penzance was the first call for ships coming from the Americas and it is thought that tobacco was first smoked in England at this tavern and that potatoes were first eaten here. Some years ago, during the course of redecorating one of the bedrooms, a door was discovered that led to a small secret closet in the roof; this, too, had probably been used by smugglers, either as a hiding-place or to secrete their contraband.

As befits such an historic building, the inn has a ghost: an old sea captain dressed in laced ruffles and a three-cornered hat, who died here. I learned when I was here in 1969 that he has not been seen in recent years but his footsteps have been heard. Both the landlord and his wife will tell you that they have heard a heavy and measured tread across the ceiling. It always comes from the direction of the upper part of the tavern and passes over the bar towards the back part of the building. The sounds never return. Once a visitor heard the footsteps and drew the attention of the landlord's wife to them, saying that he thought he was the only visitor staying at the inn at that time. He was told that he was the 'only human visitor'.
Rose Hill Private Hotel, Marazion, Penzance, Cornwall.

Peterborough, NORTHAMPTONSHIRE.

Nearby Woodcroft Manor was the scene of bitter fighting during the Civil War when Dr Michael Hudson, a King's Chaplain, took off his clerical clothes and dressed as a soldier to collect about him a band of determined men who succeeded in harassing Cromwell's troops on many occasions. At length they met an overwhelming contingent of the Protector's army and were forced to retreat to Woodcroft Manor, hotly pursued by the Roundheads. Fighting gallantly and bravely against hopeless odds, they were forced to draw back one by one through the rooms of the manor, then up the staircase and eventually out on to the roof. Each man gave his life dearly but it was all to no avail and soon Hudson was the only defender capable of putting up a fight. This he did, until he was driven back against a parapet and then over it. His sword dropped into the moat below while Hudson clung to the edge of the parapet. Still he refused to surrender; an officer cut off his fingers and with a cry he fell to his death into the night and the inky moat below. And still on summer nights, they say, the clash of steel is heard and the cries of 'Mercy! Mercy!'; perhaps the last words of the defenceless chaplain that have become impressed forever upon the atmosphere.
Great Northern Hotel, Peterborough.

Pevensey Bay, SUSSEX.

The fourteenth-century Old Mint House has a small bedroom, long reputed to be haunted by a girl in sixteenth-century costume who died there.

Although the house was built in 1342, the interior was much altered by Dr Andrew Borde, Court Physician to King Henry VIII, in 1542. Today the twenty-eight roomed mansion is full of interesting nooks and crannies and next to the Oak Room is the smallest room of all, the Haunted Chamber.

Many people claim to have seen the spectre of the girl who died in agony in this room. A few years ago the owner told me that his father had seen her and so did a local clergyman. I heard about a man who volunteered to spend a night in the room which has only one door and a single small window. He was disturbed during the night by a metallic sound which seemed to come from the direction of the little window. When he looked, he saw a face pressed against the outside of the diamond-paned glass. As he involuntarily cried out, something passed through the wall into the room and stood by his bed. He could distinctly see the figure of a young woman in an old-fashioned close-fitting bodice with tight sleeves and a dress that was very full at the hips, with a small ruff around the neck. After a moment the apparition moved back towards the window and the 'ghost hunter' took the opportunity of dashing out of the room! When he returned with witnesses the figure had vanished but he did establish that the window had not been tampered with and some threads that he had fastened across were still intact.

In 1586 the Mint House was rented by Thomas Dight, a London merchant. Here he installed his young mistress. One evening he visited the house unexpectedly and surprised the girl in the arms of a strange man whereupon Dight, in jealous fury, had his young mistress's lying tongue cut out. He then had the young people carried to what had been the minting chamber where, at his command, his servants bound the girl, forcing her to watch as they suspended her naked lover in chains from the ceiling and built a fire on the stone floor beneath him. There she had to witness the unfortunate man's slow torture by heat and smoke until death put an end to his agonies. At night the body was carried down to the town bridge and cast over the parapet to be carried out to sea; and the girl, still tied hand and foot, was thrust into that little room and left without food or light to die a lonely and painful death. Afterwards her body was buried nearby. The crime may never have been revealed had not Thomas Dight recounted the whole story to friends in a confession he made shortly before he died in 1601.

The ruins of nearby Pevensey Castle, the last stronghold of the Britons after the Roman legions had been withdrawn and the scene of the first battle of the Norman Conquest— for William the Conqueror landed in Pevensey Bay in 1066 —are reputed to be haunted by several military ghosts. The eerie sounds of fighting have been heard at night in the

vicinity of the ancient walls; it is said that on occasions an endless procession winds its way across the marshes from the sea to the castle. Armour and weapons glint in the moonlight, although no sound is heard, as the ghostly army, led by William Rufus, who once fruitlessly attacked the old castle for six days, silently disappears into the moat. There is a story, too, of the ghostly Lady Jane Pelham walking on the castle walls at night. She successfully defended the castle in the fourteenth century against an army of Kent, Surrey and Sussex men, while her husband was away in Yorkshire.
Granville Hotel, Bexhill-on-Sea, Sussex.

Pluckley, ASHFORD, KENT—KNOWN AS THE MOST HAUNTED VILLAGE IN KENT.

There is a haunting associated with the church of St Nicholas that involves the beautiful Lady Dering who died several hundred years ago. Her husband, wishing to preserve her loveliness, decreed that she should be attired in a rich gown with a red rose on her breast. Her body was placed in an airtight lead coffin; this coffin was encased in a second and a third, both of lead. The three coffins were then enclosed in an oaken one and the quadruple casket buried in the Dering vault, below the Dering Chapel in the south-east part of the church. In spite of all these encumbrances, Lady Dering is said to walk in the churchyard on certain nights, resplendent in her finery and the red rose at her breast. The story was for a long time a closely guarded secret and there have been suggestions that she may have been as wicked as she was beautiful.

Unexplained lights have been reported in the upper half of the stained glass window by the Dering Chapel; a woman's voice has been heard in the churchyard and peculiar knocking noises echo in the Dering Chapel at night-time.

The ruins of Surrenden Dering are said to be haunted by a White Lady, another former Lady Dering. Still another member of this 'haunting' family is referred to as the Red Lady, a sad, wistful figure who walks in the churchyard searching for the baby she lost.

The mellow house named Greystones has a ghostly monk;

while Rose Court is haunted by a former owner whose voice has been heard calling her dogs, as she called them so often during her lifetime. The old mill is said to be haunted by a former miller who walks when the moon is full, searching for his lost love. Opposite 'The Black Horse' is a lane where a schoolmaster once hanged himself and his ghostly form has been seen swinging from one of the overhanging trees. The ghost of a gipsy, huddled in a shawl and smoking a pipe, has been glimpsed by people taking a late walk on autumn nights near the crossroads by the little stone bridge. Nearby you can see the remains of a hollow oak tree where a highwayman met his death; he was cornered here and a sword was run through him, pinning him to this very tree. Occasionally, it is said, the whole grisly episode is re-enacted but without a sound disturbing the moonlit night.

Among other local ghosts are the phantom coach-and-horses which are said to clatter through the village on certain nights; the figure of a soldier that walks through Park Wood; a man who fell to his death at the brickworks near the station and still screams; and finally the unidentified figure of a woman in the church, in modern dress.

The George Hotel, High Street, Ashford, Kent.

Poling, NEAR FELPHAM, SUSSEX: ST JOHN'S PRIORY.

A substantial part of the ancient Commandery of the Knights Hospitallers of St John of Jerusalem are incorporated in this old house and there is said to be a vault outside the chapel walls which contains the tombs of some twelfth-century knights. On three occasions six people have heard the unexplained sounds of chanting here. Many residents of the house have frequently reported hearing ghostly music and voices, sometimes growing louder as if a procession were approaching. One authority verified the chanting as ancient Gregorian music used at funeral services. A visitor had just entered the house when he heard the chant of men's voices; he closed the door, listened for a moment and then the sounds died away. He described the experience as the most surprising and ghostly one of his life.

Norfolk Arms Hotel, Arundel, Sussex.

Poole, DORSET.

The 'Crown Hotel' in Market Street was reported to be the scene of strange happenings not long ago. They included a single note played on a piano by an invisible hand and the sound of a body being dragged across the floor.

Two young men who heard the piano 'playing' in an up-stairs stable, went to investigate and found the room empty. Later a 'fluorescent mist' was said to have drifted down the staircase, floated across the courtyard and out of the hotel entrance. The 'mist' was described as about the size of a child's head.

An Australian, staying at the hotel, decided to prove that the story was the result of imagination and painted five crosses on the door of the haunted room, closed the door, bolted it and went down to the courtyard to watch. To his horror the door opened of its own accord as he watched.

Landlord Alan Brown said that most of the mysterious noises started when the stable room was altered, although there had been unexplained sounds in the past from this part of the house, including one which sounded as though a body were being dragged across the top floor.

The Crown Hotel, Market Street, Poole, Dorset.

Potter Heigham, NORFOLK.

The famous old three-arched bridge here, known to thous-ands of yachtsmen and sailors who frequent the Broads, has long been reputed to be haunted by a striking and recurring manifestation.

The story goes back to the eighteenth century when Sir Godfrey Haslitt married the beautiful Lady Evelyn Carew, on May 31st, 1742, in Norwich Cathedral. But the wedding had been brought about, so goes the legend, by the bride's contract with the devil who demanded his price immediately after the wedding; on the stroke of midnight the bride was seized at the hall and carried, struggling and screaming, to a waiting coach with four coal-black horses stamping and snort-ing in the night air. Taking the terrified girl with them, the occupants of the coach, who looked like skeletons, tore down the drive and raced away down the road towards Potter Heigham.

Few people were abroad but those who were saw a luminous coach dash past, swaying from side to side, its wheels glowing with phosphorescence and sparks flying from them as they sped over the road, driven by a skeleton. Arriving at Potter Heigham bridge the coach swung across the narrow roadway, smashed against the wall of the bridge in the centre, broke into a thousand pieces and was flung, coach, horses, occupants and all, over the parapet and into the River Thurne below.

And each midnight of May 31st, it is said, the phantom coach repeats its fatal journey. Well-known yachtsman Charles Sampson told me that he saw the arresting spectacle in 1930 with two friends and that he knew two other people who had seen it. When I was there a few years ago, I located several local inhabitants who said they knew people who had seen the phantom coach but I was unable to trace any first-hand witnesses.

Central Hotel, St Georges Road, Great Yarmouth, Norfolk.

Raynham, NORFOLK.

Raynham Hall is the home of the famous 'Brown Lady' ghost.

Captain Marryat, the novelist, saw the ghost when he stayed at the house, occupying the room where a portrait of the Brown Lady hangs on the wall. Her identity is unknown. It was while he was walking along the corridor towards his room one evening that Captain Marryat saw the apparition. The Brown Lady grinned at him in a 'diabolical manner'. As he happened to be carrying pistols, he discharged one straight at the figure, at point-blank range, hoping to prove whether it was a ghost he saw or someone playing a trick. The figure disappeared immediately and the bullet, which he always swore passed through the figure, was found embedded in a door behind where she had appeared.

In November, 1926 Lady Townshend, staying at Raynham Hall, the seat of the Townshend family, stated that her son and a friend met the Brown Lady on a staircase; later when they saw the portrait, they both declared that this was the woman they had met, although they had never heard the ghost story.

The late Marchioness of Townshend told my friend Dennis Bardens that she had seen the Brown Lady several times and in his *Ghosts and Hauntings* he recounts the story of Colonel Loftus and a man named Hawkins who saw the figure of a woman in period dress in an upstairs corridor. Later she was seen again by the Colonel, this time face to face. He described an aristocratic-looking lady, dressed in brocade, her hair in a coif and her features lit by an unearthly light —and empty eye-sockets where her eyes should have been!

In 1936 two photographers took a series of photographs of the interior of Raynham Hall for *Country Life*. One of them, Captain Provand, had taken one shot of the ancient staircase, down which the ghost is said to have walked and was preparing to take another, when his assistant, Mr Indra Shira, remarked that he could see a shadowy form on the stairs. As the form glided down the stairs towards the photographers, another exposure was taken and when the photograph was developed, the shadowy form of a hooded female figure was discernible. The original photograph is in the *Country Life* photographic library and experts who have examined it and the plate are satisfied that there was no trickery.

Victoria Hotel, Holkham, Norfolk.

Reading, BERKSHIRE.

A four-roomed house in Oxford Road was reported to harbour the hazy figure of a grey-haired old lady a few years ago. The occupants, Mr and Mrs Edgar Morley and their son and two daughters, then aged seventeen, eleven and nine respectively, had only been at the house a week when Mrs Morley saw the figure in the kitchen. After a few minutes it vanished as she watched. She told her husband of her experience and they both laughed about it, until she saw the same figure shortly afterwards; and subsequently no less than ten times during the following three months.

Alan Morley also saw the figure and Mr Morley, a down-to-earth traffic warden, sensed rather than saw the form, while the two younger children became so frightened that they slept on a mattress in the living room.

A previous occupant of the house, elderly Mrs Davies, died here in 1961 and her description seems to fit exactly that of the ghost. Always just before it was seen or sensed there was an overwhelming scent of flowers which vanished after the ghost disappeared.

Great Western Hotel, Reading, Berks.

*Reading, BERKSHIRE.

The Roebuck Hotel, on the Thames, is haunted by mysterious footsteps which pace the corridors late at night, by unexplained hammering on doors, by disarrangement of furniture and by opening locked doors and windows. Mr Alex Wolfenden, the landlord, said in February, 1966, 'the house is definitely haunted. Nobody has actually seen a ghost but there have been some very strange things happening, particularly in the Admiral's Room, which is never occupied, and I certainly wouldn't sleep there myself.' The Admiral, after whom the room is named, died at the Roebuck over two hundred years ago in obscure circumstances, possibly being burned to death. There were four rooms in the oldest part of the ancient oak-beamed hotel that were permanently unoccupied because the landlord thought guests would be frightened by things that happen there.

The Roebuck Hotel, Reading, Berks.

*Richmond, SURREY.

The old Palace of Richmond was long said to be the scene of scandalous happenings, some concerning Queen Elizabeth I, who died here on March 24th, 1603 after having lain in a stupor for days on the point of death.

A persistent and curious story was current at the time to the effect that the ghostly figure of the great queen was repeatedly seen pacing the rooms of the palace while she was still alive but unconscious. Years later there were stories of the old gatehouse, one of the few surviving remnants of the palace, being haunted.

It was from a window over the gatehouse that the Queen's ring was thrown, after she died, to a waiting horseman, who sped the news to Scotland that James I was King of England and the reign of the Stuarts had begun.

Richmond Hill Hotel, Richmond Hill, Richmond, Surrey.

Ringcroft, GALLOWAY, SCOTLAND.

Commonly known as the Ringcroft Disturbances or the Ringcroft Poltergeist, these allegedly paranormal happenings took place in 1695. They are thoroughly attested and authenticated in a nineteen-page report published at the time and signed by the ministers of five neighbouring parishes, by the lairds of Colline and Milhouse and by other persons of repute who were eye-witnesses of the remarkable events.

There were a number of young children in the Ringcroft household of Andrew Mackie but all of them seem to have been under observation at the time of the occurrence of important phenomena. The disturbances began in February although the house had long had the reputation of being haunted. The first inexplicable incidents took place at night and outside the house when Mackie discovered that all his cattle had been let out from their sheds and their tethering ropes were broken. The same thing happened the following night when one of the beasts was found tied to an overhead beam so that its feet scarcely touched the ground.

A great quantity' of peat was then found to have been brought into the house. For several days stones were thrown all over the place—but never on a Sunday and mostly at night, although sometimes in daylight, too. A blanket and stool were combined into a shape resembling a sitting person; pot hooks and hangers disappeared and were found days later in a place that had already been searched. After an interval there was more stone-throwing and it was noticed that the stones seemed only about half their normal weight; they were now appearing more frequently—and on Sundays, too—and more especially when members of the household were at prayer.

A month after the disturbances commenced, they ceased abruptly and the family thought that their troubles were over. But 'it' returned 'more violent than ever' after seven days of peace. Stones were again thrown and more often and they seemed to be heavier for 'they hurt more when they hit'; a staff was wielded invisibly and hit witnesses several times on the shoulders and sides. People in bed were disturbed; knockings sounded on doors and furniture and things became so bad that some of the occupants were driven out of the house. Mackie himself was hit on the forehead, pushed at the shoulders and felt something like nails scratch the skin of his head. Sometimes too, people were dragged along by their clothes, including the local miller who cried out for help. The same night the children had their bed-clothes removed and they were beaten about the hips, the sound of the beatings being distinctly heard by other occupants of the house and sounding as though done by a man's hand. At the same time various objects were seen by many witnesses to move about the house of their own accord.

A voice saying 'Hush! Hush!' was now heard at the end of each sentence when the family were at prayers. Each time the dog, hearing the unfamiliar voice, would bark and run to the door. Sometimes whistles and groans were heard; fires were started, lumps of burning peat being thrown at the family while they were at prayer and 'fire-balls' fell in and about the house but fortunately they vanished as soon as they fell. Very hot stones were found in the children's beds and they were still too hot to handle nearly two hours later.

The local magistrate arranged for the examination of every person who had ever lived in the house built twenty-eight years before. During these enquiries some human bones were found buried just outside the building, giving rise to the suggestion that a murder had been committed in the house and the body buried outside. It was thought that the uneasy spirit of the victim might be the cause of all the trouble. A test, often used in witchcraft trials, where suspects were made to touch the bones, achieved no result and the next day five local ministers attempted to lay the ghost with a service of exorcism. But no sooner had they started when stones were thrown, apparently from nowhere, not only at the ministers at prayer, but all over the house. Some

Sherrington Manor, Selmeston, Sussex, where the family have no fear of their brown-clad, unidentified ghost that haunts the wide staircase.

The house near Gravesend, Kent, that used to be known as Southfleet Rectory, where a brown nun-like figure was seen for over sixty years; a figure that visitors often mistook for a nurse. *Photo: Chris Underwood*

Spinney Abbey, Wicken, Cambridgeshire, former home of Oliver Cromwell's son Henry, where there are ghostly singing monks, a mysterious hooded figure and phantom footsteps.

Sixteenth-century Thorington Hall, Stoke-by-Nayland, Suffolk, has a haunted attic and a ghost of a girl in a yellow dress. *Photo: Chris Underwood*

of the witnesses were levitated by something gripping their feet: the five ministers all attested to this phenomenon.

During the days that followed more stones and other objects were thrown about the house; children were pulled out of bed; sheep were tied together; furniture was set on fire; whistles and groans were heard; the house itself was set on fire seven times in one day; and a 'black thing' without shape but like a cloud was first seen in a corner. It increased in size so that it seemed to fill the whole house.

Next day, May 1st, 1695, the disturbances ceased as mysteriously as they had begun.

Hamilton Arms Hotel, Girvan, Ayrshire, Scotland.

Rochester Castle, ROCHESTER, KENT.

For nearly a thousand years the Norman castle keep of this impressive ruin defied the ravages of time, and of battles. Designed by Gundulf the Good it was built in 1098 and has seen many stirring times. On Good Friday in the year 1264, Simon de Montfort, Earl of Leicester, besieged the castle which was defended by Ralph de Capo, a crusader. Inside with de Capo was his betrothed, the lovely Lady Blanche de Warrene. Among the men under Simon de Montfort was one Gilbert de Clare, a knight and a rejected suitor of the Lady Blanche. When the siege was raised, de Capo left the castle to pursue the retreating rebels and de Clare, seizing his opportunity, disguised himself in a suit of armour resembling that worn by de Capo and entered the castle. Inside he sought out Lady Blanche high up on the southern battlement, watching the flight of the insurgents. Looking back at the castle de Capo saw his lady struggling in the hands of a man he knew must be an enemy. Being a renowned archer, he seized a bow and arrow from one of his men and sent an arrow speeding towards the stranger molesting his beloved. The arrow sped true to its mark but glanced off the armour de Clare was wearing and pierced the breast of the Lady Blanche, mortally wounding her.

That same night, according to reports, her ghost walked the battlements in a white robe, her raven hair streaming in the breeze, the fatal arrow still embedded in her bosom and on the anniversary of the tragedy she is still said to haunt the battlements of the old castle, bewailing the sad fate of having been killed by her lover. I traced two people who claimed to have seen her on different occasions.

A variation of this story tells of de Clare pursuing the Lady Blanche around the battlements and of her hiding within the round tower where she was found by her old suitor. According to this tale it was here that de Capo spotted him and shot the fatal arrow. Yet another version suggests that rather than risk capture, she threw herself off the top of the round tower and so met her death by suicide. At all events, there seems little doubt that she died a violent death and it seems difficult to dismiss all the odd happenings at Rochester Castle, including unexplained footsteps in this part of the ruin, as figments of the imagination.

The Old Burial Ground of St Nicholas, in the former moat of Rochester Castle, is reputed to be haunted by a white bearded figure. This is the churchyard where Charles Dickens wished to be buried and he may have been laid to rest here, the spot he loved best in his beloved Rochester, had not the burial ground been out of use at the time of his death and had not the nation thought to honour him by burial in Westminster Abbey. Yet perhaps the great novelist had his way in the end, for there are many reports of a spectre seen here at night; a spectre that takes the form of an elderly man with a beard, slowly and lovingly wandering among the tombs of long-forgotten men and women who dwelt at Rochester.

There is a story, too, that at Christmas time, when the 'moon-faced clock' over the Corn Exchange strikes midnight, the ghost of Dickens returns to this spot which he immortalized in *The Mystery of Edwin Drood*. Reports of this apparition began to circulate within a few years of Dickens's death in June, 1870.

King's Head Hotel, Rochester, Kent.

St Albans, HERTFORDSHIRE.

Battlefield House in Chequer Street, an Elizabethan half-timbered building with a modern shop front, has foundations of a very early building made from flint and stone, similar to that used for the wonderful Abbey nearby. It was probably one of the buildings belonging to the Abbey at one time. Here noises resembling galloping horses and the clash of armour are alleged to have been repeatedly heard over the years. It is interesting to recall that the house stands on the reputed site of the Battle of St Albans, one of the fierce encounters of the Wars of the Roses.

A previous occupant found the house a friendly one, free from ghosts and ghostly phenomena, but he frequently had the feeling that he was being watched. Although he instinctively looked round to see who it was, there was never anybody present. On the other hand, when he had guests in the house, they would often complain of feeling unhappy in the house and of noticing a brooding eeriness about the place. There seems to be good evidence that over the years unaccountable noises resembling the clash of weapons on armour, galloping horses and the chanting of monks, have been heard here.

St Albans is named after a Roman soldier convert who suffered martyrdom here in the year 303, the first Christian martyr in England.

Nearby Salisbury Hall, an old moated manor house was built in the seventeenth century and purchased secretly by King Charles II for Nell Gwynne, whose ghost is one of the visitors from the past to this historic house. Beneath the black and white floor in the hall, there is a Tudor floor of bricks and beneath that again, a floor of stones even older; what lies beneath *that*, nobody yet knows. It does not seem unreasonable to think that on this site there has been a building of one sort or another for many centuries.

During the Civil War Salisbury Hall was used by King Charles I as headquarters and armoury; in 1668 King Charles II found another use for it. That year he had started his affair with orange-seller Nell Gwynne, an association that lasted until the King's death sixteen years later. It was for Nell he purchased Salisbury Hall. Today you can still see the little oak-beamed cottage overlooking the moat, a property known as Nell Gwynne's Cottage, where one of the intimate and moving incidents of history is reputed to have taken place. It is said that Nell, concerned for the future of one of her children by Charles, after he had refused the boy a title, held the child out of the window of the cottage, dangling him over the moat and threatening to drop him, until Charles called out: 'Pray, spare the Duke of St Albans!'

The ghost of pretty Nell has been seen at the Hall, both on the staircase and in the panelled hall by, among others, Sir Winston Churchill's step-father, George Cornwallis-West. He told of seeing the young and beautiful figure of a woman standing in the corner of the hall. She looked intently at him, and then turned and vanished into the adjoining passage; he followed at once but could find no trace of the 'lovely girl'. Weeks later he was looking at prints of Nell Gwynne and realized how much she was like the figure he had observed. Cornwallis-West had always been very sceptical about ghosts—until he encountered Nell Gwynne at Salisbury Hall.

The present owners of the Hall, charming Mr and Mrs Walter Goldsmith, will tell you all about the ghosts there and some of the fascinating history of the beautiful house and gardens. The Edwardian era gave the Hall a revival of its great days, for Lady Randolph Churchill had married George Cornwallis-West. They had bought the properly and the society of the day came to the house: Dame Nellie Melba, Italian actress Eleonora Duse, King Edward VII himself. To write his speeches in the garden, young Winston Churchill would also come to visit his mother and step-father.

Mrs Goldsmith told me in the haunted bedroom about the unmistakable footsteps she has heard in the passage outside her bedroom door. The passage where the sounds appear to originate now ends in a bathroom but once it led into the old Tudor wing of the house, destroyed in 1818. Thinking the footsteps must be those of her husband, Mrs Goldsmith waited for them to return, expecting him to look in on her—but they did *not* return. In the morning her husband told her that he had slept all night without stirring. Soon afterwards the Goldsmiths were visited by the daughter of Sir Nigel Gresley, who lived at Salisbury Hall for five years before the Second World War. She asked Mrs Goldsmith whether she had heard the ghostly footsteps and said they were always being troubled by strange footsteps in the night when they were there.

Mr Goldsmith told me he had found a reference in an old book on the house to a cavalier who had died unpleasantly at the Hall and whose ghost, complete with a sword sticking through him, used to be seen frequently.

The bedroom over the entrance hall is also haunted. Here children have been disturbed over the years by 'something' standing by their beds, not once but on many occasions. A governess, spending a night in the same room, saw 'something terrifying' come out of the wall near the fireplace and stand by the bed. She would never spend another night in the house.

In the top storey of the house there are four rooms, their ceilings sloped to the contours of the roof. In the smallest there is a secret chamber, made in the thickness of the wall and leading up among the rafters; a 'Priest's Hole' where a hunted fugitive could be hidden and fed. In one of these roof rooms there is said to have been a suicide. Altogether, Salisbury Hall is a fascinating place, a labyrinth of secret passages, sliding panels and hidden rooms but even on the brightest summer days the shadows somehow lengthen strangely in the mellow hall and one is glad to walk in the peaceful gardens.

The Noke Hotel, St Albans, Herts.

St Ives, CORNWALL.

A recently built house here was haunted by the sound of footsteps made by high-heeled shoes. They used to pass along one particular passage, halt outside one particular door and after a moment a loud knock would sound, apparently from the direction of the door. The footsteps never receded, there never was a second knock, nor did the door ever open though perhaps other doors in the house did. At all events, there were the sounds of doors opening and closing at other times and occasionally, the sounds of footsteps heard mounting the stairs but these were never heard descending.

According to local tradition, phantom bells have long been heard in the vicinity of the famous bay. They sound way out at sea and never seem to have an explanation unless it can

be the wind playing peculiar tricks with the sound of the heavy seas rolling in from the Atlantic.
Garrack Hotel, St. Ives, Cornwall.

Saltwood, NEAR HYTHE, KENT.

Mysterious lights and a strange figure were seen in the densely wooded area around Saltwood a few years ago and there was much talk of ghosts and black magic in the village. Four teenagers, walking from Saltwood to Sandling Station, saw a ball of fire on the top of a hill about eighty feet away. Walking down a dip, they lost sight of it but when they continued up the opposite hill, a figure suddenly appeared on the road ahead, 'like a man in a red cloak carrying a lantern', one of them said. It shuffled up the hill and when it reached the railway bridge, disappeared. As they went down to the station they had to be careful not to slip on the frozen puddles, yet just outside the station, where the figure had vanished, it seemed quite warm.

A young man and his girl-friend were passing the football field at Brockhill School when they saw a strange light, a kind of glow, coming from behind some trees and lighting up the field. They could see a dark figure standing in the middle of the field. The light seemed brighter as they approached it and then, abruptly, it disappeared. The girl screamed and fainted.

There are a number of reports of a ghost being seen near Slaybrook Corner, the reputed scene of an ancient battle. The ghost may be that of William Tournay, a wealthy and eccentric landowner who died about sixty years ago and who is buried on an island in the middle of a nearby lake. According to other reports, the apparition is that of a Roman soldier.
Hotel Imperial, Hythe, Kent.

Sampford Peverell, NEAR TIVERTON, DEVON.

The scene of a classic ghost story, three years of poltergeist activity, recounted by the Rev. Caleb Colton in the *Narrative of the Sampford Ghost* (1810). The house affected was occupied by the servants and family of Mr John Chave. Here the apparition of a woman was seen by an earlier occupant who had also reported unexplained noises but these reports were discounted. A second series of disturbances began in April, 1810. The 'chambers of the house were filled, even in daytime, with thunderous noises and upon any persons stamping several times on the floors of the upstairs rooms, they would find themselves imitated—only much louder—by the mysterious agency!' There were a number of women servants and at night they were frequently beaten by invisible hands until they were black and blue. Mr Colton stated that he heard upwards of two hundred violent blows in one night delivered upon a bed, the sound resembling that of a strong man striking it with all his might, with clenched fists. One of the young servant girls, Ann Mills, received a black eye and a swelling as big as a turkey's egg on her cheek. Ann was among those who received blows from an invisible hand while in bed. Mrs Mary Dennis and young Mary Woodbury, two other servants, swore that they were beaten until they were numb and were sore for many days afterwards. The disturbances became so bad that the servants refused to use the room in which they were so severely handled whereupon Mr and Mrs Chave offered to share their own. Still, there was little peace: candles and candlesticks moved about the room of their own volition. Once Mr Chave narrowly missed being hit on the head when a large iron candlestick came hurtling at him in the dark. Colton relates how he 'often heard the curtains of the bed violently agitated, accompanied by a loud and almost indescribable motion of the rings. These curtains, four in number, were, to prevent their motion, often tied up, each in one large knot. Every curtain of that bed was agitated, and the knots thrown and whirled about with such rapidity that it would have been unpleasant to be within the sphere of their action. This lasted about two minutes and concluded with a noise resembling the tearing of linen, Mr Taylor and Mr Chave, of Mere, being also witnesses. Upon examination a rent was found across the grain of a strong new cotton curtain.'

Raps, knockings, rattling noises and a 'sound like that of a man's foot in a slipper coming downstairs and passing through a wall' were repeatedly experienced. Once, says Mr Colton, he was in the act of opening a door when there was a violent rapping on the opposite side of the same door. He paused and the rapping continued; suddenly he opened the door and peered out, candle in hand. There was nothing to see. Sometimes the noises were so violent in a room that he really thought that the walls and ceiling would collapse.

Among the independent witnesses for the Sampford ghost there is the Governor of the County Gaol, who came to see the strange happenings and brought with him a sword, which he placed at the foot of the bed, with a huge folio Bible on top of it. Both were flung through the air and dashed against the opposite wall, seven feet away. Mr Taylor, who was in the house at the time but not with the Gaol Governor, was roused by the shrieks coming from the room and when he entered he saw the sword, suspended in the air, pointing towards him. Within a moment it clattered to the floor.

Towards the end of the curious events at Sampford Peverell there were suggestions that the tenant, Mr John Chave, was faking the disturbances in order to purchase the property cheaply. When this rumour reached the people of the village and those of Tiverton, five miles away, public sympathy for the occupants of the house quickly melted away and on more than one occasion Mr Chave was very severely handled. The Rev. Caleb Colton rejected this explanation, stating that although the public were given to understand that the disturbances had ceased, in fact, as the immediate neighbourhood well knew, they continued 'with unabating influence'. Mr Chave had no intention of buying the property, said Mr Colton; indeed, he was making every effort to procure another home, on any terms. As if to confirm all this, the disturbances at length obliged the whole family to leave the house, at great loss and inconvenience. Mr Colton was criticized for his participation in the affair. It was not generally known that he offered £100 of the total of £250 to be paid to anyone who could give such information as might lead to a discovery of the answer to the mysterious events; the money was never claimed.

Years later it was discovered that the house had double walls, with a passage between, which could have consider-

ably assisted conscious trickery. There was also the possibility that the premises were used by smugglers who might have produced the weird noises for their own purpose—and, of course, many a parson was known to help the smugglers in days gone by.
Great Western Hotel, Exeter, Devon.

Sandringham, NORFOLK.

The great country house and estate, purchased by King Edward VII when Prince of Wales in 1862 and ever since a favourite royal retreat, has a ghost that usually gets up to its tricks during the Christmas holidays. There are repeated reports of 'hollow footsteps' being heard in deserted corridors in the servants quarters, of doors that open by themselves, and of lights that switch themselves on and off.

The disturbances usually begin on Christmas Eve and continue for several weeks. Among happenings for which there appear to be no explanation are Christmas cards which are found moved from one wall to another; bedclothes that are stripped off freshly-made beds and heavy breathing noises that seem to originate from a deserted room off the footmen's corridor on the second floor. A year or two ago things were so bad that housemaids refused to enter this room for cleaning and polishing unless someone else was also with them. One footman refused to sleep in the room assigned to him after he claimed to have seen something which he described as 'looking like a large paper sack breathing in and out like a grotesque lung'. He also heard heavy and regular breathing apparently emanate from the curious bulging object. King George V died here in 1936 and King George VI in 1952.
Feathers Hotel, Sandringham, Norfolk.

Sandwood Bay, Cape Wrath, SUTHERLAND, SCOTLAND.

This bleak and isolated beach on the extreme north-east tip of the mainland of Great Britain has long been reputed to be haunted and visitors to this desolate but beautiful district have brought back convincing stories of an apparition and strange happenings at the deserted cottages here.

One autumn afternoon a crofter and his son strayed into Sandwood Bay as they gathered firewood. The beach was utterly deserted as they collected the timber from long-forgotten wrecks, and they were about to set off home as evening drew on when suddenly their pony showed signs of fright and they became aware of a bearded sailor standing close to them. He was wearing sea-boots, a sailor's cap and a dark weather-stained tunic with brass buttons. The strange figure that had not been there a moment before shouted to them that the driftwood was his property and the crofter and his son promptly dropped the wood they had collected and fled.

One August afternoon the same figure was seen by a gillie and the fishing party he was accompanying: the squat figure of a sailor was first noticed close to a sandy knoll and then walking along the crest of a sand-dune before disappearing behind a hillock. Those who saw the figure particularly noticed the sailor's cap and the brass buttons on his tunic. Thinking that the man must be a poacher the gillie was sent off to find out what he could. He returned, white-faced and shaken, to report that he could find no one and there was no trace of any footprints in the sand at the spot where the figure had been seen.

Sandwood Cottage has stood here untenanted for many years, perhaps the most remote and solitary habitation in the whole of Scotland. A few years ago an old fisherman spent a night at the cottage and heard footsteps outside and a tapping at the window on the ground floor and when Angus Morrison looked towards the window he saw the face of a bearded sailor peering into the cottage. His visitor wore a peaked sailor's cap and a tunic with brass buttons, but when Angus opened the door and looked all round the cottage there was no one there. On another occasion he was awakened in the cottage by the sensation that he was being suffocated by a thick, black mass that seemed to be pressing down on him.

A local shepherd, Sandy Gunn, will tell you that he once spent a night at the same cottage and heard distinct but ghostly footsteps walking about the ground floor. He is quite satisfied that they were not caused by any human being or by an animal. It is thought that the footsteps may have some connection with a wealthy Australian who came here several times and seemed to fall completely under the spell of this fascinating spot before he died in Australia some years before the shepherd's experience.

More recently a couple of English visitors camped at Sandwood Cottage. During the night they were disturbed by fearful noises and the whole cottage seemed to vibrate with crashes and bangs that sounded like doors being flung open and slammed shut, windows being smashed and heavy, tramping footsteps, loud enough to have been made by a horse, that seemed to originate from the rooms over their heads. No explanation was ever discovered and these visitors told the local postmaster that nothing would ever persuade them to spend another night at Sandwood Cottage. *Garbet Hotel, Kinlochbervie, Sutherland, Scotland.*

Sarratt, NEAR RICKMANSWORTH, HERTFORDSHIRE.

Rose Hall was occupied during my childhood by my maternal grandparents and was the scene of the first ghost-story I ever heard.

The account of the brilliantly-coloured ghost which disturbed a visitor by leaning on the bottom of his bed is recounted by Catherine Crowe in her *Night Side of Nature*. Falling quickly asleep after a tiring journey, the visitor was first awakened by the barking of dogs and he heard his host in the adjoining bedroom, open his window and quieten them. He went to sleep again, but was soon awakened once more, this time by an extraordinary pressure upon his feet. By the light in the chimney-corner he saw the figure of a well-dressed man in the act of stooping and supporting himself on the bedstead. The figure wore a blue coat with bright gilt buttons, but the head was not visible because of the bed-curtains, looped back so that they just concealed that part of the person. Since in his haste to get to bed, the visitor had dropped his clothes at the foot of the bed, he thought at first that it must be his host come in to pick them up, which rather surprised him. But as he raised himself upright in bed and was about to enquire into the reason for the visit, the figure passed on and disappeared. Realizing that he had locked the door and becoming somewhat puzzled, the house-guest jumped out of bed and carefully searched the room. He found the doors locked on the inside as he had left them and yet he could discover no trace of his mysterious visitor. He noticed that the time was ten minutes after two and he returned to bed hoping for some rest but was unable to sleep again that night, lying till seven, puzzling his brain as to how his visitor could have entered and left the room.

In the morning, when his host and his wife asked how he slept, he mentioned first that he had been awakened by the barking of the dogs. His host told him that two strange dogs had found their way into the yard and he had called to his own animals. Then the visitor mentioned his curious experience fully expecting that this would be explained or laughed at, but to his surprise the story received great attention; he was told that there was a tradition of such a spectre haunting that room.

It seemed that many years before a gentleman so attired had been murdered in the room, under 'frightful circumstances', and his head cut off. From time to time people occupying the room claimed to see the brightly-coloured figure, but the head was never seen. As proof of the story the visitor was requested to prolong his visit to be introduced to the rector of the parish who would furnish him with such evidence as to leave no doubt in his mind but that the room was haunted. But the thought of another night in the room was too frightening and the traveller took his leave.

A short time afterwards he was dining with some ladies who came from Hertfordshire when he chanced to refer to his visit to Sarratt saying that while he was there he had met with a very extraordinary adventure which he was totally unable to explain. Thereupon one of the ladies immediately said that she hoped he had not had a visit from the headless gentleman in a blue coat and gilt buttons, who was said to have been seen by many people at that house.

Some years ago, after discovering that in the nineteenth century the ghost had been so troublesome that a prayer-meeting had been held at Rose Hall, convened for the express purpose of laying the ghost, I took the trouble to get in touch with the Secretary of the Hertfordshire Baptist Association, but he was unable to find any further information on the subject.

In 1962 I took a party of Ghost Club members to Sarratt and three of them had no difficulty in immediately locating the haunted room, although, as far as I know, nothing untoward has happened there for many years now.

The ancient little parish church of Sarratt stands a mile south of the village, on the site of a Roman cemetery. Local tradition explains the considerable distance between the village and the church by maintaining that it was found impossible to build the church in the vicinity of the village green some eight hundred years ago for each morning, after a start had been made, the stones and other materials would be found moved down the long hill a mile away. At length it was decided to bow to a possibly 'higher authority' and the church was erected in its present position. The west window is said to be older than Westminster Abbey.
Victoria Hotel, Rickmansworth, Herts.

Sawston, CAMBRIDGESHIRE.

Sawston Hall, a noble Tudor house, has been the ancestral home of the Huddleston family for over four hundred years. Yet no one, Captain Reginald Eyre-Huddleston told me, can sleep undisturbed in the haunted Tapestry Room.

In the magnificent Great Hall there is a portrait of Queen Mary Tudor. In 1553, before she became queen, she spent a night in the Tapestry Room. The scheming Duke of Northumberland sent a message asking her to go to London to see her ailing brother, King Edward VI, but not telling her that the King was already dead. Northumberland planned to imprison Mary and put his daughter-in-law, Lady Jane Grey, on the throne, to retain the power which he exercised over Edward VI. But a message reached Mary when she was at Hoddesdon warning her that Northumberland's message was a trap. She turned back to Sawston Hall, then the home of John Huddleston, a Papist, where she sought shelter for the night.

At dawn her rest in the Tapestry Room was disturbed, not by a ghost but by the arrival of a band of Northumberland's men. Hastily disguised as a milkmaid, Mary escaped in the nick of time with a few friends. At a safe distance from the house they reined in their horses and looked back at Sawston Hall: the house was in flames. Unable to find Mary, Northumberland's men had set the place alight. 'Let it burn,' Mary told her companions. 'When I am Queen, I will build Huddleston a finer house'—and she was as good as her word. Stones taken from Cambridge Castle produced the noble mansion completed in 1584, that still stands today.

The ghost of Queen Mary is said to have been seen in the house and grounds and Mrs Fuller, the Huddlestons' cook, told me that she had seen the ghost 'without the shadow of a doubt'.

'She did not speak but just drifted out of the room,' said Mrs Fuller who was born as the clock struck two. She is confident that only those born on the chime of the hour can see ghosts. 'I could never spend a night here by myself,' she added. 'I just couldn't.'

Mrs Huddleston, a grand-daughter of a former Duke of Norfolk, came here when she was first married in 1930; in those days she often heard the sound of a spinet being played when she stood at the bottom of the stairs, although at that time the only musical instrument in the house was an old harpsichord. She never had any fear of the ghostly music, although she knew it was of supernormal origin, for it was very lovely and not in the least frightening. Once too, a friend, staying at the Hall, asked about the same music that she heard and for which no explanation was ever discovered.

Major Anthony Eyre, the Captain's nephew and present owner of Sawston Hall, was at the house helping to prepare for the opening to the public a few years ago. Suddenly, while he was alone in the hall, waiting for the arrival of the young ladies who were to act as guides, he heard the unmistakable sound of girls' laughter floating down from the upper floor. An immediate search revealed nobody and it was not until some time later that the girls actually arrived. Sawston was closed to the public a couple of years ago when the ceiling of the Great Hall fell in.

Tom Corbett, the clairvoyant, spent a disturbed night in the Tapestry Room, waking each hour on the hour from four o'clock onwards, to hear someone or something fiddling with the latch of the bedroom door and footsteps prowling about the room. Traditionally, the room is haunted by a 'lady in grey' who knocks three times on the door which then opens to let the grey apparition float across the room. A former maid told her mistress that she had been in the room when the 'grey thing' passed her and she was so frightened that she ran out of the room and fell down some steps!

Father Martindale, spending a night in a room near to the Tapestry Room (which contains a canopied four-poster believed to be the actual bed in which Queen Mary slept), reported that someone rapped periodically at his bedroom door. Nothing could convince him that the sound was caused by a human being. An undergraduate, spending a night in the Tapestry Room, like Tom Corbett, found himself awakened by the sound of knocking on the door followed by someone fiddling with the latch—and then silence.
Blue Boar Hotel, Cambridge.

Sandford Orcas, NEAR SHERBORNE, DORSET.

The fine Tudor manor house here is haunted by the figure of a farmer who hanged himself from a trap-door which has since been boarded up.

Colonel Francis Claridge leased the house from the Medicott family. The Claridges became quite certain that strange things happened in the nursery wing of the house when in 1966, their daughter attempted to spend a night there but left, screaming and returned to her own room in the early hours. Although she had not seen anything, she had heard loud knocks on the door of her room and also a weird, dragging noise.

Mrs Claridge will tell you that she has several times glimpsed the white-smocked figure of the long-dead farmer 'flitting past the kitchen window between two-thirty and three-fifty-five p.m.' She has also seen, several times, an old lady in a red dress mounting a staircase in the house.

Mr and Mrs J. A. Allen, the former footman and housekeeper at the manor, were afraid to go upstairs on their own at night and thought that the stone carvings of apes above the porch 'laughed in the moonlight', while at the church across the road, 'chains and keys rattled and footsteps came running down the steps as though someone was being chased'. Mrs L. Gates of Taunton spent a night in the chilly little bedroom in the nursery wing and saw the ghost, 'at the foot of my bed, swaying and outlined against the bedroom window. He was in evening dress. His face appeared evil-looking. For what seemed quite a while, he stood there and then disappeared.'

Other disturbances include mysterious music which seems to originate from a harpsichord in an empty room; a curious haze of blue smoke appears in certain rooms; unexplained voices are heard from the inner courtyard or rear wing and footsteps pace deserted corridors. A family photograph taken by Mary Claridge in the garden shows a strange unidentified figure which appears to be wearing a white smock.

The B.B.C. went to Sandford Orcas and one of their camera team claimed to see the figure of the man which passed repeatedly the kitchen window. He appeared to be wearing a white milking smock and an old-fashioned type of farmer's hat. Local people told Colonel Claridge that a good many years ago the body of the tenant farmer at that time was found hanging in the house: he was wearing a white smock.

Half Moon Hotel, Sherborne, Dorset.

Scotney Castle, SEE *Lamberhurst*, KENT.

*Shepton Mallet, SOMERSETSHIRE.

The three-hundred-and-sixty-year-old prison, a notorious Army 'glasshouse' until 1966, is reputed to be haunted by a White Lady who was beheaded here in 1680.

In January 1967 there were reports of unaccountable bangings, the sounds of heavy breathing, the feeling that 'someone or something invisible was in one room', a chilling atmosphere that frightened those using the night duty room.

These reports of apparently inexplicable happenings became so numerous that the prison governor spent a night in the room himself and then sent a full report to the Home Office, stating: 'I was unable to find any satisfactory explanation for the happenings.' The governor asked chaplains Prebendary Leonard White and Father Ryan to speak to the worried staff and afterwards a senior warden said: 'Prebendary White told us to try to forget the incidents but it isn't easy when you've had this kind of experience. We were all scared stiff and nobody has yet come up with an explanation.'

Another officer reported an icy feeling on the back of his neck; the sensation that somebody was pushing from the other side when he was trying to lock a door, although in fact nobody was there; and having the unpleasant feeling of being pinned down by the neck. The paralysed feeling lasted throughout one night. This officer has not entered that particular room since. The attitude of the whole staff was summed up for me by one warden who stated: 'I wouldn't do another night in the duty room for £1,000.' Later the Home Office told me: 'All is now quiet there.'

Bowlish House Hotel, Coombe Lane, Shepton Mallet, Som.

Sherfield, NEAR BASINGSTOKE, HAMPSHIRE.

The owner of a fourteenth-century mill used to complain of a 'shadow' that came and stood beside him at night-time when he was stone-dressing. He said that the shadow was of a tall man with a long face and beard. He had the distinct impression that the presence was criticizing his methods of doing the work. He discovered that a man answering this description used to work at Lailey's Mill many years ago and that he was an expert stone-dresser.

Red Lion Hotel, Basingstoke, Hants.

Sherborne, DORSET.

Sir Walter Raleigh (1552-1618) lived for many years at the castle here, now a ruin. His ghost is said to walk round the old castle garden on Michaelmas Eve and to disappear in the arbour, by the tree known as Raleigh's Oak.

Half Moon Hotel, Sherborne, Dorset.

Selmeston, NEAR ALFRISTON, SUSSEX.

Years ago tall, grey-haired Cecil Chandless, Lord of the Manor, told me about the brown-clad figure that haunted his home, Sherrington Manor.

He saw the ghost several times on the staircase. One summer afternoon the family were at tea when they were surprised to hear the crunch of horses' hooves and the grind of carriage wheels which seemed to herald the arrival of a horse-drawn coach. Immediate investigation showed the drive to be deserted and nothing was ever discovered to account for the noises.

In 1963 I wrote to Mrs Chandless (her husband was then dead) to ask whether I could bring some members of The Ghost Club down to Sherrington following reports of more unexplained happenings there. Doors were said to open and close mysteriously; the swish of clothes and the tramp of heavy boots had been heard on the same staircase where Mr Chandless had seen the ghost figure, which he called 'Marmaduke'; and there were knocks and rattling noises which could not be explained.

We duly went to Sherrington Manor (and went again a few years later). We talked to Mrs Chandless and her daughter Marisa and other members of the family and household about the curious experiences that they all have had. They all fully accept the fact that they have unbidden guests and indeed would not be without them, for they feel that Sherrington is haunted by happy ghosts, as such a charming house should be.

Theresa, the Austrian maid, once heard the handle of the garden door rattle and she saw the handle turn but when she looked over the wall there was no one on the other side. She was so perturbed that she gave in her notice but Mrs Chandless persuaded her to stay and now Theresa too feels sure that the ghosts are friendly for they have never harmed or really frightened anyone.

The only unhappy element of the haunting has been outside in the lovely garden where, very occasionally, one has
the overwhelming feeling of being watched by 'someone
nasty'—particularly in a neglected corner of the ancient garden. It may be a kind of barrier of misery that dates back
to Saxon times.

Within the house odd things happen from time to time
and occasionally a ghost is seen, especially when someone
in the house is ill. Once such a person had a friendly visit
from an unknown female who leaned over her bed and
seemed to say, kindly: 'She's asleep.' Once, too, a whole
dinner party saw a figure, which certainly had no objective
reality, pass through the hall and mount the stairs.

When the family went to the New Forest during the last
war they believe that 'Marmaduke' followed them and fret-
ted to get back to Sherrington. They heard impatient knocks
and felt something invisible brush against them; they sensed
strongly that they were required to return to their Sussex
home. 'Now,' Mrs Chandless will tell you, 'none of us feels
that we could ever leave here again.'
Star Inn Hotel, Alfriston, Sussex.

Skerries, COUNTY DUBLIN, IRELAND.

A few miles inland, on a large estate, there is a field in the
centre of a plantation of trees which has not been cultivated since time immemorial. In its middle there is a large
depression covering an area of some forty-five square yards.

Legend has it that in the early days of Christianity in Ireland a holy woman called Saint Mevee and her followers had
a settlement here where many miracles were wrought. Years
later, after all traces of the original foundation had long
disappeared, the land was bought by a man who laughed at
the idea that the land was hallowed and began to plough it
up. But almost as soon as he had uttered the scornful
rhyme: 'Saint Mevee or Saint Mavoe, I'll plough this up
before I go' the ground opened and he was swallowed up
together with his horse and the plough, leaving a depression
in the field where the ground closed over them. From that

day the plot of ground has remained untilled and the depression remains to mock the unbeliever.
Shelbourne Hotel, Dublin, Ireland.

Slough, BUCKINGHAMSHIRE.

Upton Court, one of the oldest houses in the county, formerly owned by the Harewood family, has some interesting features, including a priest's hiding-place and leaded windows with quaint Flemish colourings. There is also the ghost of a woman in a bloodstained nightdress. The story of the apparition is very old and its origin is now lost, although there have been many people who claimed to have seen the singular figure in the past, usually wandering about the grounds on Friday nights.
Royal Hotel, Slough, Bucks.

Southfleet, NEAR GRAVESEND, KENT.

The former rectory at Southfleet was long reputed to be haunted by a female figure wearing a brown nun-like habit. I traced four independent witnesses for this ghost.

A former rector, the Rev. W. M. Falloon, gave me full details of the case when I went to see him on several occasions, evidence that the haunting and the appearance of the ghostly figure dates back nearly a hundred years. In the Monk's Room, where the apparition most frequently appeared, there is (or was) a stained-glass window commemorating the fact that in 1874 the Bishop of Rochester (the Rev. P. L. Claughton) visited the rectory to exorcize the ghost.

During the incumbency of the Rev. J. H. Hazel (from 1891 to 1898) several appearances of the ghost were reported. On one occasion three visitors apologized at breakfast one morning for coming to stay while there was sickness in the house. They said they had all been visited by a nurse during the night, whereupon they were told that there was no sickness in the house, and no nurse; nor had they been visited by any mortal person during the night. Mr Falloon, who saw the ghost in 1942, especially noticed several inches of white material showing at the cuffs of the figure's sleeves. This would probably account for anyone taking the figure for a nurse. The same figure, I was told, was also seen a number of times by members of the family and by visitors during the occupancy of the house by the Alcocks from 1908 to 1919.

Mrs Walcott Crockett, whose late husband, the Rev. A. W. Crockett, was Rector of Southfleet from 1920 to 1926 tells me that although they loved the old building there was certainly something strange about parts of it and she had no doubt that it was haunted. Her recollection of the origin of the haunting concerned a nurse who came to the rectory many years ago to care for a member of the family then in residence. The person who was ill, died and there was some dispute about the possession of important family documents in which the nurse was involved. Afterwards the ghostly figure of a nurse was reputed to haunt the house.

It is interesting to note that as well as being seen, sometimes as a complete ghostly figure and sometimes only partially visible and indistinct, footsteps of the ghost nurse have been heard at the rectory walking swiftly along a passage. The rustle of papers and of a starched uniform have also been heard and a clicking noise, comparable to that made by locking or unlocking a door, has occasionally been reported.

The Rev. B. S. W. Crockett, Vicar of Mickleover, Derby, and son of the late Rev. A. W. Crockett, recalls a servant seeing and describing the figure of a lady who held rustling papers in her hand and seemed to be searching for something or someone. He tells me that although the figure has been described as a nurse, he feels almost certain that she is, in fact, a nun, for mediaeval portions of the house were formerly a monastic cell attached to Rochester Priory. Mr Crockett suggests that the unhappy lady may be from a neighbouring convent.

Mrs Gertrude Dancy of Charmouth, Dorset, tells me that while she was in the employment of the Rev. and Mrs Crockett at Southfleet Rectory between 1919 and 1920 she saw the ghost on one occasion. It was about seven-thirty one evening and Mrs Dancy had to go up to the housekeeper's room to prepare her bed for the night. This room was situated in the front part of the house. While working on the bed Mrs Dancy heard a sound like paper being dragged along the passage. She went to the door to see what was happening, but nothing was visible and the noise ceased as soon as she reached the door. Returning to her task, Mrs Dancy then heard a louder noise, 'like the sound of a rustling skirt', apparently coming from outside the room. Again she went into the passage carrying a small lighted lamp with her. Mrs Dancy's report continues:

'I stood at the top of a small stair just outside the room and to my surprise saw a nurse dressed in a clean staff uniform, standing at the end of the passage. She looked very human and had a smile on her face. Feeling a little nervous at seeing her there, I very timidly walked down the three stairs and along the passage towards her. As I did so, she began to walk forward as if to meet me, then she seemed to go gently backwards, facing me all the time, until she reached the door of a small room at the end of the passage. There, to my surprise, she disappeared backwards through the door.'

Mrs Dancy immediately opened the door through which the 'nurse' had disappeared and went into the room but there was no trace of the figure she had seen, nor, indeed, of anyone. Mrs Dancy tells me that she has never forgotten the experience and is still absolutely confident that she did see this unexplained figure.

In 1920, Mr Falloon informed me, four friends visited Southfleet Rectory from Bath, and while they were standing together on the landing where Mrs Dancy saw the ghost, waiting for a key to be fetched to unlock a door, they all saw a female figure come out of the Monk's Room, walk forty-two feet along the passage, turn the corner at which they were standing, and going to a door at the end of the landing, open the door, pass inside and close the door. When the key for which they had been waiting, eventually arrived, they found to their consternation that the door which the apparition had apparently opened and closed, was in fact securely locked.

The Rev. G. A. Bingley, M.A., was Curate at Southfleet from 1923 to 1926 and during that period he resided at the old rectory. One evening, Mr Bingley tells me, he and his wife (then his fiancée) saw a 'shadowy shape' at the end of a passage about thirty feet away from where they were standing on the landing above the main staircase. The form appeared in a passage leading from the Monk's Room. On almost every occasion that this apparition has been seen, it has apparently come out of that place. A solitary exception was mentioned to me by Mr Falloon concerning the wife of a former rector who once reported seeing the figure in the act of entering the Monk's Room.

Mr Bingley described for me two other seemingly paranormal happenings. An aunt of a former rector's wife saw a similar figure to that glimpsed by Mr Bingley and his fiancée, taking shape in the dining room in broad daylight. A nursemaid once reported seeing a figure on the landing above the main staircase one evening. She described the figure she saw as a 'nurse with a flowing veil' and said 'she' crossed the landing with a 'smiling look' and disappeared through a closed door.

At noon on February 7th, 1942, the Rev. W. M. Falloon was standing in the hall when he suddenly saw what he took to be the figure of a nun between him and the window. He described her to me as being about four feet seven inches in height; dumpy in shape and wearing a brown serge overall dress, similar to the contemporary nuns' black apparel, with a brown tippet reaching to the elbows and a close-fitting brown serge cap.

The old rectory occupies the site of a former friary and tradition asserts that a nun found in the company of a monk inside the friary was bricked up alive in the cellars. Stories of the bricking-up of nuns are not infrequently encountered in nun hauntings although very sparse evidence exists to suggest that such a barbarous punishment was ever actually meted out in this country. However, on more than one occasion, bones, believed to be female, have been found in suspicious circumstances—for example in the former deanery at Exeter where such bones were discovered between two walls of a bricked-up archway.

When I mentioned this fact to Mr Falloon, he told me that about ninety years ago the west door of Southfleet Church was badly blocked with dirt and rubble. After this had been cleared away by churchwardens, they uncovered the stone lid of a sarcophagus in the pathway. This was removed and can now be seen in the Scadbury pew inside the church. An inscription around the edge states that it marks the burial place of an excommunicated monk. Perhaps, as so often happens, there was a grain of truth in the legend and a nun and a monk were indeed the chief actors in the Southfleet drama.

King's Head Hotel, Rochester, Kent.

Southampton, HAMPSHIRE.

The old Indian-style Victoria Military Hospital, Netley, built in 1856 and demolished in 1966, was long reputed to be haunted by a nurse of the Crimean War who committed suicide by throwing herself from an upstairs window after discovering that by mistake she had administered a fatal overdose of drugs to a patient.

Her ghost was always seen in one particular corridor. Officials and staff at the hospital, a clergyman, visitors and patients have all told of seeing the figure, although stories of the appearances were suppressed for many years because whenever the ghost was seen, a death took place. A service of exorcism was held here in 1951.

The apparition was reported to be particularly active when the building was being demolished and one witness stated: 'The figure was dressed in an old-style nurses' uniform of greyish-blue with a white cap and was about twenty-five feet away from me when I saw it. She walked slowly away, making no sound and disappeared down a passage that led to the chapel.'

In 1936, a night orderly saw the 'Grey Lady' pass a ward where a patient died the following morning. A night staff telephone operator, employed at the hospital for twenty-seven years, also claimed to have seen the ghost; he said that he heard the rustle of her dress as she passed and there was a perfumed scent in the air after she had disappeared.

Variations of the legend suggest that the ghost was a nursing sister who fell in love with a patient and, after finding him in the arms of another nurse, poisoned him and then committed suicide. Or that the patient died and the nurse

216

jumped from a window because of a broken heart; or that she is Florence Nightingale, who was mainly responsible for the building of the hospital and that her frequent appearances in 1966 were an endeavour to prevent its demolition. *Dolphin Hotel, Southampton, Hampshire.*

Southport, LANCASHIRE.

In 1969 something of a sensation was caused at the Palace Hotel when Mr J. Smith and his eleven-man team of demolition workers reported alarming and apparently inexplicable happenings at this thousand-room hotel.

Eerie voices were heard from empty rooms and corridors on the second floor and the four-ton lift is said to have moved up and down many times of its own volition. After conducting an investigation, the North Wales Electricity Board asserted that not an amp of power was going into the hotel; electric current having been, in fact, cut off weeks earlier.

One of the men stated that he entered the foyer in the company of eight others and they all saw the doors slam shut and the lift move up to the second floor.

A Mrs Templeman called at the hotel on business and was talking to workmen when she saw the lift suddenly begin to move upwards. She said there was no sound whatsoever; the lift moved about seven feet, almost to the second floor and then stopped. Mrs Templeman ran up to the winding room with one of the workmen. They discovered that the lift brake was still firmly at the 'on' position and there seemed no logical way that the lift could have moved mechanically. The emergency winding handle for cranking the lift had been removed by this time.

At length it was decided to cut the cables to release the lift and although this was done, the lift did not budge. Now the main shafts were cut through and still the lift would not move. It was continually thumped with twenty-eight-pound hammers for twenty-five minutes before it eventually plunged to the bottom of the lift shaft and buried itself four feet into the cellar. The workmen all agreed that it was incredible: although the lift had moved, silently and without apparent effort by itself on so many occasions, it should have been so difficult to knock down.

During the course of a television broadcast a dog was shown refusing to pass the second floor landing although it had no such objection to passing other, apparently identical landings.
Clifton Hotel, Promenade, Southport, Lancs.

Southwold, SUFFOLK.

The old vicarage, now divided into club rooms, a bus office, a wool shop and a paint shop, certainly seems to have been haunted when it was occupied by a family. The daughter of a former rector has told me of the mysterious noises—sometimes all the occupants of the house would hear sounds as though someone had fallen downstairs. But when they rushed out to offer assistance, no one was there and nothing could be found to account for the noises that had been heard. One housekeeper left because she heard what she described as the 'clanking of chains' in the unused attic. Sometimes the creak of a chair would be heard, a heavy sigh would follow and then footsteps would approach the door, followed by silence. Visitors sleeping in the four-poster bed in the spare room often told of being awakened by 'somebody standing by the bed'.
Crown Hotel, Southwold, Suffolk.

Stoke-by-Nayland, SUFFOLK.

Thorington Hall, a fine example of a gabled farm-house, was built in the sixteenth century and has a dark stairs landing where the ghost of a girl has been seen and heard.

The western wing of the property centres on a magnificent chimney stack, fifty feet high, with six octagonal shafts supplying six fireplaces on three floors. In the living room a sixteenth-century shoe, now in Colchester Museum, was found behind ornamental plaster during repairs in 1937.

A dim passage upstairs is haunted by the ghost of a girl in a brownish dress tied with a cord. Heavy and unexplained

footsteps have been heard on many occasions here and in other parts of the house.
Red Lion Hotel, Colchester, Essex.

Stow-on-the-Wold, GLOUCESTERSHIRE.

A semi-detached house in Chapen Street, occupied by Mr Stanley Pethrick (fifty-eight), his wife Nancy, and their son David (fourteen), was the scene of remarkable poltergeist activity in 1963 and 1964. Pools of water appeared unaccountably in several rooms and as soon as the water was mopped up, it reappeared and then began to seep through the walls. Three plumbers failed to find any fault with the pipes though all the floorboards in the house were ripped up. Nor could the head of the water board and a sanitary inspector find any solution. A sudden gush of water from the kitchen floor steamed up one wall as high as the ceiling; later a rhythmic tapping disturbed the occupants. Search as they would, they could not locate the source; furniture moved of its own volition; rasping sounds came from cupboards and drawers. David was tipped out of bed, sheets were ripped in half, a dressing gown flew from its hook and thrust itself under a mattress, scratching noises came from David's bed and when the furniture was moved, it was found that the headboard was gouged and scarred. Writing appeared mysteriously on the walls, wallpaper was ripped off and Mrs Pethrick saw a hand appear from the end of her son's bed. At first it was small, like a baby's hand, but it quickly grew to the size of a boy's and then to that of a large man's hand; her husband saw it, too. Then a voice spoke, always in the vicinity of David, claiming to be one of the builders of the house who had died twenty years before, on February 15th. The haunting had commenced on that date. Gradually the family learned to live with their entity but when they went on a holiday, it seemed to go with them and a church they visited 'reverberated with rappings'.
Wyck Hill House Hotel, Stow-on-the-Wold, Glos.

Stretton, RUTLANDSHIRE.

Stocken Hall Farm was, and perhaps still is, haunted by three ghosts. One is the figure of a woman, dressed in black, with touches of white, who flits away down a corridor as soon as she is seen, or passes with lowered head. At all events, her face is never visible. During the early 1900s the occupants and many visitors saw the ghost who was believed to have been a girl, strangled in one of the attics. Once a visitor reported that when she saw the girl, whom she took for a servant, she spoke to her, whereupon the figure vanished. The second ghost is that of a little white dog and this phantom, too, was seen by many people for about eighteen months at one period. Often people opened doors for it, only to find that it had suddenly disappeared. Once the then occupant of the house and her daughter were going up a narrow staircase when the creature passed them; they both felt it touching them, as it pressed tightly between them and the jamb of the door on the top of the stairs, but this time the creature was invisible. For hours afterwards, they said, they experienced a 'burning chill' where it had touched them. The third apparition was seen by three occupants of the house one December day as they were crossing the park towards Clipsham, at a quarter to three in the afternoon. The terrier they had with them pricked up his ears and showed signs of fright when they saw the figure of a man hanging from the bough of an old oak tree. He was dressed in a brown smock with something white over his face and the rails of the fence behind him could distinctly be seen through the body. When they were within about forty yards of the apparition, the figure suddenly disappeared. There is a rumour that a sheep-stealer was hanged hereabouts and a murder is known to have been committed in the park. The spot was visited on succeeding anniversaries of the date, December 22nd, but nothing further was seen. *George Hotel, Oakham, Rutland.*

Sudbury, SUFFOLK.

St Gregory's Church bell-ringers were troubled by mysterious footsteps and other unexplained noises and curious happenings when I was there a few years ago. In the circumstances related to me it was quite impossible for the footsteps, in particular, to have had a normal explanation. Preserved in St Gregory's is the head of Archbishop Simon of Sudbury, who built Sudbury Tower, Canterbury, and who was eventually beheaded.

Four Swans Hotel, Sudbury, Suffolk.

Sunderland, DURHAM.

Hylton Castle, three-and-a-half miles to the west of Sunderland, was long said to be haunted by 'the Cauld Lad of Hylton', a naked ghost which was more often heard than seen. Haunting the kitchens and lower parts of the castle, he seems to have been of the 'brownie' order for he delighted in putting things in order and only really caused mischief when he became enraged at finding no work to do. Then he would smash breakable articles, mix the cooking ingredients, overturn the utensils containing liquids and generally create havoc. Understandably, the servants soon learnt to humour him, simply by leaving work for him to do. But there are always those who will not let well alone and one of the servants heard that the way to ensure seeing such a goblin and of not being troubled with him again was to present him with a suit of clothes. Accordingly a handsome suit of Lincoln green was carefully made, complete with cloak and hood and left beside the fire and the servants hid in wait for him. Exactly at midnight the Cauld Lad appeared and stood warming himself by the fire before he caught sight of the clothes (Queen Mab's own green livery!) and promptly tried them on. Finding them a perfect fit, he gambolled about the kitchen until it was almost dawn when, drawing his cloak around him, he muttered: 'Here's a cloak, and here's a hood: The Cauld Lad of Hylton will do no more good.' With that he disappeared and there are only occasional reports of his being seen again. The precise scene of the Cauld Lad's haunting has long since vanished which is not surprising as some say the Cauld Lad is the ghost of a

young stable-boy, killed by his master in anger some five hundred years ago.
The Seaburn Hotel, Sunderland, Co. Durham.

*Sutton Place, NEAR GUILDFORD, SURREY.

This magnificent mansion with the splendid oak tables once owned by American newspaper magnate William Hearst, the priceless sixteenth-century Brussels tapestries, the gold candelabra, the art treasures—pictures, furniture and rugs, is now the home of Mr Paul Getty. With its wonderful gardens, it seems a perfect setting for a haunting and according to reports there is more than one ghost at Sutton Place.

The ghost of the long gallery for instance, although treated lightly by the present staff, was mentioned by a visitor two hundred years ago. One feels that anything might happen in this history-laden atmosphere and perhaps the servant who says she saw an unknown figure here, was not mistaken. Then there is the 'lady in white', another unidentified ghost from the past. Perhaps she is the cause of the curious noises, sounds as though furniture is being smashed, that have been heard from time to time. At all events, multi-millionaire Paul Getty is not worried. 'I am comforted by the advice of a neighbour who is reputed to have several ghosts,' he will tell you. 'He assures me that they keep their manifestations for visitors and staff and never appear before the owner of the house.'
Angel Hotel, Guildford, Surrey.

Syderstone, NORFOLK.

Ill-starred Amy Robsart, wife of Robert Dudley, afterwards Earl of Leicester, who probably contrived her murder at Cumnor Hall in conjunction with Queen Elizabeth I, lived here at Syderstone Hall before her marriage and her ghost was said to walk here before the old Hall was demolished. Then the haunting seems to have been transferred to the nearby rectory where windows used to open by themselves, after being carefully closed and bolted and other inexplicable incidents were reported from time to time.

The village green is reputed to be haunted on nights of the full moon by a ghostly highwayman suitably mounted on a ghostly horse. On occasions words like 'Your money or your life' have been heard as the figure rushes silently past. *Duke's Head Hotel, King's Lynn, Norfolk.*

Tamworth, STAFFORDSHIRE.

The Norman Castle has two ghosts: a Black Lady and a White Lady who each haunt their own parts of this historic edifice on the banks of the River Trent.

Here, on January 30th, 925, Sihtric the pagan Danish King of Northumbria was betrothed to Editha, sister of King Athelstan. Although Sihtric accepted baptism, he soon afterwards relapsed into idolatry and left Editha who founded a convent and spent the rest of her life in acts of charity and devotion. Tamworth Parish Church is dedicated to her. After the Norman Conquest, William the Conqueror gave Tamworth Castle to Robert de Marmion for his outstanding bravery at the battle of Hastings. When he took possession, Marmion expelled the nuns who fled to a nunnery at nearby Polesworth—only to meet a similar fate there, for Marmion had also been granted lands at this second place. According to legend, one night after Marmion had gone to bed, the ghost of Editha appeared to him, dressed in the habit of a nun or Black Lady and reproached him for his treatment of her nuns. She is said to have struck him with her crozier and prophesied that he would meet a terrible death unless he allowed the sisters to return to the convent at Polesworth. Bleeding from his wounds, Marmion staggered down the stairway, known to this day as the Haunted Staircase and promised to make restoration.

The story of a White Lady who haunts the Castle terrace relates how she watched from this point while her lover, Sir Tarquin, an evil Saxon Knight, was slain by Sir Lancelot in Lady Meadow below the Castle. Sir Lancelot is then supposed to have rescued forty knights from the Castle.

I am indebted to the Castle Museum Curator, Miss C. F. Tarjan, for the additional information that the Haunted

Room, where Marmion is supposed to have met the ghostly Editha, daughter of King Edward the Elder, has long been reputed to be haunted by weird sighs and groans. Some of these have been recorded on tape; a number of people claim to have had very frightening experiences there.
Castle Hotel, Tamworth, Staffs.

*Tavistock—OKEHAMPTON ROAD, DEVON.

There is a legend that occasionally, at midnight, the ghost of the Lady Howard leaves the gates of the ruined Fitzford mansion, just outside Tavistock, enters her magnificent coach drawn by four jet-black horses and sets off towards Okehampton, driven by her liveried coachman. Motorists passing the vicinity late at night have reported seeing her figure or her coach, rolling silently along the road. Some say, she is accompanied by a large black dog while others hear only the sound of horses' hooves and, perhaps, the noise of wheels.

Outside Okehampton churchyard the coach is said to stop; the huge dog plucks a single blade of grass from the churchyard and returns to the coach where Lady Howard takes it from the foam-flecked dog's mouth, presses it sadly to her bosom (another version says, she puts it between the pages of her Bible). Then the coach turns and heads back to Fitzford, as silently as it came.
Bedford Hotel, Tavistock, Devon.

Tedworth, DRUMMER OF, SEE *Tidworth*, NORTH WILTSHIRE.

*Thames Ditton, SURREY.

The Home of Compassion has a White Lady that has haunted one room for over ten years.

The present house stands on land owned and often visited by Cardinal Wolsey. The original, much larger property, had a long and interesting history. Some of King Henry VIII's officials were at Thames Ditton in the sixteenth century

Upton Court, Slough, Buckinghamshire, reputed to be haunted by the ghost of a woman in a blood-stained nightdress. *Photo: Chris Underwood by kind permission of F. R. Groves*

Walpole House, Chiswick Mall, once the home of Barbara Villiers, Duchess of Cleveland, mistress of King Charles II. Her ghost has been seen gazing wistfully out of the drawing-room windows. *Photo: Chris Underwood*

Lonely Warbleton Priory near Heathfield, Sussex, surrounded by derelict farm buildings. Two skulls used to be preserved here, said to have been those of a murderer and his victim. *Photo: Chris Underwood*

'Woodfield', Aspley Guise, Bedfordshire, where the owner tried to get his rates reduced because of the 'haunted house' reputation caused by ghostly figures, a phantom man and woman; a ghostly man on horseback and the unexplained sounds of galloping horses' hooves. *Photo: T. Sheen*

when a property then known as Stringhaw adjoined Forde's Farm. Horace Walpole, the author of *The Castle of Otranto*, visited it from nearby Strawberry Hill in the eighteenth century. Later Forde's Farm became known as Boyle's Farm although it was never really a farm in the accepted sense of the word. The place was much frequented by the nobility of the day and the Irish poet, Thomas Moore (1779-1852) attended an elaborate fête here with coloured illuminations and gondolas that carried Italian opera singers. There were character quadrilles danced by the beauties of the season and Fanny Ayton sang. The event was long remembered as the Dandies' Fête.

A century and a half later the property stood empty for several years and the estate was cut up and sold as building plots. The remainder was bought by the Church of England Community of the Compassion of Jesus and became the Home of Compassion under Mother Mary Margaret. Before long, there was talk of a mysterious figure in white who used to be glimpsed in one of the rooms. After Mother Mary Margaret died in 1933, her successor found a charming room locked and unused. She decided to make it into her private room and had it re-decorated but after one night she moved out, had the room padlocked and never used it again. The same thing happened a few years later, when a dog bristled, growled and showed signs of distress on a number of occasions and its mistress saw a white figure in the room; it was once again locked and remained unused for many years.

Mother Eva Mary told me that when she arrived at the Home, she, too, liked the locked-up room and decided to use it as her bedroom. The first night she spent there, she suddenly found herself awake in the middle of the night and saw, standing quite close to her at the side of the bed, a female figure in white. It appeared to be quite solid and didn't move or speak but looked sadly at her. Mother Eva Mary felt that it was concerned for her welfare; however, she was not frightened and became convinced that the White Lady paid her nightly visits only with love and compassion as her motives. Mother Eva Mary saw the form many, many times and expected to continue to do so for she had come to look upon the silent figure as her friend.

In 1962 my friend T. S. Mercer, the historian of Thames

Ditton, went to the Home of Compassion to photograph some mural paintings that had been uncovered by workmen stripping the walls. He took five and when they were developed, four were perfectly ordinary photographs of the murals but on the fifth he seems to have caught a fleeting apparition. He submitted the negative to a leading authority who ruled out all faults due to film, processing or camera, and maintained that some bright object had passed in front of the camera while the shutter was open. Mr Mercer himself saw nothing and the photograph remains a psychic and photographic puzzle. A few years ago Holy Communion was held for three days in succession in the haunted room, in an attempt at exorcism, but I am assured on good authority that the room is still haunted.

Mitre Hotel, Hampton Court, Middlesex.

Tidworth, NORTH; WILTSHIRE.

Formerly Tedworth and the scene of the famous poltergeist case, the 'Drummer of Tedworth' in the early 1600s. Mr John Mompesson, a local magistrate who lived at the Manor House, visited nearby Ludgarshal and heard about a travelling drummer who was demanding money. On examining the fellow's pass and warrant, Mr Mompesson found them to be fraudulent and ordered the man, one William Drury, to be sent before the Justice of the Peace. Drury confessed his fraud but earnestly begged to have his drum back which Mompesson had taken from him. He was told that if the report from Colonel Ayliff, whose drummer Drury said he was, proved to be favourable, he should have the drum back but meanwhile it would be held by the bailiff. Drury was left in the hands of the constable but the latter, it seems, soon released him.

The following month, as Mompesson was preparing for a visit to London, the bailiff sent the drum to the Manor House. When Mompesson returned from London, his wife told him that while he had been away, they had been very frightened by noises during the night-time. Soon Mompesson himself heard the noises which he described as a great knocking at the doors and the outside of the house. He investigated, with a brace of pistols, but as soon as he opened a door from which the knocking appeared to be originating the noise would be heard at another door which he would then open —but he was always unsuccessful in discovering a cause for the noise. He went outside the house and walked all round it but could find nothing although he still heard the strange and hollow sound which continued even when he returned to bed. It now seemed to come from the top of the house; eventually it decreased and after some time ceased altogether, seeming to go off into the air.

After this, the thumping and drumming noises were heard very frequently; usually five nights in a row and then there was quiet, for perhaps three nights. Always the noises sounded on the outside boards of the house. Generally they began as the family prepared for sleep, whether this was early or late.

After several weeks the noises seemed to come into the house and to be especially attracted to the room where the drum lay. Now they were heard four or five nights out of seven each week. Just before it commenced, the occupants would hear 'a hurling sound in the air over the house' and when this had gone away, they would hear the beating of a drum 'like that of a breaking up of a guard'. For two months the disturbances continued in the same room. Mr Mompesson frequently used the place himself to study the noises. Often the noises were more troublesome during the early hours of the night and after a couple of hours they would die away. It was noticed that when the noises were at their height, any dog in the house would stand stock still.

It may be significant that Mrs Mompesson was in the last months of pregnancy and the night she was away from the house, having the child, all was quiet and continued so for the next three weeks, 'until she had recovered her strength'. But then the disturbances returned in 'ruder manner' than before and seemed to follow the young children of the family about the house, annoying them and beating on their bedsteads with great violence. On holding the shaking children while they were seemingly being hit by something unseen, no blows could be felt, but the children would tremble violently. At this time the drum would beat for hours on end, sounding the 'Round-heads and Cuckolds, the

Tat-too and several other points of War, as well as any Drummer'.

Sometimes a scratching noise would be heard under the children's beds which seemed to lift them up. Later, servants complained of the same inconvenience, their beds being gently lifted up and put down again. At other times they would feel a great weight on their feet as they lay in bed.

Noticing that a loft in the house had never been troubled, the Mompessons put the children to bed there, hoping for a quiet night, but they had no sooner left the room when the trouble began in the loft, exactly as it had been experienced elsewhere in the house.

On November 5th, in daylight, a 'mighty noise' was heard and a servant in a room full of people observed two floorboards in the children's room begin to move. He asked them to approach him; whereupon the boards, by themselves, moved to within a yard of his feet. He then asked for one of them to be put into his hand and this was done. He pushed the board away from him, but it was thrust back against him and this continued at least twenty times until Mr Mompesson sent the servant away. Afterwards a 'sulphurous smell' lingered where the phenomenon had taken place.

During a visit by the local vicar the drum beat loud and clear; chairs 'walked' around the room; the children's shoes flew over the heads of those present and practically everything movable in the room moved. Part of a bedstead threw itself at the minister and hit him on the leg but so lightly that it might have been 'a lock of wool'. It was noticed that it stopped exactly where it landed on the floor, not rolling or moving at all.

Mr Mompesson now transferred the small children to a neighbour's house and took the eldest, a girl of ten, to his own bedroom. But as soon as she was in bed, the disturbances began and continued for three weeks, the drumming and other noises seeming to answer or reply to anything that was asked. The younger children were then brought back and put to bed in the parlour which had been comparatively free from trouble but even there, they were persecuted by 'something', plucking at their hair and night clothes, although no other disturbances were reported.

228

Now the drumming sound was less frequent. Instead, a noise, like the clinking of money, was heard all over the house. Less violent disturbances followed: clothes being thrown about bedrooms; articles were hidden and bedclothes were tugged off beds.

When the house was visited by a son of Sir Thomas Bennet (who had at one time employed the drummer, William Drury) he had no sooner gone to bed than the drumming started, loud and clear. At the same time, Mr Mompesson's servant John heard a rustling sound in his bechamber and felt that something dressed in silks approached his bedstead. He took up his sword, whereupon the presence left him. Shortly afterwards a singing noise was heard in one of the chimneys and lights were seen about the house, especially in the children's room. Once the light appeared in Mr Mompesson's room and he described it as blue and glimmering. After he had seen it, he noticed 'a stiffness in his eyes'. When the light had disappeared, he heard faint footsteps on the stairs as though someone crept upstairs without shoes. The maids asserted that a door opened and closed in their presence without being touched; when it opened, sounds were heard suggesting that a dozen people had entered the room, although nothing was visible. This happened, they claimed, at least ten times. Sounds were also heard inside the room as though the people who had entered were walking about, and among the sounds the maids distinguished a rustling noise, as of silk.

One morning, a little later, Mr Mompesson heard the drum at daybreak, outside the chamber he occupied; it then seemed to move to the other end of the house and then 'go off into the air'.

The entity continued to play further tricks, particularly troubling the Mompesson children when they were in bed. It seemed to pass from one bed to another, avoiding the blows that were aimed at it with a sword or other article. Sometimes a panting sound was heard, then a scratching noise and sometimes knocking and rattling. A voice cried '*a witch, a witch*' at least a hundred times. Once Mr Mompesson, seeing some wood move in the chimney, discharged a pistol and afterwards found several drops of blood in the hearth and on the stairs.

229

After the pistol shot there was calm in the house for two or three nights, but the disturbances soon returned to worry the children, sometimes carrying away a lighted candle in their room and disappearing with it up a chimney. Footsteps were heard at midnight and knocks sounded on Mr Mompesson's chamber door. When he did not reply, the footsteps moved to another room where the occupant reported an 'appearance' of 'a great body with two red and glaring eyes' standing at the foot of his bed. After staring steadily at him for a time the figure disappeared.

It soon returned to trouble the children once again, tugging at the bed and bedclothes, sometimes lifting them in their beds with such force that six men could not hold them down. Beds fascinated this poltergeist: chamberpots were emptied into them, they were strewn with ashes, a long iron pike was put into Mr Mompesson's bed and an upright knife was found in his mother's. At this time things would fly about all over the house and unexplained noises were heard day and night.

A visiting friend found all the money in his pocket turned black. Mr Mompesson discovered his horse on its back with one of its hind legs in its mouth, so tightly that it took several men to lever it out. Sometimes the house would be visited by seven or eight 'men-like shapes' which would disappear when a gun was discharged.

Meanwhile William Drury, the drummer, was committed to Gloucester Gaol for stealing. There he stated that he had plagued a man in Wiltshire and would never be quiet 'till he hath made me satisfaction for taking away my drum'. Thereupon the fellow was tried for a witch at Sarum, acquitted of that charge but sentenced to transportation, probably as a rogue and vagabond. Somehow (some said by raising storms and frightening the seamen), he contrived to be returned to these shores, whereupon the disturbances at Mr Mompesson's house, which had been quiescent while Drury was aboard ship, recommenced.

The subsequent history of William Drury—and of his drum—is not known, but the Drummer of Tedworth is a classic early account of a poltergeist infestation. It is interesting to recall that John Mompesson, a magistrate, always

maintained that the disturbances could not be explained normally.
White Hart Hotel, Salisbury, Wilts.

*Torquay, DEVON.

The Old Spanish Barn on the seafront and its immediate vicinity are haunted occasionally by the ghost of a pretty young Spanish girl. The señorita is said to have disguised herself as a page and to have arrived with her lover, a Spanish nobleman, aboard the *Nuestra Señora del Rosario,* one of the ships in the ill-fated Spanish Armada. The young lovers must have been confident of the success of the Spanish invaders and doubtless thought that in a short time they would be given some English manor house as part of the conqueror's booty. But with the defeat by Drake and the Tudor navy, their dream was shattered. Following that great victory in 1588, 397 prisoners, including the young Spanish girl and her lover, were crammed into the tithe barn at Torquay. In the appalling conditions she was one of the first prisoners to die, although she is said to have received the last rites from a priest of her own religion. However, this does not seem to have prevented her ghost from reappearing in the park on Torquay seafront and in the locality of the Spanish Barn, drifting sadly and hopelessly at the scene of her death. Motorists driving along King's Drive late on moonlit nights have reported seeing such a figure in recent years.

'Castel a Mare', Middle Warberry Road, was derelict for many years owing to the reputation of being haunted. This is the house referred to in Beverley Nichols' *Twenty-Five* and Violet Tweedale's *Ghosts I Have Seen;* the scene of the remarkable experience of Lord St Audries and Beverley Nichols and his brother in the early 1920s. Beverley Nichols himself related the story at The Ghost Club in 1965 and filled in the details for me during conversation at his delightful home on Ham Common.

It was a Sunday evening, after evensong, that the three young men found themselves outside the fearful-looking and dilapidated empty house, which was said to have long been haunted by strange sounds, screams and footsteps, following a murder there in the long distant past. Deciding to look over the house, they picked their way through the overgrown garden and entered through a window on the ground floor. They had a candle and went from room to room; each seemed more melancholy than the last. The plaster had fallen in great lumps from the ceiling, boxes and planks were scattered all over the place, wallpaper hung in strips from the rotting walls. They found themselves talking in whispers as they climbed up the narrow twisting staircase to the upper floor.

At this stage Beverley Nichols went ahead and stood waiting for his companions in the upper hall. He told me that he was not feeling at all 'creepy'; rather disappointed, in fact, that nothing frightening had happened, when he suddenly realized that his mind was working very slowly: his thoughts seemed to be reduced to a frightening slow motion. Then he became aware that the same thing was happening to his body. He felt as though a black film began to cover the left side of his brain, exactly as the time he had been anaesthetized. Just before everything would, he felt certain, go black, he managed to stagger to the window, half-fall outside and then he lost consciousness.

He awakened to find himself sitting on the grass, feeling quite normal but strangely tired. He wanted no more to do with the house but his companions who had experienced nothing strange in the place at all, were determined to return. Having established that Beverley was well again, they clambered back into the dark and silent house. After some twenty-five minutes spent in a very thorough examination of every corner of the property, including the little room from which Beverley felt the harmful 'influence' had emanated they returned to him with the conviction that there was nothing whatever to be afraid of—the house was indisputably empty.

After a while Lord St Audries announced that he was set on exploring the house alone; he felt that Beverley's brother might be a kind of 'anti-influence' keeping the ghosts off, recalling that Beverley's experience had taken place when he had been alone. So, despite the objections of his friends, he went back into the house, after agreeing to take a candle with him and to whistle every few minutes, in reply to *their* whistles, to show that he was all right.

Beverley Nichols and his brother heard their friend clamber into the house, heard his footsteps cross the plaster-covered floor of the hall and heard him climbing the stairs. They heard him walk across the upper hall and then there was silence. They presumed that he had sat down as he had said he would. After a moment they whistled and his whistle came back in reply, or seemed to, for the answering whistle seemed surprisingly faint. They whistled again and a faint echo came. This went on for some twenty minutes, the answering whistle from the direction of the house seemingly getting stronger; then both the brothers sensed that something came out of the house and past them, making no sound in the almost unearthly silence. Nothing was visible —when suddenly they heard Lord St Audries' voice: a cry, heart-rending and full of anguish; the sort of cry, Beverley Nichols said to me, a man would make who had been stabbed in the back. He and his brother scrambled to their feet and rushed to the window. The sounds of a tremendous struggle sounded from upstairs: the wildest thuds and screams, as though a terrific fight were taking place. They didn't know whether to be frightened or relieved when at length heavy footsteps staggered down the stairs and Lord St Audries, a white-faced figure, his hair, clothes and hands covered with plaster and dust emerged into the garden.

At length he was able to relate how he had found his attention being brought back time and time again to the little room Beverley had felt to be malevolent. He had sat with his eyes fixed in that direction. After a while he noticed a patch of greyish light in the darkness of the corridor; it was the door of the little room. He heard his friends' whistles and answered them for twenty minutes. Then, deciding that he had drawn a blank, he got up, having decided to return to his friends. At this moment, out of the room he had been watching, something came rushing at him, something that was black and seemed roughly the shape of a man although he could distinguish no face and the thing made no sound whatever. He found himself knocked flat on his back and a sickening and overwhelming sense of evil, as though he were struggling with something from hell, pervaded his brain.

233

He fought as he had never fought before, forcing himself to his feet and then inching himself slowly down the stairs, thinking every second that he could go on no longer. At last he reached the bottom of the stairs and blackness but he was free from his adversary. He staggered outside and met his friends coming to his help.

Later the friends discovered that the murder in the house had been a double one: a semi-insane doctor murdering first his wife and then a maid. The scene of the murders was the bathroom, the little room at the end of the corridor which had worried Beverley and Lord St Audries so much.

The house stood next to one called 'Asheldon' in Middle Warberry Road but the site has since been built upon.
Hotel Hyperion, Cockington Lane, Torquay, Devon.

Totton, HAMPSHIRE.

Testwood House, formerly a royal hunting lodge, a nobleman's country seat, a well-known gentleman's home, a country club and now the offices of the sherry shippers, Williams and Humbert, seems to harbour several ghosts.

Heavy footsteps have been heard walking along passages covered with thick carpeting, footsteps that sounded as though they were walking on boards. They seem to originate in an upstairs corridor where dogs refuse to go. One night the caretaker was making his rounds after the staff had gone home when he heard the footsteps.

A year later unexplained figures were seen outside the house. One autumn night the caretaker's sixteen-year-old daughter was returning late from a dance and had almost reached the front door of Testwood House, accompanied by her brother, when they both saw a tall man, apparently trying to open the door. As they approached, he vanished. Neither knew of any ghostly associations of the house.

Shortly afterwards the same figure was seen by a chef who happened to be working late in the kitchen. He became aware of someone standing silently beside him, watching, only a few feet away. Almost as soon as he became aware of the presence, it vanished. As the chef drove away from the house that night, the headlights of his car picked out the figure of a man on the drive, walking towards the front door. He noticed that the figure wore a top hat and long overcoat with a short cape, before it suddenly disappeared. A month later another member of the staff saw a similar figure standing by one of the entrance gates in broad daylight.

A year later the caretaker and his son were alarmed to hear their dog suddenly start barking late at night. Thinking that there must be intruders in the grounds, they ran across the yard to the main building where they found that the back door was rattling violently although there was no sign of anybody. After they had circled the building and examined all doors and windows with their torches, the caretaker's son reached the little pantry window, in the oldest part of the house. Here, although the window is unglazed and protected by a metal mesh screen and vertical bars obviating the possibility of reflection, as the torch-light fell on the window, the boy saw the unmistakable face of a young man staring out at him. The face, long and pale, with grey eyes, looked out unblinking and unmoving as the boy watched, petrified, until his father joined him whereupon the face faded away. An immediate investigation revealed that the room was heavily padlocked and no one was inside.

Discussion with former occupants of the house produced other stories of strange happenings here. The owners of the former country club spoke of an unexplained figure of a woman seen in one of the attic bedrooms and of a coach-and-four dashing up the drive. Local folk told of a murder committed here many years ago when a manservant killed a cook and dragged her body down the drive, across the main road and dumped it in a byway still known as Cook's Lane. If there is anything in this story it could account for the caped figure that haunts the front of the house; the mysterious female figure in the attic (the victim, perhaps?); the face at the pantry window (the murderer caught?); the feeling of a presence in the pantry, haunt of the cook...

In 1965 The Ghost Club visited Testwood House and several members remarked on a curious 'waiting' atmosphere in the upper parts of the interesting old house. We were able to establish that the back door fits tightly and does not rattle of its own accord.

Dolphin Hotel, Southampton, Hampshire.

Tunstead Milton, NEAR CHAPEL-EN-LE-FRITH, DERBYSHIRE.

An old farm in the locality is known as 'Dickie's' on account of 'Dickie's' skull that was kept here for so many years that no one now knows the reason for its preservation.

There is a suggestion that the skull, incomplete and in pieces, belonged to a Ned Dixon who was murdered by his cousin in the room where it is kept. Others maintain that, in spite of its name, the skull belonged to a woman. At all events, it was believed that should the skull be removed from the house, disasters and difficulties would ensue until it was brought back.

Years ago the skull gained notoriety when the London and North-Western Railway engineers had great difficulty in fixing secure foundations for a bridge as long as they were on the farm land. Eventually they had to select another site, on land belonging to another farm. The engineers ascribed their difficulties to local sand and bog but those living in the vicinity maintained that 'Dickie's' skull had been the potent deterrent.

Alma Lodge Hotel, Buxton Road, Stockport, Cheshire.

Twickenham, MIDDLESEX.

The waterfront church of St Mary's, an impressive church full of unusual features, is reputed to harbour the ghost of Alexander Pope.

The mortal remains (or most of them) of the man who gave his name to many of the roads in this area lie in the churchyard, here too is his famous grotto and the deformed and vindictive poet's restless footsteps used to be heard along the main aisle.

Thurston Hopkins, ghost-hunter and collector of ghost-lore, had no doubt about it; he told me: 'The ghost of Alexander Pope used to be seen perambulating the churchyard and the aisles, muttering and sometimes raving at the top of his voice. The apparition always faded away, accompanied by a dreadful paroxysm of coughing.'

The haunting seems to date from 1830 when Pope's grave was desecrated and his skull removed from the coffin. Certainly a skull, stated to be that of Pope, became the show-piece in the private collection of phrenologist Johann Spurzheim.

At one time the ghost of Pope was said to trouble the parson and sexton of the day, demanding to know what had become of his skull. 'Pope's ghost still walks,' Hopkins told me, 'but his figure is no longer visible; although the sound of his limping footsteps have been plainly heard on many occasions.'
Richmond Hill Hotel, Richmond Hill, Richmond, Surrey.

Ventnor, ISLE OF WIGHT, HAMPSHIRE.

Craigie Lodge, near here, was the scene of a mystery that had great publicity some forty years ago. The gardener of the tenant at that time was digging in the grounds to plant shrubs when he unearthed the lower jaw of a child which he took to his mistress, a Mrs Capell. Mrs Hugh Pollock, a psychometrist, happened to be staying with her. She placed the bone (part of a whole skeleton which was subsequently unearthed here) against her forehead and stated that another skeleton would be found lying near where the child's bone had been found. A second skeleton was duly discovered, a woman's. It is difficult to suggest a rational explanation for this prediction and its fulfilment.
Royal Hotel, Ventnor, Isle of Wight, Hampshire.

Walsall, STAFFORDSHIRE, SEE *Caldmore Green.*

Wantage, BERKSHIRE.

The village of West Hendred seems to possess the ghost of a man who died in a road accident. Mrs Margaret Prior (twenty-seven) and Mrs Marcia Colling-Hill (twenty-nine), two sisters, were driving at night near the spot when they both saw a man wearing a cap and overcoat, dash in front of their car—yet there was no collision. Mrs Prior, who was driving, said afterwards, 'I couldn't possibly have avoided hitting

him. I braked instantly as I thought I was going to kill him.
I prepared myself for the bump but nothing happened...'
Bear Hotel, Market Square, Wantage, Berks.

Warbleton Priory, SEE *Heathfield,* SUSSEX.

Washford, SOMERSET.

Historic Barton House was occupied for over forty years by
artist Edward Collier and his wife. They used to say that
ghosts 'pop up all over the place, at any time of the day or
night'. Mrs Collier said that although it was sometimes dis-
concerting when people appeared to walk through walls, the
ghosts never troubled them and in fact, they added to the
fun of living at the beautiful old house.
Luttrell Arms Hotel, Dunster, Somerset.

Waterford, MUNSTER, IRELAND.

Legend has it that a beautiful vampire lies buried here in a
little graveyard by the ruined church, near Strongbow's
Tower—still ready to kill in the unearthly fashion of vampires anyone who lingers here at night-times...
Acton's Hotel, Kinsale, Ireland.

Wayland Wood, NORFOLK.

This is the wood said to have been the original one of the
'Babes in the Wood' story. The babes were Norfolk children and here, where the uncle's ruffian servants left them to
die, two little ghostly figures are seen on misty nights, wandering silently among the trees, hand in hand, looking for a
way out. Unexplained wailing cries have been heard at
night-times in this lonely spot.
Bell Hotel, Norwich, Norfolk.

238

Wellingborough, NORTHAMPTONSHIRE.

The Lyric, formerly a cinema and later a bingo hall was the scene of a 'ghost hunt' in November 1969, following reports of the spectre of a man said to have been seen on a balcony there. The figure may have had its origin in the mysterious death of a man named Daniel who was buried in the nineteenth century, on land where the Lyric now stands. Following several reports of the figure being seen, always on the same balcony, the Rev. Cyril Payne visited the hall but refused to comment afterwards. The Catholic Bishop of Northampton would not allow a priest to attempt an exorcism. One witness described the figure as 'like a white shadow or statue that had not been unveiled'; another said: 'It scared me so much that I ran out into the street.' Messages were tapped out asking for '*Help*' and such appeals as '*Bring back priest*'. At the time a number of all-night vigils were kept at the hall by local psychical researchers who collected evidence suggesting that some para-normal activity had taken place on the foyer balcony.

Westone Hotel, Fir Tree Walk, Weston Favell, Northampton, Northants.

*West Drayton Church, MIDDLESEX.

The scene of a remarkable haunting in the eighteenth century when this delightful church was 'infested' by a large black bird for the best part of a hundred years.

People visiting the church and churchyard heard a peculiar knocking sound which seemed to emanate from the vaults under the church. Once three of them peered through the grating outside and saw a great black bird, perched on one of the coffins inside, pecking away furiously. They roused the parish clerk who told them that he had often seen the same bird, or one like it, in the vaults. His wife and daughter declared that they had seen it, too, and that it usually appeared on a Friday evening.

Once, when bell-ringers arrived at the church for practice they were met by a boy who was much agitated by a large black bird which he had seen flying about the chancel. Four

239

of the bell-ringers and two of the youths at once armed themselves with sticks and stones and set out to search for the mysterious bird. They soon found it, fluttering among the rafters; by throwing stones, they eventually drove it from one part of the church to another, hitting it twice with sticks. One of them caught it a hard knock, so that one of its wings drooped as if the creature were badly crippled; and finally, under a fusillade of blows and hits from stones it fell wounded, screaming and fluttering, into the eastern end of the church. Two of the assailants immediately drove it into a corner and vaulted over the communion rail to seize it as it sank to the floor, apparently exhausted, but as the men thrust out their hands to seize it—the bird vanished. After that it was often seen, perched on the communion rails or fluttering to and fro in the vaults.

A resident of West Drayton remarked that local people thought the spectral bird was the restless and miserable spirit of a murderer who had committed suicide and had been buried in consecrated ground at the north side of the churchyard instead of at the cross-roads, the traditional place for suicides.

When I took a party of Ghost Club members to West Drayton church in 1962 the rector, the Rev. A. H. Woodhouse, told us about the family coffins in the vault being set upright in readiness for the day of resurrection!
Skyway Hotel, Bath Road, Hayes, Middlesex.

West Grinstead, SUSSEX.

About a mile from West Grinstead there are the scanty remains of Knepp Castle, one of the six great feudal fortresses of Sussex, where a ghostly white doe is still occasionally seen nibbling the lush green grass.

According to the local legend, in the days of King John a young girl displeased one of the king's retainers when she refused to submit to his advances. He paid a local hag to bewitch the girl who was turned into a white doe. Next, for some unknown reason, the hag turned herself into a great boarhound in order to chase the little doe and keep her always on the move. The hunters of Knapp had strict orders, under pain of death, never to kill the doe but one day a youth, anxious to display his skill with the crossbow, sent an arrow through its heart and a second shaft into the great hound that was chasing it; so perished the maiden and the witch. But the ghostly doe is still seen feeding on the rich green grass in summer. In winter, usually about Christmas time, when the snow covers the ground, blood-red marks appear on the frozen snow, at the spot where the animals died.

Ye Old Kings Head Hotel, Carfax, Horsham, Sussex.

West Hartlepool, DURHAM.

In 1967 the occupants of 18, Dorset Street (Mr and Mrs Harry Parker and their two-year-old daughter) were driven out of their home and had to spend nights with their next door neighbours, because they were afraid of the house at night-time. During the course of a sitting, which they had held with friends as a joke, one person saw the outline of a man's head on the window curtains and a strip of light suddenly flashed past her. At another séance 'a figure' was seen standing in front of the fireplacc and was recognized as a deceased relative.

Grand Hotel, Hartlepool, Co. Durham.

**West Wycombe*, BUCKINGHAMSHIRE.

The fascinating fourteenth-century George and Dragon Inn is reputed to be haunted by a ghostly girl in white. There is a priest's hole here, too, and a room where Oliver Cromwell used to stay.

The girl, Susan, was a servant at the inn and her beauty attracted three local young men but she was intrigued by the visits of an unidentified but prosperous traveller. The local lads became jealous and sent a note to Susan, purporting to come from her wealthy admirer, asking her to meet him at the nearby caves, so that they could run away and get married. The three young men thought it a fine joke when Susan kept the tryst but when their mockery annoyed her and she began to throw stones at her tormentors, the affair developed into a fight and Susan fell and fractured her skull. She was carried back to the inn but died during the night, in the room which the landlord will show you. Since then her ghost has haunted the 'George and Dragon', walking along a passage in the early hours of the morning and causing a supernormal coldness in the bedroom where she breathed her last.

Falcon Hotel, High Street, High Wycombe, Bucks.

Wetheral, CUMBERLANDSHIRE.

Corby Castle, beautifully situated in a forest on the banks of the River Eden, has long been famous for an apparition known as 'the Radiant Boy'. The haunted chamber at Corby is in the old part of the house and although surrounded by delightful rooms on all sides, the only access to this particular room is through a passage cut into an eight-foot thick wall. On one wall of the room tapestry hung for many years, while the rest of the walls were decorated with family portraits and panels of embroidery giving the place an ominous and somehow oppressive feeling. Many years ago the apparition so long associated with this ancient seat was seen by a well-known and respected clergyman who was spending a night in the haunted room. He awoke soon after midnight to find the room in total darkness and yet, although there was no light, he saw an unmistakable glimmer in the middle of the room which, as he watched, increased to a bright flame. He thought for a moment that something had caught alight when, to his amazement, he saw, apparently within and part of the radiance, a beautiful boy clothed in white, 'with bright locks resembling gold' looking steadfastly at him. After a moment 'the radiant boy' glided gently and silently towards the chimney where he vanished. There was no evident place of entry or exit and, indeed, subsequent examination of the wall showed that it was quite sound and unbroken. In complete darkness once more, the visitor spent a restless night and arose at dawn, determined never to sleep in that room again. The haunted room was later used as a study and with its dark panelling presented a sombre

appearance on the brightest day although as far as I know
'the radiant boy', a rare apparition and a famous one, has
not been seen for many years now.
Crown Hotel, Wetheral, Cumb.

Weybridge, SURREY.

The famous racing track at Brooklands, now disused and
overgrown is, appropriately enough, reputed to be haunted
by a ghost in racing cap and goggles. The vast assembly
shed, known as The Vatican, juts out on to the former race-
track at the end of the Railway Straight and it is here that a
popular Brooklands figure, Percy Lambert, was thrown to his
death when a tyre burst during a record attempt. It is
thought that the mysterious figure in cap and goggles that
night-shift workers claim to have seen over the years may be
his ghost, visiting again his beloved Brooklands.
Ship Hotel, Monument Green, Weybridge, Surrey.

Whitby, YORKSHIRE.

Some of the roads hereabouts are said to be haunted by a
mischievous ghost named Hob who seems to have a grudge
against travellers and particularly motorists, for he makes
them skid into ditches, turns signposts around and lets down
the tyres of cars. At least, that's what late-night motorists to
this part of haunted Yorkshire say.
Metropole Hotel, West Cliff, Whitby, Yorks.

Wicken, CAMBRIDGESHIRE.

In the heart of the Fen country and only a mile from
Wicken Fen, the stretch of land that has remained unchanged since the days of Hereward the Wake, there stands
an isolated collection of buildings grouped round an imposing farmhouse known as Spinney Abbey. The name was
derived from the ancient priory which formerly occupied the
site. Ghostly singing monks, mysterious lights and strange

figures have been reported here.

The original Spinney Abbey was for the last fourteen years of his life the home of Oliver Cromwell's distinguished son, Henry, who settled here after he had lost his lands with the return of the Stuarts. It was here that the reputed 'stable-fork incident' took place. King Charles II, returning from Newmarket with his retinue, visited farmer Henry Cromwell, and found him farming contentedly. A member of the King's party thought it a fine jest to take up a pitch-fork and carry it before Cromwell, parodying the fact that the farmer had been mace-bearer when he was Lord Lieutenant of Ireland. The mortal remains of this well-loved son of the Protector rest in the little village church where a brass plate tells us that he was the best of Cromwell's sons. Carlyle once said that had *he* been named Protector, English history would have taken a different turn in the seventeenth century.

Now the occupants are the Fuller family and I remember that one of the first things Tom Fuller showed me were some fragmentary ruins of the old building, built in the twelfth century. Part of it was now a piggery and I was told that the pigs, although contented enough elsewhere, are often seen to be fighting whenever they occupy that part of their enclosure. I remember, too, examining the cellars, remnants of the old building with reputed secret tunnels, and seeing the remains of a grating and the attachments for primitive handcuffs showing that the cellars were used as dungeons.

One of the most frequent unexplained happenings here was a mysterious twinkling light which was often seen between the house and Spinney Bank, about a mile away. The lights have been observed within a hundred yards of Spinney Abbey and once a local man saw a light move away from him and illuminate a mill almost a mile distant. Witnesses never seemed to be able to get near the lights for as soon as they are approached, they drift away and when the observer stops, the lights seem to stop too. Such lights are often *Ignis Fatuus* (from the Latin: foolish fire), usually seen in the vicinity of marshy places and churchyards and are sometimes known as 'Will-o'-the-Wisp' and 'Jack-a-Lantern'. They are generally accepted as being a natural although incompletely understood luminosity, due perhaps to the spontaneous combustion of decomposed vegetable matter. At all events, the Fullers told me that local people will go a long way round to avoid Spinney Bank at night.

Outside the room where I learned of the many strange happenings at Spinney Abbey, Tom Fuller told me of the figure of a monk that he had seen glide slowly along the garden path and disappear at an angle of the house. The hood of the clothing which the figure wore covered its face so that no features were discernible but Mr Fuller wondered whether the ghostly monk had any connection with the murder of an abbot at the original Spinney Abbey in 1406. Other people, too, have seen a ghost friar here and sometimes ghostly footsteps, slow and measured, sound and resound about this quiet house.

One Sunday morning unexplained chanting was heard in the west part of the house by six people, including three of the children of old Robert Fuller, who were now telling me about the strange happenings they had encountered over the years. Music, faint but distinct, accompanied the Latin chanting. The whole thing was over in a few seconds but all the six people in the room at the time heard and agreed upon the unmistakable sounds. Robert Fuller himself had heard the same sounds some years before but he heard them in the stack-yard and they appeared to come from fourteen feet above the ground. 'Clear as a bell,' he said; 'pure and sweet, all in Latin; and just where the old Chapel of the Abbey used to stand.'

Mr Fuller's daughter Unis and her husband told me that they had heard something they had never been able to explain. It was a curious, uneven, rolling sound, like a coconut being rolled over the floor. After a while it ceased; then it began again and it was heard intermittently throughout that one evening, never before and never afterwards.

During the course of a night I spent in the grounds of Spinney Abbey I placed delicate thermometers at strategic spots: in the piggery where the pigs always fought, the place where the chanting had been heard, another spot where an unexplained female figure had been seen on one occasion and finally where the monk walked. Readings were carefully recorded every ten minutes throughout the night. No thermometer showed any abnormality—except one. Each of

them steadily declining from around 31°F at midnight to 24°F at six a.m. But the thermometer placed where the ghost monk walked showed a sudden and inexplicable drop in temperature of seven degrees! This occurred at two-ten a.m. and was verified by my two companions; yet the other thermometers showed no similar drop. This one was no more exposed than the others and in any case ten minutes later, this thermometer showed the temperature back to normal and in line with the others. I have thought of many possible explanations but none that I can accept as probable. It is interesting to note that some horses stabled nearby were quiet throughout the night except at the exact time at which this sudden and unexplained drop in temperature occurred. At exactly two-ten a.m. the horses suddenly made a terrific noise in their stable, kicking their stalls, whinneying and neighing loudly. Gradually they quietened down and by the time the thermometer showed a normal reading at two-twenty a.m. the horses were quiet again. Horses, like cats and dogs, are believed to be supersensitive, so perhaps some shade of a ghost passed near to me that night.
White Hart Hotel, Newmarket, Suffolk.

Willington Quay, NEAR NORTH SHIELDS, NORTHUMBERLAND.

Some old buildings at this small Tyneside town were formerly a mill house where, well over a century ago, remarkable poltergeist activity was experienced by a staunch Quaker, Joseph Proctor and his family. There is a mass of contemporary evidence for this important case of haunting which lasted for some twelve years.

The first recorded incidents at Willington Mill for which no normal explanation could be found were curious noises reported by a young nurse-maid. She described them as sounding like a dull, heavy tread of footfalls; they came from an unoccupied room. It was as though someone were pacing back and forth for ten minutes at a time. Before long all the household had heard the same sounds which continued day after day. Often the room was examined immediately the noise was heard; sometimes people sat in the room or occupied it all night; but no cause for the noise was ever discovered. It seemed impossible for the sounds to have been due to trickery. The affected room had a garret above and the roof was inaccessible from outside; the house was detached and most of the time the window was sealed up with laths and plaster while the chimney was closed and so covered with soot that even a mouse must have left traces. There was no furniture in the room and at one period the door was nailed up. No rats or other rodents were seen or heard in the house; although, as one witness said, a hundred rats could not have so shaken the floor with their weight as to cause the window to rattle as it did on numerous occasions. The noises were heard at every hour of the day but more frequently during the evening and only rarely at night.

Other noises included deadened beats, as of a mallet on a block of wood, near a bedstead in a bedroom; taps on a cradle causing vibration; footsteps on a gravel path and in a bedroom; a sound like the winding-up of a clock; the noise of a sack falling; a loud chattering and jingling; a beating noise and the sound of whistling; a voice which seemed to say 'Chuck' twice and on another occasion something like 'Never mind' and 'Come and get'.

A neighbour reported seeing a transparent female figure at a window on the second floor of the mill and the same figure was later seen by two visitors who described it as 'resembling a priest'. Two of the Proctor children saw, unknown to each other, an apparition; a cook saw 'a distinct shadow' and her bedstead was disturbed. Little Jane Proctor was frightened by the face of an old woman at the foot of her bed and on the landing, while her brother reported seeing a man with grey hair walk into his bedroom.

Once Mrs Proctor and a nurse felt themselves raised up in their beds and let down again three times. One of the boys complained of a similar experience. Another time Mrs Proctor was awakened by feeling an icy pressure on her face, over one eye, suddenly with much force and then withdrawn; she often described this experience and said she found it more distressing than anything she underwent in the house.

The Proctor's diary records these events as happening between 1835 and 1847 when, finding life in the house intolerable, they finally left. Subsequent inhabitants of the prop-

erty, who divided the mill into separate dwellings, were only occasionally disturbed by unaccountable noises and reported just once or twice seeing what were thought to be apparitions. Later there were rumours of restless nights and a few exasperating disturbances but it is probable that with the departure of the Proctor children the poltergeist could no longer produce the same effects.
The Sea Hotel, South Shields, Co. Durham.

Winchelsea, SUSSEX.

The picturesque ruins of an old Franciscan monastery, 'Friars', was once the home of two highwaymen brothers who are said still to haunt the roads hereabouts.

George and Joseph Weston lived here under assumed names and were regarded as country gentlemen, enjoying the highest reputation in Winchelsea, while at night they donned their masks and plied their nefarious trade throughout the surrounding countryside. They were apprehended in London after robbing the Bristol mail, and executed at Tyburn in 1782. But according to local observers the brothers are still to be seen from time to time, careering about the district at dead of night. One, believed to be George, has been seen in the shadow of a particular tree, armed but apparently headless, waiting for the opportunity to surprise a phantom coach. Many motorists in the district have been frightened by the sounds of galloping horses' hooves approaching them, which have ceased as mysteriously as they began.
George Hotel, Rye, Sussex.

**Windsor Castle*, WINDSOR, BERKSHIRE.

A royal palace built by William the Conqueror where many English sovereigns are buried. It has at least five ghosts: King Henry VIII, Queen Elizabeth I, King Charles I, King George III and a young guardsman who killed himself in the 1920s, while Hector Bolitho has described the ghost with whom he once shared the old Deanery in the castle grounds.

'I used to hear him in the night, walking quickly past my bedroom until he came to the three steps by the bathroom door' he told me. The odd thing was that the unseen ghost seemed to take *four* steps down before resuming his hurried pace but later it was discovered that the floor in this part of the old house had been raised from its early level and in the process one step had been eliminated.

The Cloisters near the Deanery are said to be haunted by the ghost of King Henry VIII; ghostly groans and the sound of dragging footsteps, as though made by someone suffering from gout, have been heard in these passages.

Queen Elizabeth I haunts the Royal Library (not open to the public) and witnesses include the Empress Frederick of Germany and a Lieutenant Glynn of the Grenadier Guards who heard the tap, tap of high heels sounding on bare boards when he was in the Library. The sounds came nearer and presently the tall stately figure of the Virgin Queen came into view and passed so close to him that he could have touched her. She entered an inner room from which there is no other exit and although Lieutenant Glynn followed her immediately, he found no sign of the figure he had seen in the deserted room.

The Royal Library is also said to harbour the ghost of George III, the poor old mad king whose ghost has also been seen at Kensington Palace; while a Canon's house in the castle precincts is reputed to be haunted by the ghostly form of King Charles I, recognized by the uncanny likeness to the famous Van Dyck portrait.

A young recruit of the Grenadier Guards was on duty on the Long Walk (where the ghost of Herne the Hunter has occasionally been glimpsed) when he shot himself. A few weeks later a guardsman was detailed to relieve another on this same duty and during the bright moonlit night he saw the ghostly figure of the dead guardsman. When he returned to his quarters he learned that the guardsman he had relieved had had an identical experience.
Castle Hotel, Windsor, Berks.

*Windsor Great Park, WINDSOR, BERKSHIRE.

Long reputed to be haunted by the ghost of Herne the Hunter, 'the Foul Fiend of the Forest', as Harrison Ains- worth calls him in his romance *Windsor Castle*. The appari- tion was usually seen at night-time, wearing horns and mounted on a fast horse followed by spectral hounds; the whole ghostly band seemingly engaged on a phantom hunt- ing expedition. The original Herne was a forest keeper in Great Windsor Forest, probably in the reign of Richard II. Falling into disgrace, he hanged himself, or at any rate his body was found hanging from a large oak tree which was only blown down in a storm in 1863. Queen Victoria had a new oak tree planted in the same spot for whenever dis- aster threatened the royal family or the nation, Herne's ghost was said to appear beneath the shadow of the old oak. The figure is said to have been seen in 1931 before the economic crisis, before the abdication of Edward VIII in 1936 and before the Second World War in 1939. In 1926 there was a remarkable report from Mrs Walter Legge, J.P., a member of the Windsor Board of Guardians and of the Rural District Council, who lived at Farm House, Wind- sor. She had just retired one night when she heard the sound of the baying of hounds coming from the direction of Smith's Lawn. It appeared to increase in volume and then die away in the direction of Windsor Castle. A fortnight later she heard the same sounds, exactly at midnight; and this time her daughter came into her mother's room, saying she had heard strange sounds, 'almost like Herne the Hunter's hounds'. Mrs Legge and her daughter lived at Windsor for many years afterwards but never heard the midnight baying again.

The ghost of Herne and his phantom hounds have been reported from various parts of Windsor Great Park; the great shaggy form of Herne usually being glimpsed among ancient trees and the sound of his baying hounds and a horse's gal- loping hooves have been heard suddenly and then the sounds have gradually faded away. Herne's ghost was known to Shakespeare who refers to it three times in *The Merry Wives of Windsor*. At that time the enormous oak tree,

250

known as Herne's Oak, seems to have been his special haunt.
Castle Hotel, Windsor, Berks.

Woburn Abbey, WOBURN, BEDFORDSHIRE.

The seat of the Dukes of Bedford is built on the site of a Cistercian abbey; the present structure dates from 1744 and is today one of the most popular stately homes open to the public. But the steady stream of over 25,000 visitors a week during the season has not driven away the ghosts.

In 1963 I had a long talk with His Grace the Duke of Bedford, his wife and her daughters. They all had curious and unexplained happenings to relate. The thirteenth Duke's introduction to psychic matters came when he was a young man attending a party given by Lord Tredegar, 'a very odd man who was much interested in the supernatural' and at night in one of the enormous rooms of his home in Wales, with an owl flying round the room (!) Lord Tredegar would don cabbalistic garb and tell fortunes. The strange thing was that no sooner had he begun than the temperature in the room would unmistakably drop. Everyone present agreed on this and the Duke told me that although he was right in front of a huge fire, he found himself shivering. He never forgot that visit to Wales.

In the private apartments of the Abbey, looking out over the rolling parkland, the Duke told me of an annoyingly persistent manifestation which caused them to move the site of their television room. The phenomenon, which happened times without number, was unexplained door-opening. Time after time this door would open, followed by another at the opposite end of the room, just as though someone had walked through and left the doors open. New locks were fitted; the doors were kept locked, but still they opened by themselves and in the end the wing of the house was reconstructed. Now there is an open passage where the doors of the television room used to be.

'But now the ghost has turned his attention to other doors!' went on the Duke and I heard how his son, his wife, the servants and various visitors had all told him of their bedroom doors opening mysteriously by themselves.

I was shown the beautifully-proportioned bedroom and the Duke and Duchess told me of curious incidents which they had experienced here: of the continual door-opening and what seemed like a cold, wet hand passing over one's face. It was not 'really frightening' although the dogs at Woburn didn't like the ghost. Often they would stop suddenly in one of the long corridors, crouch down with their tails between their legs, howl piteously and refuse to move. There does seem to be an indefinable atmosphere in this portion of the house, a kind of restlessness that clairvoyant Tom Corbett told me he sensed immediately on his visit to Woburn. The same feeling is prevalent in the Wood Library and in a nearby office; the Duke told me that he finds it difficult to concentrate in these rooms yet he continues to use them.

Sylvie de Cardenal, the administrator of the Stately Antique Market at Woburn was working late in her office over the courtyard one night when she noticed that the lights were showing downstairs although she distinctly recalled switching them off before coming up. She went down and was astonished to see a tall gentleman wearing a top hat walking through the market. The next day an employee was working late and when he had finished he went upstairs and asked about the mysterious gentleman in a top hat whom he had seen in the Market.

There is an isolated little summer house with an overgrown garden not far from the house which the Duke feels is haunted by an unhappy ghost; perhaps his grandmother, 'the flying Duchess', to whom the Duke has devoted a fascinating room at the Abbey. She loved the isolation of this summer house, especially towards the end of her increasingly unhappy life; and soon she took off in her Gypsy aeroplane from Woburn on the flight from which she never returned. 'I feel her presence very strongly, every time I come here,' the Duke told me.

Bedford Arms Hotel, Woburn, Bedfordshire.

Woodstock, OXFORDSHIRE.

The twelfth-century Bear Inn seems to have a haunted room where occupants find their possessions moved, hear footsteps and tell of other evidence of unseen occupants of the bedroom. During the time she stayed there in November, 1967, while making a film in the neighbourhood, actress Maggie Blye found her nights disturbed by footsteps on the creaking floorboards. Once, at two o'clock in the morning, she awakened to find the dressing-table light switched on. She stated that another member of the film unit moved out of the room after one night there and the manager, Mr Dennis Fulford-Talbot, is reported to have stated that four people in the preceding two years had told him that unexplained happenings had taken place in Room 16.
Marlborough Arms Hotel, Woodstock, Oxon.

Part II
A GAZETTEER OF SCOTTISH AND IRISH GHOSTS

For

PAMELA and CRISPIN

with love

ACKNOWLEDGEMENTS

The author gratefully acknowledges permission to use photographs in this volume from: Peter G. Currie, George J. Edwards, Alasdair Alpin MacGregor, Dame Flora MacLeod of MacLeod, Mrs J. Maxwell-Scott, Donald Ross, Board of Management for Glasgow Western and Gartnavel Hospitals, Irish Tourist Board, Northern Ireland Tourist Board and Scottish Tourist Board.

He also gratefully acknowledges invaluable help in providing information from: Lady Alexandra Airlie, Peter G. Currie, the Marquess of Dufferin and Ava, Miss Theodora FitzGibbon, Tommy Frankland, Affleck Gray, Frank W. Hansell, Norman F. Haynes, Mrs Marion Holbourn, Colin F. McIntosh, Mrs Patricia MacGregor, Dame Flora MacLeod of MacLeod, the Very Rev. Lord MacLeod of Fuinary, Mrs Cathy Mott, Commander G. R. Muir RN, W. T. G. Perrott, Captain Sir Hugh Rhys Rankin, Donald Ross, Julia Lady Seton (Julia Clements), Miss R. M. Simpson and the Earl of Southesk.

INTRODUCTION

The stories of the haunted houses of Scotland and Ireland mirror the life that was once lived in these countries. Perhaps because many of the places are remote and isolated, they have retained for a little longer some remnants of their former history. Both Scotland and Ireland are rich in legends and reputed ghosts; tales that have been handed down from past generations. The ghost stories—even the legends—often have a modicum of truth in them and they should be collected and preserved before they become submerged in the cold world of computers.

Such records of a former way of life, of old beliefs and traditions, are on the verge of oblivion. These relics of the past, once so firmly rooted that they were an accepted part of reality are now all but forgotten and when some inexplicable figure is glimpsed for a moment in some ruined castle, no one knows who that form once was or what crime or suffering may have caused the shade to reappear. I hope this book will help to remedy this state of affairs and that it will add some human element to dry histories of places and people.

I do not claim that all the entries included are factual accounts in the literal sense; but I have endeavoured to present a representative selection of traditional tales of ghostly happenings and well-authenticated instances of ghosts and hauntings, famous and little-known, arranged in alphabetical order of the place at which they are alleged to have occurred.

In December, 1970, I had occasion to write to Mr Frank W. Hansell, the factor of Drummond Castle Estates in Perthshire, and he was good enough to relate a couple of experiences which well illustrate the authenticity of ghostly happenings today:

'In the early summer of the year 1931, I was about twenty years of age, and was travelling to Perth with my father, mother, and young sister who was a teenager. While proceed-

259

ing to Perth on what is known as the Gask Road at a point East 985, North 193 (O.S. Grid reference), I noticed at the side of the road at what used to be a watering place for cattle, a female in a most peculiar costume; as a matter of fact she was dressed in the manner of what I would take to be a witch. At the time I did not mention this to anyone in the car as I was the driver. However, after proceeding about a mile or two along the road, my sister passed the remark to us all, asking if I had seen the woman who was dressed as I have described at the water hole. Of course, I had to tell her that I did. I may say that this place is very near the "Auld House of Gask" which is famous as the home of Lady Nairne who wrote some very fine Scots poetry and songs. I can give you no explanation for this as I did not get out of the car to question the woman or to see if she was actually flesh and blood.

'Shortly afterwards I was describing this incident to my dentist, an exceedingly level-headed gentleman with great knowledge, and he told me that the previous week he had seen two teenage boys from Morrison's Academy (sixth formers) and they had described to him a peculiar incident they had seen on the bridge over the River Pow, while they were fishing close by. The location of the bridge is East 93; North 25. While they were fishing, there appeared on the bridge a lady and a small child dressed in old fashioned crinoline dresses—I should say of the period 1650-1745. I understand from my dentist friend that the boys had seen the two figures, separately, and they were not together when they saw the figures on the bridge and when they met this was their first topic of discussion, each one asking the other and explaining what they had seen. My friend spoke to the boys, separately, and he was quite sure that they had seen something very strange.'

While in a few of the legends and tales of long ago it is difficult to find much substance and reality, I have included many authentic reports of Scottish 'ghosties' and Irish hauntings in past and recent times, from the curious story of disturbances at the Edinburgh home of Sir Alexander Seton after his wife surreptitiously removed an ancient bone from a tomb in Egypt to the whispering ghosts among the mummified remains in the crypt of St Michan's Church in Dublin.

Scotland and Ireland have charms that are all their own, not least perhaps because of the magic quality of so much of those majestic and sparsely populated countries whose kindly people accept without question the possibility of visitations from the dead. There are such individual inhabitants as Lucy Bruce who 'really did see fairies at the bottom of her garden'; Sir Shane Leslie who 'really did have a family banshee' and Captain Sir Hugh Rhys Rankin, Bart., F.S.A., who tells me that he has been followed by the ghost of Oliver Cromwell, seen a Campbell who killed a Stewart of Appin, watched a Norman headless lady carry her own severed head and observed time and time again a bent old hag on the seashore near Barcaldine Home Farm, Benderlock, Argyll, who was driven out of her holding way back after the '45.

Everyone knows that Ireland has leprechauns, often described as a dwarf or gnome in the form of an old man who can be induced only by threats of violence to disclose the hiding-place of his treasure. Should a leprechaun be caught by human beings, he will purchase his liberty by revealing the location of his 'crock of gold', which disappears when its hiding-place is discovered. Not everyone knows that Scotland, too, has individual ghost-like creatures: the kelpie, a ghost-horse and the water-wraith, a young woman dressed in green scowling malignantly at anyone who sees her; while the spectre of Tarbat is an example of the age-old Scottish belief that the ghost of a murdered man is earthbound for the length of time that would have been his span of life, disappearing for ever on the day that he would have died had he not been murdered.

In such places as gaunt Glamis Castle and lovely Ben Macdhui it is not difficult to believe that strange things can happen; things that cannot be explained in material or scientific terms. We may all be the better for realizing that there are some things that we cannot *yet* explain. I emphasize the 'yet' because I believe all these occurrences and experiences have 'normal' explanations; it is simply that we have not yet discovered the why and the wherefore. After all none of us has seen a radio wave, yet we have all heard voices and other sounds that have travelled along these invisible waves. It happens that I heard music in a haunted glade that I am convinced had no known origin; but there may well be some quite normal explanation, possibly on the lines of radio waves. One day we may use telepathy, extra-sensory-perception and other 'supernormal' facilities, each and every day as our natural heritage. When—or until—that day comes such experiences as those that are here collected are of considerable interest, whether as folk memories, as possible evidence of life after death, as wishful thinking or even as examples of the fantasy-ridden human mind; although I venture to suggest that none of these explanations will adequately cover all the material here included.

Since evidence is only as good as the witness concerned, it must be admitted that some of the witnesses for some of the accounts in this collection are shadowy and elusive; others, however, are very good. It should be remembered by the sceptics that such keen-minded men and women as speed king Donald Campbell, television personality Fanny Cradock, Battle-of-Britain saviour Lord Dowding, author Dennis Wheatley and John, Duke of Bedford have all told me that they have seen ghosts.

I hope, too, that these accounts will add interest and give extra enjoyment to those who know the castles, mountains and lochs of Scotland and the green hills, silent lakes and majestic coastline of Ireland, as well as those for whom the pleasures of a visit to these beautiful lands is still to come.

This book would not have been possible without the understanding and encouragement of my wife and the help of many people who have brought to my attention reputed ghosts in Scotland and Ireland and many others who have helped me with up-to-date information. I am grateful to them all and especially to my friend Donald Ross whose encyclopaedic knowledge of Scotland has been of considerable value to me. In addition, his help in supplying source material in respect of a number of cases and his interest and advice at all stages of the book is deeply appreciated.

And if by chance you ever cross the enchanted boundary and have the good fortune to experience some strange happening or have knowledge of some legend or well-attested ghost that I have not included, I shall be most interested to hear from you.

The Savage Club PETER UNDERWOOD
St James's Street,
London, S.W.1

SCOTLAND

Aberdeen

The old Auchinyell district is now occupied by houses but years ago this was a bleak and barren place with an unpleasant marsh-land area known as 'The Clash'. Bordering the south side of the marsh ran a section of the old Deeside highway to Braemar, a section where no traveller lingered on account of the eerie spectre of a cat that haunted this neighbourhood.

The several versions of the origin of the haunting all concern Menzies of Pitfodels and his cat and all have the same tragic ending. It is said that on a particularly dark night he was riding home to Pitfodels past the marsh-land with its evil reputation, when a cat suddenly sprang at him from The Clash and, flying at the unfortunate Menzies' throat, tore at it until he was dead. This cat is thought to have been a real one but no real cat was ever seen again in the vicinity although the ghostly form of a cat was said to haunt The Clash of Auchinyell for many many years afterwards.

Abergeldie, BRAEMAR

A few miles north, where the Fearder Burn joins the Dee, stood the old Mill of Inver, a haunt of the awesome spectre known as the 'Black Hand' that also appeared throughout the glen of the Fearder Burn until it was laid by miller John Davidson.

For generations the centuries-old mill (latterly serving other than its original purpose) was tenanted by a family named Davidson and one dark and wintry night in 1767 John Davidson claimed that he saw the famous 'Black Hand' while he was working in the mill. Chancing to look upwards he saw the floating apparition of a black, sinewy and hairy hand, cut off at the wrist, which had long been reputed to terrorize the local inhabitants. But John Davidson was made of sterner stuff. He immediately challenged the 'Black Hand' and, although he would never divulge the details of what took place, it seems that he had a fierce encounter with something. The following morning he was seen digging deeply in a corner of the yard and eventually he unearthed a curiously wrought basket-hilt of a broad sword. This hung for many years over the fireplace at the mill and there were no reports of the 'Black Hand' being encountered thereafter.

Alves, NEAR ELGIN, MORAYSHIRE

The dominating York Tower here, to the north-west, commemorates Frederick, Duke of York, son of King George III. It stands on the summit of the Knock of Alves, a hill long reputed to be haunted and no place to visit on dark and stormy nights when strange, indistinct shapes have been glimpsed and weird and high-pitched screeches and chuckling heard, although the Knock is indisputably devoid of human beings. This is the traditional meeting-place of Macbeth and the three 'Weird Sisters'.

Annan, DUMFRIESSHIRE

One night in April, 1962, on the stretch of the A75 between Dumfries and Annan, two brothers, Derek and Norman Ferguson, then aged twenty-two and fourteen respectively, had the most terrifying experience of their lives.

The two men had spent a short holiday touring Scotland, Derek driving his father's small saloon car. Now they were about to set off home and stopped for petrol in Dumfries. Then they embarked on what was to be a never-to-be-forgotten part of the journey, before they reached Annan, fifteen miles away.

It was almost midnight but they could see the white road stretching away ahead of them in the dry and moonlit spring night. Derek had just remarked that they seemed to be the only car on the road when what appeared to be a large hen suddenly flew towards them and then disappeared just when it seemed that it must hit the windscreen of the car. Derek swerved to avoid the bird and for a moment both the brothers were shaken, but much worse was to come.

They had hardly recovered from the surprise and shock when they saw the figure of an old woman rushing wildly towards the car, waving her spread arms—and then she, too, vanished into thin air, just as it seemed that the car must run into her. And she was followed by what appeared to be an unending stream of figures that loomed up out of nowhere: great cats, wild-looking dogs, goats, hens and other large fowl and strange creatures, including an old man with long hair who seemed to be screaming. As the horrifying sights and sounds tore at the nerves of the two frightened brothers, the car zig-zagged along the road, swerving and braking and changing course repeatedly in an effort to miss the forms that tore towards them. At first Derek, finding that the mysterious beings never made actual contact with the car, thought that it must all be his imagination but a glance at his brother, crouching wide-eyed in the seat beside him, told him that this was no hallucination: Norman was seeing the same awful phantoms.

As they proceeded through the throng of open-mouthed and wild-looking creatures, both young men noticed an appreciable drop in temperature within the car although by this time both were drenched in perspiration.

'My hands seemed to become very heavy,' Derek said afterwards, 'and it was as if some force were trying to gain control of the steering wheel; the control of the car became increasingly difficult. We seemed to be suffocating and I opened the window to get some fresh air but it was bitterly cold outside and I just hung on to the wheel as screaming, high-pitched laughter and cackling noises seemed to mock our predicament. I was absolutely certain at the time that an attempt was being made to force us off the road and I was equally certain that a fatal accident would result.'

In the end Derek stopped the car. Immediately some powerful force seemed to attack them; the two young men felt the car being bounced violently up and down on the road, rocked so forcefully from side to side that they became dizzy. As Derek felt very sick, he wrenched open the car door

269

and leaped out. Immediately all was quiet and the road and surrounding countryside was still and utterly deserted. Yet as soon as he returned to the car and slammed shut the door, the shaking and buffeting recommenced together with the unearthly and high-pitched laughter. A high wind seemed to blow up and there was the sensation of fists striking the sides, the front and back and top of the car to add to the terror of the unfortunate occupants.

Derek decided that the only thing to do was to press on home. He restarted the car and proceeded slowly through the night that was still full of the weird figures continually looming up suddenly out of nowhere and the frightening noises that seemed to come from every direction. Often the figures would stop in the path of the car, as though daring him to run them down, but although his hands and arms became almost unendurably painful with the strain, Derek kept a straight course and the figures disintegrated just as it seemed that he must slam into them. All the time Derek was conscious of his horror-stricken and strangely quiet younger brother beside him.

After a while the Ferguson brothers noticed a small red gleam ahead of them in the gathering darkness and as they drew nearer they were relieved to find that it was the tail-light of a large furniture van. Yet no sooner was Derek pleased to find some apparently normal object on that haunted road, when he realized that he was approaching it far too quickly and that there would be a collision. Exhausted physically and emotionally by the recent events he now discovered to his horror that he could not swerve or take any evasive action. His feet refused to move from the accelerator pedal. He screamed to his brother to prepare himself for a crash. And then they were upon the van and it vanished completely!

Shattered, buffeted and drained of strength, the brothers continued slowly on their way until Derek found the car had slowed down to a crawl. He realized that the noises and the high wind had died away and they found themselves approaching Annan. The whole experience had lasted nearly half an hour. Afterwards Derek congratulated himself on stopping for petrol in Dumfries; had they been unable to continue along that terrible road into Annan that night, he dreads to think what the consequences might have been.

Later Derek Ferguson talked with a friend who had been stationed near Annan during his military service in the Second World War. This man had often heard tales of witchcraft being practised in the area; while another friend stated that he had read of a phantom furniture van that was reputed to have been seen in the vicinity.

Neither of the Ferguson brothers, nor any of their family had previously any kind of psychic experience nor was it ever repeated. It is interesting that Norman was an adolescent at the time, possibly the unconscious link with the strange appearances on the lonely Annan road.

Ardrossan, AYRSHIRE

On Castle Hill remnants can still be found of the once great castle of the Montgomerys. The spot is reputed to be haunted by Sir William Wallace, the Scottish patriot who was defeated by King Edward I at Falkirk in 1298 and executed in London in 1305.

Wallace once craftily set fire to a nearby hamlet, luring there a large detachment of the English soldiers and slaughtering them one by one as they returned to the garrison. He threw the corpses into the castle dungeon, known thereafter as 'Wallace's Larder'.

Earlier still, the castle was the home of a sorcerer, known as the 'Deil o' Ardrossan' and a stone in the yard of the local church (which was destroyed in a storm in the seventeenth century) has long been regarded as marking his burial place, although according to a different tradition he was buried on the shores of Arran in a shroud made from a bull's hide. Legend has long linked the stone with disaster and it is said that should any portion of the earth be taken from under the stone and cast into the sea, a fearful tempest would devastate the sea and the land.

It is only on stormy nights that Wallace's giant figure has been seen within the precincts of his old home, glimpsed momentarily as the lightning flashes.

The wild and beautiful countryside around Loch Assynt has been haunted since a murder was committed here over a hundred-and-fifty years ago.

A pedlar by the name of Murdoch Grant amassed a considerable amount of money from trading among the lonely farmsteads; he always carried the money on his person. On the morning of March 11th, 1830, he set off to sell his wares at a wedding at Assynt. Afterwards he announced that he was going to Drumbeg and he was last seen alive, with his pedlar's pack on his back, walking in the direction of Nedd.

A month later a courting couple on the banks of Torna-Eigin saw a body floating in the clear water and when the body had been recovered from the loch, it was found to be that of the pedlar.

There was a deep wound on the dead man's head and this injury, coupled with the fact that Grant's pack was missing, pointed to foul play. Among the local men who had assisted in retrieving the body from the water was the village school-master who watched with disdain as the superstitious villagers carried out the custom of 'touch-proof'. All the bystanders were required to touch the dead body as proof of their innocence in causing the death: it was believed that in the case of a guilty person touching the body, blood would appear. Macleod, the school-master, refused to take any part in such superstition. He declared that in his opinion death was due to natural causes and the wound on the head was probably caused by the body striking rocks in the loch after death.

The local magistrates and minister were sent for and the latter, who arrived first, agreed with Macleod that the wound had probably occurred after death. Eventually the body of Murdoch Grant was buried.

Some time later the dead man's brother, Robert Grant, turned up at Assynt. He was not satisfied with the story of his brother's death and insisted on an exhumation. This was done but no new light was thrown on the affair and in spite of Macleod's repeated insistence that there was no shred of evidence to suggest any other cause of death but simple drowning, Robert Grant was still unconvinced. In particular, he was concerned that no money had been found on his brother's body. When six months passed and still there was no sign of the pedlar's pack, Robert Grant became more and more certain that his brother had been murdered.

During the course of his inquiries in the locality he talked to the village shopkeeper who told him that only that very morning school-master Macleod had dropped his purse in his shop. It had burst open and ten golden sovereigns had rolled out. This set Robert Grant thinking afresh for he knew that school-masters were not well-paid and he had already noticed that Macleod had expensive tastes; that his fondness for feminine company was costing him much more than his salary would be likely to cover. Furthermore, a number of Macleod's outstanding debts had been miraculously paid recently. Robert Grant saw a magistrate and Macleod was interviewed; his answers to the questions were evasive and he was arrested.

Now the police began to search for evidence but the absence of the dead man's pack meant that they had nothing tangible to work on. It looked as though they would have to release their prisoner when a local man named Kenneth Frazer, reputed to have the gift of second sight, came forward to say that he had seen the murder in a vision. He described the place where the deed had been done and pointed to Macleod as the murderer. In addition he told the police where the missing pack would be discovered and described its contents, including some personal items belonging to the murdered man which were found in Macleod's possession.

The police found everything exactly as the seer had foretold and before he paid for his crime Macleod confessed that he had hit Murdoch Grant over the head, robbed him of his money, hid the pack after taking some of the contents and had then thrown the body into the loch.

Thereafter for many years it was said that each March 11th, just as the watery sun sank down beyond Lochinver, at a certain spot on the mossy bank of Loch Assynt, sounds were heard of a single dreadful blow followed by a long drawn-

273

out sigh and the noise of panting and running footsteps.

The ancient castle of Ardvreck by Loch Assynt was occupied for well over a hundred years by a wicked old dowager who, among her other peculiarities, was always meddling in affairs that did not concern her and talking scandal constantly.

A gentleman and his wife who lived nearby were lucky enough to escape her serious attention for some years but on the birth of a child the husband's jealousy was awakened by insinuations put about by the old lady. He not only taxed his wife with infidelity but even threatened to destroy the infant.

In her distress the poor woman wrote to her two brothers and within a few days they both arrived to see what they could do to help. After remonstrating unsuccessfully with the husband, they decided that their only useful course would be to visit the old lady of Ardvreck. 'I plan to confront her with a person as clever as herself,' declared the younger brother darkly. He was much travelled and a student of occult arts.

The lady at the castle received the three men hospitably enough but they decided that her candour was less than complete when they eventually broached the subject of their visit. At length the younger brother suggested that they might seek the truth of the matter by calling in a mutual acquaintance. The old lady raised no objection and while the two men and the dowager were seated in the low-ceilinged hall of the castle, a large, rude chamber, roofed and floored with stone and furnished with a row of narrow, unglazed windows which looked out onto the loch, the younger brother rose quietly from his place and bending towards the floor proceeded to trace strange diagrams and figures, muttering at the same time in an unrecognized language.

The day was calm but as the young man proceeded in his mystifying practice, the still waters of the loch began to heave and swell. A 'fleece of vapour' seemed to rise from the surface of the waters and spread upwards like a cloud. As it disappeared, it was noticed that a tall, dark figure, as indistinct as the shadow of a man, now stood by the far wall of the room.

274

'Now,' said the younger brother to the husband, 'put your question and make haste.' In a timorous voice the awed man asked whether his wife had been unfaithful to him? Back came the answer that she was completely faithful. At the same time a huge wave from the loch smashed against the wall of the castle, breaking in at the hall windows and a tremendous wind, accompanied by hail, burst upon the roof of and turrets so that the very floor seemed to rise and fall beneath their feet.

'He will not leave us without payment,' said the young man, turning to the old lady. 'Whom can you best spare?'

She, terrified at the events that had been witnessed, tottered to the door and, as she opened it, a little orphan girl, whom she sheltered, came running into the hall, frightened by the storm. The lady pointed to the child. 'No,' said the dark stranger in the corner. 'I dare not take an orphan.'

As another enormous wave threw itself against the castle and came pouring in at the windows, the elder brother pointed to the old woman who had poisoned the trust between his sister and her husband. 'Take her,' he screamed; but the shadow replied quietly: 'She is mine already and her term is not quite run but I will take with me one whom your sister will miss more.' The next moment the shadowy form had disappeared, the storm abated and the puzzled party looked from one to the other. Returning home they learned that the infant, whose birth had caused so much disquiet, had died at the precise time that the dark shadow had vanished in the castle hall.

It is said that for five years afterwards only black and shrivelled grain was produced at Assynt and that no fish were taken from the loch. At the end of that period the castle of Ardvreck was destroyed in a mysterious fire, the old lady perishing in the flames, and after her death things resumed their natural course once more with the wheat ripening on the corn and fat fish again swam in the quiet loch.

Athelstaneford, EAST LOTHIAN

The legend about the origin of the national emblem of Scotland tells how the Picts and the Scots under King

Hungus saw a vision in the sky of an enormous white saltine. Strengthened by a belief that this was a sign that St Andrew would protect them, they won a decisive victory over the English King Athelstan.

It is interesting to note that the twelfth-century version of the legend relates how Hungus, after successful skirmishes with the British, spent the winter with his army near the English-Scottish border. He and seven companions were nearly blinded by a 'divine light', while the voice of St Andrew was heard 'from heaven' promising them protection and telling them that the cross of Christ would precede them as they marched on their enemies. Next day the same sign is said to have moved in front of the twelve columns of Hungus's army.

A thirteenth-century version speaks of King Hungus camping at the mouth of the River Tyne with the army he gathered against the Saxon King Athelstan and of St Andrew appearing and promising him a great victory over his enemies.

A fourteenth-century version names Athelstaneford as the place where Hungus encamped and the vision of St Andrew is related as promising victory and stating that an angel would walk in front of the soldiers.

Finally a sixteenth-century version of the legend mentions a night-time vision and St Andrew's prediction of victory over the English and in addition relates that King Hungus, awakening from the dream, found his army gazing at a shining cross in the sky.

King Athelstan is reputed to have been killed in battle by a spear piercing his body. The place where he was slain and where his army was defeated was named Athelstaneford.

Balgie, GLEN LYON, PERTHSHIRE

The Meggernie Ghost is the name given to the singular haunting associated with nearby Meggernie Castle, parts of which date back to the fifteenth century. It is an attractive French-château style building approached by a fine avenue of limes half-way up the longest glen in Scotland. The ghost is the upper half of a woman.

276

The panelled Ghost Room is high up in the baronial tower, one of the oldest parts of the castle. Among the stories of the haunting still available is one dating back to 1862 when two friends were among a number of guests at Meggernie. They were allotted a room each in the Tower. There they found a blocked-up door without even a keyhole that used to connect the rooms via a small closet.

During the darkest hours of the night one guest was awakened by what he afterwards described as an exceedingly hot kiss upon his cheek, so hot that he felt as though his face had been burned through. He leapt out of bed and saw the upper half of a woman's body drifting away from his bedside across the room where it disappeared through the blocked-up door. Within seconds he had established that the mysterious door was still firmly fastened and although he tried to reproduce the appearance he had seen by casting shadows from a lamp and moving the curtains of the window, he was quite unsuccessful. Eventually he returned to his bed and in the morning lost no time in calling to his friend in the next room to tell him that he had had a terrible experience during the night.

Before he could say any more his friend called back that he, too, had had a strange experience and suggested they told their respective tales individually to someone else in the first place so that it could not be said afterwards that they had worked their accounts together. This they did and when they compared notes it was found that both guests had had almost identical experiences, even to describing the look of despair on the beautiful face of the ghost.

The other guest wrote up his experience, giving the time of his awakening as two-thirty a.m. and recounting that the first thing he noticed was a strange pink light in the room which seemed to emanate from a female form standing at the foot of his bed. The figure moved to the side of his bed and leaned over him and then retreated as he raised himself up. For the first time he then saw that the figure had no lower half. It retreated to the closet and disappeared in the vicinity of the blocked-up door. Quickly getting out of bed he, too, established to his entire satisfaction that the closet was deserted and that there was no way out of his room. A couple of months later he met at a hotel a lady who had been to Meggernie and she told him that she too had seen a ghost there—the upper half of a woman whose appearance she described, including the look of despair on her face and the way the hair had been arranged.

Such a figure had long been said to haunt the castle rooms and corridors and in the graveyard in the park the *lower* half of a female figure had been seen many times walking among the gravestones and sometimes sitting on them. While the lower trunk was clearly visible and the legs moved about unhesitatingly, the head, shoulders and arms were missing and the mutilated trunk passing briskly over the ground, picking its way among the graves in the gathering gloom must have been a weird and fearsome sight.

A week after his experience in the Tower one of the guests was sitting alone late at night writing letters when the heavy oak door of the room suddenly flew open. At the same time the temperature in the room seemed to drop to freezing-point and although he saw nothing on this occasion, the guest had an overwhelming feeling of terror. He hastily put away his papers and could not get out of the room fast enough. On the way to his bedroom he passed along a corridor and there, looking at him through a window, he saw a face: it was the beautiful face that he and his fellow guest had seen in their respective rooms a week before! He saw it distinctly and clearly in the light from the corridor, before it faded away.

Another witness of the ghost at Meggernie was the wife of Colonel Kinloch Grant who visited the castle one autumn and awoke in the middle of the night to find a female form bending over her. She was neither frightened nor surprised for she was sleeping in the Tower part of the castle and sensed that she was seeing the ghost of a former Lady of Meggernie. She adds in her letter detailing the experience that the churchyard at Meggernie was a lovely secluded spot and she spent many a quiet hour there, often wondering why the place had such an evil reputation after dark; for nobody at the house or at the farm or indeed any of the Glen people would go there or even pass it alone after darkness.

My friend Alasdair Alpin MacGregor told me that he had obtained evidence concerning a doctor who had visited Meggernie one October evening and had spent the night there. He found himself awake in the middle of the night with the feeling that someone or something was outside his bedroom door and while waiting for a knock to summon him, he suddenly saw a human head and shoulders with nothing below them, gliding along a wall of the bedroom, high up near the ceiling. It stopped opposite and looked down at him. He stared back at the head without a body—and suddenly it was no longer there. Next morning he asked why he had been put in the haunted room and was told that no visitor was ever put in there and that the room he had occupied was in fact immediately below the haunted room. His host went on to say that knocks that could not be explained were often heard in that part of the castle. Some years before, the doctor was told, when repairs were carried out in the Tower part of the castle, a skeleton head and shoulders were discovered and these bones were taken out and buried but unlike many hauntings, the half-ghost of Meggernie was seen again.

Meggernie Castle once belonged to the Clan Menzies and a former laird is said to have committed a cruel murder that gave rise to the haunting. Insanely jealous of his beautiful young wife he murdered her in the Tower, cut her body in two and concealed the portions in the closet between the two Tower rooms. Then, spreading the word that he and his wife would be abroad for some months, he left Meggernie only returning when he felt that the danger of discovery was past and he could bury the remains of his wife. Stating that his wife had met with an accident abroad, he succeeded in conveying one half of her body to the graveyard where he buried it unobserved. He intended to do likewise with the upper part of the body but the night he chose for this task— a more dangerous one since the head would be recognizable —he was himself found dead at the entrance to the Tower in circumstances that suggested that he had been murdered; perhaps by someone who had discovered the laird's awful secret. But there was no evidence to show who murdered the murderer and the affair was allowed to rest.

Alternatively it has been suggested that the laird encountered the incomplete apparition of his young wife whom he had butchered so cruelly and met his death from shock.

And if the unfortunate lady was as free with her kisses in her life as she seems to have been in death, perhaps there was some justification for her husband's jealousy.

Ballachulish, ARGYLLSHIRE

Ballachulish House is haunted, as indeed it should be, for here, or rather in the house that formerly occupied the site, Captain Campbell was ordered to put to the sword every MacDonald under seventy years of age and the scene of the resulting massacre is less than five miles away.

The present house is said to be haunted by the ghost of a Stewart of Appin who gallops up to the house, dismounts and then vanishes as he reaches the doorway; while on the beech-lined road leading to the house the inexplicable clip-clop of horses' hooves has often been heard and here, too, a ghostly rider has been seen dismounting from his ghostly horse.

There is a story too of a phantom tinker seen near the gate of Ballachulish House on autumn evenings; and when the place was occupied by Sir Harold Boulton (who wrote *Over the Sea to Skye*) a footman complained that he had seen a ghost walk through a wall in the house.

Sir Harold always vouched for the authenticity of a very strange story. Years before he had ever heard of Ballachulish House, his mother would speak of a beautifully-situated residence about which she often thought and dreamed. So familiar did the dream-house become that she often talked about the place to the family and seemed thoroughly familiar with every corner and part of it. Imagine her surprise when she arrived at Ballachulish House to find that it was the house of her dreams! She was able to tell Lady Beresford, the owner, about a staircase that used to be a feature of the place but was long bricked-up and out of sight. Imagine her even greater surprise when Lady Beresford told her that she, Mrs Boulton, was the little lady who had haunted Ballachulish House for years!

Ballater, ABERDEENSHIRE

On the South Road there is a little stream still known as

'The Spinning Jenny Burn'. From time immemorial the figure of an old witch used to be seen sitting beside the stream, spinning; but when road-building altered the course of the burn she was reported to have moved higher up into the hills where she has reputedly been seen in recent years still spinning beside the stream.

Banff, BANFFSHIRE

Not far from here, in the beautiful and wild countryside, there is a romantic valley that is almost unchanged for hundreds of years; a valley that is haunted by a Green Lady.

The wife of a local laird had been dead some six months when one of her husband's ploughmen, returning home on horseback in the twilight of an autumn evening, was accosted, as he was about to cross a small stream, by a strange lady dressed from head to foot in green. Tall and slim, her face hidden in the mantle of her hood, she politely requested to be taken up behind the rider and carried across the stream.

There was something in the tone of her voice that chilled the hearer and, as he afterwards said, seemed to insinuate itself in the form of an icy fluid between his skull and his scalp. The request itself was odd for the stream was little more than a rivulet, small and slight, presenting no problem to the most timid traveller. However the man offered the young woman a lift, partly on account of the odd chill that ran through him when she spoke and partly because he did not wish to appear discourteous.

She lightly sprang up behind him and he then found that she was more easily seen than touched for where she came in contact with his back it felt, he asserted afterwards, as though she was a half-filled sack of wool.

As soon as they reached the other side of the stream she leapt down as lightly as she had mounted. He turned to catch a second glimpse of her, sure now that she was a creature less of this earth than himself. She turned towards him, opening as she did so the enveloping hood of her cloak, to disclose a face, thin and pale, but apparently full of life. 'My dead mistress!' exclaimed the ploughman. 'Yes, John; your

281

mistress,' replied the green ghost. 'But ride home quickly for it is getting late and you and I will be better acquainted before long.' John rode swiftly home and told his story.

Next evening, at about the same hour, two of the laird's servant girls were washing when they heard a light tap on the door. 'Come in,' one of the girls called out and in walked the Green Lady. She swept past the two wide-eyed girls and seated herself on a low bench which she had often used during her lifetime, as it gave her a good view of her servants. Now she began to question them as to how their work was going as she had often done in the past but the girls were too frightened to reply. Soon she moved with a strange half-gliding motion out of the room and into another part of the house occupied by an old nurse of whom she had been very fond. She still seemed to be interested in the old woman's welfare and remarked on the emptiness of the food cupboard!

For almost a year scarcely a day passed when the Green Lady was not seen by some of the servants though never, except for one possible exception, after the sun had risen or before it set. Evening after evening she would glide into the kitchen and enquire about the girls' work and happiness. As time passed, nearly all the people in the house became used to her presence; the servants looked upon her as a troublesome mistress they no longer needed to heed. When she arrived, they would lower their voices, thinking for a moment that it was a person of flesh and blood, then they would resume their normal chatter, remarking that it was 'only the Green Lady'.

Although shockingly pale and miserable-looking, the phantom nevertheless affected a joyous disposition and was frequently heard to chuckle and laugh—sometimes when she was not visible!

Once, provoked by the continuous silence of one of the servants, the ghost threw a pillow at the girl's head, which she caught and returned! Another time she presented her first acquaintance, the ploughman, with what appeared to be a handful of silver coins which he transferred to his pocket —only to find when he tried to spend them, that they were slivers of slate. A horseman, passing a clump of trees, found himself repeatedly struck from behind by little pellets of turf and, riding into the thicket, discovered his assailant to be the Green Lady. She never appeared to her husband, although he frequently heard the sound of her voice echoing from the lower part of the house and sometimes also the faint peal of her cold and unnatural laugh.

Then one wet and stormy day, at noon about a year after she had first been seen, she appeared in the room of the old nurse, warning her to get help quickly to save two of the children who were in danger on the rocks by the seashore. The old woman lost no time in doing as she was directed and so impressed the father with her earnestness that he set out at once. Reaching the top of the cliffs he saw, far below him, the two children clinging to the highest crags of a rock, with the restless and storm-tossed sea threatening to engulf them or pluck them from their perches. Frantic with terror for their safety he nevertheless judged that he had time to get help before the waters completely swept over the rock and sure enough no sooner had the children been snatched to safety than an immense wave, twice the height of a man, broke over the topmost part of the rock.

When she returned to her room, the old nurse found the Green Lady sitting beside the fire and there she related the reason for her restlessness after death. Ten years before, she said, a travelling pedlar broke into the fruit garden and an old ploughman was sent to drive him away, since it was a Sunday and there was no one else at home. The pedlar turned on the old servant; she went to his assistance, and in the fight that followed, the trespasser was killed. At first it was decided to take the whole matter to the laird but when the laird's lady saw the dead man's pack with its silks and velvets and a lovely piece of green satin they hit on the plan of burying the body and dividing the goods and money between them. The money was hidden in a little cavity under a tapestry in her bedroom and the green satin was made into a dress ...

As the Green Lady's story ended the old nurse watched, aghast, as the figure slowly and sadly glided away in a gleam of light that made the old woman shield her eyes with her hand. When she looked again, the Green Lady had vanished. A little hoard of gold coins was found concealed as the ghost

283

had said and some mouldering remains of the pedlar; evidence of the truth of the ghost's story.

Beauly, INVERNESS-SHIRE

The thirteenth-century remains of the Valliscaulian Priory of St John are the subject of a legend concerning a wager with the Devil that is said to be proved by the evidence of a ghostly handprint (four fingers and a thumb) on the stone doorway. The legend became known as the 'Tailor of Beauly Priory' although in fact its origin seems to go back no more than a hundred years or so. It probably has been confused with another from Argyllshire, at Ardchattan, where the same ingredients form part of a local legend.

Ben Ime, GLENCROE, ARGYLLSHIRE

A few years ago Kenneth Richmond, a lecturer at the University of Glasgow, climbed snowy Ben Ime looking for ptarmigan, the smallest British grouse that frequents the Arctic and sub-Arctic regions of the Northern hemisphere including Scotland. Instead he found a ghost.

Richmond was eating his sandwiches near the top of the mountain when he saw, plodding towards him, the figure of an old man, dressed in a bowler hat, wearing a gold watch-chain across his waistcoat and carrying a large paper parcel under his arm. 'His face was the colour of parchment,' Richmond said, 'as if he had spent his life at a city desk, yet he did not even seem to be out of breath.' The old man slowed down and then stopped and seemed to be fidgeting with the parcel. Richmond was intrigued as to what could have brought the man so far off the beaten track and after greeting his fellow-climber, he asked him which way he had come. 'From Arrochar' he was told, the village at the head of Loch Long, a long road and mountain walk away. Such a climb hardly seemed possible for an octogenarian, as the old man must have surely been. Richmond asked him whether he had noticed any birds on the way up. The man

The ruins of Baldoon Castle, Bladnoch, where the ghost of tragic Janet Dalrymple walks in white garments splashed with blood. *Photo: George J. Edwards*

Ancient Auchnadarroch, Duror, Argyllshire, in early Spring, the house has a Haunted Room where many strange things have happened and a ghost known as 'the Maid of Glen Duror'. *Photo: Alasdair Alpin MacGregor*

The beech-lined road at Ballachulish that is haunted by a ghostly horse
and rider, sometimes seen and not heard, more often heard and not seen.
Photo: Alasdair Alpin MacGregor

The Binns Tower, House
of The Binns, Blackness,
West Lothian, where the
ghost of General Tam
Dalyell has been seen,
galloping across the ruined
bridge mounted on a white
charger. *Photo: Scottish
Tourist Board*

said he had seen four speckled water-hens and he pointed out the exact spot, downhill in the direction he had apparently climbed. 'Och, well,' he remarked, looking at his pocket watch; 'I'd best be getting along. Mustn't miss my train.'

'Train from where?' asked Richmond. 'From Glasgow: six-ten from Arrochar,' the old man replied and, with a wave of his hand, turned and set off the way he had come.

Richmond looked at his watch. It was only three-thirty, but on foot the old man could not hope to catch the train he had mentioned (especially as he seemed intent on walking via Glencroe, a long way round) and, since he had left his car down in Glencroe, the lecturer felt that he must offer his strange fellow-mountaineer a lift to his station. He set off and soon caught up with the old man, but the latter would not hear of a lift, insisting that he had plenty of time and that the walk would do him good. With that the odd figure set off again leaving Richmond to resume his climbing. Looking back a moment later, Richmond was surprised at seeing no sign of the strange figure. The three-thousand feet of open, snowy slope below him appeared to be utterly deserted.

Thinking that perhaps the old man was resting behind a rock, Richmond sat down and scanned the slopes with his binoculars, watching for him to reappear but he did not see the figure again.

Later, on his way down the mountain, Richmond paused at the spot where the old man had seen the four water-hens and, sure enough, there they were. Then, as he was looking at the criss-cross pattern of ptarmigan trails in the snow, he realized that there were no human footprints in the snow other than his own leading down from the summit ridge.

It was twenty-to-six when he reached his car and he drove towards Arrochar. There he discovered that there was no train at six-ten. By this time Richmond was puzzled and he wondered whether the old man was still somewhere on the hills or perhaps had caught a bus—or maybe slipped and hurt himself. Wondering whether he should notify the police, he decided to check first with the ticket collector at the station. There he was still further puzzled to learn that no man of

285

such a description had arrived that morning, or any other morning as far as could be recollected!

'A strange business,' was Kenneth Richmond's conclusion. 'And our brief encounter will never be renewed if I can help it; since that day I have stayed away from Ben Ime.'

Ben Macdhui, THE CAIRNGORMS

The River Spey is regarded by those who should know as one of the fastest major rivers in Britain. The Grants have been associated with this valley (or 'strath') of the Spey since time immemorial and they even have a special snowdrift of their own on Cairngorm, the blue mountain, which is supposed to wax and wane with the fortunes of the clan.

One of the six main peaks of the Cairngorms and the highest in Ben Macdhui (4,296 feet) with its flat and bare summit; a mountain with a spectre known as the Big Grey Man of Ben Macdhui, whose 'existence' or presence has been vouched for by a considerable number of people over the years. The appearance of the figure and the experience of the climbers vary considerably and it seems interesting to consider some of the reports chronologically.

An early report came from Norman Collie, Professor of Organic Chemistry at the University of London (1902-1928) and Fellow of the Royal Society. He stated that in 1891 he was returning from the cairn on the summit in a mist when he heard footsteps following him, but taking steps three or four times the length of his own. He stopped and listened and peered into the mist but could see nothing. Suddenly terror seized Collie; he took to his heels and staggered blindly among the boulders for several miles until he saw the Rothiemurchus Forest ahead and realized that the mysterious footsteps were no longer following him.

In the summer of 1904 Hugh Welsh and his brother spent a fortnight camping as near the summit cairn as possible, collecting alpine plants and spiders. During their first nights at the summit of Ben Macdhui, they both heard soft footsteps following them but they never saw anything that might account for the sounds. Later they heard distinct footsteps in daylight and were conscious of 'something' near them, an

286

eerie sensation on a deserted mountain. They never saw anything that could have explained the matter.

Dr A. M. Kellas, who died during the 1921-1922 Mount Everest Reconnaissance Expedition and is buried within sight of that mountain, was a very experienced mountaineer. He claimed that one clear June night he was on the summit of Ben Macdhui with his brother; they were resting a little apart from each other. Suddenly Kellas saw a figure climb up out of the Lairig Ghru pass, wander round the cairn and then disappear again into the pass. The doctor was struck dumb in astonishment: not only by the fact that someone else was on the summit but more particularly at the enormous size of the figure for, as it passed close to the ten-foot high cairn, it seemed to be about the same height! His brother saw nothing.

George Duncan, a former Honorary Sheriff-Substitute of Aberdeen and a veteran mountaineer, told of seeing a tall figure in a black robe as he drove along the Derry road at dusk after coming off the mountain in 1914. The figure appeared to be waving long arms in a menacing fashion and Duncan felt a cold shiver run down his spine before he turned a corner and the figure was no longer in view.

In 1928 a psychic, Joan Grant and her husband were walking in brilliant sunshine in the Rothiemurchus Forest towards the Cairngorms when she was suddenly overwhelmed with terror and turned and fled back along the path they had just traversed through the forest. She was convinced that something 'utterly malign, four-legged and obscenely human, invisible and yet solid' (for she could hear the pounding of hooves), was trying to reach her. A year later one of her father's professors described an almost identical experience in the same area and there was some correspondence in *The Times*, including a letter from a reader who claimed to have been pursued by 'something'.

In 1941 Miss Wendy Wood, a well-known Scottish naturalist, fled in terror from the Lairig Ghru pass. She had just reached the entrance to the pass at night after a dull day with slight snow on the ground, when she heard a voice 'of gigantic resonance' close beside her. It sounded like Gaelic but she was too frightened to attempt any interpretation and she was trying to convince herself that it must be an echo of a deer's bark or something of the sort when she heard the sound again, right at her feet. There could be no doubt this time but that it was human speech. Still she tried to look at the mystery logically and she tramped round in widening circles in case someone was lying injured under the snow but once she was satisfied that she was not deserting anyone in distress, fear took over and she couldn't get away from the place fast enough. Then she heard gigantic footfalls which seemed to follow her hurrying footsteps and she had the impression that something was walking immediately behind her. Just as she was trying to tell herself that the footsteps were echoes of her own, she discovered that the heavy crunch-crunch behind her did not coincide with her own progress and then terror possessed her and without thought of injury to herself she stumbled down the mountain until, near White-well, a barking dog drew her mind back to the world of reality and she realized that she could no longer hear the footsteps following her.

In 1943 Alexander Tewnion, another experienced moun-taineer, naturalist and photographer, reached the summit of Ben Macdhui one October afternoon when climbing alone, just as a dense mist spread across the Lairig Ghru and en-veloped the mountain. The atmosphere became dark and gloomy and as the wind rose, Tewnion feared a storm was imminent and he retreated down the Coire Etchachan path. As he did so, he heard one loud footstep, echoing through the wind, and then another and another, spaced out at long intervals. As he carried a revolver Tewnion stopped and peered about him into the mist that was rent here and there by eddies of wind. Suddenly a huge shape loomed up, receded and then appeared to charge straight at him! Without hesi-tation he pulled out his revolver and fired three times at the figure. Still it came on and Tewnion turned and ran down the path without another backward glance, reaching Glen Derry, as he put it, 'in a time I have never bettered!'

In 1942, while at the Shelter Stone of Ben Macdhui, alone at twilight, Second World War veteran Syd Scroggie sud-denly saw a tall human figure appear out of the blackness at one side of the Loch Etchachan below and, clearly silhouetted against the water, walk with long and deliberate steps across the burns and disappear into the blackness at the other side of the loch. Noticing that the figure carried no rucksack, Scroggie was quickly over the rough ground and at the spot where the figure had crossed. No footprints were visible and there was now no sign of the mysterious figure. Scroggie began shouting but he received no reply, only the echo of his own voice. He became uneasily aware of the approaching darkness and silence surrounding him like a blanket and the brooding, watching Cairngorms. With the hair at the back of his neck beginning to bristle, Scroggie made his way back to the Shelter Stone.

These are but a few of the reports of strange experiences on the wild and stony slopes of Ben Macdhui; reports that have convinced such well-known Scotsmen as Henry Tegner that something out of the ordinary does, on occasions, take place in these Highland mountains.

Benderloch, NEAR OBAN, ARGYLLSHIRE

Sir Hubert Stewart Rankine has described a figure that disappeared into the air when he encountered it in the haunted valley of the Glendhu Burn. This is a deep and unfrequented burn that runs into the sea near Barcaldine Post Office on the coast road to Appin.

A dark, dank place with little life apart from the mournful trees, and even sheep steer clear of the neighbourhood. Local people have long shunned the valley and will tell you that they 'fear something...'

On this particular winter's day his stalker was reluctant to go into the area and after Sir Hubert had shot a stag he made his way alone down the glen, in broad daylight, towards his home.

Suddenly, when he was half-way down, he noticed a dark figure standing near a forestry hut, just above a bog. As he drew nearer, Sir Hubert saw that the figure was a youngish man, large and powerfully-built, wearing a kilt and armed with a dirk. His long hair streamed in the wind; his brogues were thick with mud and he looked puzzled and angry. It

289

was the face of the man that impressed itself on Sir Hubert's memory for it bore a fierce and scowling expression. The figure appeared to be unaware of him. The mouth, large and cruel, was crooked in a curious way and of an unusual shape. The eyes glared as if in anger or distress but no words or indeed any sound accompanied the figure as it moved with gliding steps. It seemed to follow Sir Hubert for perhaps half a mile down the burn, until he reached a cottage, the only inhabited place in the area, where the figure disappeared into thin air. One moment it was there, purposefully making its way down the valley, the next there was nothing to be seen where the greyish and almost transparent apparition had been.

Sir Hubert immediately thought of Campbell (or 'Crooked Mouth' from the Gaelic words for 'crooked' and 'mouth': cam and beul). He wondered whether this was the Campbell who was the victim of the Appin murder, an historical who-dunit that has attracted the attention of writers like Robert Louis Stevenson, Andrew Lang, Sir William MacArthur and Hugh Ross Williamson. Colin Campbell of Glenure—the Red Fox—was shot dead on May 14th, 1752; an aftermath of the troubles of '45 when the clans were suppressed, the kilt forbidden and the lands of loyal Highlanders confiscated.

The Black Isle, ROSS AND CROMARTY (See also *Cromarty*)

The Devil is said to have been in the habit of appearing here in the shape of a handsome young man, mounted on a black horse, usually in the vicinity of Mount High, four miles distant from its twin peak, Mount Eagle. Only a few years ago the older inhabitants talked of such visitations but the younger people have no time for such legends. Yet 'truth is in folklore', one historian has reminded us; 'you'll not find lies carried down the years'.

The peninsula's inhabitants included in the past Coinneach Odhar, known as the Wizard of Brahan, who had the gift of second sight and came to be regarded as an emissary of the Devil. He ended his days two hundred years ago by being burned to death in a barrel of tar at Chanonry Point, opposite Fort George on the other side of the Moray Firth. More recently a woman known as 'Red Jock's Wife' was regarded as a witch for she had the evil eye. It was said that she could turn butter bad at a glance or cause a cow to 'slip' her calf. Occasionally, however, she used her gift to good account. There is a report that after he had been kind to her by carrying her basket, a youngster named Hughie lost in the harvest field a fine silver watch which he had bought with his first wages; but after he and his family and friends had spent hours searching the stubble, Red Jock's Wife led him to it, a week after it had been lost, with her eyes closed.

Another story about Red Jock's Wife concerned the Laird of Ballincailleach, a man who was inordinately proud of his high-bred white sow named Beatrice of Ballincailleach. The laird chanced to be rude to Red Jock's Wife and refused her a fill of tobacco; an action he regretted when his sow gave birth to eleven beautiful young pigs, all born dead. A large hare was seen to dart out of the sty after the births and someone suggested that it was Red Jock's Wife in disguise since it was well known that witches could turn themselves into hares and could cause animals to be born dead.

The laird took a silver sixpence from his pocket and loaded it into his gun and he shot the hare in the leg but it ran off on three legs, through a fence and across fields, to disappear into the moor. Red Jock's Wife was not seen for some weeks afterwards. It was rumoured that she had slipped on the stairs and hurt her leg although everyone knew how it was really hurt. When she recovered she was treated with greater respect and awe than before.

At Cromarty churchyard you can see a grave that is outside the wall of the churchyard. The reason for this is said to have been the friendly quarrel between two crofters who lived on the hillside here, Donald and Sandy. They were good neighbours on the whole but could never agree on one of their boundaries, a dividing line marked only by two large boulders several hundred yards apart. Each winter, before ploughing began, first one of the neighbours and then the other, would get up early and push the boulders ten or twenty yards, seeking to enlarge their respective pieces of land by a strip some ten yards by three-hundred; until eventually one or the other would plough the first furrow one misty dawn and so confirm the land as belonging to him for twelve months of crops. The following winter the same thing would happen and for years the practice continued, until one winter Sandy died, with the boulders enlarging his land. But Donald respected his old friend for there was Sandy's widow and six children to think of so he let the stones stay although he considered that they were a dozen yards inside his land. The years passed and as he pondered on the life to come, Donald remembered that one day, so he had been taught, the trumpets would sound and the neighours, Sandy and himself, would rise from their graves. Donald pondered deeply about this and left instructions that he was to be buried outside the wall of the churchyard when he died for he reasoned that by doing so he would have a good start on Sandy who would have the high churchyard wall to climb while Donald would be rolling the boundary stones back to their rightful place!

From time immemorial there has been the belief that the Devil has appeared on Mount High and there is certainly an undefinable atmosphere here at midnight that makes such legends understandable. When the moonlight shimmers on Donald's grave and the churchyard wall, it is not difficult to imagine that any minute the silence will be broken by the sound of a trumpet and that the graves will yawn and give up their undead.

Balconie House, Cromarty, has a curious and wild legendary story associated with it and the deep and narrow gorge nearby where the River Allt Grande flows on its rocky course. It is a gloomy place that has long had a sinister reputation on account of the peculiar and strange experiences of visitors to this lonely spot.

The narrow gorge is awesome to behold with its gloomy cliffs and inaccessible caverns where the light of day never reaches, while the hoarse and hollow murmuring of waterfalls and cascades rises from the depths far below.

Back in the seventeenth century the Laird of Balconie brought home after wanderings abroad a young and beautiful wife, a reserved and quiet girl who shunned society and never talked about her life before she met the laird. For her the gorge of the Allt Grande seemed to have an overwhelming fascination and she would spend hours there each day. Gradually a great change came over her. She became more sociable, less reserved, but she had a wild air that in some mysterious way worried those with whom she came in contact. It was almost as though she were bewitched and belonged not among mortals but to some other world.

She became particularly attached to one of the maids, a pretty and simple Highland girl. One evening the two of them went to the gorge. There a dark man in green suddenly materialized, took the young bride by the hand and led her to the brink of the gorge. The maid stood rooted to the ground as her mistress, with a backward glance of infinite sadness, untied a bunch of household keys from her belt and threw them to the maid. They struck a granite boulder and an impression made on the stone is pointed out to this day as that made by the keys.

When she had picked up the keys and looked again for her mistress, the maid discovered that both figures had vanished. Terrified, she ran back to the house and panted out her story. The resulting search for the lady of Balconie House continued unabated but unsuccessfully for days.

Ten years later a Scottish fisherman, searching in the gorge for a basket of fish that he had lost, climbed down to a ledge and discovered an enormous cavern. Two black dogs rose as he entered but lay down again and let him pass. Beyond he saw his basket of fish on an iron table and, seated on an iron chair by the table, was the long lost lady of Balconie House! When the fisherman offered to take her home she pointed to the chains that fastened her to the chair which was in turn fastened to the rocky wall of the cave and replied that she would never be free. She begged him to leave quickly and she threw some meat to the dogs to keep them quiet for they were becoming restive and eyeing the intruder balefully. The fisherman therefore lost no time in picking up his basket of fish and leaving the cave, returning the way he had come, a difficult and dangerous scramble and climb. Once safe above ground, he lost no time in telling the local people of his adventure. Although many tried to locate the cavern and liberate the prisoner lady of Balconie, they all failed and she was never seen again. It was generally thought that she must have broken some pact or deal with the Devil and that in the guise of a dark man in green he or one of his demon friends had captured her.

Looking down the deep and narrow gorge today it is not too difficult to visualize such a story having a profound effect on people three hundred years ago. Even in 1970 it was possible to find inhabitants who believed that the strange noises emanating on occasions from the mysterious gorge, which produces odd acoustic effects, might be supernormal in origin.

Blackness, WEST LOTHIAN

Inland, but once connected to the port on the River Forth, stands The Binns, former home of General Tam Dalyell, still looking much as he must have proudly surveyed it after its restoration.

When he was commander-in-chief of the forces in Scotland, in 1681, he formed the regiment that became known as the Royal Scots Greys and the first musters were held here. The mansion was presented to the National Trust in 1944, after being in the Dalyell family for over three hundred years.

According to those who live on the banks of this picturesque river, the countryside is peopled with native spirits. A little old man in a brown habit is to be seen gathering sticks on the hillside above Binns; a water-sprite lures the unwary to death in the dark waters of the ancient pond below the hill. Other primitive forms are glimpsed here from time to time, perhaps survivors of the Picts who made their last stand here against the Romans. The ghost of General Dalyell himself has been seen, mounted on a white charger, galloping across the ruined bridge over the Errack Burn; in the vicinity of the Binns tower; and up the old road to his house, where the General's riding-boots and spurs are preserved to this day.

In his lifetime, it is said, Tam Dalyell used to play cards with the Devil. Once, when Tam won, the enraged Devil threw the table they had been playing on at his head but it flew past him and dropped into Sergeant's Pond, outside the house. This is one of many strange stories told about General

Dalyell, tales of which few people took much notice until, one day during the dry summer of 1878, the water of the pond was reduced to a new low and there, stuck fast in the mud at the bottom of the pond, was a heavy carved table that must have been there for all of two hundred years.

It seems that the General had another argument with the Devil over cards, resulting in Satan threatening to blow his house down upon him. General Dalyell retorted that he would build extra thick walls to protect the house. The Devil replied that he would blow down the house and the walls—to which the General answered that he would build a turret at every corner of the house to pin down the walls. Today you can see turrets at each corner of the historic old house, which certainly serve no purpose—unless they have prevented the Devil from blowing the property down!

Bladnoch, NEAR WIGTOWN, WIGTOWNSHIRE

The one street in this riverside village leads to a bridge; a left turn and the road to Baldoon Mains leads to the ivy-covered ruins of Baldoon Castle. Opposite the castle ruins, a fine old gateway gives access to the Mains (which probably belonged to the castle years ago). Looking back, the castle ruins are framed between the picturesque pillars of the gateway.

The ruins themselves, quiet and deserted and with an air of tragedy about them, are haunted by the ghost of Janet Dalrymple who walks here in the small hours, her white garments splashed with blood.

In the middle of the seventeenth century Janet, the eldest daughter of Sir James Dalrymple, was forced by her parents to marry David Dunbar, heir of Sir David Dunbar of Baldoon, although she loved the practically penniless Archibald, third Lord Rutherford. Dutifully, and worn down by her parents' persistent objections to Archibald, Janet at last married David Dunbar in the kirk of Old Luce, two miles from Carsecleugh Castle, the old home of the Dalrymples. Her two brothers took her to the church and both declared later that her hands were cold as ice on that hot summer day.

There are three main versions of the events that gave rise to the haunting. In the first version the bride stabs her bridegroom in the bridal chamber and dies insane; in the second version the bridegroom stabs the bride and is found insane; and in the third version the disappointed Archibald conceals himself in the bridal chamber and escapes through the window into the garden after stabbing the bridegroom.

Whatever the facts, Sir Walter Scott immortalized the story in *The Bride of Lammermoor* and describes how the door of the bridal chamber was broken down after hideous shrieks were heard from within and how the bridegroom was found lying across the threshold, dreadfully wounded and streaming with blood, while the bride crouched in a chimney corner, her white nightgown splashed with blood, grinning and muttering and quite insane. She never recovered and died shortly afterwards, on September 12th, 1669.

Dunbar is said to have recovered from his wounds but refused to discuss the events of his bridal night. In due course he married a daughter of the seventh Earl of Eglinton and eventually died from a fall from his horse in 1682. Archibald, Janet's true lover, never married and died in 1685.

A macabre touch is added to the story by local tradition that it was the Devil who nearly killed Dunbar and who tormented poor Janet until she was demented. Whatever the events of the night, they seem to have left their mark here forever and there are some who claim to have seen the sad and awesome ghost of Janet wandering pathetically among the quiet ruins, most often on the anniversary of her death.

Blairgowrie, PERTHSHIRE

Lovely Ardblair Castle, built on the foundations of a Pictish stronghold, is today, after careful restoration in 1890 and 1908, much as it was back in the twelfth century. In particular, the dungeon with its six-foot thick walls is almost as it must have been eight hundred years ago.

A member of the Blair family built Ardblair Castle— probably William de Blair, a courtier to the patron of the monasteries, William the Lion. Descendants of that ancient and honoured family still live there. Blairs, with neighbouring families by the names of Herons and Drummonds, bore arms to assist Robert the Bruce. It was some differences of opinion with their neighbours that traditionally caused the haunting of Ardblair Castle.

At the time of the tragedy the Blairs of Ardblair and the Drummonds of Newton were feuding. There is a long and fanciful Scots poem that tells of the Lady Jean Drummond being whisked away by the little people immediately after her wedding, for having no wedding dress she had borrowed green finery from the water kelpies and so put herself in their power. A more prosaic version of the fate of the Lady Jane tells of her deep love for a Blair which was not allowed to end in marriage because of opposition by the feuding families. In despair, the sad Lady Jane drowned herself in the surrounding marshes.

Whatever her end, the ghost of this gentle and lovely creature is said to haunt both Newton and Ardblair. She has most frequently been seen between five and six o'clock on sunny afternoons, sitting sadly on the window seat in the long gallery at Ardblair, gazing out of the window.

Her attitude and appearance are so sad that no one who sees her ever speaks to her. Wrapped up in her grief as she is, she never frightens anyone, either as she sits or as she passes through rooms and corridors without making a sound but opening and closing doors as she goes. The Blair family have always regarded the Green Lady with respect and accepted her presence because of her obvious grief and unhappiness. During the 1939-1945 War some evacuees from Glasgow were billeted in the tower and long gallery where she was most often seen. She evidently disliked their presence in the castle and although her methods were not disclosed, she seems to have caused them to leave Ardblair within a very short time.

Boat of Garten, MORAYSHIRE

A little north of Boat of Garten Bridge several parts of a stone slab can be seen in a pool on the River Spey, when the water is low, embedded in the sand. Parts of an inscription are just visible, or were when I was there a few years ago.

I made enquiries and learned that the inscription related a curious 'dividing of the waters' enabling a woman's body to be carried across the river on dry ground for burial. The stone was originally erected by William Grant on March 9th, 1865.

Over the years the name of the woman has been described differently but all the stories seem to agree that she lived at Tulloch and during her last days expressed a wish to be buried in the churchyard at Duthil, across the river. When she was told that it might not be possible if the river should be in flood, she replied, 'God will find a way,' and specified a particular part of the river where the crossing would be effected without difficulty.

After she died, the funeral party duly made for the place on the river bank that the dying woman had told them about and although the Spey was in flood, as soon as they were ready to cross the waters divided and the procession passed over with dry feet. The rector of Tulloch wrote of the 'miracle' and described the walls of water on each side of the funeral party 'like the Red Sea of old'.

It is said that salmon and other fish foundered and struggled on the wet river bed as the waters separated but when on-lookers ventured forward in the wake of the procession to capture the helpless fish, the waters closed together again and no harm came to any.

Near the existing farm of Gartenbeg the mourners set up a post with an arm indicating the place where the waters had miraculously parted, although no sign of this indication of the strange happening exists today.

The 'miracle stone' north of the bridge, was consecrated for all time—like the memorial stones of the Jordan—by a sect known as The Men, of which William Grant was a leading light. After prayer and praise it was prophesied that broom would flower to the left and to the right of the stone as a sign to disbelievers. Sceptics noted that the prophecy had every chance of being fulfilled, as indeed it was, since the slab was carefully set between two bushes of the plant. Criticism by many local people grew and resulted in the formation of an anti-stone organization whose members did all they could to discredit the alleged miracle. The local Free Church denounced the story of the crossing as an 'abominable lie' and the memorial slab as a stone that put 'lies upon God and man'. Questions were asked about the character of a woman with such apparent powers and even mutterings of witchcraft were heard.

For two years the controversy raged and then, on the morning of February 19th, 1867, the memorial stone was found broken and the pieces cast into the river. Ever since the Spey has lapped and covered and uncovered in turn the remains of the stone that was erected because of the reputed miraculous action of these waters. Whether the stone was broken and thrown into the river by human or supernormal means was never discovered but no one attempted to restore it, although years later fragments of the stone were sought by souvenir hunters. The tenants of a nearby Knock farmhouse dug up a large portion of the stone and used it as a doorstep.

Almost immediately the house was reported to be haunted by movement of objects without human contact, unexplained appearances of articles and phantom lights. Hailstones the size of a cricket ball are said to have plagued the occupants of the house in mid-summer; turnips and large stones are said to have hurtled down the farmhouse chimney and through closed windows without breaking the glass; furniture was moved up and down stairs at night-time; stones and straw were continually flying about the house and everyone was kept busy sweeping and cleaning up and replacing things in their correct places.

The local minister suggested the slow burning of a rowan tree outside the house, an ancient cure for witchcraft. Although this was done, it had no effect and, whether due to the mysterious happenings or not, the inhabitants of the house died within a short space of time with the solitary exception of one old woman who cured warts and other afflictions. She lived on, respected and feared and took whatever secrets she had about the house and its inhabitants, to the grave with her.

One of the first actions of the next tenant of Knock Farm was to return the slab of memorial stone to its resting place in the river—and from that day the curious happenings ceased.

From time to time the reputedly evil power of the stone comes back into the news. Some years ago five boys uncovered the stone from its sandy bed and within months they were all dead. In 1940 a plane returning from a bombing raid on the continent crashed on the river bank not far from the stone and it was recalled that one of the crew had meddled with the stone in his youth. Even today it is possible to find local people who regard looking at the stone as unlucky and some even believe that the stone is guarded by a giant eel which devours cattle who stray too near the mysterious Stone of Spey.

Bowland, VALE OF GALE, MIDLOTHIAN

In the middle of the nineteenth century a man named Rutherford, a member of the landed gentry class resident in this area, had a singular dream which intrigued Sir Walter Scott.

Mr Rutherford was being sued for a considerable sum of money, the accumulated arrears of tithes due. Rutherford himself was of the opinion that his father had procured these tithes by means of a process peculiar to the law of Scotland. But he was unable to find any documentary evidence among his father's papers or any confirmation from those who had transacted legal business for his father or from published records. Without anything to support his defence he was about to set out for Edinburgh when, on the eve of the law-suit, he dreamed that his late father appeared to him.

The old man, who had been dead for many years, seemed conscious of his son's troubles and told him that he had, indeed, acquired the rights of the tithes. The relevant papers were in the hands of a retired attorney, resident at Inveresk, who might well have forgotten all about the only business he ever conducted for Mr Rutherford, senior. To bring the matter to the aged lawyer's mind, Rutherford suggested to his son to remind the old man that when the account was paid there was some difficulty in getting change and the lawyer and his client spent the balance at a nearby inn.

Next morning, the dream or vision crystal-clear in his mind, young Rutherford set off early for Edinburgh, by way of Inveresk. There he succeeded in locating the lawyer in question and after mentioning the matter of the change and the drink at the inn, the old man finally recalled the matter, made an immediate search of his papers and discovering the relevant ones, was able to send Rutherford on his way to Edinburgh with the necessary documents so that he could win the case.

Braemar, ABERDEENSHIRE

Behind a shop, near the bridge over the Clunie River and not far from the cottage where Robert Louis Stevenson wrote part of *Treasure Island*, are the foundations and ruins of the eleventh-century castle of Kindrochit. Here, in the vaults, according to legend, a ghostly company sits forever round a table heaped with skulls, amid great treasure.

Kindrochit Castle was once the hunting seat and Highland residence of King Robert I of Scotland. It also had a more stern and war-like purpose. Strategically situated above the gorge of the Clunie Water, the castle served to defend the ancient mountain passes of the Cairnwell and the Tolmouth which connected the southern parts of the old kingdom with the wild and turbulent north. As its importance increased, part of the old edifice was pulled down and in 1390 a massive stone tower (the fifth largest in Scotland) was built by Sir Malcolm Drummond, the constable of the castle. Work continued for many years, some of the stones being brought over the hills from Kildrummy, where the English had the whole garrison 'hangyt and drawyn'. In 1402, however, Sir Malcolm was ambushed and murdered by a band of caterans who infested the surrounding hills.

For over a quarter of a century the Royal Standard flew from the battlements of the great tower and a massive bridge leading to the castle was built across the Clunie. The castle outworks and tower rose above the woods of Mar until, suddenly and mysteriously, disaster overtook the place. Strong and flourishing in 1400, by the beginning of the sixteenth century the castle was derelict and by 1618 the place was in utter ruin. There is a tradition that the 'Calar Mor', a terrible plague, broke out in the castle. Terrified that the pestilence might spread, the people of Braemar barricaded the gates and refused to let the garrison escape. Great cannon are said to have been dragged over the Cairnwell from Atholl and turned on the castle and so Kindrochit crashed in ruins amid the shrieks of those trapped within its walls. When we recall that as late as the sixteenth century those suspected of carrying the plague were hanged on the nearest gallows, it is by no means impossible that there is some truth in the tradition.

For years the ruins continued to crumble, the walls disappeared, trees and bushes covered the remains. In 1746 a Hanoverian soldier was lowered into the vaults to search for the castle treasure. When he was hauled up after frantic signals, he reported that in the dim light that seeped through to the vast vaults below, he saw an immense company of ghostly people seated around a table heaped with skulls.

In 1925, under the direction of Dr W. Douglas Simpson, serious excavation began. This time no such alarming discoveries were reported but among many interesting finds was the famous silver gilt Kindrochit brooch. After many difficulties and much hard work the walls of the main part of the old castle were uncovered, but more is thought to exist beneath the shop. On the opposite bank of the Clunie the remains of the old bridge were unearthed which originally led to the castle, providing its name: Ceann-Drochaide or Bridgend.

One of the principal features of St Andrew's churchyard at Braemar is the massive Farquharson vault, the burial place of John Farquharson of Inverey, 'the Black Colonel'. Here he was said to have resurrected himself three times.

Farquharson's home, Inverey Castle, was demolished by Royalist troops after the Battle of Killiecrankie in 1689. Although he had often expressed the wish to be buried in the lonely graveyard near to his ruined home, he was in due course laid to rest in the Farquharson vault in Braemar kirkyard.

The very day after the funeral passers-by were shocked to see the Black Colonel's coffin above ground outside the vault. Arrangements were hastily made for it to be re-interred. Three times the coffin was found above ground and three times it was buried, until someone recalled John Farquharson's request that his remains should lie at Inverey. A raft was constructed and the body was drawn up the River Dee to his favoured place where it was buried in the spot he had loved during his lifetime.

Many years later when two young men were digging a grave at Inverey, they accidentally broke into the Black Colonel's crumbling coffin and each man took one of the Colonel's teeth as a memento. That night the ghost of the enraged Laird of Inverey appeared to both of them and signified that the teeth were to be returned. Early next morning the grisly relics were restored to the Colonel's grave and his ghost was seen no more.

Brechin, ANGUS-SHIRE

Kinnaird Castle, the seat of the Earls of Southesk, stands in a large deer park and is the locality of a strange legend concerning a pact with the Devil and a ghostly carriage.

It was said that the body of James, the second Earl, who died in 1669, was collected by the Devil in a coach drawn by six coal-black horses. The coach, horses and all, tore away and plunged into a well near the Carnegies' family burial-ground. On wild and stormy nights the coach-and-six is reputed to repeat its journey, driving at break-neck speed past the Earl's former home and disappearing in the direction of the old burial-ground.

James Carnegie studied the Black Arts while a student at Padua. Legend has it that the Devil himself was among the professors there and that 'he' conducted a class for advanced students. The predictable fee was the soul of one pupil; the unlucky one being the last to leave the classroom on a day chosen by the Devil himself. It seems that Carnegie was the last on this occasion but he had the presence of mind to tell the Devil to take his shadow which was cast behind him as he left the room. Satan, with his liking for things of darkness, took the shadow. Consequently it is said that the second Earl of Southesk never cast a shadow after that. He used to conceal his misfortune in this respect by walking in the shade whenever possible. But the Devil seems to have won in the end.

Brechin Cathedral, now the Parish Church, was founded by King David I in 1150 and has long since been restored but the Round Tower attached to it dates from the eleventh century and is one of three such towers that survive in Scotland, probably used originally for defensive purposes. The doorway is decorated with crude Celtic carvings of the Crucifixion and fabulous monsters. A nearby valley has long been known as 'the Devil's Den'.

Callander, PERTHSHIRE

A former gamekeeper to an austere member of the Stewart family who resided here saw a ghost which caused him to mend his ways.

The keeper, James Macfarlane, was fond of the ladies in his youth and more than once he broke his master's rule that all his servants should attend family prayers each Sunday. One Sabbath night he was absent, courting a lassie beyond Doune. The head of the family, noticing his absence (and not for the first time), demanded where the 'scoundrel' was, adding vehemently: 'I wish I could give him a fright that would stop him running about courting on Sabbath nights!'

After prayers, the old man, still fuming, went to bed but soon his bedroom bell rang and when a maid-servant answered it, she found her master lying unconscious on the floor. Within minutes he was dead.

About the same time James Macfarlane, having left his sweetheart, was on his way home. As he neared Cambusmore he noticed the form of a man lying directly in his path; indeed he was almost upon it before he saw the form. At first he sprang back, startled; then, thinking it must be someone the worse for drink, he stooped to examine it, only to recoil in horror as he recognized the dead face of his master!

Knowing that his master would not be abroad at that hour on a Sunday, James's hair stood on end as he realized that the form before him was no human body. Turning away, rather than pass it, he fled from the place and took a long detour home.

Breathless and frightened, he was greeted on arrival at the house with the news that his master was dead. Whether or not the old man had his last earthly wish fulfilled, it is a fact that for the rest of his life James Macfarlane lived a pious life and never again did his courting on a Sunday. If he ever heard anyone expressing disbelief in ghosts he would shake his head and say: 'I ken well what I ha' seen myself.'

Castle Douglas, KIRKCUDBRIGHTSHIRE

A couple of miles from here, on the Kelton road, there is a little bridge that crosses a stream. This is Cuckoo Bridge and many years ago the body of a murdered baby was buried in the stream here. For years the sound of pitiful crying of an infant has been noticed by people crossing the bridge on moonlit nights and occasionally a pathetic little white shape, horrifying and hardly human, has been seen.

Corrieyarack Pass, INVERNESS-SHIRE

In the vicinity of a stream called the Allt Lagan a' Bhainne there is a broken bridge and here is the haunt of the Ghost of Corrieyarack. A suspension bridge (erected by the Scottish Rights of Way Society) now spans a stretch of the dangerous stream, all too often shrouded in mist. It is in such circumstances that a ghostly Highlander is said to loom up out of nowhere, accompanied by two great dogs, and to direct the traveller with the words: 'That way lies your road.'

The ghost only appears when the weather is misty and almost as soon as those encountering the mysterious figure become aware of the presence, the phantom figure and the silent dogs that accompany it disappear.

Craigmaddie Moor, STIRLINGSHIRE

The 'Auld Wives' Lift', three enormous drift boulders, one placed over the other two, lie at a particularly isolated spot where many visitors report a strange coldness on the warmest summer day and a sense of evil seems to overwhelm those who venture here.

The legend of the Auld Wives' Lift tells of three weird sisters, one from Baldernock, one from Strathblane and one from Campsie, who decided on a trial of strength to prove that if they were not beautiful at least they were strong. The first hoisted a great boulder on to her shoulders, walked with it far out over the moor and there dropped it to the ground; the second did just as well and placed her boulder at the side of the first one; while the third woman picked up one as large as the other two put together and *ran* with it over the moor, putting it atop her rivals' pair. On the wet and silent moor the ancient stones still stand, forming an archway for superstitious young couples to crawl through to ensure that they marry; and a constant source of argument as to which district the undoubted winner came from!

More prosaic students have pointed out that the boulders lie within a natural amphitheatre and probably formed the altar for some bleak diety eons ago. But almost everyone agrees that there is a strange atmosphere here. One feels afraid to look round quickly for fear of finding that one has slipped back into a bygone age, facing a semi-circle of primitive watching eyes and cruel little men in the amphitheatre that probably saw much bloodshed and cruelty.

Peter G. Currie who lives at Troon tells me that he first walked over Blairskaith and Craigmaddie Moors when he was eighteen, amongst the blue mountain hares (though they were still white in a late spring). Suddenly, over a low hill, he saw the Auld Wives' Lift. Not glacial (could a glacier have perched one boulder atop of another?), Peter Currie noticed the firm foundation of the stones amongst the wet sphagnum bog and the perfect central placing of the group in a natural amphitheatre; this must surely have been design, not chance. He continued: 'I climbed to the top stone, lay down on the sun-warm surface and fell asleep. I awoke to the worst attack of the horrors that I have ever had. The sky had darkened and thunder drum-rolled around the horizon. I was off that stone and over the moor so fast that my feet had no time to sink in wet peat! I'm not in the least superstitious but that place, to me, smells of blood.

'Talking about blood, I carefully examined the eastern edge of the top stone in September, 1972, where there is what has been described as a gutter cut to drain off sacrificial blood. The edge rises up to a lip (as does the western edge) but on the right there is a distinct depression down which liquid could run, although this depression may be due to natural weathering.'

Visiting the stones on September 2nd, 1972, Peter Currie had a good look at the base area around the stones and he told me that heather and sphagnum (peat or bog moss) sprouted everywhere else, but only grass grew around the three boulders. He added: 'I remember once when my wife and I traced a lost drove-road through Rothiemurchus, one of the indicators was patches of good grass, where the cattle had milled around before fording a stream, or had rested with the drovers. After two hundred years the effect of the fertilizing dung still showed. Could blood, and probably flesh and bone, show a similar difference after perhaps two thousand years? One day the surburbia of Glasgow will surround the moors, which will be drained and tamed to golf-course and building sites and the mountain hares with feet big as soup-plates will no longer be seen (there are not so many of them, even now). A prim little park will enclose the Auld Wives' Lift, and children will scramble over it, and its story will be forgotten. Yet, occasionally, if someone with sensitive nostrils passes by, he will smell blood.'

Cramond, EDINBURGH, MIDLOTHIAN

There is a fine walk here along the shore and through the woods to Queensferry. It passes Barnbougle Castle which, according to legend, gets its name from the ghostly wail of a dog that has been heard for many years and reputedly dates from the time of the Crusades.

In those days a pious and lonely man lived here whose name has only come down to us as Sir Roger. He set out to fight in the Crusades. After keeping vigil in the church of St Adamnan at Dalmeny and praying for his own safety and for the victory of the Brotherhood of the Red Cross Knights, he went to board his ship and found on the quayside his favourite hound. The dog looked so piteous and wailed so sadly at the thought of his master leaving, that Sir Roger took it with him. For years the faithful dog accompanied the noble knight as he fought bravely. Then, one dark night, the sound of a bugle rang out from the old tower on the shore where Sir Roger had embarked for Palestine. After a moment, a death-wail sounded on the wind, the awful baying of a ghostly hound. At that very moment Sir Roger lay dead on the battlefield in Syria, his loyal dog beside him. Still, on dark nights a mournful and dismal wailing noise is some-times heard that local people think is the wail of Sir Roger's hound. This is the origin of Hound Point, farther along the shore; there does seem to be evidence to suggest that in the words of the old ballad:

> 'And ever when Barnbougle's lords
> Are parting this scene below,
> Come hound and ghost to this haunted coast
> With death notes winding slow.'

Cromarty, ROSS-SHIRE

There is a wood and a moor near here, once haunted by grisly phantoms that would tear in and out of the trees and round the cairns on wild and stormy nights, cursing, laugh-ing and yelling. There are stories of ghostly knights in armour, engaged in fierce combat; of spectral old hags chuckling and chortling as they robbed dead and wounded soldiers; and of lovely young maidens who lured men to pools and swamps from which there was no escape.

One wild night a fisherman was crossing the moor and

as he passed a wood he saw in the moonlight ahead of him not the distant hills and the still moor but a wild and wide storm-tossed sea, black and foam-flecked, stretching as far as he could see. He could hear the roar of the wind and the waves; and as the moon lit up the scene, he saw a fishing boat tossed high one moment and low the next. He recognized the occupants: three were Cromarty fishermen and the fourth his own brother. Suddenly a huge wave engulfed the boat and the terrified fisherman fainted. When he recovered consciousness, he found himself back on the lonely moor; no seas within sight or sound, only the occasional fir tree and the silent landscape, stretching away into the dim distance. Had it all been a dream? The following day there was a sudden squall off Cromarty and among the casualties was a boat containing the three Cromarty fishermen he had recognized and his brother.

Behind the old town, where the ground rises abruptly to a height of nearly a hundred feet, there once stood the old and massive castle of Cromarty. For years before its demolition the rambling place was tenanted by a single elderly female retainer and a young girl whom she hired to stay with her. This girl, when she was over seventy, told of the huge chimney in the kitchen; the great hall, a dark oak-lined chamber where a hundred men had more than once exercised at the pike; and the lower vaults which she had never had the temerity to explore: vast, dark and ghostly and nearly full of long, rank grass.

Years before she went there, the place had been looked after by another female who had been foolhardy enough to sleep alone. One night she was frightened nearly out of her wits and never recovered sufficiently to relate what she had seen or heard.

At times a series of mysterious noises would echo through the upper apartments, sounds resembling a heavy man pacing the floors in the deserted castle. 'If you could have heard the shrieks, moans and long, whistling sounds that used to be heard during the winter months from the chimneys and the turrets,' the old lady said, speaking of the days when she was there as a girl, 'you would have done what I did: drew the clothes over my head as I lay listening to the strange noises

309

in the dark night; trying to get to sleep, shivering with terror.'

Once her companion was sitting in a little chamber at the foot of the great stairs when she heard a tapping against the steps and she quietly opened the door. Although the light was poor, she claimed she saw in the twilight a small white animal, something like a rabbit, rolling from step to step, head over heels and dissolving, as it bounded over the last step, into a wreath of smoke.

Another time, when a Cromarty shoemaker was passing by the front of the building one summer morning, he was astonished to see a tiny, grey-haired, grey-bearded old man, with a withered and thin face, scarcely bigger than a fist, seated at one of the windows. Half an hour later, when he returned by the same path, the shoemaker saw the same figure, wringing his hands over a little cairn in a nearby thicket, but he did not have the courage to approach it to get a better view.

The castle has long since been demolished but two curious remnants of the old building survived until a few years ago. One piece of sculpture could be seen in a vaulted passage that leads from the modern house to the road; a stone slab about five feet in length, nearly two feet wide, that once served as a lintel to one of the two chimneys in the great hall. There was a huntsman in the centre, attired in a sort of loose coat that reached to his knees, with a lance in one hand and a hunting-spear in the other. He sported a moustache and the peaked beard of the reign of Queen Mary Tudor. The lintel of the second chimney, just as interesting, was preserved at Kinbeakie Cottage in the parish of Resolis. There was an excellent lithographic print of this lintel in the museum of the Northern Institute, Inverness, but Richard Milne, the Librarian and Curator at Inverness Public Library and Museum, told me in 1972 that when the Northern Institution ceased to function, some of the museum material did not survive. What remained was acquired by the Inverness Field Club many years later but unfortunately the print of Cromarty Castle chimney lintel was not among the articles that were preserved.

When the castle was demolished in 1772 a number of earthenware urns filled with ashes and fragments of half-burned bones were dug out of the bank immediately around the building together with several stone coffins containing human skeletons, some headless, with one coffin containing a complete skeleton measuring over seven feet in length.

In 1830 a stolid and sensible Cromarty fisherman was returning home by the Inverness road after nightfall, having visited a friend in the north of the parish. It was a calm and still night with heavy clouds obscuring the moon and the fisherman walked on in a happy mood when the quiet and peaceful night was suddenly shattered by the most discordant noises that he had ever heard.

At first he supposed that a pack of hounds was in full cry in the field bordering his path and then, as the sounds faded as suddenly as they had arisen, that they were ranging the moors on the opposite side of a hill ahead of him.

Suddenly there was a fresh burst, as though the whole pack were very near at hand and baying at him through the hedge. He thrust his hands into his pockets and, drawing out a handful of crumbs, offered them to the supposed hounds but instead of open mouths and gleaming eyes he only saw a man a little ahead of him. The sounds ceased at the same time.

Thinking that the man must be the keeper of the pack, the fisherman resumed his walk homewards, noting as he did so that the silent figure ahead kept pace with him—until, reaching a gap in the hedge, he saw the man turn towards the path that he was on. Increasing the pace of his walk in the expectation of company for the rest of his journey, the fisherman was astounded, as he drew nearer to the figure, to see it grow taller and taller and then, dropping on all fours, it assumed the form of a horse!

Hurrying on his way, the horse hurried too. When the fisherman stopped, the horse also stopped. Resuming an ordinary pace, the horse walked also, step for step with him, without either passing or falling behind. He now saw that it was an ugly and misshapen beast, bristling all over with black shaggy hair and lame in one foot.

The form accompanied him until he reached the gate of a cemetery, then just outside the town, where he was momentarily blinded by what seemed to be an intensely bright flash

311

of lightning and as soon as he recovered, he found himself alone.

There is a much older story told of a man who encountered the Devil in five different shapes during a night-time journey in this part of Scotland. A few hours afterwards he lost his senses through fright; sceptics always say he lost his senses a few hours *before* his night walk!

Navity Wood, nearby, used to be haunted by the ghost of a murdered miller. A few days after the body was found on a bleak moor nearby, a postman named Munro was passing through Navity Wood one evening on the way to his home at Cromarty when he heard footsteps behind him. In the failing light he saw a tall figure which he at first thought to be a farmer friend but as the figure drew nearer, he was horrified to recognize the dead miller!

Turning tail, he fled home as fast as he could. The ghostly miller kept pace with him as he could see whenever he glanced over his shoulder. However, when he reached Cromarty churchyard, Munro was relieved to find that the frightening figure had disappeared.

The next night Munro made his way home by a different route, crossing a succession of fields instead of going through Navity Wood. As he entered a hollow that was part of the Cromarty House estate, he again saw the ghost of the dead miller, this time emerging from a clump of bushes and once more the figure followed the terrified postman. This time, reaching the low wall separating the old parish churchyard, Munro turned and faced the apparition; whereupon it spoke to him: 'Stop, stop, I must speak to you.' But Munro had had more than enough. 'I have neither the faith nor the strength to speak to the like of you,' he replied, and hurried home without another backward glance.

Next day he related his experiences to the local minister who decided that Munro was having delusions, probably due to nerves or indigestion, and poor man was told to see a doctor. Instead, he went to see an old Udoll farmer he knew who listened with interest to the story and then offered to accompany Munro through Navity Wood the following evening.

They met a few miles from Munro's home before sunset

and made their way into Navity Wood. What befell them before they reached Cromarty town they would never tell anyone, but after that night Munro made his own way through Navity Wood a score of times and never saw the apparition again.

However, both Munro and his farmer friend came to regard with suspicion an inhabitant of Cromarty who had travelled with the miller on his last journey. Both were known to have been drinking and to be somewhat quarrelsome. After the miller's body was found this last man to see him alive changed from a social and genial, if unpredictable, man to a dejected, spiritless and taciturn individual, avoiding company and seldom speaking to anyone. After a lingering illness, he died a few years later, still a young man.

Culloden Moor, INVERNESS-SHIRE

Here the fate of the house of Stewart was sealed, in a setting that has changed little since the last pitched battle in Britain was fought here on April 16th, 1746.

Bonnie Prince Charlie's nine thousand tired and hungry Highlanders met nine thousand government troops under the Duke of Cumberland, third son of King George II, and it was all over in sixty-eight minutes. The Highlanders' losses were enormous, the victors cruelly massacring their wounded enemies; the English dead only numbered fifty. A cairn and green mounds mark the soldiers' burial-places and from time to time visitors to this sorrowful place report strange happenings.

On occasions, the dim form of a battle-worn Highlander has been seen at dusk in the vicinity of the impressive cairn and one visitor, while looking closely at the Highlanders' graves here, lifted a square of Stewart tartan which had blown down from the stone on the grave-mound and distinctly saw the body of a handsome, dark-haired Highlander lying, at ease it seemed, full length on top of the mound. The visitor sensed that the figure she was looking at was dead. His clothes were dirty, muddy and of old-fashioned cut and material. His tartan was the red Stewart. As she fully realized that she was seeing something of a supernormal character, she turned and fled from the field of memories.

Dingwall, ROSS-SHIRE

This county town and royal burgh derives its name from the Norse 'Thingvollr', translated as the 'Field of the Thing' or 'Council'.

In the area where once a celebrated prophet, the Brahan Seer, roamed, now the Brahan Estate, Maryburgh, there has long been an outdoor case of mysterious breathing which has never been satisfactorily explained.

As recently as October, 1968, local papers recounted that at the foot of the imposing Brahan Rock, the two-hundred foot high rock-face at the end of a narrow and twisting cul-de-sac, up to fifty cars could usually be found each night around midnight, their occupants intent on hearing the strange noises that have variously been described as resembling snoring, whispering, breathing, panting and gasping.

A farm worker was quoted as saying that he had heard the noise regularly since coming to Brahan Lodge (a hundred yards from the cliff) five years earlier. 'We can even hear it in the house on a calm night with the windows open,' he stated. Another man in the same house, blacksmith Alan Macleod, reported: 'Along with two friends we went up the rock face one night while the breathing was being heard but each time we reached the spot we thought it was coming from, it seemed to move further up the face.'

One possible explanation would be warm air escaping from underground caverns through crevices, a theory that needs exploring. At all events the noise has been heard for many years; schoolmaster Mr J. A. Mitchell claims that a postman told him it was heard as long as eighty years ago.

Dornoch, SUTHERLANDSHIRE

This royal burgh and county town of Sutherland was once the seat of the Bishop of Caithness. It has a magnificent golf course and the prim appearance of a small cathedral town but it is distinguished as the scene, in 1772, of the last judicial execution for witchcraft to take place in Scotland. The witch was an old woman named Janet Horne who was charged with having changed her daughter into a pony to ride to the witches' meeting place, where the 'animal' was shod by the Devil. She was burnt to death and the Witches Stone, in a garden close by the golf course, recalls the event. The simple slab of rough bluish whinstone bears the date '1772' and marks the spot where the burning took place. There are those who claim that the old woman is still seen on occasions, struggling and cursing against the rising flames and smothering smoke on autumn evenings, when the moon is on the wane.

Drumelzier, NEAR PEEBLES, PEEBLES-SHIRE

Just below the churchyard here, at the side of the burn that runs through the village, lies the grave of Merlin, the wizard who worked many wonders at the court of King Arthur. He is said to have been the offspring of a Welsh maiden and a demon. Saved from evil by baptism, he retained throughout his life his father's gift of divination and the power to work magic.

One day, long ago, the stream that used to be known as Powsail Burn, overflowed violently, leaving its course and pouring into the River Tweed beside the Merlin grave. This was the day that Queen Elizabeth I died and James VI of Scotland became James I of England. Thus one of Thomas the Rhymer's prophecies was fulfilled:

'When Tweed and Powsail meet at Merlin's grave, England and Scotland shall one monarch have.'

In this quiet, secluded village, shrouded with huge trees and full of shadows, ringed with brown hills and with an air of enchantment, it is not difficult to believe in Merlin and the fulfilment of the Rhymer's prophecies.

Drymen, STIRLINGSHIRE

The partly demolished nineteenth-century Buchanan Castle once housed Rudolf Hess, Hitler's deputy leader. Today it is derelict and haunted by a strange moaning or gasping sound that is heard during the summer months. It usually begins about eleven o'clock and continues until dawn, especially on clear, still nights. The noises, which are reported to be much too regular and loud to originate from birds or animals, have been heard many times by scores of impartial witnesses, including people in houses two hundred yards away; and they have even been recorded on tape.

One witness, Mrs Ann Ostrau of Stirling Road, reported in August 1968, that she had heard the noise many times. She was emphatic that it could not be caused by birds or animals because of the loudness, 'besides it is far too regular and precise', she added, 'and the sound comes from one side, then moves round to another side.'

One possible explanation is escaping air from the many holes in the ground that may lead to underground caverns but this is only a theory which no one has yet troubled to prove or disprove. But other, apparently inexplicable incidents have been reported here; for example there is the evidence of Mr Norman McAuley who maintains that he climbed to the second floor of the castle with a friend, carrying a powerful electric torch which would not work at all on the second floor. All connections were checked and found to be in working order. On returning to the ground floor, the torch functioned perfectly.

Drynachan, NEAR FORT AUGUSTUS, INVERNESS-SHIRE

A cottage on the shores of Loch Oich, five miles from Fort Augustus, was haunted by a man in a top-hat a few years ago. At that time the place, once the home of a laird of the Clan MacDonell, was occupied by a retired gamekeeper, Andrew Ross and his family.

Culloden Cairn, site of the last pitched battle in Britain and haunted by the dim form of a battle-worn Highlander. *Photo: Scottish Tourist Board*

Meggernie Castle, Glen Lyon, Perthshire, haunted by the upper half of a woman's body. *Photo: Alasdair Alpin MacGregor*

The Auld Wives' Lift, Craigmaddie Moor, Stirlingshire, once the scene of human sacrifice; now a place of silence and superstition. *Photo: Peter G. Currie*

Culzean Castle, Dunure, Ayrshire, where in recent months a formless 'something' has been encountered in the dungeons. *Photo: Scottish Tourist Board*

Edinburgh Castle has several ghosts, including a headless drummer that has been seen in recent years. *Photo: Alasdair Alpin MacGregor*

The County Hotel, Dumfries, reputed to be haunted by the ghost of Bonnie Prince Charlie. The five windows on the first floor above the front door, are those of Prince Charlie's Room. *Photo: Alasdair Alpin MacGregor*

The Western Infirmary at Glasgow where the ghost of brain surgeon Sir William MacEwen has been seen by many nurses and doctors on night-duty. *Photo: Board of Management for Glasgow Western & Gartnavel Hospitals*

Inveraray Castle, Argyllshire, haunt of the ghostly 'Harper of Inveraray'; his harp is heard most often in the Blue Room. *Photo: Scottish Tourist Board*

At first Ross was sceptical when his wife told him she had seen the figure of the previous occupier, Angus Maclean, a jobbing carpenter who had died some forty years previously. Mrs Ross saw the ghost whom she and her husband had known, standing beside the cottage one evening. He was dressed in an old-fashioned suit and a 'lum' hat. Soon afterwards the Ross's son saw the ghost.

All the family heard unexplained sounds resembling an old person groaning as though in great pain. During his lifetime they had always found Maclean to be a kindly man and although not unduly alarmed by the disturbances, they began to think that perhaps he might have hidden something in the cottage and wanted it to be discovered. They never found anything and the noises were never explained.

Bonnie Prince Charlie rested at the same cottage during his flight from the Battle of Culloden.

Dumfries, DUMFRIESSHIRE

The County Hotel is reputed to be haunted by the ghost of Bonnie Prince Charlie.

In 1936 a visitor in the upper lounge saw a male figure, attired as a Jacobite, emerge from a doorway and stand for a few moments, deep in thought and looking very worried. He then turned and went away through the same door which, incidentally, is no longer used and now has heavy furniture barring it.

Only next day did the visitor learn that the upper lounge is known as Prince Charlie's Room; that he had been there in 1745 and slept in the room on the other side of the now-disused door.

Appropriately the floor of Prince Charlie's Room is carpeted in Royal Stewart tartan and the original panelling that Prince Charlie saw is still there.

Dunblane, PERTHSHIRE

Nearby Braco Castle seems always to have enjoyed the

reputation of being haunted, but details are scarce and as far as I can establish no real evidence exists.

The present owner, Commander G. R. Muir, R.N., tells me that his family have owned Braco Castle for some fifty-five years. Although many years ago some guests reported that their bedroom doors opened unaccountably, and some thirty years ago Commander Muir himself recalls noticing the dogs apparently observe something on the front stair 'with great fear', he neither saw nor felt anything unusual. He has no details of any other inexplicable happenings and no idea as to exactly who, or what, is supposed to haunt the castle.

The incident concerning the dogs did not take place in the oldest part of the property, which is traditionally supposed to be the part that is haunted.

Dunure, AYRSHIRE

Picturesque Culzean Castle perches on the cliff edge and was the scene of the roasting of a Stewart in 1570. Echoes of this gruesome operation have been reported in recent years.

From the fourteenth century the castle was the home of the Kennedys. It was Gilbert Kennedy, fourth Earl of Cassillis, who arranged for Allan Stewart, Commendator of Crossraguel Abbey, to be seized when he visited the property which became Crown territory after the Reformation. The unfortunate Stewart was taken to the Black Vault in the castle where he was stripped naked, bound to a spit and roasted before a great fire, being liberally basted with oil every few minutes to ensure that he did not burn. After he had prayed to be delivered from the torment by death, he signed a document surrendering the lands of the Abbey to the Earl. Six days later, however, he refused to sign a confirmatory document and the Earl ordered him to be roasted again. When near death, he signed the land away. Kennedy was fined £2,000 by the Privy Council and bound to keep the peace with Stewart, but he kept the lands and paid Stewart a life pension.

Occasionally—and particularly it seems on the quiet of a Sunday morning—the crackling and roaring sounds of a great fire have been heard from within these ancient walls, accompanied by faint, smoke-smothered screams and agonized sighs that soon fade away into silence.

The castle was rebuilt in 1777-1792 by Robert Adam. The late President Dwight D. Eisenhower used an apartment that was put at his disposal as a token of Scotland's thanks for his services as Supreme Commander of the Allied Forces in the Second World War on three occasions.

In 1972 three servants at the castle stated that they had independently seen an indistinct and inexplicable shape, on different occasions, in one of the passages in the dungeons of the castle.

Nearby is the freak hill known as 'Electric Brae'. As you travel south, you imagine your car is climbing when in fact it is going downhill.

Dunvegan, ISLE OF SKYE

Dunvegan Castle dominates this village at the head of Loch Dunvegan. The castle was formerly accessible only from the sea by a small gateway with a portcullis opening on the rocks. The present entrance is by means of a bridge thrown across a ravine which used to serve as a moat. The Fairy Bridge has long had an evil reputation and for years it was said that no horse would cross the bridge without shying. Horses and dogs are, of course, notoriously super-sensitive.

Parts of the castle, including the Tower, date back to the fifteenth century. The walls are ten-foot thick and the dungeon entered from the second floor near the drawing-room. It contains a host of interesting objects, including an Irish cup of bog-oak, the drinking horn of Rory More (Sir Roderick Macleod, the twelfth-century chief, knighted by King James VI), relics of Bonnie Prince Charlie and letters from Dr Samuel Johnson dated 1773 and Sir Walter Scott dated 1815 referring to their respective visits.

In the early sixteenth-century South Tower of this long-standing seat of the Macleod of Macleod you can see the fascinating Fairy Room containing the priceless Fairy Flag of Dunvegan. Scottish fairies, brownies and kelpies are supposed to be more malignant than their Irish brothers and are creatures of storms and tempests. The castle stands in a delightful old-fashioned garden, in charming contrast to the wilderness and wild countryside around. A waterfall in the nearby woods is known as 'Rory More's Nurse'.

Duror, NEAR BALLACHULISH, ARGYLLSHIRE

In the steep, short and lonely valley of Glen Duror, with Ben Vair rising in the background, stands Auchindarroch, one of the oldest buildings in the district. It is a rambling mansion-like property with a ghost known as 'the Maid of Glen Duror' and a low-ceilinged Haunted Room that opens off the dining-room on the ground floor and is now used as a bedroom.

The Maid of Glen Duror has often been seen hereabouts, a little woman peering through the windows on the ground floor; glimpsed for a moment inside the Haunted Room or the adjoining premises, or gliding sadly along the lower slopes of Ben Vair just behind the house. Occasionally she is seen for a moment in a lonely part of secluded Glen Duror. She is thought to be a dairymaid employed long ago by the original Stewart owner of Auchindarroch who during a great storm was swept down the glen, together with the cattle she was tending, and out into Loch Linnhe.

When I was in the vicinity a few years ago Mrs Jean Cameron told me that when she lived at Auchindarroch she had often seen the grey form of the Maid, usually at dusk.

Many are the strange happenings at this old farmhouse: doors and windows that have been left open bang to with great violence and those that have been shut continually open by themselves and then slam shut. Yet in the morning the doors and windows are always found exactly as they have been left at night. Faces peer into the house through the old windows. A peculiar chill is often noticed in the dining-room. Articles are moved and even strewn about, particularly in the Haunted Room. A ghostly old woman stands by a side door and moves across the lawn to vanish in the gloom while an unidentified hooded figure has been seen both in the dining-room and at the foot of the staircase.

Once four people heard three distinct bumps followed by three loud crashing noises. The sounds seemed to originate from the direction of the staircase but nothing could be found to account for them except perhaps three heavy paperweights that seemed to have jumped off a window sill by themselves in a bedroom where a little girl lay fast asleep.

A few weeks later a party of nine people, including a couple of Air Force officers, were guests at the farmhouse and every one of them heard three loud bumps from the room above, as if someone had dropped something deliberately three times. Yet on investigation nothing was discovered out of place. No living person was upstairs at the time. No sooner had everyone returned downstairs than another three bumps were heard and again immediate investigation produced no explanation. Yet a third time three loud bumps were heard and by now the whole party was terrified as to what was in store for them. When a final and complete tour of the property still provided no possible explanation, the guests, one after the other, made excuses and left haunted Auchindarroch.

Not long afterwards a French Air Force officer spent several nights in the Haunted Room. One night the whole house-hold was awakened by a tremendous crashing noise as though all the crockery in the house had been broken. A few moments later the occupants heard another loud sound, similar to the first. It was thought that the guest had got up in the night and stumbled into the dresser loaded with crockery and brought it crashing down and that he had banged into it again on his return journey to his room. But in the morn-ing there was no trace of anything to account for the very loud noises and the guest reported that he had enjoyed an excellent and undisturbed night!

Similar crashing noises have been heard by the occupants and by visitors to Auchindarroch on many other occasions and nothing was ever found that might account for them. Occasionally, too, a peculiar but not unpleasant perfume pervades the oldest part of the house. Alasdair Alpin Mac-Gregor told me that when he stayed there he and the only other occupant heard what sounded like an express train roar along the back of the house, which literally shook with the deafening sound. Yet when it had passed, there was no trace of anything that might have caused such a thunderous noise and in fact haunted Glen Duror seemed incredibly still and silent.

Earlston, BERWICKSHIRE

A small spur of the Eildon Hills known as Lucken Hare, the ruined grey tower, the Bogle Burn, and Eildon Tree have all ghostly associations with Thomas the Rhymer and King Arthur and his Knights. There is a strange mark on the hill-side resembling a galloping horse and rider that some people regard as a warning to those who are rash enough to intrude into the land of mystics and magicians. Thomas the Rhymer's Glen, where Thomas of Ercildoune met the Fairy Queen, is on the Abbotsford estate, in the vicinity.

The peculiar shape of the commanding Eildon Hills is said to have been caused by an evil spirit who split what had been one big hill into three at the command of Michael Scot (*c.* 1175-1234), a celebrated magician known as the 'Wizard of the North'. Many Roman remains have been found and before the Romans the priests of Baal sacrificed here to the sun-god, while on these slopes Thomas the Rhymer 'conceived and delivered' the prophecies that gave him his name.

Some two hundred years ago a horse-trader named Dick Canonbie used to bring horses to the market at Melrose. Several times a year he would ride over from his home beyond Hawick. Dick was popular with the ladies of the Melrose district and on one occasion, looking forward to a successful market next day, he persuaded an old friend, Maggie, to meet him that evening although she was now married to Sandy, a fierce and jealous man. Sandy followed Maggie that night and set about Dick who returned blow for blow and it was a bruised and battered husband who took his wife home.

That night, as Dick was settling his horses in preparation for selling them next day, Maggie burst in to warn him that Sandy and a dozen of his friends were out looking for him.

Deciding that discretion was the better part of valour, Dick lost no time in leaving Melrose and set off with his horses at speed towards Bowden Moor.

It was a pitch-black night and as he reached the western spur of the Eildons, known as Lucken Hare, he dismounted and was about to look for a spot to spend the rest of the night when the horses whinnied and shied violently at the form of an old man which had suddenly appeared close at hand. The long-haired and white-bearded figure wore a cloak that covered clothes strangely out of date; so much Dick observed as he tried to quieten the horses. Then he asked the stranger what he wanted. It seemed that the stranger wanted black horses and was prepared to pay a good price for them. Without further ado Dick sold his horses and was surprised to receive in payment gold coins bearing unicorns and bonnets, long superseded; but of their value there was no doubt and Dick was well pleased. When the stranger offered to purchase more horses one month hence Dick readily agreed.

Subsequently Dick returned several times and sold black horses to the old man, always receiving generous payment in the same old but valuable gold coins. His own horse always became terrified in the presence of the stranger and tore madly from the place as soon as the transaction was completed.

Then one midsummer night Dick asked the old man where he lived for he could see no habitation within miles. When his customer tried to put him off Dick persisted and asked whether he could not see the man's home. At length the old man agreed but warned Dick that he might see things that would test him to the utmost; should his courage fail, the consequences might be disastrous.

Dick followed the strange old man as he led the way through the deep heather and up the steep slope of Lucken Hare. Eventually they arrived at the hidden entrance to a cave which led deep into the heart of the hills, its vast interior lit by flickering lights in iron brackets fixed into the wall of the cavern.

As they advanced into the depths of the enormous cave Dick was astounded to see stall upon stall fixed into the rock and stretching as far as the eye could see, each containing a coal-black horse and at the foot of each quiet beast there lay a knight in black armour with a drawn sword in his hand. Horses and knights did not appear to be breathing although they had the appearance of life.

Deep in the heart of the cave Dick found that he had been ushered in to a vast torch-lit area, still, cold and deathly quiet. The old man led Dick forward to a great heavily carved oaken table with strange and mystic signs and symbols. Then the stranger took him firmly by the arm and pointed to a hunting horn and a sword that lay on the table.

Drawing himself up to his full height the old man spoke fiercely: 'Since you have been rash enough to intrude upon the realm of mystery and knowledge long forgotten and forsaken by the world of men, a choice is forced upon you. Either draw the sword or blow the horn. One or the other you must do. Choose well and you reign here as king; choose badly and you forfeit your life. Trifle not with me for I am Thomas of Ercildoune.'

The name of the great wizard, Thomas the Rhymer, struck terror into Dick's heart and he tried to reason which choice to make. What if the sleeping knights awakened to find him wielding a sword? Would it not be wiser to awaken them with a blow on the horn?

He took up the horn and blew. Immediately there was a tremendous roaring sound, like thunder, that filled the cave and echoing cavern; the very earth seemed to tremble; a torrent of wind rose in the depths of the subterranean caves and came rushing and shrieking upon them. In a moment horses and knights were awake and Dick hastily dropped the horn and drew the sword to defend himself as the cave became full of armed knights seemingly about to hurl themselves upon him. As he lifted the sword he became aware that the old man had disappeared but his voice echoed round the cave: 'Woe to the coward, that ever was born; Who did not draw the sword before he blew the horn.' Suddenly Dick felt the hordes of knights upon him and he was carried off his feet, swept back through the long passages and dashed senseless on the hillside.

Next morning he was found by two shepherds and although they did all they could for him, he was past human aid. In answer to their questions he gasped out his story and expired.

No trace of the entry to the cave has ever been found but a strange mark appeared on the hillside where Dick died; it resembled a galloping horse and rider and centuries of men have looked on the mark and wondered whether it is indeed evidence of a mystic realm beyond the everyday life of mankind. There are those who claim to have seen the shape of an old man by Eilden Tree on midsummer nights, while others maintain that they have either seen black-armoured knights on black horses in the vicinity of the ruined tower, or heard a screaming wind when the night is still as death on Lucken Hare.

Edinburgh.

When number 15, Learmonth Gardens was occupied by Sir Alexander Hay Seton, tenth Baronet of Abercorn and Armour bearer to the Queen, it was the scene of many strange happenings that seemed to centre on the bone of an ancient Egyptian. Certainly Sir Alexander believed that he was the subject of an Egyptian curse.

The story begins when Sir Alexander and his first wife, Zeyla, visited Egypt in 1936. They were duly impressed by such places as the Temple at Luxor and the tomb of Tutankhamun but rather disappointed with a visit to the Valley of the Kings which they undertook riding, as Sir Alexander afterwards put it, 'on a rather unpleasant camel'! However they enjoyed the bathing and good cuisine at the Mena Hotel in Cairo, close to the Sphinx and the Great Pyramid, and it was while they were there that a local guide, Abdul, offered to take the Setons to visit a tomb that was then being excavated.

This was too good an opportunity to be missed and the visit was arranged without delay. On the appointed day Abdul led them down some thirty rough-hewn steps into a chamber where a crumbling skeleton lay on a stone slab. Sir Alexander was told that the remains were those of a high-class girl, one of hundreds unearthed in the area of the Pyramids. After a look round the party made its way back up the steps and into the sunshine, but Zeyla was fascinated by the place and she slipped back to have a second look by herself.

Later that night, back at the hotel, Lady Seton showed her

husband a bone that she had taken from the tomb. 'It looked like a digestive biscuit, slightly convex and shaped like a heart,' wrote Sir Alexander in an unpublished manuscript. It was in fact a sacrum, the triangular bone at the base of the spine linking it with the pelvis.

Later, home in Edinburgh, Sir Alexander and Lady Seton showed the bone to some friends when they were talking about Egypt and its mysteries. Afterwards Sir Alexander, with mock dignity, deposited the bone in a glass case and ceremoniously placed it, temporarily, on a small table in the dining-room. Almost immediately strange things happened until Sir Alexander came to believe firmly that he was cursed for having the bone in his possession.

The same evening that he had handled the bone, just as his guests were leaving, there was a resounding crash and a huge piece of roof parapet smashed to the ground within two feet of where he stood. Next morning a chimney pot was found to have fallen to the ground, but Sir Alexander admits that it was a windy night.

A few nights later the Seton's nanny burst into their bedroom to tell them that she had heard someone moving about in the dining-room. Sir Alexander immediately went downstairs but could find nothing to account for the sounds and nothing out of place. Later the same night he heard a heavy crash himself and next day his wife accused him of upsetting the corner table, which she had found on its side, with the glass case containing the bone on the floor. The practical Sir Alexander decided that he must have set the table unevenly against the wall and that it had toppled over from vibration caused by passing traffic.

In the weeks that followed any number of odd and inexplicable noises were heard at 15 Learmonth Gardens and when a nephew, young Alasdair Black, came to stay for a few days he calmly announced one morning that when he had gone to the lower lavatory during the night he had seen 'a funny-dressed person going up the stairs.' Other visitors and servants soon claimed that they, too, saw a spectral robed figure wandering about the house at night and before long domestic help began to be a problem.

One night Sir Alexander decided to keep watch on the

Bone (he spells it with a capital B throughout his manuscript), which now resided in the upstairs drawing-room where there were also some valuable snuff-boxes. Sir Alexander carefully locked the doors and windows and kept watch from the balcony. Nothing happened for several hours and at length he decided to go to bed, only to be rudely awakened by a shout from his wife to say that someone was moving about in the room containing the Bone. Quickly picking up his revolver Sir Alexander investigated, meeting on his way a very scared Nanny who had also heard sounds of movement from the locked room. When the door was unlocked, for Sir Alexander had taken the key with him to his bedroom, they found the room looking, in his words, 'as if a battle royal had taken place!' Chairs were upset, books thrown about, furniture moved, a vase upset—and in the middle of it all the Egyptian relic alone remained untouched. Sir Alexander ascertained that the windows were still securely fastened and there seemed no possible way for any human being to have entered the room.

After a few weeks of quiet, apart from two unaccountable fires, bangings, crashes and other unexplained noises recommenced, and they always seemed to come from the direction of the drawing-room. Eventually the Setons decided to move downstairs to the sitting-room most of the articles that had been flung about, leaving just the heavy furniture in the drawing-room. The Bone in the glass case and the small table on which it stood were also moved to the sitting-room. A week later this room was found one day in a complete shambles, articles thrown about, furniture tipped over, ornaments broken, glassware smashed inside a cabinet and hardly anything in its right place. Even the table on which the Bone stood seemed to have been subjected to some kind of severe pressure for one leg was cracked.

The newspapers got hold of the story and there were headlines in Scottish papers such as 'BARONET FEARS PHARAOH CURSE ON FAMILY'. One reporter asked whether he could borrow the Bone for a few days. He returned it after a week, saying that nothing had happened while it had been in his possession but a couple of weeks later he became ill and had an emergency operation for peritonitis.

327

Shortly afterwards the Setons left their Edinburgh home. Sir Alexander explains: 'I suppose our nerves were frayed. We had a domestic scene and I went off to live at my club while Zeyla took Egidia (their five-year-old daughter) and went to stay with her family.' Meanwhile the Bone had been returned to the upstairs drawing-room. While the family nanny was alone in the house one night she heard a terrific crash from the direction of the drawing-room; she was too frightened to go upstairs. When she told Sir Alexander, he went up to explore, but the room was undisturbed, except for the Bone and the small table on which it had stood. It lay on its side, smashed and the Bone lay beside it, broken into five pieces.

Now there was talk of how the Setons should dispose of the Bone, although Lady Seton would not hear of it. One report stated that Sir Alexander had arranged for Lady Seton to make a special trip to Egypt to replace the Bone in the tomb from which she had removed it; other suggestions were that the Bone should be buried or disposed of in deep water. Sir Alexander refused many offers to purchase the relic for he was determined that no one else should endure similar experiences.

Lady Seton took the Bone to a doctor friend and asked him to mend it as well as he could. Afterwards it was placed on a table in the hall outside the dining-room. One report stated that the doctor's maid broke her leg running in terror from a mysterious robed figure while it was in her master's possession.

One evening the Setons held a dinner party and as the cheerful guests were talking and drinking merrily, the Bone and the table on which it stood suddenly hurtled across the hall and hit the opposite wall with a tremendous thump. No one was anywhere near it at the time but, perhaps understandably, something like chaos followed. The maid fainted, a cousin swooned and the party broke up in a somewhat hysterical fashion.

Now Sir Alexander decided that he must get rid of the Bone and he thought it best to do this while his wife was away from home. Accordingly he arranged for his uncle, Father Benedict of the Abbey at Fort Augustus, to come and exorcise the evil object. The solemn ceremony duly took place in Lady Seton's absence and the Bone, having been blessed, was destroyed in the presence of Sir Alexander by burning. He made sure that no part of it escaped.

The nanny, Miss Janet Clark, confirmed the end of the bone. 'I was glad when Sir Alexander decided to get rid of it,' she said in 1965. 'He brought it into the kitchen and we put it on the fire and watched it burn. It took a long time and what was left was put into a bucket with the ashes.'

Egidia is now Mrs Norman Haynes and it is to her husband, director of a printing and publishing group, that I am endebted for much of the information about this story.

Mrs Haynes, as we have seen, was only five years old at the time of the curious happenings and naturally she does not remember much about it but she recalls that she never liked the Bone. 'It was an evil thing and I always believed that there was something in the curse.'

On the other hand Sir Alexander's brother, the late Sir Bruce Seton, the eleventh Baronet, never accepted the story of the curse; before his tragic death he always felt that the various troubles that beset Sir Alexander: ill-health, financial and family difficulties, had nothing whatever to do with the Egyptian relic.

In his own narrative Sir Alexander states emphatically: 'The curse did not end with the destruction of the Bone. From 1936 onwards trouble always seemed to beset me. Zeyla never forgave me for destroying the Bone and it did not help our already rocky marriage.'

Sir Alexander and Lady Seton were in fact divorced in June 1939 and although Zeyla re-married, she had a lot of misfortune, unhappiness, poor health and eventually died while still quite young. Sir Alexander married Flavia, granddaughter of the Earl of Rosslyn in 1939 but they separated in 1953 and were divorced in 1958. Flavia, Lady Seton, died in 1959 and in 1962 Sir Alexander married Julia Clements, the lecturer and author of books on flower-arrangement. She recalls that during their honeymoon they visited the family seat at Seton Place, Longniddry, where her husband showed her the family coat of arms and the space on the chapel plaque for his own epitaph. He was, she says, outwardly always cheerful but inwardly he was deeply affected by his misfortune. He often talked about the Bone and believed that it had an evil and uncanny influence on his life. 'I was born during an earthquake,' he states in his manuscript, 'and my life has been a tremor ever since.'

Sir Alexander Seton had a premonition while on his honeymoon and he told Julia, Lady Seton that they would probably be married for only six months. In fact, he died seven months later. No one could ever convince him that there was nothing in the well-known belief that robbing a tomb brought bad luck, especially an Egyptian tomb.

There is still much of the nearby village of Colinton that the boy Robert Louis Stevenson must have known. The manse, the garden, the churchyard, even the room in which his grandfather wrote his sermons, although no longer a 'dark and cold room, with a library of bloodless books'. Parts of the place are unaltered and on the sides of what is now a doorway, one can trace the scars left by the former shelves of the cupboards of Stevenson's grandfather. Above this room is the window from which at night the novelist as a boy would gaze hopefully into the graveyard below, looking for 'spunkies' playing among the graves. The so-called 'Witches' Walk' is a narrow passage between the garden bordered by shrubbery on one side and on the other by the wall of the kirkyard. Nearby stands an enormous yew Stevenson knew and wrote about. It is here that his ghost is reported to be seen on occasions; a pale, long-haired figure, glimpsed for a moment in the shade of the great tree, sheltering perhaps from the brilliance of the sunlit lawn. A macabre relic of the past can be seen in the churchyard. It is a massive 'mort-safe', used to cover the newly-buried until the bodies were of no use to grave-robbers.

The Grassmarket, Edinburgh has a ghost, too. The notorious murderers Burke and Hare lured their victims to Tanners' Close and provided fresh bodies for dissection. Major Thomas Weir, the eloquent Presbyterian and Commander of the Town Guard, the man who led Montrose to the scaffold lived in West Bow. Weir himself was burned to death in 1670 after confessing to witchcraft and to consorting with the Devil. For over a hundred years after his death his ghost terrified the inhabitants of West Bow, for his phantom form was repeatedly seen flitting about the streets and sometimes 'fiendish laughter' would be heard coming from the locked and empty house that he had occupied until, it is said, Satan himself came to Edinburgh and carried him off in a black coach. Once towards the end of the eighteenth-century a William Patullo was delighted to rent the fine property but he only spent one night there. He recounted that as he and his wife lay in bed a strange apparition, something like a calf, came to the bedside, then set its front feet upon the bed and gazed steadfastly at the occupants. Terrified, the next day they left the house.

Edinburgh life revolved for centuries around the ancient Mercat Cross. The restored cross incorporates the original age-old shaft, supporting the unicorn and hundreds of years ago citizens heard the laws of the city proclaimed from here.

On the eve of the Battle of Flodden, on September 9th, 1513, when cannon were being removed from the castle for the use of the army, ghostly heralds are said to have appeared on the platform of the historic Mercat Cross and recited the names of those who would die in the battle where England was to lose five thousand men and Scotland their king, some ten thousand men and the flower of all the noble families of Scotland. Pitscottie, in his *Summons of Pluto*, relates that at midnight, while the artillery was rumbling out of the castle, a cry was heard at the Mercat Cross, proclaiming a summons, named and called by the proclaimer thereof, 'the summons of Pluto', which desired 'all men to compear, both earl and lord and baron and all honest gentlemen within the town, every man specified by his own name, within the space of forty days, before his Maker'. Pitscottie maintains that no man called in the summons escaped death at Flodden, except one: a certain Richard Lawson who, hearing the summons from his gallery in the High Street, called in reply: 'I appeal me from your justice, judgment and sentence, and betake me all hail to the mercy of God.' He was at Flodden and returned alive.

Among the many narrow and quaint passages or 'closes' in the old part of the city that have the reputation of harbouring ghosts, Mary King's Close was, until it disappeared during

331

reconstruction, significant for the number of terrifying apparitions that were seen there.

Among the inhabitants at one time was a respectable law agent, Thomas Coltheart, who moved to a large property in the Close despite warnings that the house was haunted. Soon after he moved in, the maid left and finding themselves unable to procure another willing to reside in the house, the Colthearts managed as well as they could on their own.

One Sunday afternoon Coltheart, who had been unwell and was resting, was listening to his wife's reading of the Scriptures. Suddenly something caught her eye and as she looked up she was horrified to see an old man's head, with a long and straggling beard, floating without a body in the air at the other side of the bed; his piercing eyes were fixed intently upon her.

She fainted with shock and fright and remained unconscious until friends called in on their way home from church. Thomas tried to convince her that she had imagined the whole thing and the rest of the evening passed without further incident.

Shortly afterwards however Coltheart awakened one night to see the same phantom head floating in mid-air over the bed and surveying him with unblinking and frightening gaze. Coltheart rose from the bed, lit a candle, awakened his wife, and began to pray. Still the apparition stayed in the room and after about an hour was joined by the head of a child, also suspended in the air, followed by an arm naked from the elbow which, despite their revulsion and reluctance, seemed anxious to shake hands with Mr and Mrs Coltheart!

Coltheart called again and again on the phantoms to relate the reason for their appearances but the hovering faces continued silently and solidly to stare at him and his wife as though they were intruders and wished them to go away.

Soon other phantoms came, including a dog which curled itself up in a chair and seemed to go to sleep. Others, more frightening, appeared until the whole room swarmed with them and then when the unfortunate couple were at their wits' end, they heard a deep and awful groan, whereupon all the apparitions vanished.

Not surprisingly the Colthearts began to make plans to

leave the house but during the whole of the extended period of negotiations for moving they saw no more apparitions and when the projected move fell through, they decided to postpone moving and in fact continued to live at the house for many years, undisturbed in any psychic sense.

Some years later, after Coltheart had died, a strange story was told concerning a client of his who lived at Tranent, ten miles from Edinburgh. This man was awakened one night by a nurse who was frightened by 'something like a child moving about the house'. Starting up and instinctively reaching for a weapon to defend the nurse and himself, he was amazed to recognize in the middle of a weird, cloud-like substance that had appeared in the bedroom, the features of his friend and legal adviser Thomas Coltheart. He had the presence of mind to ask what the trouble was and could this mean that Coltheart was dead? The apparition only shook its head twice and then melted completely away. The gentleman was much mystified and in the morning lost no time in proceeding to his friend's house in Mary King's Close, Edinburgh, where he found Mrs Coltheart mourning the recent death of her husband.

Edinburgh was also the scene of an interesting and well-attested case of premonition in the seventeenth century; an account kept both by Robert Chambers (author and co-founder with his brother of publishers W. & R. Chambers) and by Sir Walter Scott.

Lady Eleanor Campbell, youngest daughter of James, second Earl of Loudoun, was married at an early age to James, first Viscount Primrose, a man of ill-temper, dissolute habits and considerable brutality. Things came to such a pass that the gentle Lady Eleanor began to fear for her life—and not without good cause for one morning, as she was dressing, she saw, reflected in the mirror, her husband creeping stealthily towards her, knife in hand and a look of murder on his face. Terrified, Lady Eleanor, thinking only of escape, promptly jumped through the first-floor window into the street below. Fortunately she received no serious injury and she was soon in the care of relations. After such an episode any hope of reconciliation seemed doomed to failure and the ill-matched couple agreed to live apart.

Lord Primrose went abroad and for a long time the Lady Eleanor had no news of him. It was during this extended period of separation that she chanced to meet a necromancer visiting Edinburgh who declared that he was able to locate the present whereabouts of absent friends and relatives, irrespective of the distance involved.

Perhaps out of curiosity (it could hardly be from love) Lady Eleanor, together with a friend, went to the fortune-teller's lodgings in Canongate to enquire about her husband, where he was and what he was doing.

She was led to a large mirror and looking into it she distinctly saw the inside of a church where a marriage ceremony was in progress. On looking at the chief characters in the vision she was astonished to recognize her husband as the bridegroom, although the bride was a stranger to her. The ceremony had apparently just begun when a man hurried towards the bridal pair, a man whom Lady Eleanor recognized with a start as one of her brothers. He seemed, at first, to be a friend who had arrived late but, as he drew nearer to the couple about to be married, his expression changed to one of extreme anger. He drew his sword and attacked the waiting bridegroom who speedily sought to defend himself, whereupon the mirror-scene became cloudy and finally disappeared completely.

Back home, Lady Eleanor carefully wrote out a minute account of the whole affair, dated, signed and sealed it—all in the presence of a witness—and deposited it in a place of safety.

Some time later her brother visited her on his return from abroad and she enquired, during the course of conversation, whether he had happened to hear any news of her husband while he was on the continent. Her brother replied that he never wished to hear the man's name again and then, at her request, disclosed that he had in fact met Lord Primrose under somewhat strange circumstances.

While staying in Amsterdam, he became acquainted with a wealthy family whose beautiful daughter was heiress to a fortune. He learned that this girl was engaged to a Scotsman of good position who had quite recently come to live in Holland. Later he was invited to the wedding. He did, in fact, attend the ceremony, arriving late, but just in time to prevent the marriage of the Dutch girl to his own brother-in-law!

Recalling her mirror-vision and the fact that it was signed and dated, Lady Eleanor asked her brother the date of his encounter with her husband. Then she fetched a copy of her account of the vision and showed it to him; not only did it correspond in every particular with the actual experience but the date of the attempted marriage was the same as that of the vision.

The earl died in 1709 and despite many good offers, the Lady Eleanor, more than a little disillusioned with marriage, rejected them all including the well-known John Dalrymple, second Earl of Stair—though she preferred him to all the others. The earl, determined to break her resolution not to re-marry, hit upon a plan that, as one writer puts it 'marks the age as one of little delicacy'. Having bribed one of Lady Eleanor's servants to admit him to her dressing-room which overlooked the High Street, the earl, when the morning 'was somewhat advanced' showed himself *en deshabille* to the passers-by! The effect of such an exhibition upon the lady's reputation induced her to accept him as her second husband and as Countess of Stair she lived happily, outliving the earl who died in 1747. The Lady Eleanor died in Edinburgh at an advanced age in 1759.

Edinburgh Castle is reputed to harbour several ghosts, including a headless drummer who has been seen as recently as 1960. During their residence at the castle Major Griffiths and his wife were visited by their young nephew Joseph D'Acre from Kirklinton in Cumberland. One afternoon he mentioned that the following day he planned to join some other youngsters on a fishing expedition. No objection was made to this but during the night Mrs Griffiths found herself suddenly waking from a troubled dream, calling out in terror: 'The boat is sinking—oh! save them ...'

Her husband attributed the dream to apprehension about their nephew's planned fishing trip but she insisted that she had no uneasiness on that score and indeed, had thought no more about it. She was soon asleep again, only to be awakened with the same dream; the feeling of terror repeated itself no

335

less than three times during the course of that night. On the last occasion Mrs Griffiths saw the image of a boat sinking and the whole party drowned. By this time she was thoroughly alarmed and rising from her bed, she put on a dressing-gown and, not content to wait for morning, went to her nephew's bedroom persuading him with some difficulty to abandon his plans.

The next day broke fair and clear and the fishing party duly set off consisting of a Mr Patrick Cumming, Mr Colin Campbell, a boy named Cleland and two sailors. Mrs Griffiths and her nephew felt rather silly at their decision that he should not accompany the party but their minds were made up and they let things stand. At three o'clock in the afternoon a sudden squall arose from the south-east, the boat foundered and all the occupants were drowned except Campbell who was picked up after being in the water for five hours. The accident took place on August 7th, 1734 and is narrated in the *Caledonian Mercury* dated August 12th.

Edrom, near Duns, BERWICKSHIRE

Where the waters of the Whiteadder and those of the Blackadder join, stands the village of Allanton. Nearby, on the north bank of the Blackadder stood haunted Allanbank with its pathetic ghost of 'Pearlin Jean'.

In the seventeenth century Allanbank was owned by the Stuart family and one Sir Robert Stuart wooed and won Jean or Jeanne, a lovely French girl. He took her to France with him but one morning in Paris Sir Robert abruptly left the trusting girl, striding out of the house and seating himself in his coach without a backward glance. In her silks and 'pearlin' lace poor Jean ran after her lover and tried to get into the carriage, but the postillion drove on. She was thrown to the ground and the heavy wheels of the carriage passed over her head.

Back at Allanbank, where the heartless Sir Robert arrived one autumn evening at dusk, the first thing he saw, sitting on the archway high above the entrance gateway, was the figure of his murdered Jean, gazing down at him with her crushed

336

and bloody head. From then on, it is said, the sad ghost of Pearlin Jean walked the corridors of Allanbank. Sometimes only the rustling of her silks and lace would be heard; at other times her sad figure would be seen and no sound heard.

Once seven ministers attempted to exorcise the ghost but they were unsuccessful. Local people were proud of the sad but sweet Jean and when the house was demolished in the nineteenth century, many of the villagers were worried as to what would happen to 'Pearlin Jean'. They need not have worried for her ghost has been seen and heard long after all traces of the old house have disappeared; especially at dusk on autumn evenings.

'Pearlin Jean' was for years the most remarkable and best-known ghost in Scotland and it is still possible to find old inhabitants who will relate stories of eerie experiences: the rustling of silk along empty passages and up and down deserted stairways; the sound of footsteps walking backwards and forwards in certain bedrooms. The occupants became so used to the disturbances at one period that they calmly accepted and all but ignored the strange noises and continual reports of a female figure seen in the house and grounds.

For a time a picture of 'Pearlin Jean', hanging between portraits of Sir Robert and Lady Stuart, seemed to keep the ghost comparatively quiet. Then the stories started again. There was a childrens' nurse at Allanbank who arranged to meet her boy-friend in the orchard at moonlight. He arrived first and seeing a female figure wearing a light-coloured dress he hurried forward with open arms to embrace his Jenny but as he almost reached the spot, the figure vanished, to reappear again far off at the edge of the orchard. The would-be lover took to his heels but Jenny, when she did arrive, saw nothing; however she forgave her Thomas and they were eventually married.

Elgin, MORAYSHIRE

This ancient royal burgh has a history going back to 1190 and was much favoured as a royal residence, especially by James II. Part of the town was burned by the Wolf of Badenoch in 1390 and half of it sixty years later in the struggle between Huntley and Douglas. Bonnie Prince Charlie spent eleven days here at Thunderton House, later Gordon's Temperance Hotel, before fateful Culloden. Johnson and Boswell described a 'vile dinner' they had here in 1773 at the old Red Lion, still standing in the High Street. When Thunderton House Hotel was for sale in April, 1970, the proprietress, Mrs Agnes Brown, stated that she had heard the sound of bagpipes on more than one occasion in one of the second-floor bedrooms; music for which there seemed to be no normal explanation. A former member of the hotel staff whose room had been near the top of the rambling old building claimed that she heard a voice a number of times say 'Come in' as she walked along the corridor to her room, although no one was there. The wife of the previous proprietor, Mrs Lessels, said she had no doubt that the place was haunted and she and her son David saw a standard lamp rise over a foot into the air one evening; it moved across the room entirely of its own accord and landed with a thump at the opposite side undamaged, apart from the shade being dislodged.

Ethie Castle, ANGUS

In 1178 a fortified farmhouse stood here where today a fine pink castle stands, full of fine furniture—and traditional ghosts.

It is unlikely that Cardinal David Beaton, Abbot of Arbroath in 1524, built Ethie Castle although he has long been credited with that honour, for there was a great house here long before the prelate was born. It is certain, though, that he loved the place. He brought his beautiful young wife to Ethie Castle and they had seven children before he was brutally murdered at St Andrews Castle on May 29th, 1546. Soon the Cardinal's ghost was seen at Ethie and there are still occasional reports of appearances of his stately figure in the vicinity of the secret passage in the wall of the Cardinal's Chamber. There are also frequent, unexplained footsteps and a dragging noise has been heard for some minutes in an otherwise silent night. A contemporary portrait of Cardinal Beaton hangs in the dining room.

338

A more sinister story concerns the older portion of the house, part of which had been unoccupied at night for many years until a new governess arrived and spent her first night there. In the morning she complained that she had been awakened by the patter of children's feet, by heart-breaking sobs and the rattle of a wheeled toy somewhere over her head. All this happened not once but many times and when eventually some effort was made to discover the cause and locality of the disturbances, it was found that the only entrance to the room above that occupied by the new governess had long ago been bricked-up and panelled over. When the wall was broken down the skeleton of a child was discovered close to the remains of a little wooden cart. After the bones had been buried the distressing sounds were heard no more.

Fearn, ROSS AND CROMARTY

There are a few green mounds and traces of an old hawthorn hedge at a spot where the parish of Nigg borders that of Fearn; the last reminders of a ghost that walked here for years and perhaps still walks.

King Charles II, during his exile in France, procured a contribution of £10,000 from the Scots who at that time wandered as itinerant traders throughout Poland. One of these men returned to his native land in his old age, possessed it is said, of such considerable wealth that he was known locally as 'the rich Polander'.

He died suddenly and in his will, the only thing in his strongbox, he bequeathed large sums to various relatives whose whereabouts were unknown. Some people thought that he had loaned money in the neighbourhood; others that he had a brother in Poland to whom he had entrusted the greater part of his money but who had been robbed and murdered by bandits on the continent.

In the midst of such speculation the 'rich Polander' himself, it seems, returned to try to settle the matter. The rough pasture, near the green mounds that were formerly part of his house, was then a lawn with a gate in the eastern corner and another in the west corner. Between them a road ran

339

passing in front of the old man's house. For years the apparition of the 'rich Polander' was seen, evening after evening, walking along this road. It always approached from the east, lingered for a while in front of the building that stood empty and silent and then glided away to the west, disappearing as it passed through the western gate.

Dozens of people saw the figure; scores more heard about it, but no one had the courage to approach the ghost and perhaps try to find out about the legacies which it is said, remain unpaid to this day. One witness saw the apparition in bright moonlight and described the richly-embroidered waistcoat, the white cravat and the 'small clothes' of crimson velvet, together with the laced hat and broad shoe-buckles. The thin, withered hands were clearly distinguishable but the features 'wholly invisible'.

Also in Fearn there used to be a cottage half-way up the hill with an old elm tree beside it, a cottage that was once occupied by a farmer and his wife, a bad-tempered, one-eyed woman. The farmer had been married before and his son of five years and a daughter of seven found their stepmother hard and unkind; the little girl was shrewd enough to remark on one occasion, when she was beaten by her stepmother for tasting a piece of cake straight from the oven, that her second mother could see better with one eye than her first mother could with two!

The dead children's mother, an industrious and devoted housewife, had left behind her a large store of blankets and bedlinen; yet the children's bed, for the summer and autumn after the second marriage of their father, was only covered with a few worn-out rags. When winter set in, the little ones would lie in each others arms for the early part of each night, shivering with cold. Then, for a week, they found when they awakened each morning that they were closely wrapped up in some of their mother's best blankets.

The stepmother stormed and raged and replaced the blankets in the big store chest, furnished with lock and key, but it was all in vain and each morning the blankets were regularly back on the children's bed. The poor children were threatened and beaten but they could give no account of the matter other than they were very cold when they fell asleep but were warm and comfortable when they awoke.

Then one night the girl was able to explain the mystery. Her brother had fallen asleep but she was cold, bitterly cold and lay awake deep into the night. Suddenly the bedroom door opened and there entered a lady clothed in a long white dress. As she went to the chest, the lock sprang open and she withdrew some blankets, wrapped them around the children, kissed the boy and was about to kiss the girl when the child recognized her mother's features. Turning, the figure vanished into the darkness and thereafter the children were allowed to have warm bedclothes on their beds.

There is yet another ghost story associated with Fearn concerning a farmer who had buried his wife one day and the same evening called on a young woman with whom he had become friendly. She lived in a cottage almost adjoining Fearn burial ground. The couple were getting along famously and soon after midnight the young woman was seated on the farmer's knee close to a window that opened to the burial ground. When the mother of the girl came upon them unexpectedly, she was shocked by their levity and reminded the farmer that the corpse of his recently deceased wife lay not forty yards from where they sat, 'in its entireness and almost still warm with life'. 'No' replied the farmer, 'entire she may be but cold she certainly is for she was cold enough long before we laid her there.' As he spoke he turned towards the window and there, looking at him through the panes of glass, he saw the face of his dead and recently buried wife!

Hurrying home the farmer became ill and died of a brain fever only a fortnight later—after which widowers in these parts were noticeably less hasty in courting their second wives for years afterwards!

Fettercairn, KINCARDINESHIRE

An old hostelry used to stand on the south side of a nearby summit and many years ago when the Reverend Dr Rule was Chancellor of Edinburgh University, he and his *entourage* sought shelter there while on their way to Aberdeen.

As the hostelry happened to be full, the landlord suggested

341

that Dr Rule might care to accommodate himself in an empty house close by where the landlord said he would gladly light fires and ensure that bedclothes, candles and other necessities were available. 'But,' he added, 'I must warn you, sir, that the house is haunted!'

Dr Rule was not in the least perturbed by this information but his servants were loath to accompany him and they found lodgings among the hospitable local people, leaving the Chancellor to spend the night alone. Being weary from his journey, he retired as soon as the rooms were ready, undressed, blew out the candle and went to bed. But an hour or so later he awakened to find a ghostly figure in the room. It approached the bed-side table, took up the candle, lit it from the embers of the fire and then turned to leave the room, beckoning to Dr Rule to follow! Instead the doctor, deciding with Falstaff that discretion was the better part of valour, remained in his bed and 'commended himself to God's keeping'.

The ghost seemed to realize that Dr Rule was reluctant to leave his bed and evidently resolved on more positive action for as Dr Rule watched, with wide eyes, the apparition placed a poker in the fire and, when it was red-hot, withdrew it and laid it on the floor pointing towards the bed.

At this Dr Rule decided that he had no choice in the matter. He rose and followed the ghost which led him out of the bedroom and down a flight of stairs; at the foot of which it placed the candle on the floor—and vanished! Dr Rule, with commendable calmness, picked up the candle and returned to his room where he pondered on the matter and decided that his spectral visitor had tried to convey some message to him. He thought it might concern murder. He spent the rest of the night undisturbed.

In the morning he enquired of the landlord as to whether he knew of any unsolved crimes in the district and although the good doctor was reassured on this point, he nevertheless felt sure that he was right. Determined to see whether he could discover anything about the matter himself, he made arrangements to spend the week-end in the area and announced that he would preach at the church on the Sunday. He added that he hoped the landlord would do all he could to ensure a good attendance. Word quickly spread that the well-known divine was to be heard at church and when Sunday arrived, Dr Rule, to his satisfaction, found a large congregation.

He took for his sermon the subject of conscience and must have been most impressive and lucid for at the end of the service an old man came to him and said, with tears in his eyes, that he could keep silent no longer. He told Dr Rule that as a young man he had assisted in the building of a house (the house in which the Chancellor had spent his disturbed night); that he and another man had quarrelled and fought and, more by accident than intention, the other man had been killed. Terrified of the consequences, he had quickly dug a hole at the foot of the stairs in the house and there buried his victim.

A skeleton was later unearthed at the foot of the stairs in the haunted house and after the bones had been buried in the churchyard, the ghost was never reported again.

An account of the affair is preserved among the old church records at Fettercairn.

Forfar, ANGUS-SHIRE

A grove in the beautiful Vale of Strathmore is haunted by the ghost of a penitent girl.

One day she had met in this grove Edmund Graeme, the only son of a laird. He had fallen in love with her and they would often keep their trysts in this romantic grove on the laird's estate. Soon they became engaged to be married but then, one evening, when he went there for a pre-arranged meeting, it was to learn that she had been unfaithful to him.

The shock nearly broke his heart. Before long, the ghostly sounds that are always heard before the death of a Graeme terrified the family and servants and soon Edmund Graeme was dead.

Hardly had he breathed his last before the girl he loved so much came to him, full of remorse. Distraught at being too late, she kissed the still lips and bade the attendants meet her in the grove that night to receive instructions about the burial of her beloved.

343

On the stroke of midnight Edmund Graeme's servants met the girl in the grove. She persuaded them to promise to bring the next night to the same grove the body of Edmund, in a double coffin. As they arrived with the coffin, again at midnight, the girl emerged from the trees clad in a white shroud. She told the attendants that it was here that she had first met Edmund Graeme, here that he had learned of her unfaithfulness, and here that he and she would be buried.

So saying she stepped into the coffin, lay down by the side of her dead lover and bade the servants put on the lid and bury them both on the spot. Too terrified to disobey, the servants carried out her instructions and the deed was done.

Ever since that day the glade has been haunted and whenever a girl passes through it at night, the ghost of the penitent betrothed of Edmund Graeme appears and warns her never to be unfaithful to the man she loves.

Fyvie, ABERDEENSHIRE

The magnificent fourteenth-century Fyvie Castle, formerly the seat of the Lord and Lady Leith of Fyvie, is probably built on the site of an even earlier castle. It is haunted by a weeping stone and a phantom trumpeter and it has a ghost room, a murder room and a secret chamber.

Beautifully situated near the river Ythan in a wooded valley, the impressive castle was given by King Richard III to Sir James Lindsay from whose family it passed to Sir Henry Preston of Craigmillar who distinguished himself at the battle of Otterburn in 1388.

While Sir Henry Preston was demolishing a nearby monastery and using the stones to construct what is now known as the Preston Tower, he had no less a visitor than Thomas the Rhymer, Scotland's prolific prophet, poet and bard, whose abilities are said to date from his contact with the Queen of the Fairies in the Eildon Hills.

It chanced that during the transference of many weighty stones three fell into the river and were lost; a circumstance that did not put Sir Henry in a good mood. When Thomas the Rhymer appeared at the castle at this inopportune moment to request a night's shelter, he was not admitted and the great gate was shut in his face.

Always quick to take offence, Thomas proceeded to pronounce a curse in front of the awed spectators who had hurriedly gathered to catch a glimpse of the famous wizard. He declared that until the three stones had been recovered, the Fyvie property would never descend in direct line for more than two generations. As he spoke a violent storm burst over the castle; the wind and rain drenching the watchers who noticed, with amazement, that the spot where the Rhymer stood was calm and dry.

Two of the lost stones were eventually recovered but the third was never found. Of the two retrieved one was found to have moisture on it and so it remained ever after no matter how dry and warm the weather might be. Thus the name 'Castle of the Weeping Stone' became attached to Fyvie: weeping perhaps on account of the missing stone and the curse.

Sir Henry Preston had only a daughter and she married into the Meldrum family to whom the castle passed on his death. Later it was sold to Alexander Seton, third son of the sixth Lord. He was created Lord Fyvie and Earl of Dunfermline. It was a Seton who rescued Bruce from the English but they always considered that the family was blighted as long as they remained at Fyvie because of Thomas the Rhymer's curse. Indeed, the estate was forfeited when the fourth Lord Fyvie espoused the Jacobite cause. William, second Earl of Aberdeen, became the owner in 1726 and he bequeathed it to his son by his third wife. The direct line died out, I understand, after two generations.

It was during the eighteenth century that the Phantom Trumpeter first made his appearance. Among the several stories in circulation to account for this famous ghost perhaps the most commonly accepted concerns Andrew Lammie, a trumpeter in the service of the castle who fell in love with Agnes Smith, the daughter of a prosperous local miller. Agnes's parents did not approve of the match and so the couple used to meet in secret. There is no telling how the affair would have ended had not the Laird of Fyvie himself desired Agnes for a mistress. Learning of the clandestine meetings, he arranged for Andrew to be seized and transported to the West Indies. However, after a few years in slavery, he managed to escape and returned to Scotland to look for his beloved Agnes, only to learn that she had died of a broken heart. The shock took its toll on Andrew's weakened frame and soon he, too, died. On his deathbed he cursed the Laird of Fyvie and swore that the sound of a trumpet would henceforth foretell the death of every Laird of Fyvie and would be heard both within and outside the castle walls.

It is said that shortly after the death of Andrew Lammie the haunting of Fyvie began and for many years afterwards the harrowing blast of a trumpet would be heard at dead of night before the death of a laird. Sometimes a tall and menacing figure, a shadowy man clad in a picturesque tartan, would be seen in the vicinity of the castle walls; a figure that had no reality and which disappeared into thin air when approached.

A variant of this story tells of the parents of Agnes Smith, angry with her for loving Andrew Lammie and rejecting the powerful Laird of Fyvie, actually being responsible for her death. In any case, the story of the love between Agnes and Andrew is immortalized in an Aberdeenshire ballad entitled 'Mill O'Tifty's Annie'; the poet substituting fictional names for the real characters.

On the summit of one of the castle's turrets is a stone effigy thought to represent Andrew Lammie and the trumpet in his hand points in the direction of a monument erected in Fyvie churchyard to the memory of his beloved Agnes Smith.

Another ghost at Fyvie Castle is the Green Lady who, Elliott O'Donnell told me a few years ago, is still seen from time to time. She emerges from the room known as the 'Haunted Chamber' and, gliding noiselessly through the winding stairways and panelled rooms, descending and ascending stairways, she returns at length to the Haunted Chamber, to disappear until the next time. Some years ago a monster fungus developed in the old gun room and when the giant growth was eventually removed the masons and carpenters discovered a complete skeleton. After these bones were unearthed a number of disturbances were reported, including re-appearances of the ghostly Green Lady. One of the maids at the castle (who had stoutly maintained that she did not believe in ghosts) lay in bed one night and saw a 'white object' step out of the wall of her room near the head of the bed. Too terrified even to cry out, she saw that the figure resembled a lady dressed in a wide and flowing whitish-green gown. The apparition 'sailed' rather than walked across the chamber, turned once and seemed to look sadly at the terrified occupant of the room, then disappeared through a closed door. Other witnesses told of meeting the Green Lady wandering through the corridors of the castle, a lonely and silent figure, disappearing into solid walls of panelling. After the Lord of the time gave instructions for the skeleton to be replaced in the wall where it had been discovered, there were fewer reported appearances of the mysterious Green Lady.

No one seems to know who the Green Lady might be; perhaps she is connected with another mystery here, a secret room which, according to rumour, has been kept locked for many years. It is believed that should the room be opened, grave misfortune will befall the inhabitants of Fyvie Castle. Some people think that the room contains ill-gotten treasure; others that it holds the bones of victims of some dreadful family tragedy; yet others that it is the entrance to dungeons where dark and awful deeds were committed long, long ago.

Galashiels, SELKIRKSHIRE

Ancient Buckholm Tower stands in this deserted landscape, a sentinel looking out over the valley of the Gala, a silent reminder of dreadful deeds.

The Laird of Buckholm, nearly two-hundred years ago, was named Pringle. He was a dark, evil man who had so ill-treated his wife and young son that they had left him. No woman was safe in the house and his cruelty was a byword for miles around. There was nothing he enjoyed more than employing his two ferocious hounds in hunting down Covenanters, outlawed religious dissenters.

One June day a troop of dragoons were in the vicinity in order to surprise an assembly of Covenanters who were due to hold one of their clandestine meetings on nearby Ladhope

Moor. Pringle was known as a loyal supporter of the Government so the dragoon captain came to Buckholm Tower for his help and advice as to the most likely spot on the wide moor that the Covenanters would choose.

Pringle was delighted. He had little doubt as to the place and after the troops were refreshed, he eagerly led them to Ladhope Moor. His guess was right but the Covenanters must have received warning for they had fled, leaving behind one old man, Geordie Elliot, whose wife had served Mrs Pringle at the Tower in happier days, and whose son, Willie, had stayed to help his father when the old man had fallen from his horse. Both were known Covenanters.

The wicked laird of Buckholm was in favour of dispatching the two men without argument but Captain Bruce of the Dragoons suspected that the men might be persuaded to disclose information about their fellow-Covenanters and he persuaded Pringle to keep them prisoner at Buckholm for the night. Next day an escort would collect them.

After the captain and his dragoons had departed, Pringle had the two men thrown into the tower dungeons which exist to this day, gloomy and damp with an ominous row of iron hooks suspended from the roof where hams and salted beef would hang in Pringle's happier days. There is also (or was) a bloodstained beam nothing would clean, a grim reminder of dreadful happenings.

With his prisoners safe Pringle sat down to celebrate the capture of the two Covenanters. His secret supply of French brandy dwindled alarmingly as he treated himself to glass after glass. The hours passed and Pringle still drank his brandy alone and became more ill-tempered with each glass.

At length he lurched to his feet and made for the dungeons. At the massive doorway he encountered several of his servants who had been disturbed by calls for 'Help' from the dark dungeons. It sounded, they said, as though old Geordie was in a bad way and his son was calling for assistance.

Pringle pushed his men to one side, opened the dungeon door and pulling it close after him, disappeared, cursing and staggering, into the gloomy interior. Quaking with apprehension the loyal servants listened to the raised voices, then the sounds of heavy blows, a dragging noise and strangled screams

348

Haunted Iona; Inner Hebrides, the holy island with phantom bells and the ghosts of Viking longboats. *Photo: Scottish Tourist Board*

Isle of Iona, Inner Hebrides, where ghostly music has been reported, twinkling blue lights have been seen, and the fatal 'call' still claims its victims. *Photo: Scottish Tourist Board*

St Michael's Church, Linlithgow, West Lothian, where, it is well documented, a ghost warned King James IV of Scotland of his defeat and death at Flodden. *Photo: Scottish Tourist Board*

Abbotsford, Melrose, Roxburghshire, which Sir Walter Scott built, lived in, died in, and now haunts. *Photo: Mrs J. Maxwell-Scott*

before silence and the re-appearance of the laird, panting, wide-eyed and cursing all and sundry. He stumbled out of the dungeon and was about to return to his study for more brandy when a knock sounded on the entrance door of the tower. Pringle stopped in his tracks and one of his servants hurriedly opened the great door. Outside stood an old woman, dignified and accusing. Pringle recognized Geordie's wife, Isobel. She had come in search of her husband and her son.

'Ye want to see your menfolk, do ye?' snarled Pringle, pointing to the dungeons. 'Come with me, then. By God, ye shall see them!'

He dragged the old woman with him and they disappeared through the dungeon doorway. Again he slammed the door shut behind him. A moment later a piercing scream broke from old Isobel's lips, for there, suspended on the cruel hooks, were the bodies of her husband and her son. Scream after scream echoed from the dungeon as the distraught woman stumbled out and collapsed, sobbing at the tower doorway. Now Pringle emerged from the dungeon, laughing hideously and shouting something about 'Swine should be treated as swine ...'

He paused as he saw Isobel, a pathetic heap, sobbing and shuddering in her sorrow. He stood over her, remorseless, calling her an old witch. For a moment the watching servants thought he was going to strike her but after a moment the sobbing ceased and the old woman slowly dragged herself to her feet. Her eyes burned with hatred. She faced the drunken laird fearlessly and cursed him quietly, invoking the vengeance of God for what he had done. 'May the memory of yer evil deeds haunt ye for ever, like the hounds of hell,' she said. 'May they pursue ye waking and sleeping and may ye find no rest in this life or through eternity.' The next moment she was gone.

Thereafter the laird of Buckholm was a haunted man. Whatever potency the curse may have had, Pringle certainly believed that he was hunted by ghostly hounds, not perpetually but at any time of the day or night the horror would be upon him. He would suddenly turn in his chair, eyes staring, and lash out at some invisible presence; he would wake from his sleep screaming that dogs were at his throat. Time after

349

time his servants would burst in on him after hearing his screams and cries for help, to find him beating about himself with his arms in all directions as though warding off attacks from all sides. Often he would return to the tower, having obviously ridden long and hard, fling himself from his panting horse and clamour for protection from the fearful things that he said had chased him.

Before long he died, wretched in mind and body, full of haunting horror and his last moments saw his body racked by convulsions, for all the world as though he were worried and badgered to death.

The months passed and as the anniversary of the laird's death approached, the atmosphere at Buckholm Tower seemed charged with expectation. Three days before the date on which he had died one of the servants swore that he had heard the baying of hounds and the cries of a man fleeing for his life, a mile or so from the tower. The pursuit seemed to pass close to him and faded away in the direction of Buckholm although he saw nothing to account for the fearsome noises.

The next night everyone at the tower heard the baying of hounds and a voice calling for help. The sounds drew nearer and nearer until the chase seemed to arrive at the very door of Buckholm and then came the noise of loud beating on the door and a man's voice imploring refuge; a strange, hollow voice that sounded like the late laird of Buckholm. Yet, when the door was opened the sounds ceased and the courtyard was seen to be totally deserted.

On the night of the anniversary of Pringle's death the baying of hounds and the piteous cries for help were heard yet again and this time they seemed to come from the dungeon. They grew louder and more terrible until finally someone was brave enough to open the dungeon door. Still the awful sounds came from within, although nothing was visible in the darkness. The door was shut again and then lingering footsteps were heard, heavy crashing noises and sudden thuds sounded from within the dungeon; then the tower seemed to vibrate with repeated heavy blows on the dungeon door as though someone wanted desperately to get out.

The awful noise continued for hours with no one daring to open the dungeon door again. At the time that Pringle had breathed his last, the battering noise ceased, a long-drawn-out sobbing sigh was heard and then silence.

Each year on the anniversary of the death of the laird of Buckholm noises resembling the baying of hounds, cries for help, heavy footsteps and thuds on the dungeon door are said to be heard, in varying intensity, by those who venture here after darkness has fallen.

Garleton Hill, near Hoddington, EAST LOTHIAN

The mansion-house called Garleton was said to be haunted by a mysterious tall man who walked about the old house with heavy footsteps, trying to persuade someone to listen to his long tale of woe. Foundations of the haunted house that took a long time to die can still be traced.

Towards the end of the eighteenth century one of the still-habitable wings of the decaying house was occupied by the eccentric Miss Janet Hepburn, a tall, thin woman who walked the countryside at all times of the day and night, dressed in black from head to foot and invariably carrying a cane with a gold chain and tassel.

One night, or rather morning, for it was just before sunrise, she had seated herself on a grassy knoll not far from her home when she was approached by a strange man whose looks she did not like at all. He was tall and pale with piercing eyes and he seemed most anxious to convey something to Miss Hepburn. But such a dislike had she taken to the odd figure which she had neither seen nor heard approach but suddenly found close to her, that she waved her cane at him and set off home. Looking back a moment later she discovered that the man was nowhere in sight.

That night Janet Hepburn took care to lock and bolt all her doors and windows and even put the key of the front door under her pillow for she found herself unable to forget the strange man. Living alone with only a maid, she feared that he might have followed her in some way and found out where she lived.

In the middle of the night she awakened to hear the sound of the front door opening, followed by heavy footsteps climb-

351

ing the stairs towards her room. The footsteps ceased and she then heard the sounds of movement within her bedroom. 'Who's that?' she called out, with as much defiance in her voice as she could muster. And the man who had accosted her the day before stood by her bed! 'This is my home,' he said in deep and hollow tones, and there was an indescribable sadness about his presence and his voice. 'I have a long story to tell you.'

Janet Hepburn felt sure that her visitor was a burglar. She pointed to her jewel box and told the man to take what he wanted and be gone. He shook his head and said that he only wanted to talk to her. Frightened and uneasy beyond words, Miss Hepburn told him that she would never listen to his story and waved him away. Without another word the strange figure turned and left the room. She heard heavy footsteps echo through the old house as he slowly made his way downstairs and out of the house. She only breathed again when she heard the front door slam shut.

For the rest of the night she tossed and turned, dreading that she would again hear the heavy footsteps and see the tall, sad man at her bedside. Yet she decided not to disturb her maid.

In the morning however she told her about the night's events and learned that the maid also had heard footsteps at the dead of night and also a man's voice; but thinking she must be dreaming, she had gone back to sleep. Now both women hurriedly looked everywhere to see what was missing but all the valuables were untouched, the front door was still locked and bolted and all the windows fastened.

In the years that followed heavy footsteps were heard from time to time at dead of night or very early in the morning but no trace of any intruder was ever found; locked doors and windows were never tampered with but, perhaps because Miss Hepburn had been so insistent that she would not listen to the visitor's story, the figure was never seen again.

Geanies, ROSS-SHIRE

Some years ago a cottage a mile away from the estate lodge,

occupied by a labourer and his wife, their two boys and elderly grandparents, was haunted by an invisible presence that knocked, threw things about and pinched people in bed.

The disturbances were investigated by Professor George J. Romanes, F.R.S., Professor of Physiology and a friend of Charles Darwin. An element of intelligence was observed for some strange scratchings were heard on an outside wall. When Professor Romanes asked whether his height could be indicated, a long scratch was heard; and when a similar question was asked regarding Mrs Romanes, a short scratch came— thus crudely but correctly asserting that while the Professor was tall, his wife was short! These noises and the knockings were heard when the boys were at school.

The movement in the beds seemed to be perceptible *under* the ticking of the mattress, almost as though a small animal were trapped there. There was gentle heaving and faint movement. Many times occupants of the cottage maintained that their sleep was disturbed by the pinching of invisible fingers. Incessant knocking accompanied this manifestation and sometimes the old man's night-cap would be snatched from his head and tossed to the floor.

Rabbit-traps placed on the bed were found flung to the floor with the wires broken and when the mattress was taken out of doors, split open and the stuffing removed and carefully examined, nothing untoward was discovered. Yet when it was re-stuffed and replaced on the bedstead, the movements returned exactly as before.

Professor Romanes and a friend spent a night at the cottage but nothing of a mysterious nature occurred during their visit and later the disturbances ceased. No explanation was ever discovered.

Gladhouse Reservoir, Moorfoot Hills, near EDINBURGH

The reservoir covers land where once Hoolet House stood, a small farmstead long occupied by a miserable middle-aged man who had no known relatives and few friends. His widely separated neighbours who knew him by sight, were surprised beyond words when he returned from a visit to Falkirk with a young bride. Now Hoolet House had servants and for a time there was light and gaiety but within a few months the fifty-year-old bridegroom was once again morose, irritable and unsociable.

The servants left one after the other and fresh ones stayed only a short time, except for a young Irishman. He alone seemed to remain faithful and the farmer only awoke to the young man's real reason for staying at the lonely old house when, after a long day at market he returned to his farmhouse to find his wife missing, together with the young Irishman and some £200.

The disgruntled farmer organized searches high and low for the guilty pair but without success. It began to be generally assumed that they had left Britain for one of the colonies, although curious stories began to circulate about the couple being seen in the vicinity of the old farmhouse and of the figures disappearing when they were approached. Such reports grew more and more numerous until the phantoms of Hoolet House were well-known in the neighbourhood and no one ventured that way after dark, if they could help it.

Soon the animals on the farm were stricken with a strange and deadly malady so that the farmer was hard put to it to bury the animals single-handed and he was forced to hire men to help him with the unpleasant work. It was as they were about to bury the last horse, having moved to another part of the farm from that to which they had been directed, that a shout from the farmer ordered them to stop digging. But it was too late; already a human hand was unearthed and before long the mutilated bodies of the farmer's wife and the Irish servant were uncovered.

Suspicion soon fell on the sullen and unpopular farmer but before the law could take its course he fled and was never seen again in the locality.

Hoolet House remained empty. The land was divided between neighbouring farms and as time passed, the very stones of the house were used for dykes and dividing walls. By the time the reservoir was constructed, hardly anything of the former house remained. And after the bodies of the young couple were uncovered and re-interned in consecrated ground

354

there were no further reports of the phantoms of Hoolet House.

Glamis, ANGUS

It is an unforgettable experience to approach Glamis Castle along the tree-lined drive on a shimmering summer's day. The haunted castle, solid and silent in the sunshine, has about it an air of mystery even under these conditions.

This splendid seat of the Earls of Strathmore is mentioned in thirteenth-century records; Shakespeare refers to it in *Macbeth*; and it was the birthplace of Princess Margaret.

What a place Glamis is for those who love mysteries! There is the Haunted Chamber; ringed stones in several of the bedroom floors now cleverly covered with built-in cupboards which are always full; the unexplained noises and strange nocturnal visitors that occupants have heard and seen; the fearsome appearance of huge and bearded 'Earl Beardie' who is reputed to have played cards with the Devil, and lost; the mysterious rooms that seem to have no doors; the everlasting blood-stain in King Malcolm's room where Malcolm II was murdered in the eleventh century (no amount of scrubbing and cleaning would remove it so in the end the whole floor was boarded over!); the pathetic and shy Grey or White Lady who is still seen quite often in the vicinity of the chapel dedicated to St Michael; the unrecognized tall figure in a long coat, fastened at the neck, which always enters a locked door halfway up a certain winding stair; the shadowy figures that are always being seen flitting about the castle; the bedroom door that opened every night whether it was locked, bolted or had furniture piled against it ... eventually the wall was taken down and the door removed. There is the Queen Mother's bathroom where no one could sleep soundly when it was a bedroom; the tongueless woman who looks out of a barred window or runs across the park pointing to her bleeding mouth; and the ghostly little Black Boy who sits on a stone seat by the door into the Queen Mother's sitting-room and is supposed to be a Negro servant who was unkindly treated over two hundred years ago.

There is even a vampire legend at Glamis. A woman servant who was caught in the act of sucking the blood from one of her victims was hustled into a secret room and left to die—but that is not one of the ways to rid the world of a vampire; and legend has it that her secret tomb is still open somewhere in Glamis and her menace still potent. Then there is the mystery of the number of rooms at Glamis and the story that house guests once hung towels out of every window from within the castle but when they went outside they discovered that no towel fluttered from any of the dark windows in one very old square tower, nor could they find a way into that particular tower.

The Haunted Chamber, sealed for years by walling, its position known only to a few, is thought to have got its name in the feuding days when a number of the Ogilvy clan, fleeing from the Lindsays, sought shelter at Glamis Castle. Although the owner at the time admitted them, he had no sympathy for their feud and on the pretence of hiding them, he secured them in a remote chamber of the rambling castle and there left them to starve. The chamber, it is said, still contains the remains of the unfortunate men and when many years ago, the earl of the day was much disturbed by strange night-time noises, Lord Strathmore and some companions went to the Haunted Chamber. He collapsed, however, when he encountered the contents of the unventilated chamber. Today the white-walled, bare chamber has a sense of brooding uneasiness.

A Dr Lee records that when a woman and her young son were staying at the castle and the child was asleep in an adjoining dressing-room, the woman suddenly felt a blast of cold air which extinguished a night-light at her bedside but did not disturb the light in the room where the child was sleeping. The woman saw a tall figure in armour pass silently from her room into the dressing-room where the child awoke with a shriek. When the lady comforted her child, she learned that he had seen what he described as 'a giant' who came into the room and leaned over the bed, peering closely at him.

High up in the uninhabited tower is the room where the ghost of 'Earl Beardie' gambles with the Devil. Earl Beardie was an ancient Lord Crawford who quarrelled with the Lord Glamis of the day as they gambled. Beardie, a huge man, was thrown down the stone staircase, only to return, according to legend, stamping his feet and roaring with rage, bellowing that if no man would play with him, he'd play with the Devil himself. Instantly a tall, dark man in a cloak strode in and play began. No one knows what happened but the man was never seen again and Earl Beardie died shortly afterwards. Ever after the ghost of Earl Beardie gambled, stamped and swore with 'something' in the empty room with two doors and an ominous trap-door. Even today servants at the castle maintain that they hear at night the rattle of dice, heavy stamping noises and the sound of men cursing from the direction of the empty room. A former Lord Castletown's daughter awoke during a night she was spending at Glamis to see the figure of a huge old man seated in front of the fire in her bedroom and when he turned to look at her, she saw that his face was that of a dead man. Dr Nicholson, a Dean of Brechin, occupying a room off the central staircase, awoke to see a tall figure in a cloak standing by his bed. The figure disappeared through a wall—a ghost that the Bishop of Brechin, Dr Forbes, was to encounter the very next night.

Once three sets of rooms on the Clock Landing were allotted respectively to Lady Strathmore's sister, Mrs John Streatfeild and her husband; the Trevanions, Lord Strathmore's sister; and Mr and Mrs Munro from Lindertis who occupied the Red Room with their young son sleeping in an adjoining room. During the night Mrs Munro was awakened by someone bending over her, and a beard brushing her face. She awoke her husband and they both plainly saw a figure pass into their son's room; he immediately shrieked with terror and rushed into his parent's chamber, declaring that he had seen a giant. The time was four o'clock. In the morning Mrs Trevanion related that she and her husband had been awakened during the night by the restlessness of her little dog and they had both heard a tremendous crashing noise followed by the sound of a clock striking four times. The following night the three couples sat up to watch and although they saw nothing on that occasion they all heard a loud crashing noise from the direction of the landing and as they were examining the area with its great old clock, the hour of four boomed out.

Lady Granville, elder sister of the Queen Mother, told my friend James Wentworth Day that when she lived at Glamis, children often woke up at night in the upper rooms, screaming that a huge, bearded man had leaned over their beds and looked at them. All furniture has long been taken out of these rooms and they are never used in these days; nor is the Hangman's Chamber which is said to be haunted by a butler who hanged himself there. Sir Shane Leslie told me that the ghost of Earl Beardie had been seen by his Aunt Mary when she was a visitor at Glamis.

There are many accounts of a White or Grey Lady being seen at Glamis Castle; one account relates that the figure was seen by three people at the same time, from different vantage points; and there are persistent accounts of a strange, elusive, racing figure nicknamed 'Jack the Runner' who speeds across the park on moonlit nights.

I was told more about the Grey Lady when my wife and I were at Glamis. Lady Granville was in the chapel one sunny day when she saw a grey figure kneeling in one of the pews and although the detail of the dress the figure was wearing was quite clear, Lady Granville noticed that the sun shone through the figure and made a pattern on the floor. The last Lord Strathmore saw the Grey Lady in similar circumstances. He was checking the details of some of the interesting de Wint pictures in the chapel one afternoon when he turned round and saw the figure in grey, kneeling in one of the pews. Not wishing to disturb her, Lord Strathmore tiptoed quietly away. My wife and I silently examined the pictures in this quiet little chapel when we were there but we saw no ghost.

And then there is the famous 'monster' legend. It is said that nearly two hundred years ago a 'monster' or frightfully deformed child was born within the family, a grotesque and bloated being that grew up in a hidden room to a large size and possessed enormous strength; a closely guarded secret known only to successive heirs and the faithful factors of the estate. The creature is said to have lived to an incredible age; one person who should know maintains that he died in

1921. That some such secret lies buried in the hundred-odd rooms and incredibly thick walls of Glamis, seems certain. Listen to Lady Granville again: 'We were never allowed to talk about it when we were children ... my father and grandfather refused absolutely to discuss it.' The last Lord Strathmore felt sure that a corpse or coffin was buried somewhere in the walls and the walk, high up on the roof, is still known as the Mad Earl's Walk, perpetuating the legend and dating perhaps from an escape attempt or the place where the poor monster was exercised.

Haunted and romantic Glamis Castle has many secrets and many ghosts.

Glasgow

The second largest city in Great Britain with over a fifth of the total population of Scotland; its name is derived from the Celtic meaning 'dear, green spot'. In the high-standing thirteenth-century cathedral a rare fifteenth-century rood-screen depicts the seven deadly sins; the tomb of St Mungo who founded a bishopric here in AD 543 (the saint's well is nearby) and the strange 'Rob Roy's Pillar' from behind which a mysterious stranger conveyed a warning to Frank Osbaldistone in Scott's romantic tale. The city has also a haunted infirmary and a number of haunted houses.

The ghost at Glasgow's Western Infirmary is said to be Sir William MacEwen, the brain surgeon who died some fifty years ago. Shortly before his death at the age of seventy-six, Sir William declined to perform an operation for severe headaches on a young artist. After he left the surgeon, the artist, suffering from one of his violent headaches, fell to his death down four flights of stairs at the Infirmary. The ghost that has been seen here from time to time in the corridors of the hospital is thought to be the remorse-filled spirit of Sir William, returning to the scene of the tragedy.

Quite recently a young nurse reported seeing a white-coated figure coming towards her one night along one of the dimly-lit passage-ways. When the form almost reached the door of the operating theatre, it vanished.

Many hospitals have ghosts. The authorities are invariably

359

sceptical and say that such stories are put about as a joke to frighten new night-staff. The nurses hope that the officials are right but evidence, such as that for the ghost of Sir William, mounts steadily and is not easily explained away.

Elliott O'Donnell once told me of a visit he made at a haunted house in Duke Street, Glasgow, which he first heard about from a solicitor who had visited the property with the idea of renting it, until he encountered something unexpected.

Almost as soon as he let himself into the empty house he heard footsteps that seemed to follow him as he climbed the stairs and explored the various rooms. At first he thought the sounds must be some peculiar acoustic result of the deserted house. But when he stamped his foot there was no answering echo although the footsteps continued to follow him when he resumed his exploration. Gradually, as a level-headed man, he began to feel that there was something strange about the place for although it was a warm and sunny summer's day he felt icy cold. As he walked along a passage with a large uncurtained window behind him letting in the summer sun, he suddenly saw on the wall ahead of him the shadow of a man—not his own! This figure had its arms outstretched and, with a shudder, the solicitor noticed that while the right hand seemed normal, there was no left hand at all!

Thoroughly frightened now, he turned and ran out of the house. But during the days that followed he found himself thinking more and more about it, reminding himself of its advantages, its low price and its sense of mystery. Within a few weeks he had taken the property and moved in with his wife and family.

For a while all went well. Then one morning the children's nursemaid burst into his study looking distressed. It seemed that the children were playing with something in the nursery that looked like a dog, and yet wasn't one! As he entered the nursery, the solicitor saw the blurred outline of a large dog come out of the room where the children were. Far from being frightened they were delighted with their new-found 'play-thing' although they told their father that it was a 'funny dog' because it never wagged its tail and they could never get near enough to touch it.

That same night, as he went to switch off the light after working late, he found his outstretched hand caught by something large and soft which had no fingers. The light went off as he screamed in surprise; his hand was released and he heard a tremendous crashing sound from the room above where his wife was already in bed.

Rushing upstairs he found his wife sitting up in bed, apparently still fast asleep but talking to a vague dark shape that crouched on the floor at the foot of the bed. As he approached, it seemed to disappear into the wall.

The sleeping woman now awoke and implored her husband to take her away from the house. She had dreamed of a murder being committed in the room and she described the murderer approaching her with outstretched hands. Next day the solicitor and his family moved out of the haunted house.

Elliott O'Donnell told me of the short time he spent there one night. Soon after arriving at the house a loud knock sounded at the front door and he found a policeman who was suspicious at seeing a light moving about in the empty house. O'Donnell soon reassured him that he was no intruder and when he explained that he intended to spend a night at the place the police officer commented that he had little to fear with a dog 'like that one' to keep him company, pointing towards the stairs. O'Donnell looked up and saw a huge, shadowy, dog-like shape half-way up the stairs. As they watched, it seemed to retreat and disappear into the wall. At the same time O'Donnell told me that he sensed an overwhelming air of evil. Acting on the spur of the moment, he explained to the policeman that there was no physical dog in the house and he hurriedly left with him. The distinguished writer on the occult told me he always regretted leaving the house that night although at the time he felt that he just could not stay a moment longer. He never had the opportunity of visiting the house again.

A correspondent has related peculiar happenings experienced some years ago in a council flat where she and her husband moved with their six-month-old baby, having looked forward for a long time to a home of their own.

Their happiness was, however, short-lived, for before long

they both began to notice strange bumps and knocks at night-time which could not be accounted for; furniture and other articles apparently moving of their own accord. The constant knowledge that something inexplicable might happen at any time of the day or night began to tell on their nerves and soon they fled to live with relatives.

A party of investigators sat all night in the deserted flat, hearing and seeing nothing unusual. They tried again and this time they certainly had a most extraordinary experience. Inexplicable bangs and crashing noises echoed through the flat at irregular times and for irregular periods; articles moved of their own volition, including a pair of iron fire-tongs which behaved as though propelled by invisible hands.

A medium was invited to join the next all-night sitting and in a dark room, while in trance, he spoke in what sounded like the croaking voice of an old woman. The communicating entity seemed agitated, her words were jumbled and disjointed but at length the sitters established the fact that she was worried about a baby; the child had something wrong with its throat and must be taken to hospital immediately, 'she' insisted, or it would die. 'She' identified herself as a relative of the young couple who had been driven from the flat and claimed that 'she' had caused the disturbances in an effort to attract their attention.

When the couple heard about the warning they were sceptical, for their child seemed perfectly fit, but they arranged for an X-ray examination and the same day surgeons removed a small obstruction from the baby's throat which, had it moved towards the windpipe, could have caused suffocation.

The vicinity of George Street was, it seems, haunted a few years ago by two ghosts, dressed in the fashion of the eighteenth century. They were seen by a man at two o'clock one morning as he walked home from late shift-work. He said afterwards that he heard no sound but suddenly became aware of two men, dressed in the clothes of two hundred years ago, walking beside him; 'going about their own amicable business' as he put it, obviously chatting pleasantly to each other although no sound of any kind reached the witness. Within a few seconds the ghosts faded and vanished.

Far from being frightened or upset the down-to-earth work-man stated that he had enjoyed the experience and rather hoped that it might be repeated!

Glen Shira, NEAR INVERARAY, ARGYLLSHIRE

One warm and sunny day in 1765 a man accompanied his father, a farmer from Glen Aray, to nearby Glen Shira, where both had business to attend to. They had walked there by crossing the hill between the two places and having finished by mid-day, they decided to return by way of Inveraray.

They reached the Gairan Bridge and turned north, when they were astonished to see a great number of men under arms marching on foot towards them. The men marched in regular order from the Quay, along the shore and high road, crossing the River Apay near the town, at the spot where a bridge was later constructed—and still there appeared to be no end to the column.

Father and son stood and watched the vast army for a considerable time and, as far as they could see, the column of men came marching towards them from the distance. At last the two men walked on, stopping now and again, with the marching men constantly in their view. They counted six-teen or seventeen pairs of colours. They clearly saw the soldiers, six or seven abreast, with children and women on each side, some carrying pots and pans. The soldiers were clothed in red and the bright sun of the summer day gleamed on the muskets and bayonets. At one point the two men noticed an animal that looked like a deer or possibly a horse, in the middle of a circle of soldiers who seemed to be forcing the animal forward with their bayonets which they used to stab and prod the tired beast.

The older man had served with Argyll's Highlanders in the rising of 1745 and in answer to his son's questions he said that he supposed the army 'had come from Ireland and had landed in Kintyre and that it was proceeding to England'. He considered the number of men to be greater than all the combatants at the battle of Culloden.

363

The two men had now reached the Thorn Bush, between the Gairan Bridge and the gate of the Deer Park and were able to observe the marching men minutely. There was an officer on a grey horse (the only mounted man they saw) and from his appearance they considered that he must be the commander-in-chief. He wore a gold-laced hat and a blue hussar-cloak with wide and loose open sleeves, all lined with red; and boots and spurs.

The younger man now began to fear that the army might possibly attempt to take him along with them if they noticed him so he climbed over a stone dyke that fenced the Deer Park from the road. His father, being an older man, had no such fears and he continued on his way, by now untroubled by the marching men.

After walking behind the dyke for a time, the younger man reached a clump of bushes. There he stopped and looked back to see how far the army had progressed when, to his utter astonishment, he found that they had all vanished and not a soul was to be seen! Rushing back to his father he asked what had become of the army of marching men. Only then, it seemed, did the older man become aware that the army was no longer there. He could offer no explanation and, like his son, was utterly astounded at the disappearance of the vast army.

So the two men proceeded to Inveraray, meeting on their way an old acquaintance from Glen Shira. He was driving a horse before him and both father and son thought that this was the same animal that they had seen being driven along by the army. The son asked the old man, whose name was Stewart, what had become of the marching men who had recently travelled along the road. Stewart seemed puzzled by the question and replied that he had seen no one since leaving Inveraray but it was such a warm day, the air so close and sultry, that he felt hardly able to breathe. His horse too had become so feeble that he had felt obliged to dismount and drive the animal before him.

It seemed that only the two men in this remote part of Scotland had seen the phantom army but they were both honest and upright men, seemingly incapable of inventing such a pointless story. They often recounted their experience

364

and no one to whom they told it ever doubted that they were telling the truth.

Glencorse, MIDLOTHIAN

A little over a century and a half ago, on the site of the present barracks, stood Greenlaw House, a fine mansion set among fir trees; a property that was used to house French prisoners during the later years of the Napoleonic War.

The prisoners enjoyed considerable freedom and were permitted to wander without escort throughout the house and grounds. One young officer, strolling through the peaceful glades of nearby Frith Woods, met one day the daughter of a local farmer. Their friendship developed rapidly and soon they were meeting and walking together in the privacy of the woods. But one evening, as they walked hand-in-hand, they were suddenly confronted by the girl's father and a young man who was his choice for his daughter's hand. Without a word they set about the startled Frenchman who defended himself bravely but was no match for the two enraged Scots. Before long the luckless man lay dead at the feet of the grief-stricken girl, who sobbed and struggled as she was dragged home and locked in her room.

Late at night, however, she escaped and fled from the house. In the morning when her absence was discovered an immediate search was instituted. Before long the dead body of the broken-hearted girl was found at the foot of a rocky gorge on the North Esk, a spot known to this day as Lover's Leap.

On numerous occasions, since the tragic death of the unhappy maid, the sad figure of a girl has been reported in the Frith Woods; sometimes standing as if waiting for her lover from France, but more often glimpsed running wildly, her hair dishevelled and blown by the wind, towards the place where her lover was killed before her eyes. Occasionally, too, she is seen sobbing silently and sorrowfully beneath a tree near this haunted spot.

Glenluce, WIGTOWNSHIRE

For four long years, during the seventeenth century, a ghost plagued the cottage of weaver Gilbert Campbell. The visitant earned the name of the 'Deil of Glenluce' and became the talk of all Scotland when exorcism by Presbyterian ministers had no effect.

The disturbances seem to date from the time that a wandering beggar named Alexander Agnew called at the Campbell cottage and was sent away empty-handed. Agnew had long enjoyed an evil reputation and on this occasion he loudly abused the family and threatened them with ill-fortune.

Gilbert Campbell's son, Tom, on vacation from Glasgow University at the time, soon complained that he was followed by a 'spirit' that made loud noises and shrill whistlings whenever he moved about the house or yard. His sister Jennet, too, complained that she was troubled by an invisible 'demon' that had threatened to 'cast her into the well'.

Through the long winter nights the family became increasingly plagued by what they called 'restless spirits' who hurled stones at doors and through windows, destroyed materials and property, tore to shreds clothing that members of the family were wearing and interfered with Gilbert Campbell's work, severing the warps and threads as he laboured at his loom. Bedclothes were repeatedly dragged off the cots of the smaller children; chests and trunks were opened and their contents thrown out and scattered about the rooms; loud and mysterious noises were reported at all times of the day and night.

The disturbances became so troublesome and frightening for the younger members of the family that the Campbells were at last compelled to send their children away and it is reported that when only adults occupied the house, all was quiet. But soon Tom returned from Glasgow on another vacation; almost immediately the 'haunting' recommenced and reached a hitherto unparalleled intensity including one occasion when the cottage was set alight and narrowly escaped complete destruction.

Having come to the conclusion that their son Tom was the main object of the 'spirit's' malice, Campbell and his wife asked the local minister to take the lad into his house. This was done but the disturbances at Campbell's cottage continued unabated and at length several ministers convened a solemn meeting at the haunted house. Tom was brought along and there followed a long and complicated series of alleged conversations with the haunting 'spirit' (which claimed to have a commission from Heaven to vex the family). During the course of these communications several witches of Glenluce were named and the 'ghost' requested a spade to dig a grave for itself! One minister suggested that the 'voice spoke out of the children of the family': an insinuation which the haunting entity much resented. Soon afterwards this particular clergymen fell to loud praying when he claimed to see the apparition of a hand and arm.

Still the trouble continued and a meeting of the local presbytery at Glenluce to free the weaver's cottage from the 'evil spirit' had no effect. Soon the children claimed that they were thrashed daily 'with heavy staves' and their parents were also assaulted and knocked about. More stones were thrown and considerable damage caused, including some small fires, before the manifestations suddenly ceased; after which the family lived on in the house for many years without further trouble.

It was later discovered that Agnew, the tramp who had predicted the whole affair, was hanged at Dumfries on a charge of atheism and as he died, the disturbances ceased.

Glenshee, PERTHSHIRE

In this desolate and wild stretch of mountain and bog the ghost of a murdered English soldier used to walk.

In 1749 Sergeant Arthur Davies of General Guise's Regiment of Foot was in charge of a patrol of eight men sent from Aberdeen twice-weekly to meet another patrol at Glenshee. With memories of the '45 still vivid in everyone's memories, their duties were to ensure that Perthshire inhabitants did not carry arms or wear the kilt.

Sergeant Davies was a keen sportsman and known to be in the habit of wandering away from his men in pursuit of game although he had been warned that this part of the country could be dangerous for lone Englishmen. At all events, when Davies' patrol reached Glenshee, Davies himself was missing and he was never seen again. The fact that his wife, then staying near Braemar, asserted that he had on him over fifteen guineas in gold, some silver, a silver watch, two gold rings and other valuables, soon gave rise to suspicions that he had been murdered. But where was the body? And what connection, if any, was there between the missing English sergeant and the naked ghost seen occasionally in a wild and lonely spot, a ghost that vanished when it was approached?

Nine months after the disappearance a Glen Dee man, Donald Farquharson, received a visit from someone named Alexander MacPherson who told him that he was 'much troubled' by the ghost of Sergeant Davies. He stated that one night when he was in bed, the missing sergeant had appeared in his room, dressed in a blue coat and declared who 'he' was. Later the ghost returned, this time naked, and asked for its bones to be buried. It told MacPherson to visit Farquharson and said it would show them both where they were. Farquharson was sceptical but agreed to go with MacPherson. They were led to a local spot known as 'the Hill of Christie' where they found, half-hidden, the much-decayed remains of the murdered man with remnants of his blue coat and other clothes but no valuables. They buried the bones on the spot.

Suspicion in respect of the missing Sergeant Davies fell on a man of questionable character named Duncan Terig who, although previously penniless, had been known in recent months to have money to spend. In addition he had married and Farquharson testified that one of the gold rings on Mrs Terig's fingers was similar to one worn by Sergeant Davies.

Five years after Davies disappeared the authorities arrested Terig and also a man named Alexander MacDonald. They were sent to the Tolbooth in Edinburgh and tried for murder. Things looked black for the two men in the dock. It was quickly shown that accounts of their movements at the time of Davies' disappearance disagreed and was at variance with other evidence. Terig was shown to have attempted to silence

368

one witness and altogether so damning was the case against the men that even their own counsels believed them to be guilty.

When the matter of the ghost was discussed, however, the affair took a totally unexpected course. Isobel MacHardie, a former employee of Alexander MacPherson, testified that she too had seen the ghost when she was in bed at one end of the room and MacPherson in bed at the other end. She saw 'something naked come in at the door' which frightened her so much that she drew the clothes over her head. Next morning she asked MacPherson what it was that she had seen and he told her not to worry for it would not trouble them any more.

Whereupon the jury, without exception, found the two men 'not guilty'.

Gourock, RENFREWSHIRE

Where the Clyde swerves sharply south, heading for the open sea, there stands on a grassy plot a seven-foot high block of grey mica schist, known as Granny Kempock. It is a stone which has long been held in superstitious awe, heightened by the fact that the plot of ground has a condition of tenure attached forbidding any building there in perpetuity.

The Granny Kempock stone may mark the site of a Druidical altar and among local seafaring folk there seems to have been always a belief that Granny Kempock ruled the seas and controlled the weather. Years ago the fishermen would bring gifts and a basket of sand from the river shore to sprinkle at the foot of the stone as they circled it several times, imploring calm seas, good weather and big catches.

Newlyweds besought Granny Kempock's help as they set out on the voyage of matrimony; they, too, asked for a calm and fruitful expedition as they walked round and round the stone, hand in hand.

In 1662 Mary Lamont confessed to having danced round the talisman with the Devil as her partner. She said they had plotted to cast the stone into the sea to bring harm and bad fortune to the fishing boats and fishing folk. There are those who maintain that dim and silent figures still ceremoniously circle the mute stone on nights of the full moon.

Granton, MIDLOTHIAN

On the shore road between Granton and Cramond rise a pair of quaint and ornately-topped stone pillars with a wooden gate between them. This is the old sea-gate of Caroline Park, the well-preserved house that was built by George Mackenzie, Viscount Tarbat, first Earl of Cromartie. He called the place Royston. John, second Duke of Argyll, bought it with its priest's hiding-hole and secret passage and renamed it Caroline Park, after the reigning queen.

About a hundred years ago the resident was Lady John Scott of Spottiswoode. It is said that she left behind a green ghost and a mysterious bumping sound like a cannon-ball bouncing along the white-panelled Aurora drawing-room. Here she would sit, the portraits of exiled Stewart kings lining the walls, playing her harp and singing fine Scots songs she wrote and composed herself: 'Ettrick' and 'Durisdeer'. It was her genius that transformed 'Annie Laurie' into the present well-known song.

One still night at about eleven o'clock Lady John was sitting in the Aurora Room when the unearthly noise was heard for the first time. A window suddenly burst open and a cannon-ball came bouncing into the room. In three leaps it bumped across the floor and came to rest at the foot of a draught-screen. Lady John rang the bell and her servants answered her summons but by the time they arrived the window was shut fast and there was no sign of any cannon-ball.

In 1879 a governess heard the same sounds and witnessed precisely the same sight when she was alone in the same room, which has no apartment above it. She would never sit alone in the Aurora drawing-room afterwards.

After that date the noise became almost commonplace and resident servants grew quite accustomed to the strange sounds that emanated from the empty room.

When Lady John Scott was at Caroline Park there was an

old moss-covered well on the east side of the house and in the little square courtyard there used to be a wrought-iron bell-pull. At midnight on certain dates the green ghost of a former Lady Royston is said to emerge slowly from the well in emerald robes covered with mystic designs and float to the front door of the house. There she disappears, only to re-appear in the little courtyard and ring the old bell.

Lady John's grand-niece, Margaret Warrender, always maintained that when she stayed at the old house she used to lie awake night after night and hear the tolling of the bell, when everyone else in the house was in bed and asleep and when there was no breath of wind. The green lady may still walk occasionally and the bell may still toll without being pulled by human hand.

Haddington, EAST LOTHIAN

The parish church of St Mary, formerly a fourteenth-century abbey, stands on the riverbank. It is also known as Lucerna Laudoniae, the Lamp of Lothian, a title that originally belonged to the now-vanished church of Haddington's Franciscan monastery, sacked in 1355.

The hereditary burial chapel of the Maitlands, earls of Lauderdale, is behind the iron-studded door in the south wall and the coffins of these famous statesmen lie in the vault beneath. There is John, the seventeenth-century Lord Maitland of Thirlestone, Lord High Chancellor of Scotland; his son John, the second Lord Maitland and first earl; James, the eighth earl, Baronet of Nova Scotia and Standard Bearer of Scotland; a later John, Duke of Lauderdale, the most learned and powerful minister of his age, whose funeral cost £2,800 and was attended by over 2,000 horsemen. A large leaden urn, containing the brain and intestines of the Duke, was placed near the coffin.

This coffin was found in different positions whenever the vault was visited. This fact fed other stories suggesting that the duke did not rest and that his ghost was often abroad, until it was discovered that the flood-waters had probably moved the coffin. The figure of the grim-faced duke, still reported to be seen from time to time in the vicinity of the chapel, has never been explained.

Hermitage Castle, see NEWCASTLETON, ROXBURGHSHIRE

Inveraray, ARGYLLSHIRE

Passing through Inveraray a couple of years ago my wife and I called at Inveraray Castle, the home of the Dukes of Argyll, and the haunt of the strange little 'Harper of Inveraray'. Rob Roy MacGregor's dirk handle and sporran are among the relics displayed at Inveraray Castle; the ruins of Rob Roy's house are five miles away at the Falls of Aray.

The part of turreted Inveraray Castle in the area of the Green Library has long been said to be haunted by a loud crashing sound. One Sunday evening, according to a former duke of Argyll, a tremendous commotion, like books being thrown violently to the floor, continued for over an hour. Nothing was found to account for the disturbance.

Usually only the family hear the sounds even when other people are present, although friends and visitors shared the experience on occasions. Nothing is ever moved and nothing has ever been discovered that might account for the loud sounds that have been reported from time to time for nearly a hundred years. The sound of harp music used to be heard in the area of the Blue Room, although no harp was in the castle at the time.

The Harper is said to be the ghost of a man who was hanged at Inveraray when Montrose's men were hunting the first marquess of Argyll. In fact, Argyll lived to see Montrose hanged in the Grassmarket at Edinburgh.

Occasionally the Harper is also seen. It has been noticed that he always wears the Campbell tartan and never harms or frightens anyone; he has most frequently been seen by the successive duchesses of Argyll and only rarely by the dukes. A number of women visitors have seen and heard 'the Harper', noticeably at the time of a duke's death and during a ducal funeral.

372

Iona, Isle of; INNER HEBRIDES

This holy island with its mellow ruins and burial-ground containing the tombs of some sixty Scottish, Irish and Norwegian kings, and the ancient monastery founded by Saint Columba who came here in the year 563, has plenty of ghosts from the silent Viking longboats and the massacred monks on the White Sands to phantom bells, ghostly music and twinkling blue lights. The strange and sometimes terrible enchantment and 'call' of this strange and irresistible island persists.

I have been receiving first-hand accounts of the ghosts of Iona for over twenty years, since I first heard about the strange happenings from my friend Tommy Frankland, a former Royal Air Force officer. I recall that we discussed Iona and its mysteries for hours in such varied surroundings as a haunted church on the Essex marshes, Tommy's Cadogan Square flat and my home, at that time not far from the river at Richmond.

Many are the reports of ghostly monks seen here over the years, often at certain spots where the local people will not venture at night-time, such as the Angels' Hill, almost in the centre of the island, where many odd things have happened. Miss Lucy Bruce, who had a home on Iona, told me that she had seen ghostly monks on several occasions on the island, both indoors and outside. She said that they were always Columban monks, with brown robes and a hempen rope about the waist; they never spoke or made any sound, appearing to be unconscious of the presence of human beings. The ghost monks of Iona have only appeared since the time of the Reformation when great numbers of the sacred crosses marking the monks' graves were cast into the sea. Twinkling blue lights have often been reported when the ghostly monks have been seen.

Tommy told me about a sighting of the famous fleet of ghost Viking longboats at the well-known White Sands, a spot popular with artists. John MacMillan, at that time like Tommy, a member of the Iona Community (the brotherhood of ministers and laymen whose summer work consists of restoring the early Columban buildings on Iona) was walking one evening in midsummer along the road from the old abbey towards the north end of the island. (He rarely went towards the south end which has an evil reputation locally: Lucy Bruce used to refer to crowds of elementals in the south of the island and John MacMillan always said that he could smell death there.)

As he walked John saw a croft, perhaps half a mile from the abbey, and thought he would call on Mrs Ferguson, an elderly and blind lady whom he had come to know during his six years' association with the Iona Community. To his astonishment, he couldn't find her croft. He realized with growing apprehension that he could not locate the croft of his friend John Campbell either. Surely it stood down there on that deserted grassy plain. He continued on his way towards the White Sands, becoming more and more puzzled at the apparent disappearance of familiar landmarks. Had he stepped back in time, before the crofts were there?

Suddenly as he approached the White Sands, sparkling in the bright moonlight, he saw a fleet of Viking longboats emerge from behind a islet off the north of Iona, Eilean Annraidh, and make for the north shore. He counted the ships, fourteen of them and he watched the oars swoop gracefully through the water. He saw the Viking emblems on the great square sails and the fierce-looking men, who seemed to be shouting and gesticulating as they neared the shore where a group of monks stood apprehensively. John MacMillan heard no sound himself. Aghast, he watched as the invaders flung themselves upon the defenceless monks, slaughtered them and then set off over the hill towards the abbey. Time had no reality for the spellbound watcher and he could never say whether a moment or an hour elapsed before he saw the Vikings reappear with the monks' cattle and precious possessions, while the sky behind them turned to a red glow as the abbey went up in flames. Still John MacMillan watched as the cattle and valuables were loaded on to the longboats and, the silent invaders aboard, the ships pushed off into the dark sea and the White Sands were again deserted.

374

That evening John MacMillan sketched the coloured emblems that he had seen decorating the mysterious long-boats. Subsequent consultation with the appropriate authority at the British Museum dated the designs as belonging to the late tenth century.

As a matter of historical fact on Christmas Eve in the year 986 a party of marauding Danes did descend on the island at the place now known as the White Sands and there slew the abbot and fifteen of his brethren, afterwards plundering and setting fire to the abbey.

Among other witnesses who claim to have seen the ghostly Viking invasion at the White Sands there is the Edinburgh artist F. C. B. Cadell and a party of three visitors who watched what they thought must be a rehearsal for a pageant or a film.

Tommy Frankland had two experiences on Iona which he is totally unable to explain. One afternoon he encountered an invisible presence half-way up the original old wooden stairs in the abbey buildings; something that made it impossible to proceed, a force the like of which he had never met before—and hopes never to meet again. Tommy is no light-weight but whatever it was on the stairway that bright and sunny afternoon, it stopped him in his tracks and he had no choice but to retreat and make his way out into the grounds. After a time he felt able to attempt the stairs again and this time no presence, visible or invisible, barred his way.

Another afternoon, in the company of two nuns, Tommy walked to Columba Bay where they found some of the lovely green Iona stones. On the way back to the Bishop's House they halted for a moment on a high headland that separates Larachan Bay from the Bay of Coracles. Looking back towards Larachan all of them saw three columns of smoke apparently emanating from a deserted spot some distance away. The smoke rose straight upwards to a height of some twenty feet. With typical curiosity Tommy made extensive investigations and enquiries but he was totally unable to find any explanation for the three distinct columns of smoke that day. One of the nuns said that it was the most extraordinary thing she had ever seen.

One other incident always puzzled Tommy. He was among

a group of students, young and old, in the library at the Bishop's House one evening when he and others present noticed an elderly clergyman standing by the open window that looks out towards the Sound of Iona. The man stood absolutely still, his whole being focused on the quiet bay. After a while he left the room and Tommy saw him walking quickly towards the ebbing sea. There, without a moment's hesitation, he walked straight into the water and he was waist-deep before Tommy reached the shore, shouting and calling to the man to come back. After what seemed an eternity the man turned; at last he seemed to hear the calling and shouting and he slowly made his way back. Afterwards he said that he had seen the abbey as it had been a thousand years ago and he had thought he would walk along the causeway, which has long since disappeared. Until he heard his name being called, he had no idea that he was in the water.

And what about the famous 'call' of Iona? The enchantment that can be fatal? Perhaps it is best described in the true story, told to me by Lucy Bruce, concerning a young Italian lady, Marie Emily Fornario, who came here because, far away in her Mediterranean home, she heard a 'call', the Call of the Island. For a while she enjoyed the peace and tranquillity of this unforgettable place. She wrote poetry with a strange, mystical quality about it; she interested herself in the legends and folklore of the island. This beautiful and gentle soul soon became absorbed by the eerie and mysterious places of Iona; especially a bleak and lonely spot which has no real track leading to it where, it is said, the spirits of the dead hold sway. One day the lady said that she must leave the island at once. Her bags were packed and her belongings were taken down to the pier but it was a Sunday and there was no way of leaving the island until the following day. Marie returned to her room and some hours later opened her door to say that her departure was no longer necessary. Her things were brought back into the house and unpacked.

Next morning Marie had disappeared. She was found two days later, naked and quite dead. A silver chain she wore had turned black. There was a knife in one of her hands and her head rested on the other. She had died of exposure and exhaustion in the place where the spirits of the dead are

376

said to roam: perhaps she had answered their call that moonlit night when she had walked out, unseen and unheard, to die on their ancient ground.

Haunting and haunted Iona has ghostly monks in procession and solitary; faëry music; evil elementals; invisible presences; mysterious twinkling lights; ghostly music; phantom Viking longboats; and the uncanny 'call' that will not be denied.

Jedburgh, ROXBURGHSHIRE

All traces of Jedburgh Castle have now disappeared and its site has been occupied by a succession of buildings (including the old prison) but none of them can boast an apparition as fearful as that which interrupted a ball many, many years ago.

Time was when Jedburgh enjoyed an important place in Scottish history and, after it was surrendered to England by the treaty of Falaise in 1174 as security for the ransom of William the Lion, was a favourite residence of royalty. Malcolm IV died here in 1165. Alexander II and Alexander III were often here and it was during the second wedding feast of the childless Alexander III in October, 1285, that the grisly and singular spectre is said to have appeared—an occurrence that may have given Edgar Allan Poe the idea for his macabre story *The Masque of the Red Death.*

The wedding festivities were at their height when a strange figure was noticed by the startled guests, an awesome form that seemed to glide through the throng of guests, tall and gaunt and shrouded from head to foot in grave-clothes, while a mask resembling the face of a corpse concealed the identity of the wearer.

Soon the king noticed the weird figure that dampened the festive air. He gave orders for the person to be seized and unmasked and hanged at sunrise from the battlements for insulting him with such blasphemous mockery on his wedding day. At his words the group of pale courtiers made movements in the direction of the intruder but some nameless horror held them back. None laid a hand on the mysterious figure; indeed, the entire assembly shrank back to the walls

377

of the room and the grim figure made its solemn way with unhurried steps in the direction of the king. At last his immediate guards flung themselves forward only to gasp in unutterable horror at finding the grave-clothes and corpse-like mask which they seized, 'untenanted by any tangible form'.

Nothing further is known of the strange spectre but it was, perhaps not unnaturally, regarded as portending some great calamity. The seer and prophet, Thomas the Rhymer, informed the Earl of March, in the presence of some of the earl's relations and household, that March 16th would be 'the stormiest day that ever was witnessed in Scotland'. In fact the day dawned clear and bright and many scoffed at the prophecy, when news came that the king was dead. 'That was the storm I meant,' said the Rhymer, 'and there was never a tempest which will bring more ill luck to Scotland.' Indeed, the news caused distraction among the people and civil war between the claimants to the throne of Scotland.

Alexander III, riding between Burntisland and Kinghorn in failing light, was thrown from his horse over a cliff and killed in his forty-fifth year, a few months after his second marriage. Many people recalled the ominous presence at the king's wedding and felt that it had foretold his early death.

Killiecrankie, Pass of, PERTHSHIRE

The battle of Killiecrankie took place on July 27th, 1689, when William III's troops under General Mackay were routed by three thousand Highlanders under John Graham of Claverhouse, Viscount Dundee, for James II; 'Bonnie Dundee' himself fell mortally wounded almost at the moment of victory.

The battle itself was fought on the hillside above the main road a mile north of the pass through which King William's men advanced to engage the Jacobites and shortly afterwards returned in retreat as they fled from the torrent of bare-footed red coats and tartans that swept down the valley.

Each July 27th, I have been told, a red glow hangs over the scene of the conflict; a phantom light that many people, but not everyone, can see in the valley through which the High-landers charged. The mysterious glow is thought by local people to have its origin in a vision seen by Viscount Dundee on the eve of the battle.

As he slept, Dundee saw a man whose head poured with blood standing at his bedside, bidding him to get up and follow where he led. Dundee awoke but seeing no one, inter-preted the vision as a dream and returned to sleep. But again he was awakened by the same voice and the same figure; this time the form pointed to its bloody head and seemed to implore Dundee to rise and follow. Now Dundee did get up and ascertained from the guard that no one had entered his tent. Satisfied, he once more returned to his bed but for the third time the same form appeared to him, bidding him arise and pointing towards the plain of Killiecrankie, seeming to indicate that he would meet Dundee there. When the figure had disappeared Dundee got up, dressed and discussed the strange vision with a Highland chief who agreed never to speak of the matter if the coming battle should prove success-ful for the Highlanders.

On the day of the battle Dundee was reluctant to descend from the high ground. Perhaps he had a premonition of his own death or maybe he wished to wait until darkness before coming to close quarters with the enemy so that his troops could find shelter in the mountains if they were defeated. At all events, it was sunset before he gave the order to charge. Within minutes King William's forces were defeated and beginning to flee when, almost as if by accident, a fatal shot struck Dundee in the side.

Kilmacolm, RENFREWSHIRE

A ruined wall is all that now remains of haunted Duchal Castle in Strathgryfe. Once it stood, proud and invincible, at the junction of two burns, the Green Water and the Blacketty Water.

The ghost was an excommunicated monk who would be seen sitting on the castle outbuildings, jeering at inhabitants. The form, described as 'foul and gross', was seen, heard and

379

even touched by scores of people in the thirteenth century. Arrows that found their mark melted as they struck home and only the eldest son of the Knight of Duchal Castle, an exceptionally pure-hearted individual, was able to defy the troublesome ghost with any success. One night he lay in wait for the foul fiend and wrestled with 'him' as soon as he appeared but the following morning the brave young knight's body was found in the wrecked hall. The ghost was never seen thereafter.

It was at Duchal Castle that a son of King James IV was born to Marian Boyd; a man who became Archbishop of St Andrews at eighteen, founded St Leonard's College there and died with his father at the Battle of Flodden.

Kinross, KINROSS-SHIRE

The minister's house at this country town on the shore of Loch Leven (Mary Queen of Scots was imprisoned in the fifteenth-century castle) was infested by a typical poltergeist in the year 1718 when the parish minister, a Mr McGill, was plagued almost beyond endurance.

Initially some missing silver spoons were located in a barn, buried among straw, and although McGill readily admitted that this incident could have had a normal explanation, the disturbances quickly took a more serious turn. (It is interesting to notice that in poltergeist cases it is often the first incidents that are the easiest to explain.) Before long McGill discovered that at every meal pins of various sizes were mixed in his food! Even boiled eggs bristled with them! His wife decided to supervise the cooking of her husband's food herself but to her consternation she found a dish that she had most carefully prepared with her own hands—full of pins!

Soon there were other inconveniences and difficulties to contend with. Linen hung out to dry was found to be torn to shreds and before long clothes, even as they lay in cupboards where they were stored, were found rent and in some cases destroyed beyond repair. Visitors complained that their clothes suddenly developed cuts and clips. Everyone noticed that this spiteful and annoying occurrence happened most

380

Hermitage Castle, near Newcastleton, Roxburghshire (as 'restored' for the film *Mary Queen of Scots* 1971), where the ghosts include a figure in blood-stained armour; Soulis the Bad frolicking with evil spirits; Alexander Ramsey who died of starvation here in the dungeon, and a headless apparition. *Photo: Donald Ross*

Dunstaffnage Castle, near Oban, Argyllshire, haunted by a 'Green Lady' and where poltergeist-like activities repeatedly disturbed the Campbell children. *Photo: Scottish Tourist Board*

Haunted Dunvegan Castle, Sligichan, Isle of Skye, has a bridge that no horse could cross. *Photo: Scottish Tourist Board*

The famed Fairy Flag preserved at Dunvegan Castle, Isle of Skye. *Photo: Dame Flora MacLeod of MacLeod*

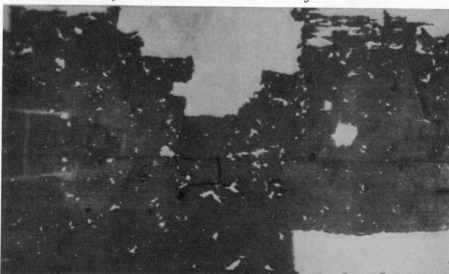

frequently in the parlour of the house; either as they sat there or as they passed through the room.

Once the minister's Bible was thrown on to the fire but it was recovered unharmed. On the other hand when some silver spoons were inexplicably thrown into the fire, they melted instantly. As with most poltergeist cases, the affair ceased as inexplicably as it began.

Kintraw, at the head of Loch Craignish, ARGYLLSHIRE

In the valley of the River Barbreck in this delightful and thinly populated district of heathery rocks and low hills between Ardfern and Ford, a mysterious figure known as the 'hooded maiden' has long been reported by local people and, occasionally, by visitors.

The area where the figure has been seen lies within the Barbreck estate with its Georgian house and vast acreage of moor and river and loch fishing (Craignish is a sea-loch with wooded islets). Consequently it is fishermen, shepherds and ghillies who have seen 'her' most often.

The 'hooded maiden' invariably wears a plaid of dark but unidentified tartan. Her hair is long and seems to cling to her face, framing the pale, sad features of the young girl. Who she is or what she waits for, nobody knows. She is always seen seated on a rock and she always disappears as soon as she is approached.

Kirriemuir, ANGUS

Cortachy Castle, seat of the earls of Airlie, is haunted by a drummer. The sound of his drumming has long been regarded as heralding the death of a member of the Ogilvy family.

The tradition is thought to have its origin in a drummer-boy who angered a former Lord Airlie. He was put to death by being thrust into his own drum and thrown from the window of the castle tower. Here is the chamber where the ghostly music most often seems to originate. Before his death the drummer is said to have threatened to haunt the family if his life was taken. He seems to have been as good as his word for the drum is reported to have been heard before the deaths of members of the family on a number of occasions over many years.

One account tells of a visitor to Cortachy Castle hearing, while she dressed for dinner on the evening of her arrival, a strain of music which seemed to originate below her window and which finally resolved into the well-defined sound of a drum.

She mentioned the matter at dinner and made enquiries about a drummer playing near the castle. She noticed that Lord Airlie turned pale at her words while Lady Airlie looked distressed and several of the other guests seemed embarrassed. She therefore changed the subject, but later that evening she asked a member of the family about the mysterious music and the effect it seemed to have on Lord and Lady Airlie. She was then told about the legend of the drummer-boy who is reputed to play a drum about the house whenever a death is impending in the family; and that it had been heard before the death of the previous Countess.

The visitor was much concerned at having unintentionally caused distress to her hosts. When she again heard the ghostly drummer the next day, she made her apologies and left Cortachy, stopping on her way back to Dundee to call on some friends to whom she related her experiences. Within a short time Lady Airlie with whom she had stayed was dead, leaving a note referring to the drummer having been heard by a guest and adding that she knew the drum had sounded for her.

Five years later a member of the Earl of Airlie's shooting party heard a swell of faint music accompanied by a distant drum; sounds which were totally inexplicable as far as he could establish. The following day the Earl of Airlie died.

Thirty years later Lady Dalkeith and Lady Skelmersdale heard drumming music which sounded like the traditional Airlie Drummer. The death of Lord Airlie took place the same night in America and it was established that the drumming sound was heard approximately an hour before his death.

After the death of the twelfth earl in 1968, his widow, whose son Mr Angus Ogilvy is married to the Princess Alexandra, informed me that she did not know of anyone who had heard the drum on that occasion.

Lasswade, NEAR DALKEITH, MIDLOTHIANSHIRE

Romantically situated on the river bank Lasswade lies below you from whatever direction you approach. The old and now disused parish church overlooks the little town. Here lie buried Henry Dundas, first Viscount Melville, whose lofty column graces St Andrew Square, Edinburgh: a man known as the uncrowned king of Scotland.

A much enlarged cottage, opposite the gates of Dunesk House, was the first married home of Sir Walter Scott. He lived very happily here for six years and it is not difficult to place some of the scenes from his famous books.

A mile away, De Quincey Cottage was the home of Thomas De Quincey for the last nineteen years of his life. It is said that his ghost is often to be seen wandering about in the vicinity of his cottage and along the banks of the River Esk as far as Lasswade, usually in the small, dark hours, wildly flourishing a lantern he used to carry during his long and treasured night walks.

Lendalfoot, AYRSHIRE

The tall fragments of a grey building perched high on a hill overlooking the cleft of Lendal Water is all that now remains of Carleton Castle.

The area is haunted from time to time by mysterious shrill cries and strangely fading screams. This is the castle, immortalized in a ballad, where a baron lived who disposed of seven wives by throwing them over the cliff; but his eighth, May Cullean, was more than a match for him and pushed *him* to his death.

Linlithgow, WEST LOTHIANSHIRE

The parish church of St Michael's was the scene of one of the best-authenticated instances of a purposeful apparition.

A ghostly old man, dressed in a long, blue gown, is said to have appeared here to King James IV of Scotland while the monarch was at evening worship, warning the king of his defeat and death at Flodden in 1513. The bare-headed figure, carrying a pikestaff, told the king not to march into England and then disappeared. Those who were with the king at the time included David Lindsay, the Scottish poet, a man of complete integrity, who vouched for the story. The odd figure appeared and disappeared in circumstances that cannot be explained in any rational way. The prophesy was fulfilled exactly for James was not to be dissuaded; the great army marched south and into the tragedy of Flodden Field.

There is a room in the fine loch-side fifteenth-century palace known as Queen Margaret's Bower where the queen waited in vain for the king's return from Flodden. Here, too, you can see the room where Mary Queen of Scots was born on December 7th, 1542.

Lismore Island, ARGYLLSHIRE

The picturesque ruins of Caifen Castle, on the west coast of the island, just across from Clachan, was named after a prince.

Caifen was the son of a Norse king and he lived at the castle with his beautiful sister Beothail, who was as gentle as her brother was warlike. While he never seemed to allow his galleys to rest and was known as a hard master but a fair one, Beothail became betrothed to a son of Lochlann. When her beloved was killed in battle, the fair princess died of a broken heart and she was buried at nearby Eirebal.

But death did not bring her peace and her voice was often to be heard crying in the wind. She wanted to be buried in Norway beside her lover.

At length a ship came to Caifen Castle, Beothail's body was disinterred, washed in the holy well, taken on the long voyage to Lochlann and there the bodies of the lovers were laid beside one another.

Still Beothail did not rest and her form was seen pointing to a missing bone in her left foot. Again the ship went to Caifen and in the holy well where the body had been washed, poor Beothail's small toe bone was found and was at length buried in the lovers' grave in far away Norway. Thereafter there was peace for Beothail.

In Lismore there is still a well known as the Well of the Bones of Beothail.

Little Loch Broom, ROSS AND CROMARTY

On the wild, northern shore, not far from the mouth of the loch, a solitary cottage once sheltered George, first earl of Cromartie, when he was Sir George Mackenzie. The croft was the scene of a prophetic vision.

Sir George, a loyal Royalist, was engaged in raising troops for the king shortly before the Restoration of the Monarchy and, with some friends, chanced to find themselves storm-bound on the north shore of Little Loch Broom.

They sought shelter in a lonely loch-side cottage and after a while spent in chatting among themselves and the residents, Sir George's servant, an old Highlander, went out to attend to the horses. On his return, he hurried to his master's side as soon as he entered the room and urged him to rise from the chair he was occupying, saying that he could see a dead man seated on the vacant chair beside him. Everyone present rose to their feet at the words but they only saw the empty chair. The vision of a dead man was visible only to the old Highlander who described the figure as a pitiful sight, his head bound with a blood-stained bandage, his ashen face streaked with dried blood and one of his arms hanging broken at his side.

Next day a party of horsemen passed along the steep side of a hill in the neighbourhood when one of the horses stumbled and threw its rider. The man, grievously injured by the fall, was carried unconscious to the cottage. On being brought into the primitive dwelling in a death-like condition, he was placed in the identical chair which the Highlander had seen occupied by a dead man in his vision. The man's head was found to be deeply gashed and one of his arms was broken but he did eventually recover. Contemporary evidence includes a letter from Sir George Mackenzie relating the story to the celebrated Robert Boyle.

Lockerbie, DUMFRIESSHIRE

Five miles north, west of the Glasgow road, beside a loop in the River Annan stands Jardine Hall, seat of the Jardine family. Opposite stands Spedlin's Tower, haunted for centuries by an unpleasant ghost that terrified the countryfolk hereabouts.

Many years ago the laird of Applegarth was Sir Alexander Jardine, the first baronet, who had occasion to punish a miller named Porteous. He confined him in the dungeon of the Tower, after the miller had, for some unknown reason, set his cottage alight.

One day Sir Alexander had to go to Edinburgh on urgent business and in his haste he took with him the key of the dungeon. As soon as he discovered what he had done, he sent the key back post-haste but it was too late; the unlucky miller had died of starvation. Indeed, it is said that the dying man was so ravaged by hunger that he had gnawed at his own hands and feet in the last throes of torment.

Soon after the miller's death Sir Alexander's household was plagued by his ghost. A loud battering noise would be heard at the door to the dungeon, late at night, and a hollow voice would call piteously: 'Let me out ... let me out ... I'm dying of hunger ...' When mischievous children of the household inserted a stick through the keyhole, it is said that the hungry ghost stripped the bark in an instant.

It was discovered that if an ancient 'black letter' Bible was left in a niche by the dungeon doorway, all was quiet; but when it was removed for re-binding, the ghost, it seems, returned. By this time the Jardine family had moved to the new residence on the other side of the River Annan. The ghost is reported to have followed them, entering the baronet's bedroom and creating such a noise and disturbance that no time was lost in restoring the Bible to its place. As soon as this was done, peace was restored.

Maxton, ROXBURGHSHIRE

Near here, on the banks of the River Tweed, stand the ruins of Littledean Tower, the scene of strange happenings long ago that are echoed here on certain stormy nights.

One of the last lairds of a once proud and powerful family was a dark and handsome but wicked man whose gentle wife Margaret sought solace in quiet prayer. Her cruel husband was hated by his servants, suffered by his friends and feared by the young maids of the locality.

As time passed and stories of his cruelty grew and spread, especially after he had caused the death of a stable boy in a fit of anger, his former associates kept away and his wild parties began to be peopled with the lowest and worst characters in the area. Margaret, much distressed, began to leave him to his own devices and her absence was often the cause of ribald jokes. One evening a certain 'gentleman' who was commonly believed to be the black sheep of a famous family, a man who had an eye for the ladies, taunted the laird about his wife's absence at the 'dinner party' whereupon the host, more drunk than sober, fetched his frightened wife and commanded her to greet his motley collection of friends. Terrified but proud, Margaret refused and the guests, mustering together such dignity as they could, left embarrassed as the laird swore and screamed at his wife. He raved and cursed at her after they had left, calling her everything from unfaithful to useless, 'I'd rather be wedded to a fiend from Hell than to you,' he screamed, 'She'd have more warmth about her, at any rate ...'

This was too much for the gentle Margaret. She raised herself from the floor where she had slumped in despair and looked her husband straight in the eyes. 'You will live to regret those words', she said and walked to her room with dignity, leaving him to fume and curse to himself.

The laird called for more brandy but his wife's words and her sober looks troubled him. Before long he called for a horse and, drunk as he was, he rode off into the night not caring which direction he took. Soon it began to rain in torrents and looking for some shelter he turned into a small wood where he found himself in a clearing, with a wretched and crumbling cottage at the far end. As he approached, figures seemed to recede into the shadows leaving one woman sitting on a stool, spinning, just inside the cottage. When the woman turned towards him the laird thought that never had he seen such a lovely face. He struggled to speak as the beautiful woman smiled at him in the shadows. Then, lifting the thread that she was spinning, the woman held it high towards him and snapped it in two, laughing in his face. For the first time the laird noticed the restive snorting and stamping of his horse; at the same time he felt some strange force beginning to hold him captive in the glade. With an effort he tore himself away, mounted his horse and rode out of the wood.

In the days that followed he could not forget the beautiful woman he had seen and in a sort of sickness he searched again and again for the wood into which he had strayed that stormy night. Then one evening, after spending hours in fruitless search for the mysterious place, he was almost home when he noticed a movement beside a cluster of trees by the river bank, only a few hundred yards from Littledean Tower. He looked again; it was the same woman. Quickly he dismounted, went into her open arms and together they walked into the silent trees. Thereafter he would meet the mysterious woman almost daily for she was ready and eager to satisfy his every desire, almost under the windows of the Tower, although she would never agree to meet him elsewhere.

Soon the inevitable happened. The pair were seen and seen again. The scandal spread and the story reached Margaret's ears. She faced her husband and threw the rings he had given her at his feet. She had decided to leave him but two of her friends from the old days counselled her to wait until they had trapped the woman to discover who she was. One evening, having seen her enter the little knot of trees,

they circled the plantation and then met in the middle—
but the only living thing that came out of the trees was a
hare that scampered away across the fields.

Hours passed and the laird returned home, later than he
had ever been before. He looked shaken to the core,
frightened out of his wits. He bade the servants withdraw
in a hushed voice and whispered to Margaret: 'Devils, Devils,
Devils everywhere ...' His wife shrank away from him and
after she had led him silently into the great hall, he told her
his story.

He said that he had been riding home in the twilight when
he had passed a hare which, to his surprise, followed him.
Presently another joined it and then another and another,
until a whole flock surrounded him as he rode on, his horse
sweating with fear. After a time he tried to trample on them
but he never succeeded in touching one. He found that however fast he travelled, the hares kept pace with him and soon
some began to leap across his saddle bow. Drawing his sword
he slashed at them but they were hard to hit. At length he
did strike one, more daring than the rest and severed its paw
which fell into his empty pistol holder. At this the whole pack
suddenly made off and looking about him, he discovered that
he was in the vicinity of Midlem, reputed home of many
witches and miles from Littledean Tower.

As he concluded his story, Margaret asked to see the hare's
paw and a moment later her husband withdrew his hand
sharply from the gun holster where the paw had fallen, ex-
claiming that it had bitten him! When tipped from the
holder it was found to be a woman's hand, wearing a ring
that Margaret recognized.

The laird drew his sword and speared the hand that
seemed to squirm as he pierced it, then he sped with it to the
nearby river where he scrambled down the bank and swung
the hand off his sword with all his strength far out into the
deep water, hearing it splash in the darkness. Hurrying back
up the steep bank of the river side, he was making his way
home in the darkness when he realized that he was close to
the little cluster of trees where he used to meet the mysterious
woman. Something led him in among the trees and he saw the
woman, huddled on the ground with her back towards him.

As he approached she turned to face him and to his horror he saw that she was no longer young and beautiful; instead, he found himself looking into the face of a hag: bitter, ugly and ghastly in the moonlight. Her eyes glowed with hatred and she held up her right arm to show him a raw and bleeding stump. He sensed rather than heard her tell him that he had taken her hand and he would never be parted from it.

Somehow he stumbled back to Littledean Tower, a silent, broken man. He slowly made his way to his bed-chamber and, refusing food or drink, sat slumped in front of the fire, puzzling over the events that had befallen him. After an hour or so he chanced to notice a lump in the pocket of the riding jacket that he still wore and thrusting his hand inside drew out the hand that he had thrown far out into the river! Rushing to the window, he tore it open and threw it out into the darkness.

Dreading the dreams that would mar his sleep, he put off going to bed until dawn streaked the sky. When he eventually stretched out on the bedstead, he reached beneath the pillow —and encountered the hand again! He snatched up the awful thing and threw it into the fire, watching as it crackled and burnt to a cinder.

Next morning the laird did not appear for breakfast and when eventually Margaret had servants break down the door of his chamber, they found the bedclothes dragged off the bed in the direction of the hearth and in front of the cold fire lay his dead body with marks on his throat that suggested that a hand had choked the life out of him.

On stormy nights the ghostly figure of the laird is still to be seen sometimes, mounted on a phantom horse, plunging madly through the wind and rain.

Melrose, ROXBURGHSHIRE

Nearby Abbotsford House is the large and turreted mansion built by Sir Walter Scott between 1817 and 1825. If concentrated thought and excessive single-mindedness coupled with love and death, can bring about ghosts and hauntings then Abbotsford should be haunted. The silent figure that has been seen on rare occasions in the dining-room (where Scott died) may be the ghost of the great novelist who built his life's dream in the baronial style—and out of his hard-earned savings. A year after the house was completed, financial ruin overtook poor Scott and although the house and estate were restored to him by his creditors in 1830, he died on September 21st, 1830, on a bed placed near the window in the dining-room, where he could view the fast-flowing River Tweed.

The property was formerly a small farm which Scott bought in 1811 and it was during the alterations, in 1818, that Sir Walter reported a 'violent noise, like drawing heavy boards along the new part of the house.' Next night he heard the noise again, at the same time, two o'clock in the morning. He quietly reached for 'Beardie's broadsword' and thoroughly investigated the rooms and half-built passages where the noise seemed to originate; but he could discover nothing that might account for the sounds. It is interesting to record that George Bullock, Scott's agent who was responsible for the early alterations at Abbotsford, died suddenly when the mysterious disturbances were at their height.

Today the house is owned by Mrs J. Maxwell-Scott, a descendant in the female line, and parts of the large and picturesque house, including the haunted dining-room, are open to the public. In addition to many fascinating mementoes of the famous novelist, historian and poet, there is a fine collection of Scottish historical relics.

Montrose, ANGUS

The old aerodrome here has long been reputed to be haunted by two ghosts, one a pilot from an aircraft that crashed in 1913 and the other a wartime officer of the Second World War who was also killed in a crash here.

A fighter pilot whose squadron was sent to Montrose during the winter of 1940 to rest after the Battle of Britain, related his experiences which are said to have their origin in the earlier crash which took place at the perimeter of the airfield, the plane bursting into flames and leaving practically no wreckage or remains, except for the ghost of the pilot, a figure in flying kit that disappears near the Old Mess.

Men of the squadron stationed here in 1940 said that they saw the ghost and the figure was seen five times by Major Cyril Foggin in August 1916 and by the Commanding Officer and several instructors during the autumn of that year. Once he seems to have flown his ghostly biplane to the danger of a Hurricane, witnessed by scores of airmen.

It happened that one night the squadron were summoned from their beds by the warning that a marauding Heinkel was somewhere over the aerodrome. A Hurricane taxied out in an attempt to intercept it. Half-an-hour later the pilot reported 'No joy' and was instructed to return to base. No chances were taken by lighting up the airfield in case another enemy aircraft was somewhere aloft and only a twin row of glim-lights were laid along the grass to guide the Hurricane in. The pilot was experienced, a regular service sergeant-pilot; hard-headed, unimaginative and very reliable, who should have had no difficulty in landing in these conditions. Scores of the airmen watched the glow of the Hurricane's exhaust as the plane crossed the boundary. The pilot touched down—and then, with a roar, he opened up the engine and disappeared again into the night. The ground crew decided he must have thought that he was not aligned correctly with the flarepath and, sure enough, he approached again, this time with his navigation lights on; but again, just as he was about to land, he opened his throttle wide and roared away, climbing over the sea.

The ground crew decided that they must take a risk and put on the Chance light, a type of horizontal searchlight, bathing the whole path of the landing-ground in a wide ray of yellow-white light. This time the Hurricane made a perfect landing, taxied in and shut off the engine as ground-crew and airmen gathered round. The hood slid back and the pilot tore off his helmet in annoyance and shouted: 'The fool! Who was the fool who cut me out?' Someone said that no one had cut him out. 'Of course someone did,' replied the angry pilot. 'Why do you think I went round again? Some madman in a biplane baulked me just as I was touching down—a thing like a Tiger Moth.' 'There's no one else flying' replied the flight commander quietly. 'Besides there isn't a biplane on the station.' Only the wind blew in the darkness of the night and in silence pilot and airmen returned to the crew-room. The only explanation seemed to be that the phantom airman was keeping his hand in.

One morning in the summer of 1942 an unpopular flight-lieutenant took off from this airfield and crashed within seconds, being killed instantly. He had earned for himself a reputation as a stickler for discipline and was disliked by the ground staff because he seemed to find fault whenever he could. About a week before the fatal flight he had been involved in a scene with a fitter working on the aircraft he was about to fly, shouting at the man for some trivial offence and putting him on a charge. The man, not surprisingly perhaps, felt that he had been unfairly treated. He nursed a grudge against the flight-lieutenant and he serviced the plane a week later when the officer took off and was killed.

A routine inquiry failed to reveal the cause of the crash and the unofficial view held on the airfield was that the fitter had 'doctored' the plane; but this was never proved although the fitter certainly had both opportunity and motive.

Everybody thought that the affair had ended, until some airmen reported seeing a ghost. Other reports followed and the mysterious figure, dressed in a flying suit and goggles, was glimpsed by many servicemen. Soon the ghost airman became accepted and almost part of normal life at the station. The flight-lieutenant had come back, it was thought, to haunt the fitter who had caused his death; and new arrivals at the station were warned to watch out for the ghost airman at night-time.

Four years later, in 1946, an experienced serviceman who had seen action in France, Belgium, Holland, Germany, Denmark and Japan arrived at Montrose. He was told about the ghost and laughed at the story for he had heard many weird and wonderful war stories and had learned to take them with a pinch of salt. Then he was put on guard duty.

Guard duty at Montrose in those days meant armed patrol in twos, taking in the airfield, aircraft and the hangars. The way to the hangars lay by a morgue, which everyone gave a wide berth. But on this particular night an aircraft had just landed and had been parked close to the control tower and opposite the morgue; the new arrival was detailed to keep a special eye on it.

At three in the morning he and his companion were standing on guard close to the aircraft. A quiet smoke seemed to be in order and it was arranged that they would each nip round the corner to smoke a cigarette. The new arrival's mate went first and as the new man stood there alone, the doors of the morgue (which had been checked and found secure only moments before) suddenly flew open and a figure emerged, an airman with a dead-white face wearing goggles, helmet and a flying suit. The new guard's rifle clattered to the ground and he stared at the figure, frozen to the spot. Then, as suddenly as it had appeared, the figure vanished; with a loud bang the doors slammed shut and everything was quiet again.

Soon the mate returned from his smoke but the experienced and tough war veteran never related what he had seen to any of the airmen at the station. He was wondering, for one thing, whether the whole business hadn't been a hoax. Only years later, talking to another man who had been stationed at Montrose, did he learn that the ghostly flight lieutenant had years before emerged from a building later converted into the morgue, to walk to the plane for his last flight. Sir Peter Masefield saw the 1913 accident re-enacted in May 1963, fifty years to the day after it happened.

Morar, INVERNESS-SHIRE

A correspondent told me an experience that befell her at a small local hotel, overlooking the beautiful white sands at the mouth of the river near the extraordinarily deep Loch Morar. This loch, only thirty feet above sea level, has a depth of a hundred-and-eighty fathoms and it is said to be the deepest hollow on any part of the European plateau except for the submarine valley that skirts the south part of Scandinavia.

My informant told me that during the early part of the Second World War she and a girl friend shared a room here for one night. As they moved around, preparing to retire by the light of two candles for there was no electricity, they became increasingly aware of sounds suggesting the presence of someone else in the room with them. It seemed to be some-one tramping about in heavy boots, moving objects and creaking the floorboards. The girls said nothing to each other and finally they went to bed, both feeling very nervous. Lying still, they listened intently.

Now that they were making no noise at all themselves, the third presence in the room was quite clear and definite. My informant tells me that she was petrified with fright, unable to stir although longing to reach out and relight the candle. Her companion started to scream and clung to her friend. The noise set off a dog barking wildly, that was tied up outside somewhere, but no one attended to it nor came to see what was the matter with the screaming girl. Throughout the night they saw nothing, either by candlelight or in the darkness, but for hours they heard heavy footsteps circling around the room, and round their bed, pausing occasionally to touch things.

In the morning they rose early and left the hotel without saying anything about their experience; but they gained the impression that the residents who must have heard some of the commotion, probably knew the reason and were not surprised—nor inclined to be disturbed or discuss the matter. The bedroom was at the back of the hotel, where a grassy slope rose steeply behind the building.

Motherwell, LANARKSHIRE

Here, deep in the coal-mining area of Scotland, there is, appropriately enough, a ghost that wears dungarees and boots. It was reported in November, 1968, from the Ravenscraig Steel Works, and workmen stated that the apparition, which sometimes seemed to resemble a complete workman and at other times appeared to be headless, was always seen in the vicinity of Number 2 blast-furnace.

Mull, Isle of, ARGYLLSHIRE

Lochbuie, in the south-east of the largest island of the Inner Hebrides, is associated with one of the best-known family ghosts in Scotland. The desolate road through the great glen here, travelled from time immemorial by pilgrims to Iona, is haunted by a headless horseman whose appearance heralds a death in the Ewen family.

Due north of Lochbuie stretches a chain of tarns and on the farthest north of these, Loch Sguabain, stands a ruined castle built so long ago that nobody can say with certainty just when it was erected. But here before the middle of the sixteenth century lived Eoghan a' Chin Bhig, Ewen of the Little Head and his wife, the proud daughter of a laird. Some say her father was MacDougal of Lorne, others claim he was chief of the MacLaines; at all events she was forever grumbling about her circumstances since marrying Ewen and goading her husband to wrest the estate from her father. One day there was a stormy confrontation between Ewen and his father-in-law and soon afterwards Ewen began to collect followers for a show-down with the laird.

The evening before the conflict in 1538 Ewen is said to have seen a little woman by a stream. She was dressed in green and was busy rubbing away at a bundle of blood-stained shirts. Ewen realized that she was a fairy-figure and asked her whose shirts she was washing. 'The shirts of those who will fall in the fight' came the reply and when Ewen asked whether his shirt was among them, he was told that it was, 'but', added the fairy woman, 'if your wife offers you bread and cheese with her own hand, without your asking for it, on the morning of the conflict, you will win the fight.'

On the morning that the armies were to meet Ewen's wife was in a bad temper; she offered her husband neither bread nor cheese and he dared not ask for it. He and his men fought bravely and desperately but they were no match for their adversaries and at last Ewen met his end. His head was cut clean from his body and his black horse galloped away with its headless rider on its back.

And always now, before a Ewen dies, a ghostly headless horseman is said to ride, sometimes seen and sometimes only heard, down Glen More, on the shores of Loch Sguabain near the ruined castle or at Lochbuie where the phantom is regarded as an ill omen fortelling sickness to one of the Ewen family. Certainly the headless horseman was seen and heard before the death of three Ewens within living memory. Although the galloping feet of the ghostly black horse seem to thunder over the ground, no hoof-prints are ever found to mark the soft earth.

One old member of the family used to complain before he died that he constantly heard a horse galloping close at hand and after his death unexplained noises and movements of furniture took place in the room where his body lay while servants and others passing the door told of weird screechings and the presence of ghostly hands which were attributed to Ewen of the Little Head.

Lochbuie House used to be haunted by a phantom black dog which Dr Duncan MacDonald encountered on a visit to the house. Another medico, Dr Reginald MacDonald, also met the Black Dog of Lochbuie; while a guest at Lochbuie House once recorded briefly the presence of a ghost dog that was seen and heard, 'so horrible' that the visitor felt unable even to write about the experience.

Nannau, MERIONETHSHIRE

The old residence of the Vaughan family, said to stand upon the highest ground of any country seat in the land, is haunted to this day by the victim of a murder long, long ago.

In those days the occupant was one Howel Sele, a first cousin of the Welsh prince, Owen Glendower; but the cousins had never been good friends. Their antagonism came to a climax, according to legend, when they were out together hunting, while guests of the Abbot of Kymmer who was striving to reconcile the two kinsmen.

As they rested on their way Owen noticed a doe feeding down below them and remarked that here was a fine mark for Howel who was regarded as one of the best archers of the day. Without a word Howel took aim on the doe and then suddenly turned and shot the arrow straight at Glendower!

The prince, however, wore armour beneath his clothes and the arrow glanced harmlessly off him. Enraged at his kinsman's treachery, he drew his sword and after a short and sharp exchange, killed Howel. Once the deed was done there was no undoing it, but where to hide the body? Medog, Glendower's companion, who had been following at a distance, now reached the scene of the fight and suggested that a nearby blasted oak tree would conveniently contain Howel's body in its hollow interior.

In the days that followed Howel's servants searched for him high and low while his sorrowing wife shut herself up in solitude in the gloomy castle. The years passed with no news of the missing Lord of Nannau, although from time to time there were terrifying accounts of the ghostly form of the chief being seen in the vicinity of his ancestral home. Some witnesses maintained that he stalked the upper stories of the castle on dark nights, others that he haunted the grounds of the ancient house he loved, others again that they saw him on a nearby mountain, and still others on a neighbouring shore. There were persistent stories of hollow groans and strange, incoherent mutterings heard in the locality of the blasted oak. His old nurse in particular, used to say that she often saw his form flitting about the garden on moonlit nights and that she heard his unmistakable footsteps about the house.

After some ten years Glendower died and on his deathbed besought Madog to reveal his secret to Howel's widow and give the remains a Christian burial. Madog carried out his friend's wishes, revealing to the horrified and still hoping wife that she was indeed a widow. Then he led Howel's retainers to the hollow oak which was rent open to reveal the bleaching skeleton.

The remains were borne home and duly buried but still the ghost of the vanquished Lord of Nannau was seen from time to time, while the blasted oak, until its fall and destruction on July 13, 1813, was referred to as 'the hollow oak of the demons'; a tree haunted by a gruesome secret for over ten years.

In this wild and beautiful border country known as Liddesdale, a valley traversed by Liddel Water, stands, on bleak moorland the remains of squat, massive and haunted Hermitage Castle.

The oldest part was built early in the thirteenth century by Nicholas de Soulis probably for the purpose of repelling the frequent assaults of the English. In the reign of Robert Bruce (1274-1329) the castle was held by William de Soulis, known as the Bad Lord Soulis and he is said to haunt the place to this day.

Soulis the Bad was reputed to have studied sorcery under the celebrated wizard Michael Scot (c.1175-1234) in the mysterious Eildon Hills. On his return to Hermitage Castle he practised Black Magic and was credited with many evil and blood-thirsty crimes, including the murder of the Cout of Keilder (Keeldar Mangerton), so-called because of his enormous size and strength.

It would seem that one day the Cout was invited to visit the notorious Lord Soulis. In spite of warning from his wife and a well-known local seer, the 'Brown Man of the Moors', he accepted the invitation to Hermitage relying on his strength and charmed weapons for protection.

After feasting and making merry the treacherous Lord Soulis gave a secret signal to his men who had been seated between each of the visitors. In a moment all of the guests had been stabbed and were either dead or dying, but the Cout of Keilder, ever mindful of the unreliable Soulis, saw the signal, sprang on to the table and escaped in the tumult, reaching the door of the dining chamber by running along the laden tables. He fought his way from the room and out of the castle, pursued by the retainers of Soulis; but in attempting to leap to safety over the river, he fell into the deep waters and was held under by the spears of his adversaries until he drowned. To this day the place is known as Cout's Pool.

Near to the castle keep, in the ancient burial ground, the gigantic grave of the Cout is still pointed out to visitors, indicated by two stones set far apart, one said to mark his head and the other his feet.

But the death of the Cout brought about the end of the Bad Lord Soulis for so terror-stricken were the local inhabitants after the treacherous murder of Cout's men that they petitioned the king for permission to destroy him. King Robert I of Scotland, irritated by constant complaints about Soulis is said to have replied: 'Hang him, boil him, do anything you like to him but for Heaven's sake let me hear no more about him.'

More than satisfied with such an answer, the petitioners returned to Liddesdale and lost no time in taking Soulis by surprise. They dragged him, none too gently, to the ancient circle of stones known as Nine Stone Rig (of which remnants still remain) and there they thrust him head foremost into a cauldron of molten lead.

Robert the Bruce quickly repented of having spoken hastily. Fearful, lest the headstrong men of Liddesdale should take his words literally and actually boil Soulis, he despatched messengers to prevent such a frightful act taking place. But they were too late—awful retribution had already overtaken Soulis the Bad.

So runs the legend although it is by no means certain that Soulis met such a horrible end. According to historical records, he was arrested for conspiring against Robert the Bruce in an attempt to get the crown for himself on the grounds that he was descended from an illegitimate daughter of Alexander II, and ended his life imprisoned in Dumbarton Castle. Yet the more dramatic version has been accepted for hundreds of years. Whatever his end may have been, it is believed to this day that Soulis haunts Hermitage Castle because of the wicked deeds he perpetrated there and that he is destined to do so until Doomsday. There used to be stories of a room in the castle that was sealed where, on certain nights of the year, his ghost returned and frolicked with other evil spirits. Local inhabitants and visitors who have chanced to be within the castle precincts, or even passing near the building on these unspecified nights, testified that they heard unearthly screams and diabolical laughter.

Another ghost of Hermitage Castle is that of the gallant

Alexander Ramsey, Sheriff of Tevitdale, who was decoyed to Hermitage Castle by his one-time companion-in-arms, Sir William Douglas, Lord of Hermitage and natural son of the king from whom he had received the castle in 1358. There the noble sheriff was set upon, thrown into a dungeon and left to die of starvation.

Poor Ramsey is thought to have prolonged his misery by eating grains of corn that fell from the granary situated above his dungeon for during the early days of the last century a mason broke down part of the wall of the old granary for the purpose of using the stone and found, when he explored the dungeon he had unearthed, a quantity of chaff, some human bones and a rusty sword. Even today it is possible to meet local people who maintain that they have heard heart-rending cries, groans and anguished whispering, when they visit the gaunt but proud structure at night-time.

Sir William Douglas forfeited the castle in 1491 when he was caught in treachery and it was subsequently bestowed upon the Earl of Bothwell. When the Bothwells were in turn disgraced, King James VI gave the property to the Buccleuch family who retained it until it passed to the nation.

Other reported ghosts at Hermitage Castle where, over the years, a great number of men and women have met cruel and violent deaths, include a regal figure in white who may be Mary Queen of Scots. She was here when James, Earl of Bothwell, owned the castle and lay seriously wounded and thought to be dying. There are rumours, too, of unidentified and terrifying ghosts in blood-stained armour glimpsed for a moment or two only, within the castle precincts both on dark and stormy nights and during the hours or daylight whenever there is lightning and the clash of thunder in the area. Vague and unsubstantiated reports of headless apparitions have also been associated with this picturesque but grim castle in Liddesdale.

Nigg, near Fearn, ROSS AND CROMARTY

An old cottage with a curious ghost story used to stand on a ridge known locally as the Hill of Nigg. Remnants of the cottage, which almost overhung the sea, could still be traced a few years ago.

There were once two young girls who grew up together and were much attached to each other. One day they visited the home of a relative who had recently died. They were shocked and distressed at the light-heartedness and indifference shown by some women employed in dressing the body. The two friends agreed that, should one outlive the other, the survivor, and no one else, would lay out the corpse of her friend.

Some years later one of the girls was the mistress of a solitary farmhouse on the Hill of Nigg. One day she was informed, by chance, that her old companion who had also married a farmer and lived in the neighbourhood of nearby Fearn, had died in childbirth the previous night. Recalling her promise, she spent an anxious day worrying about the matter for she was unable to fulfil her pledge. She now had an infant who needed attention and no one with whom she could leave the small child; her maid had gone out only shortly before she heard the sad news, having gone to a neighbouring fair; her husband and his ploughman had also gone there. She resigned herself to the fact that she could not keep the pact that had been made but told herself that her friend had probably forgotten all about the childhood promise long ago.

Evening drew on and her thoughts turned again and again to her friend and the unfulfilled promise. She went out and stood on a little hillock beside the cottage, giving her a view over the moor her husband and servants would cross on their way home. After a while she saw a female figure approaching through the deepening twilight and, supposing that it was her maid and unwilling to appear anxious for her return, she went back into the house.

As she entered she noticed that some nearby farm animals were restive, as though some stranger were about. But she continued on her way and entered the cottage where she was astonished to find the figure that she had spotted out on the moor! Now, close at hand, she saw that the tall figure was wrapped from head to foot in a winding sheet. It stood, silent and unmoving as she halted, stunned with surprise, in the doorway. Slowly the figure crossed in front of the fireplace towards a chair where it seated itself, raised its chalk-white arms and uncovered its face, disclosing the features of the deceased girlhood friend. To add to the horror there was an expression of anger on the features, lit up by the flames of the fire. As the dead and glassy eyes turned to her old friend, the housewife instinctively snatched up her child from the cot in the corner of the room and gazed, fascinated, at the apparition. She said afterwards that she could distinguish every fold of the winding-sheet; she described the dead, black hair drooped carelessly over the forehead; the livid and un-breathing lips drawn apart, as if no friendly hand had closed them after the last agony; and the reflection of the flames seemed to rise and fall within the eyes, varying by its cease-less flicker the statue-like rigidity of the features.

As the fire burned slowly down, the woman threw some sticks on to keep the flames burning, without taking her eyes from the frightening spectre in front of her. She had almost exhausted the firewood and was dreading the thought of being left in the darkness with the silent form of her old friend, when she heard voices approaching the cottage.

At the same time the apparition rose from the chair and glided towards the door where the farm animals again set up a commotion as she passed. This time a cow kicked out at it with one of its back legs and, uttering a faint shriek, the phantom disappeared.

The farmer entered the cottage in time to see his wife fall to the floor in a swoon. Having recovered, next day she set out to pay her last respects to her old friend and on examining the body, she discovered on it the unmistakable mark of a cow's foot.

Oban, ARGYLLSHIRE

A couple of miles to the north, on the banks of Loch Etive, and commanding the entry to the loch, stands the ruined castle of Dunstaffnage. According to tradition it was once the royal seat of the Dalriadan kings, built by Evanus at the time of Julius Caesar. For long it housed the famous Stone of Scone, thought by some to have been the stone that was the pillow of Jacob when he dreamed of a ladder to Heaven, the coronation stone of Scottish and English kings from time immemorial. The stone was moved to Scone near Perth and then to Westminster Abbey, by King Edward I, in 1296.

Dunstaffnage Castle, captured by Robert the Bruce in 1308, became the stronghold of the Campbells and the MacDougals; then an English military station during the risings of 1715 and 1745, while Flora Macdonald, the Jacobite rescuer of Bonnie Prince Charlie, was imprisoned here for ten days in 1746. One of the old guns among the ruins was raised from a Spanish galleon in Tobermory Bay.

With such a history and background small wonder that the ruins are haunted. When the Campbells lived at the castle a notorious phantom, 'the Green Lady' haunted the place. She was known as the Scannag or Elle maid. The reason for her haunting is now forgotten, but the figure invariably exhibited sorrow before the death of a member of the family and joy before an event which brought happiness to the family. In addition, the appearance was sometimes accompanied with poltergeist-like activities. There are many accounts of 'something' teasing children of the Campbell family when they were in bed, especially the younger folk, of loud stamping and banging on the flooring which seemed to shake the rooms and disturbed many a night's rest.

Pencaitland, EAST LOTHIANSHIRE

Haunted and romantic Pencaet Castle has several ghosts including one known to the family as 'gentleman John' who is believed to be a former occupant; a royal ghost in the 'shape' of King Charles I who may have visited and whose bed is certainly here; and more than one unidentified figure.

The late Professor Holbourn acquired the property now known as Pencaet Castle or Fountainhall House in 1923. His widow Mrs Marion Holbourn has been good enough to pass on to me many details of the apparently paranormal manifestations that have taken place at the picturesque rubble-built structure boasting a forestair leading from the courtyard and a circular tower. The early sixteenth-century structure is practically in its original condition.

There are many things of interest at Pencaet apart from the ghosts: a crusader's helmet, a Spanish treasure chest, part of the chair used by Mary Queen of Scots when she abdicated the throne, sixteenth-century tapestries and much furniture in keeping with the period. Also, a four-poster, presented to Professor Holbourn by his students that is reputed to have once been occupied by King Charles I. Altogether Pencaet Castle is acknowledged to be one of the most interesting mansions of southern Scotland and I am indebted to the Society for the Recording of Abnormal Happenings and to Edinburgh Psychic College for permission to include details from their reports devoted to paranormal activity at Pencaet.

The property was at one time owned by Sir Andrew Dick Lauder who was terrified as a child at seeing an apparition standing by the fireplace in an upper room. Another former occupant, John Cockburn, either committed murder or was himself murdered centuries ago by one John Seton, to whom he was related by marriage. Cockburn is credited with being the instigator of some of the disturbances here, including most of the various inexplicable noises of many kinds that have been heard by numerous people on many occasions.

Sounds of footsteps have frequently been heard echoing through the castle together with the sounds of furniture being moved. Such noises were heard in 1923 soon after the Holbourns moved in. Next year various people occupying the house while Professor and Mrs Holbourn were visiting the Island of Foula, complained of loud shrieks and groans. Doors, securely closed at night, were found open in the morning, even when they had been locked and barred. One girl refused to sleep another night in the place after a full night of strange sounds and unexplained happenings.

As time passed the noises and disturbances became less violent and assuming that the originator was John Cockburn, Professor Holbourn would call out whenever a continuous rattling or tapping was heard: 'Now John, that's childish. Stop it.' And the sounds invariably ceased. Such a well-behaved ghost soon became known as 'the perfect gentleman'.

On Christmas Eve, 1923, the family and guests were

gathered around a roaring fire in the music room, singing carols, when in full view of them all and verified by everyone present, a piece of carved oak bearing the family crest emerged from its place on the wall, paused for a moment and then returned to its normal position. The size of the block was seven inches by six inches. This manifestation was regarded as a greeting to the new inhabitants.

After the four-poster bedstead was brought into the house noises, comparable to someone moving about the room, using the bed and shifting the furniture, seemed to emanate from the King Charles Room. The magnificent bedstead has elaborate carving on the bottom standards which are believed to be taken from the death-mask of King Charles I. Professor Holbourn and his wife occupied the chamber below the King Charles Room for a time and often they heard noises that sounded like someone surreptitiously groping and stumbling above them. The entity haunting the room is thought to be the ghost of Charles I himself, beheaded in 1649.

The royal bedstead appears to have been the scene of paranormal activity. In 1924 a visitor was taken to see the room. The bedclothes were found to have been violently disarranged, giving the impression that the bed had been slept in. A Mrs Anderson, who was responsible for keeping the room tidy, asserted that she had left the place, only minutes before 'in a decent and proper condition'. Shortly afterwards another visitor, entering the King Charles room to take a photograph also found the bed apparently unmade. Again, Mrs Anderson was certain that she had in fact made the bed and left it tidy. The photographer discovered that his photograph was under-exposed and when he returned to take another, once again the bedclothes were found disarranged on the haunted bed. On this occasion, after the bed had been re-made, precautions were taken by locking the two doors giving access to the room and ensuring that all the windows were secured; in addition two bricks were placed against the main door. Next day the bricks were found to have been moved and although the doors were still locked and the windows fastened, the bedclothes were disturbed yet again.

Miss Avis Dolphin (now Mrs Foley), a survivor of the *S.S. Lusitania* disaster, when nearly two-thousand lives were lost,

406

lived at Pencaet Castle with the Holbourns for some years. One night, while occupying the King Charles Room, she awakened Professor and Mrs Holbourn, who were sleeping in the room directly below, to say that someone was moving about downstairs. Professor Holbourn got up at once; they went down together to find out what was happening. After an unsuccessful search for the perpetrator of the noises, they were returning upstairs, when they both heard, as they reached the first floor, unmistakable creaking sounds, as of a heavy person turning and tossing in the King Charles bed so recently vacated by Avis Dolphin. On another occasion Avis Dolphin felt a light touch on her neck as she mounted the stairs in the darkness; she described the feeling as if some-one drew the tip of a finger across the throat—light but un-mistakable.

About the same period, Marion Holbourn told me, she sometimes saw faint but distinct lights shining in various passages throughout the old house. One night the sound of birds wings were heard beating violently against the castle windows, terribly loud and insistent. Next day a cousin of the Holbourns who had been staying at Pencaet, died in hospital.

Some time later an elderly lady, recovering from an illness, was occupying the King Charles Room and Mrs Holbourn's brother was at the time using the bedroom immediately beneath this haunted chamber. One morning at about five o'clock he awakened his sister to let her know that judging by the sounds he had heard from the room above his, he thought the old lady had fallen out of bed and was trying to get help. On reaching the King Charles Room Marion Holbourn found the old lady fast asleep.

Many objects have been moved mysteriously at Pencaet, apparently without human intervention, including large and heavy furniture. A big antique cabinet was shifted from its accustomed place by the wall. A brass ewer and basin, brought to England by Mrs Holbourn's grandfather from Turkey, was found to have been placed on top of a tall cabinet, the ewer on its side.

During the time that Marion Holbourn's son was a student at Edinburgh College of Art, nine students from the college visited Pencaet Castle to rehearse the play, *Ladies in Retirement*. Mrs Holbourn, spending the night in the Music Room, heard the most appalling noises; her son and daughter-in-law, occupying the dining-room, also heard them and were, in fact, kept awake much of the night. In the morning the two students in the apartment immediately above the Music Room were asked how they had fared during the night. They replied that their sleep had been much disturbed; they had assumed that some of the other students were playing pranks. They had decided to ignore the noises and assured Mrs Holbourn that they themselves had kept quiet all night. The two students who spent the night in the King Charles Room, situated above that occupied by Mr Holbourn (junior) and his wife, asserted that they had been continuously disturbed and had hardly closed their eyes all night. They, too, had suspected a practical joker but had not themselves moved about or made any noise. They complained of the extreme coldness in the room they occupied and described a broad 'and ghastly' stain they had both seen to appear when the commotion was at its height. In the morning when they examined the wall where they had seen the mark during the night, they could find nothing to account for their nocturnal experience. Among the noises they described (and this has been reported on other occasions at Pencaet) was one that sounded like something heavy and soft being pulled slowly across the room at about midnight, accompanied by stealthy footsteps.

One of the occupants of this room at another time had with her a square and most reliable clock that had worked well for many years. At Pencaet it stopped; altogether, it never went for more than five minutes all the time she was at the castle. Marion Holbourn told me that she, too, found difficulty in keeping clocks working when they were placed on a particular wall of the dining-room; once even a watch hung there stopped.

A convincing account of paranormal footsteps was given to me by Marion Holbourn. They were experienced the night of Professor Holbourn's funeral by his widow and their son. Firm and distinct, they appeared to approach the front door along a path and the door was heard to open and shut. Young

Holbourn immediately searched thoroughly but could find nothing to account for the noise, although he did find the pet cat hiding beneath a table in a terrified condition.

Mrs Marion Holbourn was away from Pencaet Castle for a period at one time and the house was occupied by her son. Mr Alasdair Holbourn, Mrs Holbourn's bedridden mother, her nurse and the housekeeper, Bella Leadbetter. Miss Leadbetter, occupying the room next to the bathroom, called out on one occasion to Alasdair to enquire whether he was having a bath as she could hear the hot water running. Actually he was outside the house at the time. He replied in the negative and said he would see if it was the nurse. He discovered that she had been in bed for an hour. Entering the bathroom, he found the place full of steam with the windows and mirror blurred but the bath absolutely dry! He also discovered a strange piece of soap which none of the occupants of the house claimed or could explain. Next morning Bella reported that her bath towel had disappeared and it was never recovered.

A Siamese cat was concerned in an incident which took place in the chamber known as the Middle Room. One night Alasdair Holbourn heard the cat scratching at one of the two doors situated at opposite ends of the room. Rising to open the door, he was about a yard away when the door suddenly threw itself open and at the same time the door at the opposite end of the room also opened and the sound of running footsteps faded away down the passage. Of the cat there was no sign.

An Edinburgh medium visited Pencaet one day and as a result of the various 'impressions' she obtained during a complete tour of the mansion, she had no hesitation in pointing to the late Professor Holbourn as being responsible for the paranormal footsteps and a number of other unexplained happenings.

A curious 'spontaneous manifestation' occurred when a party of members of the East Lothian Antiquarian and Field Naturalists Society were being conducted through the low-beamed Library at the top of the castle. A domed glass, encasing a model of the castle made years before by Alasdair Holbourn, suddenly cracked for no apparent reason and broke into several pieces. No one was within a dozen feet of the model at the time.

In one letter to me Mrs Holbourn related that the ghost had been active again. She felt that unusual displacement of air might account for some of the reported 'manifestations' and that the forty-one doors in the castle and many more windows had always suggested to her that there could be a normal explanation for some of the curious happenings. Yet she readily admitted the difficulty of explaining the apparition of a small man dressed in a cloak who was seen by her daughter-in-law to emerge from a cupboard and walk the whole length of a room before disappearing into a solid wall. Similarly the actual movement of heavy furniture, the stopping of clocks and such activities as the movement of the wooden panel are difficult to associate with draughty doors and ill-fitting windows.

In August, 1972, Mrs Marion Holbourn told me she was really convinced that there were ghosts at Pencaet after the Charles I bedstead was disturbed. A very reliable person was involved. The Holbourns were away on holiday but they left in the house Marion Holbourn's cousin, who lived with them. He looked into the bedroom one morning and saw that the bed was unmade. He told the daily help, who declared that she had made it. He took her to the room and showed her the bed and she said she must have forgotten. They made the bed together, but next day it was again unmade. The cousin became frightened and, the bed re-made, he barricaded the windows and locked both doors. When the Holbourns returned home he took them up to the bedroom; together they unlocked the room and looked inside. The bed was again in wild disorder!

There is yet another ghost at Pencaet: an ancient beggar who practised wizardry years ago, named Alexander Hamilton. He is said to have been turned away empty-handed from the castle; in revenge he came back with a blue thread and 'with murderous intent' wound the thread about the gates of the mansion. A day or two later the chatelaine and her eldest daughter fell victims to a mysterious illness and both died. Hamilton lost his life on Castle Hill at Edinburgh but it may be that his ghost returns on certain nights for from time to time a mysterious and unexplained shadowy form has been seen about the castle gates. I find that King Charles I visited nearby Winton House in 1633, so it is by no means impossible that he called at Pencaet.

Penicuik, MIDLOTHIAN

Some five miles south the obsolete Mount Lothian Quarry has long been reputed to be haunted by a galloping horseman.

In the late 1800's, when the quarry was being worked, the lime-burners finished work at dusk. There were recurrent stories of their being startled by the figure of a galloping horseman that disappeared in the direction of Peebles.

Sometimes, late on dark nights, the 'clip-clop' of horses' hooves indicated the return of the mysterious rider. Those who saw the figure on the occasions when the horse and rider travelled north, quite oblivious to any human watcher, swore that as the galloping horse and intent rider approached the quarry they both leapt high into the air while at the same time a blood-curdling scream rent the air. Then there was silence and the figures were seen no more.

The locally accepted story to account for the singular spectacle concerned a young farm labourer who used to 'borrow' a horse from his master for the purpose of visiting his lady love at a farm near Eddleston on the Peebles Road.

One night, at a corner near the quarry, he came upon a heavily-laden cart that had toppled on to its side, trapping both horse and driver. But despite the driver's anxious cries for help, the love-lorn young ploughman turned a deaf ear and hastened on his way. A few hours later, when he returned, he again passed the upset cart and rode past it. But this time the cart-driver recognized the young man in the bright moonlight. When next morning the injured man was found by the quarrymen on their way to work he only lived long enough to tell his story, deeply tinged with the bitterness he felt for the heartless young labourer.

Very soon the young man found himself without a friend in the district. After he lost both his job and his girl-friend, he took to poaching. One morning his body was found; no one ever knew whether he had died by accident, suicide or murder. Due to strong local feeling his body was not buried in consecrated ground but on a piece of waste land where the estates of Frith, Whitehill and Roseberry meet. It is hereabouts that clear moonlit nights are still disturbed by the occasional figure of a hurrying horseman, by the clip and clatter of horses' hooves—a phantom horseman hurrying home with the horse before it is missed by its owner.

While in the vicinity, it is worth visiting nearby Roslin Chapel. Here, although they have no ghost, there is a remarkable sculptural decoration, probably by Spanish craftsmen, representing such subjects as the Seven Deadly Sins, the Seven Cardinal Virtues and the Dance of Death. The Prentice Pillar is said to derive its name from the fact that an apprentice produced it in the absence of his master who, on his return from abroad, slew the 'prentice' with his mallet in a fit of jealousy—so perhaps there should be a ghost here, anyway!

Perth, PERTHSHIRE

A ghost here appeared night after night because it owed a small sum of money!

In July 1838 the Rev. Charles McKay, a Catholic priest, left Edinburgh to take charge of the Perthshire missions. On arrival he received a call from a Presbyterian woman named Anne Simpson who said she had been waiting more than a week to see a priest. He learned that she had been much troubled for several nights by the apparition of a dead woman who had materialized in her bedroom. McKay asked the woman whether she was a Catholic and when she replied that she was a Presbyterian, he asked why she had sent for him? Anne Simpson replied that her 'visitor' had besought her to get a Catholic priest who would pay a certain sum of money that she owed; then she could rest in peace. The priest asked what the sum of money amounted to and was told three shillings and tenpence.

Anne Simpson did not know to whom the money was owed but she was quite emphatic that the visitation was no dream, insisting that she could get no rest because the figure

412

The haunted ruins of the Cathedral at St Andrews, Fifeshire, where a ghostly lady wearing a veil and carrying a book was seen by two students in 1968. *Photo: Scottish Tourist Board*

Ballachulish House, Argyllshire, where the ghost of a phantom tinker stands by the gate on Autumn evenings. *Photo: Alasdair Alpin MacGregor*

Stirling Castle where appearances of the ghostly 'Green Lady' are taken seriously since sightings have heralded several serious fires. There was once a real 'Green Lady' who rescued Mary Queen of Scots from a burning bedstead. *Photo: Scottish Tourist Board*

Fitzwilliam Square, Dublin, has an old house haunted by a ghost known as 'Lady Reid'; a ghost that so terrified servants that they made a point of never entering one particular room when they were alone. *Photo: Irish Tourist Board*

appeared to her night after night. She recognized her as a woman named Maloy whom she had often seen going in and out of the army barracks, near her own lodgings.

The Rev. Charles McKay made enquiries and discovered that a washer-woman from the barracks, named Maloy, had indeed died. He located a grocer with whom she had dealt and who was not aware of her death. Asking him whether she owed him anything, the grocer turned up his books and revealed that Mrs Maloy's unpaid account had amounted to exactly three shillings and tenpence. McKay paid the sum. Shortly afterwards Anne Simpson came to tell him that she was no longer troubled by the ghost of Mrs Maloy; although she did not know that McKay had discovered the debt and paid it. The full story was told in a letter from the Rev. Charles McKay to the Countess of Shrewsbury, dated October 21st, 1842.

Ringcroft of Stocking, Rerrick, KIRKCUDBRIGHTSHIRE

Ringcroft has now disappeared but it is possible to locate the parish of Rerrick where, nearly three hundred years ago, a poltergeist manifestation was experienced by fifteen responsible people, including six clergymen. The case, written up at the time with great care and attention to detail, came to be regarded as a classic poltergeist infestation.

We have a record of the strange happenings from the pen of the Rev. Alexander Telfair, the parish minister, who published a pamphlet in 1695 recounting the disturbances at the home of Andrew Mackie, a mason.

Initially it was the Mackie's animals that suffered. Live-stock was found with the tethers cut or loosened; although these were renewed or strengthened, the same thing happened even when the animals were moved from their accustomed grazing grounds. One morning an animal was discovered suspended from a beam at the back of the house with its feet hardly touching the ground.

Shortly afterwards, in the middle of a quiet spring-time night, the sleeping family awakened to find the house full of smoke. They discovered that a basket full of peats had been tipped out on the living-room floor and set alight.

A few days afterwards, on March 7th, inexplicable stone-throwing began and continued unabated for five days. The stones felt half their normal weight when they were picked up. A month later the same thing happened; one large stone flew upwards from the floor with such force that it almost penetrated the thatched roof. As it fell back to the floor, breaking in a number of pieces, one struck the Rev. James Monteith, minister of Borgue, in the back.

It was during the early days of the infestation, too, that the Mackie children went running to their parents one evening, frightened by the sight of a shrouded body they found seated by the fireplace when they came into the house. Their awed faces convinced Andrew Mackie that they had indeed encountered something that scared them. He hastened to the house with the children cowering behind him but whatever had terrified them had by then disappeared. Next day a shepherd's staff and some kitchen utensils were discovered to be missing; later they were found in the shuttered and locked loft.

After church the following Sunday Mr Mackie remarked on the strange happenings to his minister, the Rev. Alexander Telfair, who listened attentively and later visited the house, staying for some time to exorcise the ghost by prayer. Practically nothing of a ghostly nature happened until the rector was on the point of leaving when two small stones dropped on to the roof of the house and the whole family ran outside to complain that the evil ghost had returned. Mr Telfair immediately went back inside and prayed but even as he did so a number of small stones were thrown at him, seemingly from nowhere. A few found their mark but without harming him. Soon afterwards, on March 18th, bigger stones were hurled and during the night of March 21st, which the rector spent at the home of the Mackie family, there was considerable alarm throughout most of his stay. The minister was struck by a stick wielded by unseen hands, not once but several times; articles and furniture in one of the bedrooms were moved and seemed to be alive, to the great consternation of the occupants of the house, the minister and three neighbours who were present. Later the same night, when engaged in yet another attempt at exorcism, the Rev. Alexander Telfair became aware of a slight pressure on his arm and, looking down, he saw a little white hand and arm that vanished as he watched.

Thereafter the ghost seemed to become more powerful and more vindictive. There were numerous reports, not only from the various members of the family affected but also from friends and neighbours who came to assist, of stones being thrown at them, articles moving suddenly when they were about to be touched and people being hit by sticks and stones. Once Andrew Mackie was hit on the forehead by a stone and when he tried to dodge some of the repeated missiles with a heavy stick, 'something' gripped him by the hair and scratched him with its finger nails. At night-time the sleeping children would be awakened by a great noise caused by a stout stick rattling and banging on the wooden chest beside their beds; bedclothes would be repeatedly dragged off the beds and prayer times were disturbed by a noise described as 'whisht—whisht—whisht'.

After Mackie and his neighbour Charles MacLennan went to Buittle and related the story of the disturbances to a gathering of clergymen, two of the ministers, Andrew Ewart of Kells and John Murdo of Crossmichael, returned with Mackie to Ringcroft. Here they fasted and prayed in turns throughout the night, but to no avail and they themselves were repeatedly struck by stones that flew at them from nowhere. Ewart was hit so hard on the head that he bled.

That night no member of the household escaped the attention of the ghost. While they were all collected together for evening prayer a peat, alight and burning, was flung among them and as they rose from their knees, stones showered on them from every angle.

During the next few days a barn full of straw was set alight; two attempts to set fire to the house were quashed with the speedy help of neighbours, and William MacMinn, the blacksmith, received a wound on the head from a flying stone.

One evening as Andrew Mackie and his wife were carrying peat into the house, Mrs Mackie stumbled over a slab of the stone floor and discovered to her surprise that the stone

415

was loose for up to that time both she and her husband had always found it perfectly firm. When they had finished moving the peat, Mrs Mackie turned her attention to the loose stone and, finding that it raised easily, discovered beneath it seven small bloodstained stones and some flesh, enclosed in a piece of old paper. The Rev. Alexander Telfair recounts that the blood was 'fresh and bright'. Mrs Mackie believed that her interference with these hidden articles resulted in the appearance on the children's bed of a stone so hot that it burned a hole in the bed-clothes; it was still too hot to handle when a neighbour was called to the scene.

A letter written in blood was next found by Andrew Mackie; stone-throwing was resumed; a barn door was discovered to have been inexplicably smashed; there was more fire-raising; a spade and a sieve were thrown about the house. When Mackie succeeded in catching hold of the sieve, the greater part of it was forcibly snatched from him, leaving the rim in his hand. A visitor received a blow on the head that caused bleeding. During the following days there was continual whistling, groaning noises and stone-throwing at prayer times. Sometimes an invisible force shook the kneeling men backwards and forwards and tried to lift them bodily.

Sheep were found tied together in pairs; ropes were deposited in unusual places and a voice declared that God had directed it to warn the land to repent before dire judgment fell. There were more attempts at setting the house alight and one gable-end of the property was pulled down so that the Mackie family had to shelter for the night in a stable.

Finally the entity or being responsible for all the trouble was apparently seen in the barn at Ringcroft by five of the local inhabitants. They described it as a black thing that seemed to increase in size to such an extent that they thought it would fill the building. They were terrified but this appearance seemed to signal the end of the disturbances for though next day, May 1st, 1695, an empty sheep-shelter was gutted by fire, thereafter nothing of an extraordinary nature was reported.

The site of Ringcroft of Stocking is marked by three trees that stand a short distance up a side road not far from Auchencairn village. They are known locally as The Ghost

Trees. Some of the foundations of Mackie's haunted farm-house can still be located in what is now pasture land.

Roslin, MIDLOTHIANSHIRE

To the south, on the banks of the North Esk, it is still possible to trace remains of Woodhouselee Castle, the 'haunted Wood-houselee' of Scott's ballad. It stood here on a slope of the Pentland Hills and was persistently haunted by the Lady Bothwell, with a child in her arms. There are reports that she has been seen in the present New Woodhouselee.

The ghost story has its origin in a murder or assassination. There is no doubt that Hamilton of Bothwellhaugh shot and killed the Regent Moray as he passed through Linlithgow on January 23, 1570. He claimed justification, for while Hamilton was away from home, a favourite of the Regent seized his house, turning out Lady Bothwell and her infant into the cold night where, stark naked, they were found next morning, the child dead and the Lady Bothwell mad.

In the vicinity of the hollow glen beside the river this dastardly act used to be re-enacted: the stark and silent ghost of the mad Lady Bothwell rushing about on cold, moonlit nights. The apparition was seen so often some years ago that the singular appearances ceased to attract attention and came to be accepted by the inhabitants. This pitiful ghosts seems to have disappeared now although it is still possible to trace people who remember and have seen it.

St Andrews, FIFESHIRE

The town is said to get its name from the shipwreck in the fourth century of a ship carrying the relics of St Andrew himself, but it is not his ghost that haunts the ruined cathedral. Rather, it is an unidentified lady in a long white dress with a veil, holding a book in her clasped hands. In May, 1968, she was reported to have been seen near the Round Tower by an arts student, Miss Alison Grant and by medical student Mark Hodges.

Sanday Island, ORKNEY

In October, 1970, Mrs Anne Searancke and her family moved
into a lovely old cottage that stands by itself with glorious
views extending almost the entire fourteen miles' length of
the island. They had been there only a couple of days when
they heard faltering footsteps accompanied by a strange tapping noise. They could discover no cause or reason for the
sounds which were heard most often at night but sometimes
during the day. Then the sound of an organ playing was
added—with no such instrument for miles. No recorded
music was being played and no organ music was being broadcast at the time. Soon afterwards a friend, staying for the
week-end, went for a walk in the evening and on his return
saw a figure entering the back door. Realizing that it was no
member of the family he quietly followed and watched as
the female figure entered the house, crossed the kitchen and
stood silent and unmoving in front of the stove. As quietly
as he could he rushed away to get his camera but as he
turned to look again at the mysterious figure, he discovered
that it had disappeared. Afterwards several members of the
family saw the same apparition: an old woman in a long
dress with her hair curled behind her head and a shawl
thrown around her shoulders. One of the rooms in the cottage
is reported to have a most unpleasant atmosphere and dogs
have refused to enter the room which has a cupboard, omi-
nously bricked-up. It seems that one previous occupant of
the house used to walk about the place with faltering footsteps and tapping stick, as she was almost blind.

Sandwood Bay, Cape Wrath, SUNDERLAND

This extreme north-east tip of Scotland is a strange and
isolated place where one can walk for a whole day among
the rocky hills and great lumps of stone slowly disintegrating
through the ages, without meeting another living soul. But,
if repeated reports are reliable, one might meet the ghost of
an irascible old sailor.

Here the utter silence of miles of deserted sand beaches is

broken by the continual roar of breaking waves and the high-pitched screaming of gulls, bringing to mind the age-old belief of sailors that these birds were the souls of drowned mariners.

A few years ago a crofter and his son were out with their pony gathering driftwood for fuel. On this particular occasion they wandered further than usual and were busy near the sea-shore in this wild and desolate place—over fifty miles from the nearest railway station. They had collected a good supply of timber and kindling from unfrequented Sandwood Bay and were thinking that it was time to turn towards Old-shore More and home, for the watery sun was sinking and darkness would be all about them soon, when they became aware that their pony, a quiet and calm creature, had turned suddenly restive. The next moment father and son both became aware at the same time of a large and bearded man, dressed in the uniform of a sailor, standing close beside them on the sands. Before they could recover from their surprise at the soundless and sudden appearance, the figure commanded them in a loud voice to take their hands off what did not belong to them and to leave his property.

Horror-struck, for they both immediately felt that there was something uncanny and inexplicable about the sudden appearance of the mysterious figure in that deserted place, the two men dropped the wood they had spent hours gathering. Then they fled from the presence of the sailor—although not before both had noticed the brass buttons on his tunic, the worn sea-boots, the faded sailor's cap and the dark, weather-beaten clothing.

A few months later, early one afternoon, a similar figure was encountered by all the members of a fishing party from Kinlochbervie, as they rounded one of the big sand-dunes that dot the beach of Sandwood. Each member of the party clearly saw the figure striding along the crest of a sandy knoll; they all noticed the sailor's cap and saw the glint of brass buttons in the sunlight, before he disappeared behind a hillock. The gillie had his stalking-glass on the form and thinking it must be a poacher, he went off to track him down and see what the man was up to. The experienced and level-headed gillie returned, ashen-faced and puzzled, to report that there was no one in the bay at all except themselves, nor were there any footmarks or other indications that there had been anyone where they had all seen the figure.

High on a ridge facing Cape Wrath Lighthouse amid bracken and heather and about a mile from the sand-dunes of the bay stand the remains of Sandwood Cottage, untenanted now for many years; probably the most remote and solitary habitation on the mainland of Scotland. No road or even path leads to it and on the north side of Loch Sandwood there is only one other habitation, a deserted shepherd's bothy that is also reputed to be haunted.

Once an old shepherd, who had been with the sheep all day, decided to sleep in Sandwood Cottage overnight—and later told this story: 'I entered the cottage as dusk was falling and after making myself a cup of tea, I locked and bolted the front door and went upstairs to the room above the kitchen, took off my clothes, extinguished the candle and went to bed. Just as I was going to sleep, I heard steps, distinct footfalls padding about below. I got out of bed and put my ear to the bedroom door and distinctly heard footsteps padding about below me, seeming to go from room to room and back again, time after time. I said to myself that's queer, for I bolted the door; surely I didn't lock someone into the house who entered before I did: but who on earth would be near Sandwood of all places at this time of night? As the tramp, tramp, tramp continued, I dressed, lit the candle, quietly opened the door and proceeded to search every room in the place. I found nothing to account for the noises which had ceased as I descended the stairs. I went back to bed and heard nothing more.' Nothing could convince the old man but that something sub-human was with him in the cottage that night and he even had an explanation for the cause of the footsteps.

Some years before a wealthy Australian had stayed at Sandwood Cottage while fishing Sandwood Loch. He seemed to have fallen completely under the spell of the place and had come back again and again whenever he could, year after year; each time he was more loath to leave. Soon after the last of his visits to this bleak but beautiful area, he died in Australia and the old shepherd believed that his spirit returned to the place he loved so much.

420

One night an old fisherman found himself in the bay and as it was so late, he decided to spend the night in Sandwood Cottage. He had been helping to collect some sheep for a friend and he made himself as comfortable as he could in a room on the ground floor. Around midnight he was awakened by his dog barking and he heard distinct, firm footsteps apparently approaching the outside of the cottage, followed by a knock on the window-pane of the room he was occupying. Looking towards the window he saw clearly in the moonlight the face of a bearded sailor gazing into the cottage. The fisherman particularly noticed the short black coat that the figure was wearing, the brass buttons and the peaked cap. When he opened the door to see who his visitor might be, he could find no trace of any living soul. He carefully searched the whole cottage, inside and out, but saw no one and found nothing to account for the figure he had seen.

One other night the same man spent at Sandwood Cottage, alone, in the same room. This time he awoke at dead of night with the awful feeling that a thick and heavy black mass, like a blanket, was pressing down on top of him. The sensation of being suffocated was not a pleasant one and the old fisherman made sure that he never spent another night at the haunted cottage.

Not long ago two walkers from Surrey made their way from Durness to the Cape Wrath lighthouse and then, following the coast-line southwards, planned to reach Kinlochbervie in time to catch the morning bus to Lairg. But they were very tired—so when they saw Sandwood Cottage as the sun went down, they decided to spend the night there and continue in the morning.

Next day, having fled the cottage at dawn, they told a local postmaster, the first person they met, about the ghastly time they had had in Sandwood Cottage. In the middle of the night they were roused from their slumbers by a fearful noise so loud that it seemed as though all the windows and doors in the place were being smashed; the whole cottage vibrated as if in a violent storm. While the rocking and crashing sounds still continued a noise like a horse stamping and pawing seemed to come from the room above them. As near as they could judge, the noise lasted four or five minutes and during this time every part of the cottage seemed to come apart and close up again; the very foundations appeared to rock and sway and the two hikers were so terrified that they could not move. Afterwards they sat, huddled together, dreading further disturbances, until dawn broke and they, like others before and after them, fled from the haunted cottage at Sandwood Bay, the cottage that does not like to be visited.

Quite recently I heard of an Edinburgh woman who received a small piece of wood from the broken staircase at Sandwood Cottage, as a souvenir of the remotest dwelling in Scotland. Since the remnant of the cottage has been in her possession she has had several alarming experiences in her London flat, while some very strange things have also happened in her Edinburgh house. Crockery has tumbled to the floor for no apparent reason, knocks and the sound of heavy footsteps have been heard at night-time; once she noticed a strong smell of alcohol and tobacco and caught a glimpse of a bearded sailor who turned and faced her before disappearing near her sitting-room window. The odd thing is that the recipient of this piece of wood from Sandwood Bay, a much respected member of society not prone to exaggeration, has never visited the cottage herself yet she asserts that the portion of wood itself now rattles and moves on occasions. She keeps the relic locked up in a drawer and says wild horses could not drag her to haunted Sandwood Bay.

Selkirk, SELKIRKSHIRE

Some three miles to the east there are a succession of stagnant pools bordered by rushes and a few gnarled alder trees growing out of the peaty slime. It is an unobtrusive piece of marsh-ground that has a beauty and mystery all its own, especially at dusk when a mist often hovers there. Ghostly whispers and half-interpreted sounds have been reported and some unexplained figures have been seen at the place called Murder Moss, or Murder Swamp.

It is said that over two hundred years ago, in the black year of 1745 when the English were continually crossing the Scottish border, sacking and burning, one of the villages so attacked was Bowden where there dwelt a certain Davie Bonnington who had a lovely young daughter. Eighteen-year-old Kirsty had many local suitors but only one found favour with her father, a prosperous but forbidding and morose man known as Geordie o' the Mill. He was a strong and rough man, somewhat feared on account of his habit of disappearing for days at a time on his horse. Where he went no one guessed although his knowledge of the surrounding countryside was unequalled.

Kirsty, perhaps in deference to her father's wishes or perhaps because the mature Geordie fascinated her, did not discourage his wooing, until there returned to Bowden, Will Hob who had left the village as a boy of fifteen and came back a prosperous and handsome man; a man who was enchanted by Kirsty's beauty.

Before long the young pair were often walking together over the Common on summer evenings or sitting by the village stream. Geordie, whom Will disliked from the start, seemed to bear no resentment, always greeted the couple politely and made no show of disappointment when the couple announced their forthcoming wedding-day.

On the eve of the wedding friends and neighbours had gathered, as was the custom, at Bonnington's home to sing and dance and drink and eat as an expression of their good wishes. It was a wild and stormy night and the revelry was at its height when the distant sounds of galloping horses and shouting told the villagers that the dreaded English raiders were upon them. Hurriedly, lights were extinguished and men and women struggled to return to their homes or run to the moor to hide. Will took Kirsty's hand and led her through the confusion and darkness to the back of the house where his horse was stalled. He mounted, drew Kirsty up behind him and told her to 'hold tight' for he knew that their only hope of safety lay in instant flight. Suddenly the shape of a mounted man loomed up in the darkness which, with relief, they recognized as Geordie. 'Oh! Geordie, save us' cried Kirsty. 'Right', replied Geordie, 'I'll save you. There's a fine shelter I know where you'll never be found. Come on.' So saying he laid hold of the reins of Will's horse and galloped off with the lovers into the darkness, across the wild countryside that he alone knew so well. A number of villagers saw them depart.

Next day Geordie returned to the village but without either Kirsty or Will. He said that he had set them on the way to Leith and Davie Bonnington started out to look for his daughter. At length he returned to say that he could find no trace of them; all successive searches and extensive enquiries failed to locate the missing pair.

As time passed, suspicion grew that Geordie was responsible for their disappearance; it was even whispered that he had enticed the English to the village and that he had betrayed the young couple to them. Then, months later, a still more sinister suspicion was aroused by the finding of a woman's handkerchief which a village lad fished out of one of the pools outside the village; a handkerchief that was recognized as having belonged to Kirsty.

Geordie had no friend in the village and he grew more and more sullen and morose. He seemed to be a haunted man and it was noticed that ever more frequently would he ride westward out of the village in the direction of the lonely pools and marshes. Finally he was seen no more but a few days later the same lad who had returned to the village with Kirsty's handkerchief, came running into the village terror-stricken by what he had seen. He had again visited the silent pools and was half-scared out of his wits. The villagers could get little sense out of the ashen-faced lad, so a party of the men set out and reached the lonely pools as darkness fell. There, in the moonlight and through the swirling mists, they clearly saw the figure of a man submerged in the water to his waist, motionless and silent, his eyes protruding with terror, glazed and staring ... it was Geordie!

Those were superstitious days and it was commonly believed that the man who had caused the death of the young lovers had been forced to revisit the scene of his crime and that he, too, had become inexplicably engulfed in the treacherous swamp. Thereafter the place was known as Murder Moss and people who venture there on moonlight nights say that they hear ghostly whispers and long drawn-out sighs. Occasionally, as darkness gathers about the black pools, phantom forms seem to stalk among the rushes at this scene of tragedy.

From time immemorial there have been stories of phantom kilted armies on Skye. One of the more recent accounts concerns two young men: Sir Patrick Skipwith and a student from Oxford who were making a geological survey of the island.

They were camped in a deserted glen at Harta Corrie when something awakened Sir Patrick soon after midnight. He got up and went outside where he was astonished to see groups of kilted men, dozens of them, scrambling along the mountainside within fifty yards of the two tents. He was about to call out when he suddenly realized that he could hear no sound. He woke his friend and together they watched the kilted men for nearly ten minutes before the figures faded away and were gone.

Some nights later Sir Patrick and his friend camped again in the vicinity of Harta Corrie, celebrated in the history of the island for the Bloody Stone that marks the scene of a bitter battle between the MacDonalds and the MacLeods some three hundred years ago. Again, in the early hours of the morning, they both saw the kilted Highlanders, a phantom army in retreat, in bright moonlight.

The island also has a phantom car that travels at great speed along the hill road from Sligachan. All witnesses agree that the car is a 1934 Austin with lights blazing but no driver. The soundless form vanishes suddenly.

One of the first reports came from Dr Allan MacDonald who saw the 'car' in 1941. 'I was motoring along the road,' he said, 'when I noticed a car travelling very quickly towards me over the hill. Its speed really was terrific and I drew in to let it pass but it never came abreast of me. I waited a while, then proceeded forward and found that the car had completely vanished! There was simply nowhere for it to have gone.'

Donald MacKinnon from Sconsa also saw the same car quite clearly and saw it vanish before his eyes; his son Donald John MacKinnon also saw it, travelling far too quickly for a normal car.

Lieutenant Donald Campbell, of the island's Observer Corps, was driving home to Broadford from Portree when he saw the 'car' tearing towards him with lights blazing—but it never passed him. It vanished before reaching him: one moment it was there, the next it was gone, although there was nowhere for it to have gone to.

Postman Neil MacDiarmid saw it too. He said at the time: 'I had been out with mail to Sligachan. There had been a full moon but it had gone down. As I drove along a cold chill suddenly swept over me. I looked to the shore side and saw an old Austin travelling very fast with one light burning bright at the front and a kind of dim glow inside the car. I could plainly see that there was nobody at the wheel. It tore ahead of me and veered to the right; and then just disappeared.'

Stirling, STIRLINGSHIRE

The castle, built on the site of a Roman station, occupies a commanding position on the River Forth with remarkable views from the walls, including the field of the Battle of Bannockburn (1314). Many foul and bloody deeds have been perpetrated here over the years and many are the reports of ghosts and ghostly happenings within these ancient walls.

Perhaps the best known ghost is the castle's Green Lady, a phantom reputed for centuries to walk these sombre passages and corridors and to appear in the most unexpected places. Reports in quite recent times include the experience of an army cook, busy in the officers' mess kitchen, until he became aware of the feeling that he was being watched. When he turned round, he was startled to find a misty-green figure of a lady standing at his elbow, apparently absorbed in his activities. Dinner was late that night for the cook fainted with fright and afterwards swore that he knew nothing of the Green Lady ghost until he saw 'her' himself.

There is a story that the real 'Green Lady' was an attendant to Mary Queen of Scots and that one night she had a premonition that the Queen was in danger. She rose from her bed and rushed to the Royal bedchamber to find the draperies of the four-poster on fire and the Queen asleep inside.

Any appearance of the Green Lady is taken seriously at Stirling Castle for it seems that many of these have heralded a disaster of some kind. Serious fires at Stirling have followed a reported sighting of the silent figure and it is recorded that after the Queen was rescued from the burning bedstead, she recalled a prophecy that her life would be endangered by fire while she was at Stirling Castle.

Alternatively, it has been suggested that the original Green Lady was the daughter of a governor of the castle who was betrothed to an officer garrisoned at the castle who was accidentally killed by her father. In despair and anguish the unfortunate girl is said to have thrown herself from the battlements to her death on the rocks hundreds of feet below.

The massive section in the Upper Square of the castle, known as the Governor's Block, has a room at the top of a flight of stairs where footsteps echo across the ceiling although there is no room, passage or corridor above the apartment. In 1946 the footsteps were heard at infrequent intervals by an officer of the Argyll and Sutherland Highlanders and in 1956 by a major occupying the room, a particularly hard-bitten officer who had fought in Burma and many other parts of the world; not a man who frightens easily.

In the regimental history a curious incident is recorded which may be connected with the mysterious footsteps. In the 1820s there was a 'sentry beat' along the battlement that existed at that time 'above the Governor's Block'. One night a sentry taking over guard duty found the previous guardsman dead at his post, slouched on the ground, mouth open, a look of utter terror on his face. There is no explanation, no record of a medical report, just a note of several subsequent 'disciplinary cases', before sentry duty above the haunted Governor's Block was discontinued.

Strachur, ARGYLLSHIRE

There is a curious story of a remarkable vision associated with the Manse at Strachur.

A certain captain spent a single night here when the

property was occupied by some of his relatives. The house had no reputation of being haunted at the time.

Soon after retiring, the visitor was surprised to see the bed curtains open and somebody look in on him. Assuming that one of the residents must be unaware of his visit, he took no notice but when the 'visitor' returned two or three times, the captain at length called out from his bed: 'What do you want?' 'I come,' replied the form in a hollow voice, 'to tell you that this day twelvemonth you will be with your father.'

Although his father was dead, the captain was not particularly disturbed and decided that he had experienced an hallucination or dream of some kind. He lost no sleep over the matter, although he did relate the experience to his host in the morning.

It so happened that a year later to the day he was again at the Manse of Strachur, on his way north to cross the ferry at Craigie. The day was stormy but he decided to proceed. His kinsman accompanied him to the ferry but on arrival they discovered that the boat was moored at the side of the lake; the boatman assured them that it was impossible to cross until the storm lifted. The captain had important business to attend to and insisted on being ferried across. After much argument it was arranged that the old ferryman's son would attempt the crossing. The captain stepped into the boat— with the ominous warning that they would never reach the other side and that both he and the young man would both be drowned.

The boat set off with the captain, his servant and horse. Although the distance was not great the storm grew in intensity and half-way across it was found impossible to proceed. After all efforts at tacking had failed, it was decided to return to the point of departure but during the turning the boat capsized throwing the three men and the horse into the water. The captain, who was a strong swimmer and not afraid for himself, shouted to his servant to keep hold of the horse for safety. Then he set out to swim to the shore, no great distance —but he was encumbered by a heavy topcoat, his boots and his spurs. He seemed to be winning until his coat caught in his spurs and he was gradually dragged below the water. Although he reached the shore, where his relative had anxiously watched the mishap, it was only to make a gesture before he expired which seemed to say, 'You see, it was to be!'

The young boatman was also drowned although the servant, aided by the horse, escaped.

Stranraer, WIGTOWNSHIRE

The oddly shaped peninsula known as The Rhinns of Galloway is a green and enchanted land. It may well be that long ago the arm of land that joins the mainland of Wigtownshire lay under water and The Rhinns was an island.

There are numerous remnants of ancient earthworks, castles and early Christian relics here. The road to the north tip runs by the west coast of Loch Ryan; the main road more or less ends at the village of Kirkcolm. It is said that a former minister of the village had so powerful a voice that his sermons could be heard at Cairn Ryan, on the other side of the loch!

His strong voice was the means of exorcising the ghost that sorely troubled the district for many years. Caldenoch Castle seems to have been the home of the ghost but it is credited with seizing old women whenever it could and dousing them in any burn or water that might be handy. Attempts by other clergymen had always been frustrated by the ghost who out-sang the psalms and drowned the prayers of those who tried to lay it; but the minister with his formidable voice was too much for the troublesome ghost. After a night trying to out-sing the new clergyman it gave up and was duly exorcised—or at any rate troubled the area no more.

Strath Conon, ROSS AND CROMARTY

A stretch of the beautiful River Conon with its deep and wide ford, not far from the seventeenth-century (moderized) Brahan Castle (built by the first Earl of Seaforth), has long had the reputation of being haunted by a water-wraith.

Legends abound and many of the fatal accidents that used

to occur near Conon House were said to have been due to the murderous malice of this local 'elemental'.

One of the most reliable accounts of such a spectre concerns a servant of a Lord Seaforth who, late one night after a party, was accompanied on his way by two friends. In the light of the full moon the servant, described as a young and vigorous man, mounted on a powerful horse, entered the ford and rode in a slanting direction across the full stream. When he was nearly halfway across a loud cry of terror, followed by a frightful snorting and plunging of the horse, alarmed the servant's companions waiting to follow in his footsteps. Wide-eyed, they watched what appeared to be a tall, dark figure start out of the water, lay hold of their friend and drag him off the horse and into the water! A moment later they watched the terrified horse struggle towards the opposite bank while its ill-fated rider wrestled with some invisible adversary in the stream for a few seconds and then disappeared for ever beneath the water.

Tain, ROSS AND CROMARTY

Ancient Balnagowan Castle is haunted by at least two ghosts: wicked 'Black Andrew' and a murdered Scottish princess. There are several skeletons somewhere within these grey-pink walls, the remains of the Scottish princess, a man who died of the plague and one of the Rosses who were here for centuries.

My friend James Wentworth Day has told me of the night he heard footsteps, heavy and ponderous, that clumped along the Red Corridor and woke him at midnight. The footsteps were also heard by actress Hermione Baddeley who was staying at the castle at the same time and by another guest, Lady Duff. They have been heard, too, by the housekeeper whose family have served at Balnagowan for three centuries.

The footsteps are said to be those of 'Black Andrew' whose real name was Andrew Munro, a laird in a little fortress in the middle of the sixteenth century. He is reputed to have made the village women work in the harvest field stark naked and he was credited with murders and rapes for miles around.

430

Eventually the Chief of Clan Ross put an end to 'Black Andrew'; he was thrown out of a high window with a rope around his neck and breathed his last gasp dangling outside one of the bedroom windows of the Red Corridor. Always a 'devil for the women', he comes back and walks the Red Corridor (so it is said) whenever a new lady visitor stays at the castle.

Jimmy Wentworth Day told me that he was shown up to Muniment Room at the top of the tower, accompanied by a black Labrador owned by Bill Hunter who manages the estate. At the threshold of the room the dog suddenly stopped in its tracks; its hackles rose, it growled in terror, snapped and backed away. 'He always does that,' his owner said. 'I'm certain this is the room where they put the rope round "Black Andrew's" neck and pushed him out of the window. The dog knows.'

Lady John Conyngham once saw the ghost of the murdered Scottish princess. She was alone in the castle at the time and was eating her dinner when she heard a rustling sound, as of a dress. She turned and saw a female figure dressed in grey emerge from a corner of the room. The apparition had copper-gold hair and green eyes. She seemed to be a very friendly and gentle ghost. She silently beckoned to Lady John who rose from the table and followed the figure into the drawing-room where it disappeared.

There is no portrait of the mysterious Scottish princess at Balnagowan but a hairy old man with burning and malevolent eyes glowers at all who pass along the Red Corridor; almost as though 'Black Andrew' still watched for women as he did all through his evil life.

Tarbat, NEAR FEARN, ROSS AND CROMARTY

There used to be a muddy lake in the north of the parish of Tarbat which shrank considerably during the summer months, with the remains of a farmhouse still discernible near one edge.

Long ago a young pedlar who was well known in the district disappeared without trace. Some years later, during

431

a dry summer which reduced the lake to half its normal size and depth, a human skeleton was found amid the mud and rushes at the bottom. Long before this discovery, however, the farmhouse near the lake was reputed to be haunted by a restless and mischievous spectre, which appeared to be wearing some kind of grey woven material. So troublesome did the ghost become inside the house that the property was soon deserted, began to fall into decay and for over half a century no one lived there.

Then a young man bought the site and remains of the cottage, rebuilt it and moved in with his young wife. On the third evening of their married life the young couple were disturbed by strange noises apparently emanating from an adjoining room. Shortly afterwards the door of their bedroom opened and a figure entered, dressed in some grey plaid or material. The young man leapt from the bed and made for the intruder, calling as he went: 'Who are you? Who are you?' The spectre stepped back and replied in a deep voice: 'I am the unhappy pedlar who was murdered sixty years ago in this very room and my body was thrown into the lake yonder. But I shall trouble you no more. The murderer is now dead and in two hours the permitted time of my wanderings on earth will be over for had I escaped the cruel knife, I would have died in bed this evening, a grey-haired old man.'

The form slowly disappeared as it spoke and from that night was never seen or heard again.

Tiree, Isle of, ARGYLLSHIRE

A wild and lonely beach on the northern shore has long been reputed to be haunted by a phantom black dog. It has the unnerving habit of following people and occasionally barking once or twice; a weird, echoing bark never forgotten by those who hear it. If a third bark is heard, according to tradition, the phantom dog will overtake the hearer.

The same form has been seen on the moor near Kennavarra, crouching near a sand-dune. One witness, the morning after he had seen the figure, went to the spot in daylight and discovered the prints of huge paws at the place where he had seen the Black Dog.

A similar ghost-dog is said to haunt another part of the island, in the south-west; a strange, wild place known as Hynish Hill where it was seen and heard by two boys some years ago. A curious, naked, semi-human form with a grotesque head and face is seen sometimes in broad daylight on a sea-girt rock close to Balvaig.

There is on Tiree a cavern known as the Lair of the Faëry Dog. Loud and unexplained barking, as of a huge dog-like creature, has been repeatedly heard here by the islanders and, occasionally, by visitors.

Watherston, MIDLOTHIAN

A phantom lorry is said to travel along the busy road between Edinburgh and Stow and its unaccountable presence has been the source of many local reports, published in the Edinburgh papers in recent years.

One such report dates from a warm and sunny day not long ago when a local inhabitant noticed the swift and silent approach of a lorry travelling in the direction of Edinburgh, driven by an evil-looking man. The witness watched the rather old-fashioned lorry make its quiet but quick way along what was little more than a sheep-track to Watherston Hill where it joined the main road. Several Scottish newspapers published readers' accounts of a similar vehicle on this particular stretch of road where, it has been noticed, a number of accidents have occurred that could be explained by motorists following this phantom lorry round a bend and off the road.

I approached the spot with some caution when my wife and I travelled over this stretch of road in 1970 and it was just as well that I did—for we suddenly came upon an accident as we rounded a blind corner. Whether or not this particular mishap was caused by the phantom lorry I do not know.

Whitburn, WEST LOTHIAN

A few years ago the Town Council of this coal and iron district investigated a psychic manifestation at the home of a Mrs Maule and Mrs McClusky in Townhead Gardens.

The two ladies shared the house and became so mystified by apparently inexplicable rappings that Mrs Maule's son went for the police—and returned with two Town Councillors. These practical and hard-headed men searched until three o'clock in the morning in an attempt to discover the source of the noises.

During the course of their investigation they made what was described as 'Miner's Taps': three taps, followed by two short taps. Each time they received answering taps which seemed to originate in the vicinity of a bed occupied by Mrs McClusky's twelve-year-old daughter who disclaimed responsibility for the knockings.

On the following night a further enquiry produced the same result. Afterwards one of the councillors stated that old mine workings ran underneath the house but added that they were about two hundred fathoms down. 'It doesn't seem possible that sound could travel that far through the ground,' he added. 'In any case there are no men working there.'

Mrs McClusky said that the curious tappings began on a Monday and, before they started, vibrations were felt throughout the house. On the Thursday of the same week a further investigation was carried out but this time nothing was heard and thereafter all was quiet.

There has long been a theory that occasional raps and other noises and perhaps displacement of objects may be due to geophysical causes such as underground streams, tides and earth movement. In the case of this particular report it sounds very much as though some such explanation may be applicable.

IRELAND

Antrim, CO. ANTRIM

Derelict Antrim Castle dates from 1662; it was rebuilt in 1816 after a fire and was again destroyed accidentally by fire in 1922. A loud hissing or breathing sound, apparently localized in the right wing of these picturesque ruins, has been reported by hundreds of people. Intrepid investigators have ascended the castle walls with ropes and ladders to dislodge owls and other night birds but have failed to discover the origin of the noise. Underground caverns and porous stonework might possibly repay study.

Birr, CO. OFFALY

Grim, grey and bare, nearby Leap Castle, commanding a fine view of the Slieve Bloom mountains to the east, has been described as the worst haunted mansion in the British Isles.

One of the ancient strongholds of the O'Carrolls, Leap was badly damaged by fire in 1923 but originally the central portion (which comprised the entrance hall) was a square and solid castle of the usual type. Later wings were added on either side, one of which terminates in what is known as the Priest's House. The whole edifice is built on rock and gives the impression of enormous strength.

There is an age-old story that treasure is hidden at Leap Castle. Legend has it that a former inhabitant, due to be taken to Dublin to be tried on a charge of rebellion and fearful that he would not return, made the most of the time left to him by burying somewhere a crock or earthware pot full of gold and precious jewels. After years of imprisonment he did, in fact, return home but his long and cruel confinement had deranged his brain and he could never remember where he had hidden his wealth so skilfully.

From time to time various methods have been tried to locate the treasure but so far all have been unsuccessful. One lady who was psychic, though she did not find the money

437

and jewels, as she made her way through the wide hall, suddenly walked towards one wall, laid her hand on the old stones and said: 'There is something uncanny here but I don't know what it is.' It was at this spot in the walls of the castle that two skeletons were discovered, walled up.

The top storey of the central tower is known as the Chapel; it is a big, well-lighted chamber and was probably used for religious purposes at one time. At one end of the apartment there is, or was, an *oubliette*, a secret dungeon into which prisoners were thrown through a trap-door and then conveniently 'forgotten'. Often people walking along nearby roads, or in the neighbouring fields, have seen the windows of this chapel lighted up for a few seconds at a time as it would be if many lights were suddenly brought into the chamber. The possibility that the lights originate from servants can be discounted for I have been told that for years they shunned that part of the castle after dark.

One psychic message at a séance stated that the Leap treasure would be found in the chapel room under 'the tessellated pavement near the altar'. But no trace can now be found of any altar in the apartment, nor any chequered pavement unless this lies beneath the mass of debris where a former roof collapsed. It would be well-nigh impossible to establish this fact now.

Many visitors to Leap Castle have had experiences that they cannot explain. After staying at the castle one man wrote to say that he found himself awake in the night with an extraordinary and violent cold feeling in the region of his heart. As he turned in his bed to ease the pain, he became aware of a tall female figure, clothed from head to foot in some red material, with her right hand raised menacingly in the air. The figure seemed to be illuminated from within itself. As the visitor lit a match and prepared to get out of bed, he realized that the room was empty. He put out the light and went back to bed and although he did not see the 'Red Lady' again, he experienced several times the same cold feeling that seemed to grip his heart, while his body seemed warm to his touch.

Then there is the inexplicable and unpleasant 'something' that is usually referred to as 'It'. Several owners, residents and visitors have described identical experiences of this vile ghost. Not many years ago the lady of the house was in the gallery that runs round one side of the hall and connects with some of the bedrooms. She was leaning over the balustrade, looking down into the ancient hall and thinking of nothing in particular when suddenly she felt two bony hands laid on her shoulders! Twisting sharply round she saw 'It' standing close beside her. It seemed to be human in shape but only about four feet high; the eyes were like two black holes in the face. She had the impression that the whole figure was made of cotton-wool but the most objectionable part of the experience was the accompanying smell, a most appalling stench such as one would expect from a decaying corpse. After a moment the figure and the odour vanished as inexplicably as they had arrived, but it was a long time before the lady recovered from the shock of encountering the nauseating presence of the nameless horror.

There are other ghosts at Leap Castle. A shaven monk wearing a cowl walks near one window of the Priest's House and makes his way out through another window. There is an invisible presence that has the habit of lying on the bed beside a human occupant, leaving a deep impression on the bedclothes afterwards and the feeling of a great weight on the bed at the time; a very frightening experience. A quiet little elderly man has also been seen here, dressed in old-fashioned cut-away coat, bright green in colour with brown breeches and shining buckle shoes. He suddenly appears and disappears just as suddenly, sometimes accompanied by a quaint old lady, dressed in similar ancient-style clothes. It is thought that they are the ghosts of some long-past servants or visitors, who met their ends unexpectedly and probably violently in this sombre castle.

Bushmills, CO. ANTRIM

Two miles west of this pleasant town, whose River Bush gave its name to a famous pot-still whiskey, stands the extraordinary and romantic ruin of Dunluce Castle, the 'mermaid's fort'. It is perched on a precipitous detached basaltic rock

439

high above the sea, separated from the mainland by a deep chasm twenty feet wide; a gulf that in ancient times was spanned by a drawbridge and is now crossed by a narrow wooden bridge that has tried the nerves of many people.

The 'strong fort' was probably built in the fourteenth century by Richard de Burgh, Earl of Ulster or by the Mac-Quillans (or MacUillins) who certainly held for centuries the castle built on the site of a very ancient Irish fortress, until the almost impregnable bastion was taken by the Mac-Donnells in 1558. Sorley Boye ('Yellow Charles') MacDonnell was conspicuous in the struggle against the English and although Sir John Perrot took the castle in 1584 after a nine-months' siege, Sorley Boys recaptured it and made peace with the English. His son Randal was created Viscount Dunluce and Earl of Antrim by King James I. The castle was abandoned and allowed to fall into decay during the seventeenth century.

The castle, long reputed to be haunted by the restless ghost of Richard de Burgh who walks on stormy nights, originally consisted of five circular towers joined by a strong curtain wall with a platform inside and openings in the battlements for the use of archers. Only two of these circular towers remain with parts of two others. It is noticeable that in view of its exceptionally isolated position no castle keep was necessary.

The ghost of the original owner is said to be doomed to remain earthbound for ever because of the unmentionable crimes he committed during his lifetime. There are some people who credit him with causing part of the castle to fall over the cliff into the sea one stormy night in 1639, carrying with it eight people. The famous Giant's Causeway (*q.v.*), an incredible formation resulting from the slow cooling into crystalline form of volcanic lava, may be seen here and should on no account be missed.

Celbridge, CO. KILDARE

The fine house to the north-east of this pretty village (where once Esther Vanhomrigh, Swift's 'Vanessa' lived—her hopeless passion for Swift hastened her death) is called Castletown House. It has a ghost that walked down stairs before they were built and once, it seems, the house was visited by the Devil himself.

William Conolly, speaker of the Irish Parliament, 1715-29, said to have been the richest man in Ireland, built the great house in 1722. Having no heir, he left the property to his favourite nephew, William Conolly of Leixlip Castle. In 1733 he had married Lady Anne Wentworth, daughter of the Earl of Stafford, and it was she who first saw the ghost that walked down stairs that were not there.

Castletown House has always been proverbial for its hospitality. George Moore spent a fortnight here and said afterwards: 'I have wined and dined *par excellence....* I venture to say that the hospitality of this splendid house is so unbounded that even in Ireland it will long be remembered.'

But once the hospitality was abused during an encounter between young Squire Thomas Conolly, son of William who had inherited the house and a stranger, one cold and wet November evening in 1767.

One afternoon that month he had walked with his wife, Lady Louisa, in the garden of their home. She reminded him that his mother had written in her journal of the 'tall and shadowy man' she had seen standing on the top gallery, before the staircase had been built. She had described the figure pausing for a moment against the light of the window and then, with a high-pitched laugh, walk arrogantly, with mincing steps, down the staircase that was not there. Lady Anne had the impression that the man was marking Castletown House for his own; that the ghost was taking possession. The figure, its derisive laughter still ringing through the hall, seemed to have the power of sight—even foresight— since it confidently descended a staircase that did not exist, taking the right turns and following the shallow treads. When the staircase was actually built ten years later (at a time when Lady Anne was away from the house), its graceful and gently mounting sweep and two turnings corresponded exactly to the way the mysterious and chuckling figure had manoeuvred the invisible staircase.

A few days later there was a meet of the Kildare Hounds

441

at Garanagh Cross, two miles from Celbridge. It was a wild, windy and wet morning after a storm that had lasted most of the night. Only a handful of the hardiest sportsmen followed the first 'find' through Garanagh Woods. The fox proved to be as tiresome as the weather, doubling and redoubling on its tracks until the hounds were dizzy. Afternoon began to wane and cold, driving rain added to the discomfort of the hunt. One by one they went off home to dry clothes and a warm fire until by late afternoon there were no more than five or six huntsmen straggling across the ploughed fields by Rantully Hill.

At a point where the 'Dublin Gap' crossed the Portarlington road Squire Conolly noticed for the first time a man riding a spirited black horse that seemed as fresh as his own horse had been when the day began. The squire looked hard at the rider but could not recognize him as being one of the field that morning.

He turned in his saddle and called out a greeting, asking whether the huntsman was a stranger to Kildare as he did not recognize him. The tall stranger smiled or rather grinned, disclosing abnormally long and yellow teeth, but neither spoke nor acknowledged the greeting, merely pointing away ahead of him. As he did so, he turned his horse sharply and set off at a canter up the steep hill. At the same time the hounds, over the hill, set up a great noise that could only mean that they were about to make a kill.

Without a second thought, for he did not want the whole day to be a wasted one, the squire set off in pursuit, determined to be in at the kill himself. As he breasted the hill, he reined in his horse in surprise at the sight that met his gaze. The stranger, dismounted, stood a little distance away, his feet firmly apart and holding above his head with both hands, a bloody fox, oblivious of its gore dribbling down from his grey beaver hat on to his grey hunting jacket and thigh boots. Still grinning, the man snipped off the brush with his sharp teeth and offered it to the squire. Puzzled, the squire looked about him; the stranger's horse stood proudly nearby but otherwise the hill was deserted. Hounds deserting a kill? It was impossible.

As Squire Conolly turned away from the nauseating sight,

442

the man called out to him in a high, false and unpleasant voice: 'Conolly, if you will not accept the brush, will you offer me a cup of something hot at your great house—Castletown?'

Squire Conolly never refused hospitality to anyone and, unattractive as he found the man and his manners, he could not deny so direct a request. He bade the man follow him and take a cup of hot rum toddy with the rest of the huntsmen.

As they entered the high hall of Castletown House, Conolly noticed that the stranger's eyes darted to the window at the top of the staircase, a window that had given light to the gallery before the staircase was built. Then the squire watched as the stranger's eyes followed down, step by step it seemed, the massive sweep of the great staircase. A hissing laugh burst from the stranger's lips as he minced across the hall floor towards a chair near the roaring fire.

Several of the squire's friends were already seated about the hall, warming themselves with hot drink while servants busied themselves removing the men's wet boots. As a servant approached the stranger, stretched out now in a comfortable chair, he was rudely ordered away; the odd and high-pitched voice told the servant that its owner was feeling drowsy and did not want to be disturbed.

For the first time, as the man's eyes closed, Squire Conolly looked hard at him and he now saw, in the well-lighted hall, that the man was as hairy as a dog. Long, stiff hairs sprouted from his nostrils and great curling tufts of hair hung out of his ears. Even his hands, long-nailed and with tapered fingers, were matted with hair!

An awful suspicion crossed the squire's mind and as the stranger slept, he ordered a servant to remove carefully one of the man's boots. As the steaming boot was drawn from the man's foot—a hairy hoof was disclosed, black and cloven!

Apparently oblivious to the commotion the stranger slept on and Squire Conolly hastily sent a groom to Celbridge to fetch a priest. Just as the holy man arrived, the stranger awakened from his sleep. As soon as he saw that his boot had been removed, he leapt to his 'feet' and, with gait even more unseemly wearing only one boot, he limped towards the fireplace. There, spreading his arms on the mantelpiece, he dared the priest to do his worst. At the squire's entreaty to exorcise the fiend, the priest mumbled an incantation, but he was too gentle and his words had no effect except to provoke the Devil to laughter.

Angered by this reception, the priest called on the figure to be gone in the name of all that was holy but still the hall shook with Satanic laughter from the figure in front of the fireplace. This was too much for the priest who threw his missal at the leering face. The book missed its mark and smashed the mirror hanging over the fireplace but this attack had the desired effect for the fiend leaped high into the air and disappeared in a cloud of sulphurous fumes. His vanishing point was a blackened crack in the creamy marble of the hearthstone that remained to remind successive occupants of Castletown House of the strange happenings there one November day in 1767.

Cloncurry, CO. KILDARE

There is a strange ruined church here and a curious mound or barrow with a tree growing on top of it. Nearby stretches what used to be the dreary wasteland known as the Bog of Allen, now largely reclaimed as pasture. This most-famous of all Irish peat-bogs was once a place of brown turf and stagnant water; it is still a place of ghosts.

One of the many stories of weird experiences concerns a young man on a walking tour who ran into foul weather in the bleak and lonely place. The rain poured down so hard that he could hardly get his breath and within a few minutes it became so dark that he found it difficult to pick his way in the treacherous bog-ridden countryside. For a brief moment he glimpsed a hut or cabin and, hoping for shelter of some kind, he made his way towards the building. On arrival he found to his disappointment that it was unoccupied and in a ruinous condition. Without a door or glass in the windows, an earth floor and only half a roof, it offered small comfort but it was somewhere to shelter until the frightful downpour eased and he prepared to spend an hour or two there.

Making himself as comfortable as he could, he ate some

St Michan's Church, Dublin, where the peculiar dryness of the atmosphere has preserved corpses in the vaults – where curious whispering sounds have been reported, and movement of one corpse. *Photo: Irish Tourist Board*

The vaults of St Michan's Church, Dublin, where bodies have lain for centuries without any signs of decomposition and where one corpse is alleged to walk. *Photo: Irish Tourist Board*

Haunted Lake Leane, Killarney, Co. Kerry, where the ghost of Irish hero O'Donoghue is said to glide over the waters each May 1st. *Photo: Irish Tourist Board*

Blarney Castle, five miles from Cork. The Blarney Stone here has a world-wide reputation of imparting, to those who kiss it, irresistible powers of eloquence and persuasion. *Photo: Irish Tourist Board*

sodden sandwiches and was standing against the rotten wall, sheltering beneath what was left of the overhanging roof, gazing at the depressing and barren landscape all around him when his attention was drawn to a dark and swiftly flowing river that wound its sinuous way through the wasteland. A kind of black haze seemed to be rising from one particular part of the river. It was like a fog and yet it was not fog. He pondered about what it might be but found himself baffled. He had never seen anything like it before and the very strangeness of it gave him an eerie feeling. It seemed to waver this way and that, almost as though undecided which direction to take. Then, after remaining motionless for a moment, it began to move towards the lonely watcher in the ruined hut.

He watched, fascinated, as slowly, noiselessly and somehow furtively, it came towards him, a tall, shapeless black cloud, opaque, impenetrable and indefinable. Alone in that forsaken spot he began to feel uneasy as it grew nearer. He became more and more sure that it was not merely a vapour or mist but rather that it had an intelligence of sorts, that it had seen him and that it was evil.

He became conscious of the fact that he was frightened and yet he could not take his eyes away from the approaching mass, creeping slowly but surely ever nearer to him. His sense of self-preservation told him to run but when he tried to move, to shrink to one side or hide or, better still, to run, he found that he was powerless to move a limb. He had no alternative but to remain, his heart beating faster and faster as the haze drew closer and closer.

The next moment it had reached him. He had no power to ward it off, to resist the indefinable horror that seemed about to envelop him. It was as high as the cabin, devoid of any scent or smell, unsubstantial but not transparent, immaterial but not without a sense of purpose. It seemed to have arms that reached out and thrust him to one side as the shapeless haze passed him and disappeared into the cabin.

For a moment he stood taking deep breaths—he realized that he must have stopped breathing as the fog or haze reached and passed him—and then he turned to see where it had gone. It had passed through the hut or cabin and was

445

moving resolutely into the heart of the Bog of Allen. He stood and watched as it slowly disappeared into the gloom and shadows of that dreadful place.

Thinking about the experience afterwards he said that he thought it might be some elemental river spirit, a sexless, melancholy, soulless being that roamed forever in the desolate and doleful area that was the Bog of Allen.

Connemara, CO. GALWAY

Connemara was one of the last ancient kingdoms of Ireland to accept English customs; in this country of austere beauty, matched only in Greece, small boys were still dressed in skirts in recent years to deceive the fairies.

Renvyle House, now an hotel, was the scene of séances in the late nineteen-twenties conducted by W. B. Yeats and attended by people like James Joyce, Augustus John and Oliver St John Gogarty who owned Renvyle; many people believe that the place is still haunted, some that it is the most haunted house in all Ireland. The present house is about fifty years old and was built by Sir Edward Lutyens on the site of an old Gogarty residence that was burned down in the days of the Irish Troubles.

Yeats is credited with personally raising the ghost of a previous occupant of the house, a man who is said to have strangled himself with his bare hands and whose restless ghost still walks here. More than one visitor has insisted on changing rooms but few ever offer any explanation for wanting to move; often they accept inferior accommodation without protest.

A previous employee at the hotel, beautifully situated between lake and sea, recalls that the whole house had a peculiar and indefinite, almost expectant atmosphere. One particular room always seemed to have been the centre of the disturbances. This is I think No. 27 on the first floor in the centre of the hotel. The informant well recalls several visitors who occupied the room reporting that there seemed to be a non-human 'something' in the room. Once the apartment happened to be occupied by a sensible lady who chanced to be a personal acquaintance of the hotel employee and she repeatedly complained that sometimes a man looked over her shoulder as she was seated at the mirror making up her face. Another time, when the room was occupied by the wife of a well-known musician, she expostulated about seeing the reflection of a tall well-dressed man in dark clothes. In fact, a dozen or so visitors, all without previous knowledge of the reputation of the room, reported almost identical experiences. After the employee and his wife had themselves experienced 'unpleasant sensations', they persuaded a local priest to visit the hotel and say Mass in the room. In the middle of the Eucharist a violent thunderstorm suddenly blew up and everyone began to feel that things were getting out of control. The service ended and the priest left but there was no lasting benefit.

Once, when the haunted room was occupied by a very level-headed couple, a loud clinking noise disturbed their rest; a noise that sounded so close that it seemed to originate from the pillow on which their heads were lying. No explanation was ever discovered.

More recently, a frightened maid reported that she had encountered a strange man in one of the upstairs corridors; a man who disappeared into thin air as she watched.

Oliver St John Gogarty related in an article published in an American magazine some twenty years ago the story of Yeats and the Ghost of Renvyle. Once Mrs Yeats, who possessed mediumistic powers, saw a ghostly face at the window of her room. Another time, during the course of a séance held in a room upstairs, the restive spirit of a young man manifested, a man who had died by his own hand in the room where the séance was held.

A Welsh medium encountered what may have been the same ghost and had the overwhelming impression of madness. He saw the figure, almost boy-like, dressed in brown velvet and a white shirt, standing beside a chair. The medium had the feeling that something awful was about to happen. Slowly the apparition lifted its hands to its neck and squeezed. The body was violently agitated and it seemed certain to the medium that a suicide had taken place in the room.

447

Yeats believed he reached the suicide through automatic writing and learned that the ghost objected to strangers occupying the room. In return, Yeats demanded that the ghost should cease to frighten children; he must not moan in the chimneys and fireplace or wander about the house scaring people with his unexpected appearances and disappearances and he must not move furniture or otherwise terrify those who occupied adjoining rooms.

For a while there was comparative peace as the agreed terms were honoured on both sides but soon a curious stranger succeeded in obtaining permission to occupy the room in question and altogether things are said to have been as disturbed as ever before they gradually faded. Instead a tall figure, thought to be Yeats himself, is still occasionally reported at Renvyle.

Cork, CO. CORK

One of the most charming cities in Ireland, although its ancient churches and abbeys, its old walls and its mellowed castles have all vanished, there are a number of ghosts and hauntings associated with the place and with the nearby fifteenth-century Blarney Castle.

Elliott O'Donnell told me of one interesting haunting he heard about from his grandmother who had known the people concerned. About a hundred years ago there lived in Cork an orphan girl named Amelia Jenkyns who was employed as a maid by a wealthy widow, Mrs Bishop. The lady also employed a young man named Andy O'Leary to do odd jobs around the house. Andy and Amelia became good friends and after a time began to wonder what their mistress did most days when she would have a cup of coffee in the morning and then leave the house, always dressed fashionably and looking very smart. They learned that she was often seen at one of the finest hotels in Cork. They were puzzled, too, by the fact that she possessed wardrobes of fine clothes, purchased from some of the best shops in Ireland.

One dress in particular was admired by Amelia; it was red with large buttons all the way down the front and a very pretty little collar. Amelia had noticed it one morning and she was holding it against herself and admiring it when Mrs Bishop came into the room. She was very annoyed and threatened to beat Amelia if she ever caught her touching any of her clothes again. The red dress was snatched away and put inside a wardrobe in a locked room. But she never forgot the angry and cruel look in her mistress's eyes.

Time passed and periodically Amelia and Andy would talk about the red dress and the locked room, wondering what other clothes were kept there. They were also puzzled about the kind of man Mr Bishop had been. One day they asked the milkman who told them that he remembered a distinguished-looking man with white hair who looked old enough to be Mrs Bishop's father. He seemed to be independent and always had plenty of money. In those days Mr and Mrs Bishop used to winter in the South of France and while they were on one of these visits Mr Bishop died and was buried abroad.

Not long after they had received this information and let their imagination run riot, their thoughts turning again to the mysterious locked room, Amelia and Andy had a further subject to talk about together. One night Amelia had a strange dream in which Mrs Bishop took a key from a secret cavity beside the drawing-room fireplace and proceeded to unlock the room containing the red dress. In her dream Amelia followed her mistress and tried to slip into the room behind her but she was unsuccessful and found the door slammed in her face. All that she had glimpsed through the open door had been a great four-poster bedstead. Standing listening outside the room Amelia had heard the clink of coins and on the spur of the moment she had put her eye to the keyhole whereupon she had felt something hot burning her eye and this woke her up.

The dream made a great impression on her; she and Andy would talk about it time and time again. They became convinced that Mrs Bishop was a miser and that she kept hoards of money in the locked room. Gradually they became possessed with the idea of getting in, taking some of the money and running away together.

More than once Amelia set out to see if there was a secret

449

cavity near the drawing-room fireplace but she either became frightened by memory of the cruel look she had once seen in Mrs Bishop's eyes or something happened to prevent her reaching the spot she had seen so plainly in her dream. Once she thought she heard ominous raps that seemed to follow her as she stealthily crossed the hall towards the drawing-room; another time, as she was creeping downstairs, she thought she heard footsteps following her and she rushed back to her room in terror. Then one day she and Andy entered the drawing-room when Mrs Bishop was out.

They had been talking about all the wonderful things in the world that they had never seen. Amelia, who had never been to the theatre, decided to do some play-acting. As she had gone out, Mrs Bishop had said that she would not be back until evening and half-laughing and half-serious Amelia said she would dress-up in some of Mrs Bishop's lovely clothes.

She ran up to Mrs Bishop's room and picked up a silk dress. She put it on and strutted about the room. She took a big hat and put that on too. She rouged her face, pulled on a pair of French boots with high heels and went downstairs to show Andy. He was delighted and in all the excitement they decided to see whether there was a key to the locked room, as in Amelia's dream.

Hardly daring to breathe they stole across the hall and reached the drawing-room. At the door they stopped and after a moment Amelia tapped, gently at first and then more loudly. There was no sound from within the room. They opened the door and went in. Amelia went straight across to the fireplace and to the spot she had so clearly seen in her dream. She picked at a board and it opened. *Inside was a key.*

Shivering with excitement she snatched it up and ran with Andy to the mysterious locked room upstairs. Laughing and giggling to overcome their fear they inserted the key in the lock. It turned and they slowly opened the door and entered the room.

In the middle of the room, exactly as Amelia had seen in her dream, stood a massive four-poster bedstead with the curtains drawn back. Also in the room there were a couple

450

of heavily carved chairs, an enormous gilt-framed mirror and in the corner a safe.

Amelia posed in front of the mirror, mimicking Mrs Bishop and admiring herself in the dress and hat, with Andy looking over her shoulder into the mirror with her. They saw the bedstead reflected in the mirror behind them and at the same moment they both saw that it was occupied. An old man lay on the bed on his back, apparently asleep. He had white hair and a long white moustache. As they stared, open-mouthed and suddenly silent, they saw what appeared to be a large cupboard that they had not previously noticed. The door opened and a lady emerged—it was Mrs Bishop! And yet, like the figure on the bed, there was something odd and unreal about her. She was dressed in a blue evening gown and she sparkled with jewellery: a beautiful necklace and brooch, rings and a magnificent bracelet. The figure tip-toed towards the bedstead, picked up a pillow and with a cruel, almost insane look on her face that Amelia recognized, placed the pillow carefully over the face of the sleeping man, pressing down with all her strength. Amelia uttered an involuntary scream whereupon both figures vanished and Amelia and Andy found themselves again alone in the room.

They looked at each other. Each was thinking the same thing. They had witnessed a ghostly re-enactment of what had once happened—Mrs Bishop had murdered her husband in that bedstead!

Amelia was the first to speak. In a voice that she hardly recognized as her own she said to Andy: 'I'll get the money and then we'll run away from here.' Andy only nodded; he found himself unable to speak.

Amelia tried the safe and after some searching she must have touched a hidden spring for the door flew open. Inside there were lots of jewellery and piles of gold coins. Neither had ever seen such riches. Greedily Amelia thrust rings on her fingers, bracelets on her wrists and necklaces over her head. In an ecstasy of delight she was dancing round the room when the door opened and Mrs Bishop stood there! Quick as a flash Andy slipped behind the open door. This was the real Mrs Bishop dressed as she had been when she went out a few hours before!

She was livid with rage. She made Amelia remove the jewellery, the hat, the dress, the boots; then catching hold of the girl's wrists in a cruel grip, she pulled her out of the room. Hardly daring to breathe, for Mrs Bishop had not seen him, Andy followed, ever ready to hide should his mistress glance back. But she was too intent on revenge; she took the weeping Amelia out of the house, saying never a word but determined and utterly relentless. Through the bright moonlit streets of Cork they went and Andy saw that they were heading for the river.

Arriving at the banks of the Lee Mrs Bishop did not hesitate. She hustled Amelia towards a small yacht moored close by, and stepping aboard, dragged the terrified girl after her. Frightened but loyal, Andy crept close and through a porthole he saw Mrs Bishop force Amelia on to her knees. Taking a piece of wire Mrs Bishop coiled it round the neck of poor Amelia and drew it tighter and tighter. Rigid with terror Andy watched as Amelia fell lifeless to the floor, realizing in an awful flash of comprehension that Mrs Bishop knew exactly what she was doing. Amelia had no relatives, no friends, no one who would make enquiries about her. In a torment of remorse at not going to her aid, he crept away and fled back to the house. He did not know what to do.

Mrs Bishop returned, composed and acting as though nothing had happened. She told him that Amelia had run away but would probably be back with them soon. Andy just nodded and went on with his work. He spoke to no one until about two weeks later when he told O'Donnell's grandmother, for whom he occasionally ran errands. Unbelieving at first, for Andy's story was incoherent and unconvincing, she at length told the police. They questioned Andy who was still very frightened and his confused and unlikely story was not treated seriously. Nevertheless they saw Mrs Bishop and believed her when she told them that Amelia had run away, a thing she had done once or twice before. No further steps were taken in the matter.

Some weeks later Amelia's body was found in the River Lee, too decomposed to establish how she had met her death other than by drowning; but for years afterwards when the moon was full there were reports of a ghostly figure haunting the banks of the Lee; a poorly-clad young girl in black with a white, bloated face and a very frightened look in her eyes.

Five miles from Cork the square keep of Blarney Castle nestles on a lonely stretch of countryside overlooking the River Marta; its walls eighteen-feet thick and a hundred and twenty feet high, with delightful views of the surrounding country from the top. The well-known Blarney Stone is in fact the sill of one of the machicolated battlements about twenty feet from the summit on the south side. The age-old custom of kissing the stone to acquire irresistible powers of persuasive eloquence, used to be accomplished by dangling head down, one's legs held by a guide. The term 'blarney' was used by Queen Elizabeth I in referring to evasive answers she met from the castle owner at that time, McCarthy Mór, Lord of Muskerry, a descendant of Cormac Laidhir McCarthy who founded in 1446 the earlier castle that once occupied the site. There is an ancient rhyme that tells of the power of the stone:

> There is a stone there
> That whoever kisses,
> Oh, he never misses
> To grow eloquent.
> 'Tis he may clamber
> To a lady's chamber
> Or become a member
> of Parliament.

Derrygonelly, near Enniskillen, CO, FERMANAGH

A farmer's cottage a couple of miles from Derrygonelly was the scene of a number of inexplicable happenings witnessed by Professor Sir William Barrett, F.R.S., an early Member of the Ghost Club (founded in 1862) and a former president of the Society for Psychical Research.

The three-roomed cottage consisted of a large living-room and two bedrooms, one of which was occupied by the farmer and his only son and the other by the farmer's four daughters. The eldest daughter, Maggie, was nearly twenty at the time of the disturbances; she was the apparent focus of the phenomena which generally began after all the occupants had retired to bed for the night.

The first noises were described as rappings and scratchings that sometimes lasted all through the night. Not unnaturally, these sounds were at first blamed on rats and mice but before long articles in the cottage were found to have been moved; boots, clothing, candles and cooking utensils being found outside the cottage in the morning after a night of bangs, raps and inexplicable noises.

The farmer, a Methodist by religion, sought advice and according to directions laid a Bible in the affected bedroom, its pages held open by means of a heavy stone. Far from having the desired effect the stone was lifted off the book and seventeen pages torn out.

Things became so bad that no lamp or candle would remain in the cottage and even a lamp borrowed from a neighbour and specially blessed and sprinkled with holy water by a priest disappeared during the night and was never seen again.

Sir William Barrett visited the cottage with a Mr Thomas Plunkett of Enniskillen and reported: 'After the children, except the boy, had gone to bed, Maggie lay down on the bed without undressing, so that her hands and feet could be observed. The rest of us sat round the kitchen fire, when faint raps, rapidly increasing in loudness, were heard coming apparently from the walls, the ceiling and various parts of the inner room, the door of which was open. On entering the bedroom with a light the noises at first ceased but recommenced when I put the light on the window-sill in the kitchen-cum-livingroom. I had the boy and his father by my side, and asked Mr Plunkett to look round the house outside. Standing in the doorway leading to the affected bedroom, the noises recommenced; the light was gradually brought nearer, and after much patience I was able to bring the light into the bedroom whilst the disturbances were still loudly going on. At last I was able to go up to the side of the bed, with the lighted candle in my hand, and closely observed each of the occupants lying on the bed. The younger children were apparently asleep, and Maggie was motionless; nevertheless, knocks were going on everywhere around, on the chairs,

454

the bedstead, the walls and the ceiling. The closest scrutiny failed to detect any movement on the part of those present that could account for the noises, which were accompanied by a scratching or tearing sound. Suddenly a large pebble fell in my presence on to the bed; no one had moved to dislodge it, even if it had been placed for the purpose. When I replaced the candle on the window-sill of the kitchen, the knocks became still louder, like those made by a heavy carpenter's hammer driving nails into flooring.'

Afterwards Sir William Barrett paid three visits on consecutive nights to the cottage with Mr Plunkett and the Rev. Maxwell Close, M.A., a fellow-member of the Society for Psychical Research. Each time they all heard noises they could not explain although more than once they carried out a complete search of the cottage and garden.

When the farmer told the visitors that sometimes the ghost answered questions by means of raps ('although it tells lies as often as the truth'), Sir William asked *mentally* for a certain number of raps. Immediately the correct number was heard. He repeated this experiment on four occasions, with different numbers and the resulting raps were always the number he had thought of.

The end of the disturbances came when the Rev. Maxwell Close, at the request of the farmer, read some passages from the Bible, followed by the Lord's Prayer, to the accompaniment of many knockings and scratching noises. At first these were so loud that the parson's words could hardly be heard; but gradually the noises became quieter and ceased—and no further trouble was reported.

Dublin, CO. DUBLIN

There is a redbrick Georgian house in the district of Rathmines, occupied by a German professor in 1970 that has long been haunted. The writers James Joyce (1882-1941) and J. M. Synge (1871-1909) were born in the district. But the disturbances seem to be concerned rather with the living than the dead for it has been noticed that unexplained happenings often took place when the professor was absent from

455

the premises. On one occasion he returned home to find the house flooded from burst pipes. Another time electrical wall sockets seemed curiously 'alive' with sparks jumping from them when plugs were inserted, yet nothing happened when an electrician examined them and he could find no fault in the electric circuit.

When the professor, who was a widower, went away on holiday a friend (who was very sceptical of the paranormal) stayed at the house to look after it. He soon became aware of doors all over the house unaccountably opening and closing by themselves. Repeated study and investigation failed to solve the mystery. He also found the house inexplicably cold and often encountered a draught in the most unlikely places.

One night, while reading in bed, he watched with widening eyes as his bedroom door slowly and noiselessly opened. After a moment he got out of bed and closed the door, after ascertaining that nobody was in the house. Making sure that the door was securely shut, he returned to bed. Moments later, as he watched, the door opened again. This continued time after time until the visitor decided to ignore the matter and leaving the door open he went to sleep. In the morning when he awakened it was shut tight.

On his return home the professor related a dream which he felt might have some bearing on the curious happenings at the house. In the dream his wife, who had been dead for some years, appeared with a vividness that haunted him so much that he modelled a statue on the dream appearance; a statue that has a prominent place in the hall of the house to this day—so perhaps the happenings are related to a dead person after all.

St Michan's Church in Church Street is famous for its vaults containing mummified bodies. It is not surprising that there have been occasional reports of strange and inexplicable happenings here.

Most of the accounts are vague but one visitor told me that while she and her husband were being shown the macabre remains, they all heard bursts of incessant loud whispering, as though a number of people were engaged in a violent argument in the dry and still atmosphere. The verger told them that the sounds were heard quite often but no explanation was forthcoming. They gained the impression that it was one of those things that are not discussed. Another visitor maintains that there is one 'mummy' or his ethereal counterpart, that has been seen in several of the family vaults. Certainly, visitors often become confused when they ask about these particular remains and then find that the body is no longer in the position that it had occupied a short time previously.

There are about thirty mummies in open coffins in the vaults of this small and unpretentious church built on the site of an ancient oak forest which, for some obscure reason, has made the air in the vaults incredibly dry. There is row upon row of perfectly preserved bodies, dark brown with age. The coffins often disintegrate but the bodies remain. Some years ago a visitor placed a bunch of flowers near some of the pathetic human remains—and bodies within a distance of six feet started to decay, affected by the water in the flowers.

An old house in Fitzwilliam Square has long been haunted by a ghost known as 'Lady Reid', an entity that is blamed for lost objects, articles that are moved from their accustomed positions and various noises and disturbances for which no rational explanation can be found.

Mrs Burnett Smith (the Scottish writer known as Annie S. Swan) told me that during several visits to the house when it was occupied by family friends, she experienced happenings which she was totally unable to explain and for which the inhabitants of the house invariably blamed 'Lady Reid'.

During the course of one visit Mrs Burnett Smith occupied a bedroom with her hostess and in the night a terrific noise awakened her. She discovered that a Venetian blind had been pulled up. It seemed impossible that it had been done by human hands but Mrs Burnett Smith's hostess was by no means surprised at such happenings, which she said occurred all the time. She merely remarked, 'Oh, it's just Lady Reid,' and went back to sleep.

During the course of her stay on one occasion Mrs Burnett Smith was to learn more about 'Lady Reid's' activities, which she related to me in a calm and detached tone, carrying great conviction and utter acceptance. A blue dinner dress disappeared from a settee and was later found underneath a bed, tightly rolled up and badly creased. One night all the shoes belonging to everyone in the house were moved into one room. Nocturnal noises, for which no explanation was ever discovered, were a common experience. Scores of articles were found moved from their accustomed places, usually during the night. Toilet requisites and dressing-tables seemed to hold a particular attraction for 'Lady Reid'.

The guest-room was particularly plagued and things became so bad at one time that no one would enter it by themselves. Servants, attending to the making of beds in the morning and again, turning down the beds in the evening, would make a point of 'doing' this room in pairs, mounting the stairs to the guest-room hand in hand and crossing themselves at every step. A serious investigation of this room would have been interesting but Mrs Burnett Smith's attempts in this direction on my behalf were unsuccessful. The occupants rather enjoyed their ghost and were reluctant to do anything that might annoy her.

When Number 118 Summerhill was being demolished in 1966 the workmen had considerable trouble with ghosts. Six local men claimed they were persistently kept from completing the demolition. Ultimately they refused to work on the property at all unless they were all together on the same floor—and in daylight. They claimed to have seen the apparition of a tall man on three separate occasions. One of the men, William McGregor, collapsed in a faint when he saw what he described as a tall man wearing a striped shirt. His fellow workman, Mr Joseph Byrne, claimed that he saw a similar figure in the basement, while a Mr Kearney asserted that he had seen the same apparition on three occasions and each time on a different floor of the haunted house.

Elliott O'Donnell once talked to me about a house that used to stand near St Shepherds Grove haunted by the ghost of an unidentified old woman.

The house, it appears, had stood empty for years before a retired colonel rented it furnished for a year, although it had neither gas nor electricity. Colonel Ward's wife and children moved in early one December and it was arranged that the colonel, who had some business to attend to abroad, would join them as soon as he could; certainly in time for the family to spend Christmas together in their new home.

A few days after they had moved into the house Mrs Ward was quietly doing some embroidery in front of the fire one evening when the children were in bed. Suddenly she was surprised to hear a sharp rap on the front door. Wondering who it could possibly be, she listened carefully, recalling that it was the servants' day off. After a moment there was another knock, sharp and somehow authoritative, sounding as though it was made with bare knuckles.

Mrs Ward put her embroidery on one side and answered the door. Standing on the step was an old woman wearing a lace mob-cap and dressed in strangely old-fashioned clothes. She was ugly, even repulsive. Mrs Ward was about to shut the door in her face, for the old woman had said not a word but simply peered into the house behind her. Now she quickly raised a skinny hand in a menacing fashion, leered stupidly, pushed past Mrs Ward and ran across the hall and up the stairs with remarkable agility for someone of her apparent age. Startled, Mrs Ward watched her as she seemed to enter one of the maids' rooms; deciding that she must be a friend or relative of the servant, she closed the door and went back to her embroidery.

Next day Colonel Ward arrived and the same night he sat up late, working on some papers. It was past midnight when he picked up a candle and went into the hall on his way upstairs to bed. As he was about to mount the first step he thought he heard a movement from the direction of the front door. Turning, he found himself face to face with the old hag whom his wife had seen the previous evening. He said afterwards that an odd light seemed to envelop the figure and her pale old eyes seemed to glow maliciously as they met the colonel's surprised gaze.

'Who are you?' demanded the colonel, thrusting the candle towards the woman, but she made no reply and suddenly rushed past him, leering in his face as she did so and ran up the stairs. Near a bend in the stairway she paused, turned, shook a fist at the colonel, turned away from him and vanished. The colonel searched carefully everywhere but could find no trace of the mysterious figure.

The following day Mrs Ward's brother, Jack Deane,

arrived from Sandhurst to spend Christmas in Dublin. That evening he saw the old woman, whom he took to be a servant, as he was carrying his boots to the kitchen to be cleaned. When he addressed the woman, she stared back insolently at him and did not answer so he tossed a boot towards her, saying, 'Here, clean these, I said.' To his astonishment the boot appeared to pass clean through the woman. He threw the other boot and the same thing happened. Hardly able to believe his eyes, Jack took a step towards the woman whereupon she slowly disappeared as he watched.

As soon as he saw his sister next morning Jack said he thought he must have been overdoing it at Sandhurst and must be suffering from hallucinations. Only then did Mrs Ward tell him that both she and her husband had seen the same figure and were equally unable to account for her appearance or disappearance.

Next day all three were in the hall in the evening discussing the party they had arranged for the children the following day when they heard rattling sounds of glass and china. They had previously laid out the china and glasses on a table in the drawing-room and they all hastened there to see what was happening. As they opened the door they were startled by a tremendous crashing sound. They could do nothing but stand in the doorway and watch as all the china and glass on the table slid to the floor and smashed upon itself.

As they looked round the room they were amazed to see, lying on the floor by the fireplace, the hideous sight of the body of a boy aged about twelve years, almost covered in blood. Bending over the body, a look of murderous triumph on her face, was a young woman, dressed in clothes of a bygone age, her jewellery and gold ornaments glittering in the weird and inexplicable light that played over the whole scene, while to one side crouched the old hag, leering and swaying backwards and forwards with glee; a devilish and nauseating scene. As the three people stood horror-stricken in the doorway, the whole room darkened, the figures disappeared and an uncanny silence reigned.

Although it was Christmas, next day the Wards moved out of that haunted house.

Haunted Lough Derg, Co. Tipperary. Those who have met the unidentified ghosts here or heard faint voices and music from the still waters have never forgotten the experience. *Photo: Irish Tourist Board*

Lough Derg near Killaloe, Co. Clare, haunted by a phantom boat on still moonlit nights, and several indefinite and wispy figures who haunt the quiet places of this still lake. *Photo: Irish Tourist Board*

The remains of Aughnanure Castle, Oughterard, Co. Galway, where banshees wail before the death of an O'Flaherty chief. *Photo: Irish Tourist Board*

Lough Gur Castle, Co. Limerick where the last Earl of Desmond appears once every seven years mounted on a coal-black horse. *Photo: Irish Tourist Board*

Eringle Truagh, CO. MONAGHAN

The old church has long disappeared and only a couple of ivy-covered gables remained a few years ago to mark the site of the churchyard that was famous for its 'phantom of death'.

William Carleton (1794-1869) the Irish novelist, youngest of fourteen children of a farmer, who acquired an insight into the ideas and feelings of Irish peasantry that has never been equalled, became interested in the haunting, visited Eringle Truagh and wrote afterwards:

> I have been shown the grave of a young person about eighteen years of age, who was said about four months before to have fallen a victim to the phantom, and it is not more than ten weeks since a man in the same parish declared that he gave a promise and fatal kiss to the ghost and consequently looked upon himself as lost. He took a fever and was buried on the day appointed for the meeting, which was exactly a month from the time of his contact with the spirit. Incredulous as it may seem the friends of these two persons declared, at least those of the young man did, to myself that particulars of the meetings with the phantom were detailed repeatedly by the two persons without variation. There are several other cases of the same kind mentioned, but the two alluded to are the only ones that came within my personal knowledge.

The centuries-old tradition that this churchyard was haunted by a handsome young person is one of the most interesting cases of haunting in the annals of Irish ghost-lore. The phantom of death usually appeared in the churchyard and only after the funeral of an inhabitant of Eringle Truagh. To men the phantom appeared as a beautiful young girl and to girls as a handsome young man.

Through all the scores of reports of the appearance of this phantom runs a strikingly similar story. A man or woman, present at the burial of a local person, would linger on in the churchyard after everyone else had left, thinking perhaps

461

to delay for a little while the last parting from someone near or dear to them.

Suddenly they would be confronted by a strikingly beautiful girl (or if it was a woman by a singularly handsome man). In either case the stranger would show the mourner great sympathy and comfort by assuring the bereaved that the dead person was far happier than he or she would have been had they lived. Gradually the sympathetic words and actions would console the sad mourner. As the two progressed towards the church and then sat side by side in the porch or on the low churchyard wall in the dying sunlight, the magnetic attraction of the mysterious comforter would begin to work its power. From a gentle hand clasp to an arm around the shoulder, from a gentle squeeze of the waist to a light kiss and before long the couple would forget everything but themselves. Alone together in the dusk passionate embraces would follow one after the other until, almost as in a dream, they would make desperate and wonderful love together in the deserted churchyard.

Afterwards, as they promised eternal love for each other, a pact would be made to meet again in the churchyard four weeks hence. After a lingering kiss, the former mourner would depart in a quandary of sadness and happiness. If he, or she, should chance to look back they would see no sign of the mysterious and beautiful lover. Perhaps then, but only then, would they recall the awful story of the traditional phantom of death in Eringle Truagh churchyard; wide-eyed and panic-stricken, they would rush to relatives, friends, and the parish priest, imploring for something to be done to save them.

But neither prayers, nor the love and friendship of any mortal could save them. The shock that they had suffered and the suspense of waiting for the four weeks to pass would make them ill; they would fade and die and, on the very date that they had pledged to meet the phantom, they would be taken to the churchyard in a coffin.

There are a few records of the phantom appearing outside the churchyard at weddings, christenings and dances. But always the last kiss sealed a promise to meet in the churchyard four weeks hence—and always the promise was kept by the mortal arriving on the agreed day, for burial.

Giant's Causeway, CO. ANTRIM

This impressive promontory of closely packed greyish-brown basalt columns, the result of crystallization of molten lava thrown up during a volcanic eruption in the Tertiary period, is one of the natural wonders of the world.

There are in all some 40,000 hexagonal and pentagonal columns, perfectly articulated by means of convex and concave joints and the causeway extends almost half a mile into the sea. The bright red bands in the cliffs represent quiescent periods between volcanic eruptions.

The legendary origin of the Giant's Causeway suggests that it was built by Finn M'Coul or Fingal as a bridge between Ireland and Scotland for the giants of those days to cross from Antrim to Staffa, where Fingal's Cave on the Hebridean island has a similar fantastically old and primitive atmosphere.

In this area of ruined castles, high towering cliffs and bays that are the graveyards of many stout ships (including at least one vessel from the Spanish Armada) it is not surprising that there are stories of strange mutterings and indistinct words being heard suddenly for a moment and then fading away with the wind. There are weirdly loud and echoing footsteps, heard when they are least expected. Some of the feaures of the Causeway: the Wishing Well, the Giant's Organ, the Wishing Chair, Lord Antrim's Parlour, the Lady's Fan, the Mitre and the Coffin, are said to change shape inexplicably at night and disappear occasionally altogether for a while.

Kilkenny City, CO. KILKENNY

This city on the River Nore, once divided into two districts, Englishtown and Irishtown, has a thirteenth-century cathedral, ruins of a Dominican and of a Franciscan monastery, a college attended by satirist Jonathan Swift (1667-1745)— and a ghostly woman on crutches.

This singular figure, tall and thin, wears a long coat, no stockings and has long, white, flowing hair. She has been seen repeatedly in the vicinity of St John's Parochial Hall. A young nurse and her boyfriend saw the figure pass their parked car in May 1967, after they were alerted by a barking dog. As the figure passed they were able to see it clearly, although they could not distinguish the face. A moment later the road was deserted. Frightened, the couple drove a short distance along the road and when they stopped again the same figure appeared, passed the car again—and promptly disappeared.

Other witnesses for the strange figure include a priest and a local couple who have seen the apparition on a number of occasions, usually in the springtime.

Killarney, CO. KERRY

The Irish hero O'Donoghue is said to haunt this world-renowned beauty spot, beloved by Scott, Wordsworth, Tennyson and Thackeray, mounted on his favourite white horse.

At dawn each May 1st his ghost is reputed to glide over the waters of Lough Leane, preceded by groups of youths and maidens who scatter wreaths of spring flowers in his path.

Among a number of legends associated with the lake and the O'Donoghues, there is one concerning a beautiful young girl who became so completely possessed by her love for the visionary chieftain and his snow-white steed that, sick with love for the unattainable, she threw herself, one May-day dawn, into the lough so that she might join him.

The legend is immortalized in Thomas Moore's 'O'Donoghue's Mistress':

> Of all the fair months, that round the sun
> In light-linked dance their circles run,
> Sweet May, sweet May, shine thou for me!
> For still when they earliest beams arise,
> That youth who beneath the blue lake lies,
> Sweet May, sweet May, returns to me.

Of all the smooth lakes, where daylight leaves
His lingering smile on golden eaves,
Fair lake, fair lake, thou'rt dear to me;
For when the last April sun grows dim,
Thy Naiads prepare his steed for him
Who dwells, who dwells, bright lake, in thee.

Of all the proud steeds that ever bare
Young plumèd chiefs on sea or shore,
White steed, white steed, most joy to thee,
Who still, with the first young glance of spring,
From under that glorious lake dost bring,
Proud steed, proud steed, my love to me.

While white as the sail some bark unfurls,
When newly launched, thy long mane curls,
Fair steed, fair steed, as white and free;
And spirits from all the lake's deep bowers
Glide o'er the blue wave scattering flowers,
Fair steed, around my love and thee.

Of all the sweet deaths that maidens die,
Whose lovers beneath the cold waves lie,
Most sweet, most sweet that death will be,
Which under the next May evenings' light,
When thou and thy steed are lost to sight,
Dear love, dear love, I'll die for thee.

There is a statue of Thomas Moore (1779-1852) in the centre of Dublin City. And the Killarney boatmen still refer to the crested waves that rise from time to time upon the lough as 'O'Donoghue's white horses'.

Kinsale, CO. CORK

This picturesque little port, a maze of narrow streets and steep passages, has a rocky coast with a lighthouse which is the first sight of Britain for ships coming from the United States of America. Here the *Lusitania* was sunk in 1915 and three of the victims are buried in the churchyard, including an unidentified woman.

Charles, or Kinsale, Fort is one of the first examples of military architecture in the world; it dates from 1677, and it is haunted by a 'White Lady'.

The traditional story of the origin of the haunting concerns a certain Colonel Warrender, a man known for his severe disciplinarian outlook. Warrender was appointed governor soon after the fort was built. He had a daughter, a girl with the unusual Christian name of 'Wilful' who became engaged to be married to a Sir Trevor Ashurst. On the evening of their wedding day, as they strolled along the battlements of the fort, hand in hand, in the still, warm evening, Wilful pointed to some unusual flowers growing on the rocks below the fort. As they passed a sentry the young bride expressed a wish to have the flowers. The sentry, smiling at the newly-weds, volunteered to climb down and pick the flowers, if Sir Trevor would take his place while he did so.

Eager to please his bride Sir Trevor quickly buttoned on the sentry's coat and took his musket while the soldier went in search of a rope to lower himself over the side of the fort. Having secured his line the soldier disappeared over the parapet and Sir Trevor took up sentry duty. Time passed and Wilful began to complain of the chilly night air. Sir Trevor knew that he must wait for the return of the soldier but his young bride went inside to their apartment. Still the sentry did not return and Sir Trevor, heavy with exhaustion after a tiring day and the jollification of the occasion, soon dozed off to sleep.

He was still asleep when the governor made one of his accustomed rounds of the sentries and receiving no answer to his challenge, he perceived that the man was asleep, whereupon he drew a pistol and shot his son-in-law through the heart.

As soon as she learned of the fate that had overtaken her husband, the distracted bride rushed from the apartment and threw herself over the battlements. On learning of the double tragedy her father shot himself during that awful night.

Over the years there has been some variation in the details of the story. Other accounts give the governor's name as

Browne; the initial victim as the governor's son and date the affair around the middle of the eighteenth century. All agree, however, that the ghostly White Lady has its origin in the suicide of a young bride on her wedding day and there are many reports of the sighting of this ghost.

After service in the Peninsular War of 1808-14 a certain Major Black became Fort Major at Kinsale. He related an experience which befell him to a number of his friends and to his physician, Dr Craig, who published the story in *Real Pictures of Clerical Life in Ireland*.

One summer evening Major Black went to the hall door of his apartment at Charles Fort and was astounded to see a lady enter through the doorway and walk up the stairs. At first he thought she must be the wife of an officer who had somehow entered the wrong apartment, but as he looked closely at her mounting the stairs without making a sound, he observed that she was dressed entirely in white, in a very old-fashioned style. Filled with curiosity but with never a thought of anything ghostly, he hurried upstairs and followed her within seconds into one of the bedrooms; yet on entering the room he could not find the slightest trace of anyone. Only then did he recall the story of the mysterious White Lady, reputed to have long haunted Charles Fort.

On another occasion Major Black recounted that two of his sergeants were packing some articles for him. One of the men had his little daughter with him and the child suddenly asked: 'Who is that White Lady bending over the banisters and looking down at us?' The two men looked up and saw nothing but the child insisted that she had seen a young lady, dressed all in white, smiling down at her.

Some years later a married staff officer and his wife, living in the apartments known as the 'Governor's House', were awakened by their children's nurse who had been sleeping in a room adjoining the apartment known as the 'White Lady's Room'. The nurse said she had been lying awake, listening to the children's deep and regular breathing when she suddenly saw the figure of a lady clothed in white glide noiselessly from the direction of the White Lady's Room towards the cot containing the youngest child. After gazing

467

at the child for a moment, the figure placed its hand upon the child's wrist, wherepon it immediately started and cried out: 'Take your cold hand from my wrist!' The next moment the White Lady disappeared.

About a hundred years ago a certain Captain Marvell Hull and his friend, Lieutenant Hartland, were on their way to the captain's room for a drink together. As they reached a small landing on the staircase they both saw in front of them a woman in a white dress. A moment before she had not been there and they had heard no sound. Startled by the sudden and inexplicable appearance, the two officers stopped in their tracks, whereupon the figure turned, looked at them, then passed them silently and disappeared through a locked door. Afterwards they said that the face was that of a beautiful young woman, but colourless and with a corpselike appearance.

Fifty or so years ago a surgeon had a more terrifying experience. He had quarters at the fort and returned from snipe-shooting as the fort mess bugle rang out. He hastened to his rooms to change but when he failed to appear for the meal, one of his brother officers went in search of him and found him lying senseless at the bottom of the steps leading to his rooms. On recovering consciousness he related that as he hurriedly stooped down to retrieve the key of his door, which he kept under the mat, he felt himself dragged violently across the hall and flung down a flight of steps. As he fell, he caught sight of a white figure which he thought looked like a woman in a wedding-dress.

Not long after the surgeon's experience a Captain Jarves was puzzled one evening to hear a strange rattling noise as he approached his bedroom at the fort and he caught a glimpse of a white figure hurrying away. When he attempted to open the bedroom door to see what was happening, it seemed to be locked and he could not open it. Thinking that some of his brother officers were playing a joke on him, he called out and tried to force the door inwards. At this a gust of wind suddenly passed him and some unseen power flung him down the stairs where he lay senseless for some time.

In recent years visitors have reported seeing a vague white form in the vicinity of Charles Fort, especially on still summer evenings; a form that disappears almost as soon as one becomes aware that it is there.

Lough Derg, ON THE BORDERS OF CO. CLARE, CO. GALWAY AND CO. TIPPERARY

The lowest and the largest of the great lakes formed by the River Shannon. It is said to be haunted by several ghosts; indefinite, wispy figures from the past who have never been identified but those who meet such forms along the shores of this beautiful lake never forget the encounters.

The lake is also said to have a phantom boat which always travels northwards, with the sound of its oars dipping the water and faint voices and music plainly audible to passers-by on dark nights, when the boat itself is not visible. Those who have seen the boat, on still moonlit nights, have always said that it appeared to be deserted although the rhythmic oars carried it swiftly over the deep and dark waters. Once an Englishman, seeing the strange boat with no visible being aboard, threw a stone at it—whereupon the stone was thrown back at him with great violence. He also heard peals of mocking laughter which frightened him so that he fled and has never since returned to the haunted lake.

Lough Gur, CO. LIMERICK

A pretty lake where, according to legend, the last of the Desmonds holds eternal court beneath the waves, emerging every seventh year on a silver-shod steed. On the banks of the lake there are castles and cramogs, dolmens, circles and raths; it is an area much associated with the distant past and perhaps it is not to be wondered at that some faint remnants of bygone ages linger in this beautiful and unspoilt spot.

It is said that the last Earl of Desmond, as famed for his magical practises as for his doughty deeds in battle, one day brought his young and lovely bride to his castle. Being as innocent as she was beautiful and ignorant of the forces of magic she came one morning to the chamber where her husband studied and practised the black arts, imploring him to let her see some of the wonders which he said he could perform. For a time he refused but he was much in love and could deny his young bride nothing for very long; so eventually he agreed but warned her that whatever happened she was not to speak or utter a sound. She gave him her solemn promise and with a last warning gesture he moved into the centre of the chamber, muttered an incantation—and feathers sprouted thickly all over him. His face contracted and became hooked, his head shrank, his arms disappeared; the air became filled with a cadaverous smell and in the place of her husband, a huge vulture rose in his place. It swept round the room on heavy, beating wings, threatening every now and then to pounce with its great claws and beak. But still, with tremendous effort, the Countess remained still and calm and she uttered not a sound. The vulture alighted on the floor near the door, ruffed up its feathers, shook itself, shrank and then swelled in a peculiar way; the next moment a hideous and horribly deformed hag crouched in its place, the flabby and discoloured skin hanging about her face, with thin, yellow hair and great bloodshot eyes. Dwarfish in stature, she waddled towards the Countess on tiny, thick crutches, her toothless mouth slobbering, her grimaces and contortions becoming more and more frightening as she approached. Suddenly, a few feet from the Countess (still by superhuman effort keeping motionless and silent) the hag gave a screech and collapsed on the floor.

No sooner had she done so than she turned into an enormous snake, rising up and towering over the Countess, seemingly about to strike at any moment. At the instant that the creature struck the snake changed into her husband who stood before his wife, a finger to his lips, motioning her to remain silent. He then lay full length on the floor and began to stretch himself from the waist: his legs and lower trunk slithered at alarming speed away from the rest of his body while his head and chest drew away in the opposite direction until his feet touched one end of the chamber and his head the other. As his head rolled and seemed about to become detached from his body the Countess's fortitude gave way and she screamed with every ounce of her strength. Immeditely the walls slid downwards, the whole edifice sank into Lough Gur and the dark waters closed over the castle.

One night in every seven years the ghost of the last Earl of Desmond—and some say his lovely wife, too—emerge from their watery grave. Mounted on a coal-black horse they ride back and forth across the waters with the silver shoes of the horse shining in the moonlight. As dawn breaks, they plunge back into the depths of Lough Gur for another seven years and they are doomed to return again and again until the silver shoes of their steed wear out.

Oughterard, CO. GALWAY

Nearby are the ruins of the principal stronghold of the O'Flahertys, Aughnanure Castle. This family was such a scourge in the Middle Ages that the whole area of the rock-bound uplands of Iar Connacht was known as the country of the Flahertys. Over the west gate of Galway City stood the inscription: 'From the fury of the O'Flahertys Good Lord deliver us.'

The great banqueting hall and keep tower of Aughnanure Castle date from the sixteenth century. It is from here that an O'Flaherty was setting out one night on a foraging expedition when he heard the family banshee singing sadly from one of the castle turrets. He said nothing to his wife but the following night she, too, heard the lament. Two days later her husband's body was brought back to the castle; he had been killed in a clan feud. Here too, it is said, several banshees were heard singing sorrowfully before the death of the wife of an O'Flaherty clan chief.

Portlaw, CO. WATERFORD

Curraghmore House, to the west, is the seat of the Marquess of Waterford and memorial to the famous legend of 'The Tyrone Ghost'. A manuscript account of the tale, firmly accepted by successive generations, is preserved at Curraghmore. It was written by the Lady Elizabeth Cobb, grand-

471

daughter of the Lady Beresford to whom Lord Tyrone is said to have appeared after his death.

Lady Beresford's son, Lord Tyrone, and her daughter, Lady Riverston (who both died in 1763) were with their mother at the time of her death. They removed from her wrist the black tape which she had worn on all occasions and at all times, even at Court, a fact repeatedly vouched for by witnesses. There existed for many years an oil painting of this Lady Beresford at Tyrone House, Dublin, with a black ribbon visible on one wrist. This painting, incidentally, disappeared in a peculiar manner. It hung, with other family portraits, in the main drawing-room at Tyrone House and when Henry, Marquis of Waterford, sold the family's town residence to the Government, he arranged for Mr Watkins, a well-known dealer in pictures, to collect the paintings and objets d'art for removal to Curraghmore. Mr Watkins was interested in the legend and saw to it that this particular picture was carefully packed for transportation. When the consignment was received at Curraghmore, however, the picture had disappeared and in spite of considerable exertions and inquiries on the part of Mr Watkins and the Tyrone family, it has not been located to this day.

John le Poer, Lord Decies (1665-1693) succeeded as Lord Tyrone in 1690 and is the ghost of the story. This Lord Tyrone made a serious pact with Nicola Hamilton, the daughter of Hugh, Lord Glenawley (who married Sir Tristram Beresford in 1687) that whichever of them should die first, would—if possible—appear to the other with the object of proving life after death.

In October 1693 Sir Tristram and Lady Beresford were visiting the latter's sister, Lady MacGill at Gill Hall. One morning Sir Tristram rose early leaving Lady Beresford asleep and went for a walk before breakfast. On his return his wife joined him and their hostess but she seemed agitated and embarrassed. Her husband asked after her health and questioned her as to what had happened to her wrist which he and others present had noticed was tied up with black ribbon. Lady Beresford implored her husband and others not to question her, either then or later about the reason she wore the ribbon, adding, 'You will never more see me without it.'

472

After breakfast she was anxious to know whether the post had arrived. It had not and Sir Tristram asked her whether she was expecting any particular letter that day. She replied that she expected to hear of Lord Tyrone's death, which she felt certain had taken place on the previous Tuesday.

Sir Tristram concluded that his wife must have had a vivid dream and said so, adding that he had never considered her to be a superstitious person but perhaps he should now revise his opinion!

Within minutes a servant brought in the post including one envelope sealed with black wax. 'As I expected,' exclaimed Lady Beresford, 'he is dead.' The letter was from Lord Tyrone's steward to inform them that his master had died in Dublin on Tuesday, October 14th, at 4 p.m.

Sir Tristram consoled his wife, distraught at the news and yet somehow relieved and easier now that her uncertainty had become fact. She then told her husband that she was with child, adding that she would have a son. A boy was born the following July; Sir Tristram survived the birth by only a few years.

Lady Beresford continued to reside, with her young family, at their home in Co. Derry. She seldom went out and had few friends, with the exception of a Mr and Mrs Jackson of Coleraine. Mr Jackson was a leading local citizen and, through his mother, related to Sir Tristram. Mrs Jackson was descended from Sir Adam Lofters, and a relation of theirs, Richard Gorges, married Lady Beresford some three years later, in 1704.

They had a son and two daughters before his wild and dissolute conduct forced Lady Beresford to seek a separation which she obtained. Four years later her husband, then General Gorges, expressed repeated regret for his misdeeds. On the strength of solemn promises for the future, Lady Beresford agreed to his return and she became the mother of another boy. A month after the birth of this infant, on the occasion of Lady Beresford's birthday, she sent for her eldest son, Sir Marcus Beresford, then twenty years old and her married daughter Lady Riverston. She also invited Dr King, archbishop of Dublin (an old friend) and the elderly clergyman who had christened her and who had always maintained a kindly interest in her life.

During the course of conversation with the clergyman Lady Beresford remarked that she was forty-eight that day, whereupon her old friend said 'no' she was forty-seven. He went on to say that Lady Beresford's mother had a discussion with him once about her daughter's age and he consulted the registry; so he could say with complete certainty that she was forty-seven that day. This news brought consternation to Lady Beresford who told her friend that what he had said was in effect a death warrant. She implored him to leave her for she was convinced that she did not have long to live and had a number of things to settle before she died. She asked for her son and daughter to be sent to her immediately.

When her two children were in her presence Lady Beresford told them that she had something of great importance to communicate—before she died. She reminded her son and daughter of the friendship and affection that existed in their early life between Lord Tyrone and herself. She revealed the pact they had made that whichever of the two died first should, if possible, appear to the other as proof of life after death. One night, Lady Beresford said, many years after this, she was sleeping with the children's father at Gill Hall when she suddenly found herself awake and saw Lord Tyrone sitting on her side of the bed. Lord Tyrone told her that he had died the previous Tuesday at four o'clock and said he had been permitted to appear to assure her of the truth of life after death. He was further allowed to inform her that she was with child and would produce a son who would marry an heiress, that Sir Tristram would not live long and that she would re-marry and die from the effects of child-bearing in her forty-seventh year.

Lady Beresford begged Lord Tyrone for some convincing sign or proof of his presence so that in the morning she would know that it had not been a dream; whereupon Lord Tyrone hooked up the bed hangings in an unusual manner through an iron hook and wrote his signature in her pocket book. But still she was not satisfied and, after she had asked for still more substantial proof, placed his hand, which was as cold as marble, on her wrist for a moment and immediately the

474

sinews shrank and the nerves withered at the touch. Warning her never to let anyone see the mark, Lord Tyrone vanished. In the morning, after Sir Tristram had gone for an early walk, Lady Beresford arose and with great difficulty succeeded in unhooking the bed curtains. She bound up her wrist with black ribbon and went down to breakfast, quite certain that Lord Tyrone was indeed dead and had visited her that night. She stated that under the impression she had passed her forty-seventh birthday, she had consented to a reconciliation with her husband but now that she knew she was only forty-seven that day, she was certain she was about to die. She instructed her two children, after her death, to unbind the black ribbon and look at her wrist before it was consumed in her coffin.

An hour later Lady Beresford was dead and after everyone had left the bedroom, her son and daughter untied the black ribbon and found their mother's wrist to be exactly as she had described it; the nerves withered and the sinews shrunk. She was buried by her clergyman friend in the Cathedral of St Patrick, Dublin, in the Earl of Cork's tomb, where she lies to this day.

Lady Beresford's son Sir Marcus later married Lord Tyrone's daughter and both he and his sister always swore to the truth of the story for the rest of their lives. Lady Elizabeth Cobb, grand-daughter of Lady Beresford, preserved both the ribbon and the notebook with the signature of a ghost, for many years at her home in Bath.

Randalstown, NEAR ANTRIM, CO. ANTRIM

During the summer months there are motorboat trips from Antrim, with its beautiful French garden and one of the only two complete Round Towers in Ulster, to Shane's Castle by Lough Neagh. This is the largest inland lake in the British Isles; the waters are reputed to have petrifying qualities and pieces of fossilized wood are often to be found on its shores.

Sixteenth-century Shane's Castle was built on the site of the Castle of Edenduffcarrick, mentioned in the Annals of

Ulster under the date of 1470 and destroyed in 1490. Shane's Castle was the ancient stronghold of Shane O'Neill of the O'Neills of Clandeboye and the estate is still owned by Lord O'Neill. Although most of the later castle was destroyed by fire in 1922, a fine square tower still exists and in the remaining south wall, about thirty feet from the ground there is the sculptured head known as the Black Head of the O'Neills. For centuries there has been a tradition that if this head should be injured, the O'Neill family would come to an end.

The O'Neills have a banshee which has been known to appear at Shane's Castle in the form of a beautiful young woman, seen in one particular room at the castle, pacing to and fro, wringing her hands in sadness and singing a soulful lament. Such an appearance invariably heralded the death of the member of the O'Neill family who heard the banshee wailing. It is related that a young O'Neill once heard the singing voice just before he set out on a long journey; a few days later he ran into an unexpected skirmish and was killed.

Rathfarnham, CO. DUBLIN

The pond in the grounds of the old castle is haunted by the ghost of a dog.

In the severe winter of 1840-41 a skating party was enjoying the seasonal weather. Among the skaters was a man who had with him a 'very fine curly-coated retriever dog', and the animal seemed to be enjoying the fun as much as its master. At the height of the sport the ice gave way and the man disappeared into the freezing water. Without hesitation the dog went after his master but both man and dog were drowned.

A monument was erected to perpetuate the dog's heroic self-sacrifice and although today no more than the pedestal remains, the ghost of the faithful dog haunts the grounds of the castle; its form has also been seen many times on the public road between the gates of the sixteenth-century castle and Dodder Bridge.

Rathlin Island, CO. ANTRIM

Five miles north of Ballycastle, across a tide-race that can often be treacherous and is always exciting, this island, shaped like 'an Irish stocking', has seen many historical events. Now its massive cliffs offer sanctuary to numerous sea birds.

The island has often served as a stepping-stone between Scotland and Ireland. One of Marconi's early successful attempts at radio communication took place between Ballycastle and Rathlin and there is a cave near the lighthouse which has long been regarded as the place where Robert the Bruce (1274-1329, King of Scotland) had his famous encounter with a spider. The king's body was buried at Dunfermline, his heart at Melrose.

There are those who maintain that the ghost of Robert Bruce has been glimpsed, motionless, at the shadowy far end of a cave on Rathlin Island where, reputedly, he so often silently meditated during his lifetime. If his ghost has been seen here, it is such an indistinct, wispy, half-materialization that no witness is entirely sure whether shadows and uncertain light cannot account for what they have seen.

Skerries, CO. DUBLIN

A few miles inland there is a field, part of a large estate, that has not been cultivated or used since time immemorial. It comprises a clearing in the centre of a luxurious plantation and it has been suggested that the trees were originally planted to conceal the unused and unusable land.

In the centre of the field there is a very large depression which extends to an area of some forty square yards and has a depth of about two feet. Legend has it that in the very early days of Christianity in Ireland a devout and holy woman and her selected followers had a foundation here. The woman was called Maeve or Mavoe or Mevee (referred to in those days as Saint Mevee) and her establishment were known for their piety and goodness and for the many miracles for which they

477

are said to have been responsible, miracles that made the very ground here hallowed and secret.

Years passed and the well-loved foundation of Sister Mevee was no more than a memory when the land passed into the possession of a man who laughed at local awe and superstition concerning the holy field.

Time and again he was quietly warned against desecrating the soil but undeterred he put plough to it and began to work, repeating a mocking ditty as he strode across the virgin soil: 'Saint Mevee or Saint Mavoe, I'll plough this up before I go.' Hardly had he reached the centre of the field before the ground opened and swallowed him, together with the horse and plough, closing over them, leaving the depression in the untilled field that can be seen to this day.

Strabane, CO. TYRONE

The railway station here has (or had) a ghost that was seen by many local workmen.

One report described the appearance of the ghost to three people two nights running. The three men, named Pinkerton, Madden and Oliphant, were working in the engine house one October night when, soon after midnight, they heard a tremendous knocking noise which seemed to come from all the doors of the workshop, accompanied by unearthly and blood-curdling yells and screams. They went to one of the doors and wrenched it open and saw there the form of a massive man, staring at them. They shouted for help and a nearby signalman came running to their aid, armed with a crowbar. He made a dash at the figure but even his crowbar had no effect and the mysterious form hovered about the shed until shortly after two-thirty in the morning. All four men swore that they had seen the figure in good moonlight and inside the workshop; they were so terrified towards the end of the experience that they climbed up on to the engine they were supposed to be cleaning and hid on the roof until the form disappeared.

Next night the same figure appeared at one-thirty in the morning. On this occasion Oliphant, determined to discover whether the figure was material, succeeded in approaching to within a couple of yards of the form, but when the 'ghost' uttered terrible yells he collapsed. Pinkerton tried to continue with his work but the frightening figure drifted towards him and gazed into his face so that Pinkerton fell against the engine in his fright. Seven workmen saw the 'ghost' and afterwards found that their clothes, tools and personal belongings had all been thrown about the engine house.

One of the other engine-cleaners stated that once he saw the 'ghost' run up a ladder leading to a water-tank, where it disappeared; another said he thought it seemed to disappear through a window, high up near the ceiling of the workshop.

It was discovered that many years earlier a man had been murdered near the spot where the ghost first appeared. But no description of the murder victim seems to have been obtained so it is difficult to say whether this tragedy had any connection with the figure of a heavily-built man that was repeatedly seen—on one occasion by seven witnesses.

Tuamgraney, CO. CLARE

In this wild and romantic mountain country, where you can still walk for a day without meeting a living soul, there is a small lake known as Tier McBran. Great cliffs rise sheer from the water's edge and on the summit of one bluff there are the ruins of an old castle. The lake itself has long been a mystery for no visible streams flow into it or out of it and it has never been fully explained where its constant water comes from. It is also said to be unfathomable and there is a strange legend associated with these still waters.

Before recorded history when the Fians, a legendary band of warriors, are said to have roamed these parts, a chieftain was out hunting one day when he saw a beautiful white hart suddenly emerge from a shrubbery, its horns and hooves gleaming like gold. Spotting the hunting chieftain it fled like the wind. He and his fellow huntsmen pursued it, hour after hour, losing sight of the creature and then finding it again. On and on went the hunt and one by one the followers gave up in exhaustion until only the chieftain and his favourite hound Bran remained, following the elusive and apparently tireless hart.

Just as the sun was setting, the hart was trapped on a high cliff overlooking the lake. As the delighted chieftain went forward for the kill, the little white hart paused for a moment, took a last look at its tormentor, and then leaped down and vanished into the green waters far below. Without hesitation Bran followed it and the chieftain looked down to see what had happened. Astounded, he saw that the hart had changed into a lovely golden-haired girl dressed in white who caught hold of Bran and sank with him to the unknown depths of the lake.

Thereafter the lake was always regarded as being haunted and few people ventured there after nightfall or even dared to fish in daylight. There are those who maintain to this day that they have seen a giant hunting hound poised on the cliff edge at sunset, a hound that vanished as the sun disappeared beyond the horizon. The cliff from which Bran sprang is known to this day as Craig-a-Bran.

There is a wooded hollow near Tuamgraney (with its interesting twelfth-century church) where many visitors and local people have reported curious happenings often at the end of October, around Hallowe'en.

It is a wild and unspoilt part of the country, fascinating and primitive, yet imparting to the visitor a feeling of awe and foreboding. An air of expectancy seems to linger here and stories of phantom forests and weird experiences abound.

There is, for example, the story of a young man who lived at Tuamgraney and who had once or twice found himself in the vicinity of this strange wooded hollow. But he always became depressed and unusually conscious of himself, so that he invariably turned aside and travelled another way.

One afternoon, however, he determined to walk through the hollow. It was a lush October day, the countryside full of autumn beauty. The place seemed peaceful enough and as he entered the hollow and began to descend through the quiet trees, he thought to himself that he did not feel the acute oppression that he had always noticed when he had been there before.

Suddenly, almost as though he had passed from this world

480

into another, he experienced an overwhelming feeling of sadness and something like terror. He stopped and almost turned back but as he was determined this time to walk through the haunted place, keeping an eye on every tree and bush around him, he cautiously went forward, suddenly realizing that he was walking almost on tip-toe as though not to disturb something. As he plunged deeper and deeper into the wood he noticed that there were no birds—in fact no sound at all. He felt as though he were the only person alive in the world.

Still he walked warily on, deeper and deeper into the dim hollow, forcing his way through tall grass and bushes. Then he noticed that the overgrown path ahead of him was bathed in a pale light. He stopped for a moment, uncertain what to do. He couldn't understand where the pale but distinct light was coming from. As he stood still the silence seemed to close in on him and he became conscious of the fact that he had been making the only sounds he had heard for some time. Evening had fallen quickly and there was no moon. Nor was there any hooting of owls, no fluttering of wings, no rustling of grass, leaves or branches; simply utter and complete silence.

He looked more carefully around him. The trees looked somehow strange, tall and slender, waving their long branches like arms, silently and menacingly towards him. He remembered tales of frightful rites being practised in this area long ago, of pagan worship and human sacrifice; of death to those who entered the sacred groves. Now he seemed to feel hidden eyes watching his every movement as he hesitatingly made his way forward again, telling himself that he would soon be out of the hollow and into the countryside he knew.

Suddenly he saw a movement just ahead of him. A large bush moved and a dog poked its head through the foliage and stared at him. He fought to control his fright and told himself that some stray dog lived in the hollow; but all the time he was looking at the animal and at the expression of evil in its eyes as their gaze met. It showed its fangs and then suddenly vanished.

Before he could overcome his surprise a big black hare leaped on to the path in front of him, gave him one long look that he felt to be an expression of warning and hate

481

rather than fear; then the creature bounded away out of sight. An enormous straw-coloured cat with bushy coat and slowly waving tail sprang from a tree on to the path ahead of him. It arched its back, glared at him, spat silently, snarled like a tiger and then turned and walked away into the under-growth.

Other animals appeared from time to time, suddenly and silently, each looking at him with hate before disappearing again into the thick woods. He was sure that lots of other eyes were watching him as he walked on, ever on his guard but determined to make his way through the haunted wood.

The ground began to rise and thankfully he decided that he was coming out of the hollow, when the path turned and he found himself in a glade. No trees grew here but they surrounded the glade so that they seemed to form an audience for a spectacle. Then he saw that the glade or arena was occupied by two animals engaged in a violent yet one-sided struggle. A beautiful and graceful hind, its eyes wide with fright, was being attacked by a ferocious black ram. There seemed to be something overwhelmingly evil, even satanic, about the coal-black ram. Appalled, yet fascinated, the young man watched the unequal struggle. The repeated butting of the ram gave the hind no chance to escape and, beaten to its knees, it gave a pitiful look towards the human being who was watching its torture; its eyes, almost human in expression, imploring for help. Alerted by the mute appeal, the young man snatched up a heavy stick and threw himself between the animals. Just as the ram was making another charge on the helpless hind, he struck at it with all his might but found that his stick struck nothing but the air. The next moment he felt the pain as the ram butted him savagely and then he knew no more.

When he recovered consciousness he found himself lying on the side of a bare and hollow piece of ground. There was hardly a tree in sight. He thought that he must have dreamed the whole experience but when he moved to get to his feet, he discovered that he was very sore, as though he had been butted. He made his way home, thoughtfully and painfully, leaving behind him the haunted hollow.

When he recounted his experience, or dream, to his uncle,

482

who had lived in the locality all his life and remembered stories of the phantom forest that older folk had talked about when he was a child, he learned that such experiences as his used to befall many people who ventured into that strange place around Hallowe'en.

Waterford, CO. WATERFORD

There was a Danish settlement here in 853. King John established a mint at Waterford that issued coins for two hundred years; Cromwell was forced to abandon a siege of the town in 1649, while King James II received a famous welcome here. There is a curious monument to the Rice family in the Christ Church Cathedral with a 'memento mori' representing a decomposing corpse. Ancient Reginald's Tower, probably built in 1003, has a great hall in which the marriage of Strongbow and Eva was celebrated in 1171. With such a history, small wonder that Waterford has a number of ghosts, among them the well-documented return of the dead Jack Hayson.

One Christmas Eve, in a small house close to the River Suir, Eli Hayson was about to go to sleep at nearly midnight when he was surprised to hear the sound of running footsteps along the nearby waterfront. Something made Eli get up and look out of the window on to the bright moonlit quay where he saw several vessels moored and, racing towards his house from the river, a young man in a grey jersey and dark trousers. As the figure ran frantically towards the house, Eli recognized his twin brother Jack, a seaman whom he thought to be on the *Thomas Emery* at Cork.

He was about to leave the window to unbolt the door for his brother when he noticed several other dark figures behind Jack, seemingly rising from the water and making after him. Eli tried to shout a warning but found himself rooted to the spot and unable to make a sound. He saw Jack reach the door and attempt to wrench it open; then the forms closed in on him, clutching and overpowering the terrified and panting man. Eli plainly saw his brother's face convulsed with terror and fear and he heard a single scream: 'For God's

483

sake help me!' but still he could not move an inch. Within seconds the moon disappeared behind a cloud and all was quiet. When the moon reappeared the waterfront was deserted. Eli came to himself and hurried to the door but there was no sign of his brother nor anything to account for what he had seen and heard. Deciding that he must have had a nightmare, he crept back to bed and was soon asleep.

Within a couple of days news came from the captain of the *Thomas Emery* to say that Jack, walking in his sleep, had fallen overboard and drowned. Eli and his father attended the inquest at Cork where Mr Hayson testified that he had never known either of his sons to walk in their sleep but several of the ship's crew swore that they had seen Jack get up from his bunk at night and walk about the vessel and a verdict of 'Found Drowned' was returned. The family were far from satisfied; they made extensive enquiries from the captain and various members of the crew of the *Thomas Emery* to try to discover what had really happened on the fateful night but all to no avail.

During the years that followed Mr Hayson, senior, died and Eli, left alone in the world, had long given up all hope of solving the mystery of his brother's death when a possible explanation was brought to his notice.

One evening he was having a drink at a bar in Cork, as was his custom and where he was well-known, when the landlord mentioned that an old inhabitant of the town might be able to tell him something of interest. He would say no more but suggested that Eli lose no time in visiting the old man who, it seemed, did not have long to live.

Eli left the bar at once and called at the address given to him by the landlord. There he met a gentle old man named Webster who, however, seemed reluctant to talk once he learned the name of his visitor. At length, in the middle of idle chatter, he said that he would like to tell Eli something that his son, Tom a watchman on the quay who had died a couple of months before, had been worried about; something that he had seen twenty years earlier and had done nothing about.

It seemed that around midnight one Christmas Eve he had been sitting dozing in front of a brazier, by the side of a

484

shed on the quay, when he was roused by the sound of stealthy footsteps. He got up cautiously, on the look-out for thieves and saw three extraordinary figures walking along the water's edge. Although they had the bodies of men and were clad in sailors' clothing, their heads were those of animals, apes and stags.

For a moment Tom was petrified with fright and surprise but curiosity overcame his fear; making sure that he was not seen, he crept round the side of the shed and followed the strange figures. He saw them descend the quay steps, board a dingy and row off in the direction of a schooner moored nearby. As soon as he saw them board the ship, he jumped into another boat and rowed himself across. Reaching the schooner, he hauled himself aboard and hid among some of the ship's gear and barrels that lay in the stern of the vessel.

He had hardly settled in his hiding place when his blood nearly froze as he heard loud shrieks of terror accompanied by agonized moans and groans. A moment later a young man of about his own age came leaping up the companion ladder, raced across the deck for his life—with the grotesque trio that Tom had seen ashore at his heels.

It was a moonlit night and as the running man raced towards him Tom could see the awful fear on the man's terrified face. 'Help!' he screamed, 'For God's sake, help me!' Tom rushed from his hiding place but before he could do anything more the frenzied man had jumped overboard. Tom prepared himself to dive in to do what he could to help but found himself held fast by the three pursuing figures. Now that he was close to them Tom saw that they were indeed men but that they each wore a mummer's mask. It quickly transpired that the whole affair was a plot to get rid of the young man who, in some way that was not revealed, had incurred the bitter animosity of three of his fellow-seamen.

Two of the men were for getting rid of Tom at once but the third, who seemed to be the leader, persuaded them to spare him on condition that he took a solemn oath never to relate what he had seen. Tom took the oath and amid ghastly threats of what would happen if he ever breathed a word about the affair, he was allowed to go. Only years later, still tormented by the awful look on the terrified man's face, did Tom tell his father about the matter, making him swear never to tell a soul as long as he was alive.

Eli asked whether the old man could establish the exact date of his son's experience and reaching into a chest of drawers Matthew Webster brought forth a pocket book and showed Eli the date. It was the night that he had seen the figure of his brother trying to get into his cottage.

Legend has it that a female vampire is buried at a spot near Strongbow's Tree or Tower, in the little graveyard of a ruined church and that her fatal beauty still lures men to this sinister spot when darkness falls.

Westport, CO. MAYO

About eight miles west, rising in isolation over Clew Bay, stands the graceful cone of Croagh Patrick, the Rech (i.e. rock) of St Patrick, Ireland's holiest mountain of 2,510 feet, an object of pilgrimage since the Middle Ages. On occasions 100,000 people have been known to make the ascent on the last Sunday in July, Garland Sunday, many bare-footed in accordance with tradition.

At the summit which commands a superb view of the Connemara mountains to the south and Achill Island and even Slieve League (1,972 feet) away across Donegal Bay, there is a little oratory and a statue of the saint. Here St Patrick, according to ancient belief, spent the forty days of Lent in the year 441 praying, fasting and banishing from the whole land every snake and other noxious reptile. Certainly Ireland is today one of the few countries without snakes, toads, polecats, weasels and moles. St Patrick is said to have achieved this result by ringing a bell and then throwing it over a precipice, where it was followed by a swarm of venomous creatures. The bell was returned to his hand each time by angels until the extermination was complete.

There have been a number of reports that elderly pilgrims, while making the strenuous climb, have seen or sensed a gentle and white-robed figure at their side, a manifestation that they have found comforting and helpful on the long ascent to the summit of Croagh Patrick. On occasions the faint sounds of a ringing bell have been heard in the vicinity of the chapel on the summit when few pilgrims are there but it has only been heard during the month of March or early April, in fact during the forty days of Lent.

Wexford, CO. WEXFORD

It was at a large country house called Tullamore, not far from Wexford, the picturesque country town and seaport, that Lord Dufferin, ex-Viceroy of India, saw an apparition that probably saved his life.

A brave and cool soldier, a much-travelled man of the world, self-possessed and unimaginative, he had been relaxing in Ireland after years in India when he was invited to join the house-party of an old friend.

It was close to midnight as Lord Dufferin made his way along the mellowed passage and up the great staircase to his bedroom. He was in a pleasant and cheerful frame of mind as he entered the spacious room with a cheerful log fire blazing in the wide hearth. He felt at peace with the world and having prepared for bed he thought he would read for a while before settling down to sleep.

After half an hour or so he put the book aside but found himself strangely awake and restless. He dozed a little but soon awakened, twisting and turning; a most unusual state of affairs for a calm, clear-headed and practical man who normally fell asleep as soon as his head touched the pillow and slept soundly till morning. But this night, in 1890, something was wrong and Lord Dufferin eventually felt so restless and disturbed that he got up from his bed.

Crossing the room he reached the window and looked out over the moonlit lawns. It was a cloudless night and the full moon flooded the gardens beneath his window. He could see every rise and fall of the sweeping lawns, the well-cropped shrubs and the neat paths. Nothing moved and Lord Dufferin stood for some minutes contemplating the beauty of the night scene; silent, still and mysterious.

Suddenly a movement caught his eye and he watched, fascinated, as the figure of a man stepped from deep shadow into the moonlight. He walked slowly and purposefully straight across the wide lawn, bent almost double by the weight of a long and heavy box that he carried on his back. When the man was in the middle of the lawn, in full view of the watcher at the bedroom window, he stopped, lifted his head and looked straight at Lord Dufferin.

The moon shone down on the man's features and at the sight the hard-headed ex-Viceroy took an involuntary step backwards. So horrible was the face that he shuddered as their eyes met and he was later to describe the face as 'full of horror and malevolence'.

Resuming his task, the man turned away from the window and walked on across the lawn until he was lost in the dark shrubbery; but not before Lord Dufferin, with a quickening of his breath, realized that the object the man was carrying on his back was a coffin!

Lord Dufferin looked at his watch as he turned away from the window. It was nearly two o'clock in the morning and the whole house seemed to be asleep; it was as quiet as death. He turned again and looked out of the window but all was quiet and peaceful and deserted out there now. There was no doubt in his mind but that he had seen a real person in the garden; for there had been nothing ghostly about the figure he had seen, it had even cast a shadow he had noticed. Nevertheless, he experienced an eeriness such as he had never known before, a feeling that made him realize that he was cold. He returned to his bed and slept soundly for the rest of the night.

Next morning Lord Dufferin recounted his night's experience at the breakfast table. No one took seriously his account of seeing a hideously ugly man carrying a coffin across the lawns at two o'clock in the morning and he was assured that the house had no history of a ghost.

In the years that followed, Lord Dufferin often stayed at Tullamore and occupied the same bedroom but he never again experienced the cold restlessness that had disturbed him on his first visit to the house. And he never again saw the dreadful figure on the lawn—or did he?

Following a number of diplomatic engagements Lord Dufferin was appointed Ambassador to France. One morning, when he was to address an important gathering of diplomats on the fifth floor of a Paris hotel, he arrived with his secretary and was escorted by the manager to the lift. The lift rattled to a stop, the doors opened. Lord Dufferin, deep in conversation with his secretary, hardly noticed that a number of people entered the lift ahead of him. Then he stepped forward and as he did so he saw the uniformed lift attendant for the first time. The man was facing him and at the sudden shock and amazement, Lord Dufferin stepped back and out of the lift: for the face of the lift attendant was the face of the man he had seen in Ireland carrying a coffin across the lawn.

Now once again Lord Dufferin felt a chill dread seep into him. He was visibly shaken and much to the astonishment of the hotel manager, waved the lift away. As he waited for it to return after depositing the occupants at the various floors, Lord Dufferin heard a sudden harsh clang, then a loud banging noise followed by an awful screech and a tremendous thud that seemed to vibrate through the hotel.

The lift had just reached the fifth floor after leaving Lord Dufferin but the doors were never opened there. The wire suspension cable snapped and the loaded lift plunged to the bottom of the shaft. Five people died, among them the lift operator whose face had stopped Lord Dufferin from entering the fatal lift.

Later Lord Dufferin discovered that the lift operator had only been engaged for that single day, replacing the regular attendant; and no one ever discovered his real name or where he came from.

A later Marquess of Dufferin and Ava said a few years ago: 'The story is perfectly true but my grandfather could never explain it. We have always believed the story and puzzled about it, because he did not believe in ghosts.'

A Selection of the Best Books on Ghosts and Hauntings.

DENNIS BARDENS, *Ghosts and Hauntings*, London 1965

SIR ERNEST BENNETT, *Apparitions and Haunted Houses*, London 1939

JOSEPH BRADDOCK, *Haunted Houses*, London 1956

HEREWARD CARRINGTON AND NANDOR FODOR, *The Story of the Poltergeist Down the Centuries*, London 1953

B. ABDY COLLINS, *The Cheltenham Ghost*, London 1948

J. WENTWORTH DAY, *Here are Ghosts and Witches*, London 1954

J. WENTWORTH DAY, *A Ghost-Hunter's Game Book*, London 1958

NANDOR FODOR, *On the Trail of the Poltergeist*, London 1959

A. GOODRICH-FREER & JOHN, MARQUESS OF BUTE, *The Alleged Haunting of B—— House*, London 1899

DOUGLAS GRANT, *The Cock Lane Ghost*, London 1965

LORD HALIFAX'S *Ghost Book*, London 1936

CHARLES G. HARPER, *Haunted Houses*, London 1907

JOHN HARRIES, *The Ghost Hunter's Road Book*, London 1968

CHRISTINA HOLE, *Haunted England*, London 1940

R. THURSTON HOPKINS, *Ghosts Over England*, London 1953

JOHN H. INGRAM, *The Haunted Homes and Family Traditions of Great Britain*, London 1912

ANDREW LANG, *The Book of Dreams and Ghosts*, London 1899

SHANE LESLIE'S *Ghost Book*, London 1955

T. C. LETHBRIDGE, *Ghost and Ghoul*, London 1961

ALASDAIR ALPIN MACGREGOR, *The Ghost Book*, London 1955

ALASDAIR ALPIN MACGREGOR, *Phantom Footsteps*, London 1959

ANDREW MACKENZIE, *The Unexplained*, London 1966

ERIC MAPLE, *The Realm of Ghosts*, London 1964

DIANA NORMAN, *The Stately Ghosts of England*, London 1963

ELLIOTT O'DONNELL, *Haunted Churches*, London 1939

ELLIOTT O'DONNELL, *Haunted Britain*, London 1949

HARRY PRICE, *Confessions of a Ghost-Hunter*, London 1936

HARRY PRICE, '*The Most Haunted House in England*', London 1940

HARRY PRICE, *Poltergeist Over England*, London 1945

HARRY PRICE, *The End of Borley Rectory*, London 1947

W. H. SALTER, *Ghosts and Apparitions*, London 1938

PHILIP W. SERGEANT, *Historic British Ghosts*, London N.D.

SACHEVERELL SITWELL, *Poltergeists*, London 1940

WILLIAM OLIVER STEVENS, *Unbidden Guests*, London 1949

A. M. W. STIRLING, *Ghosts Vivisected*, London 1957

G. N. M. TYRRELL, *Apparitions*, London 1943, 1953

INDEX